SCOTLAND

Shetland Islands

ATLANTIC OCEAN

Orkney Islands

OUTER HEBRIDES

THE HIGHLANDS

Loch Ness

Fort Augustus

Fort William

▲ Ben Nevis

Aberdeen

NORTH SEA

Forth Bridge

Glasgow   Livingston   **Edinburgh**

SCOTLAND

The British Isles

ENGLAND

LEARNING ENGLISH

GREEN LINE NEW 4

Ausgabe für Bayern

von

Stephanie Ashford
Rosemary Hellyer-Jones
Marion Horner

Ernst Klett Schulbuchverlage
Stuttgart · Leipzig

LEARNING ENGLISH GREEN LINE NEW 4
Ausgabe für Bayern

von
Stephanie Ashford, Brigachtal; Rosemary Hellyer-Jones M.A., Ehingen (Donau); Marion Horner M.A., Cambridge; sowie Peter Lampater, Ehingen (Donau)

Beratende Mitarbeit
Dr. Thomas Becker, Nürnberg; Anne Marie Deißenböck, München; Waltraud Gschwendner, München; Gerhard Nickl, Nürnberg; Wolfgang Poeppel, Augsburg

Illustrationen
Elsie Lennox, London (Zeichnungen); Christian Dekelver, Weinstadt (Grafik); Dorothee Wolters, Köln (Zeichnungen im Vokabular und der Grammatik)

CDs
 Begleit-CD zum Schülerbuch für zu Hause und für den Unterricht mit Texten, Liedern, Ausspracheübungen (Klettnummer 547248)

 CD mit den Hörtexten für den Unterricht (Klettnummer 547249)

Lernsoftware
Zu diesem Band gibt es ein multimediales Lernprogramm. Dieses Programm bietet abwechslungsreiche Übungsformen zu Vokabular, Grammatik, Kommunikation und ein Lexikon mit dem Wortschatz des Lehrwerks.

1. Auflage 1 5 4 3 2 1 | 2010 09 08 07 06

Alle Drucke dieser Auflage sind unverändert und können im Unterricht nebeneinander verwendet werden. Die letzte Zahl bezeichnet das Jahr des Druckes.

Das Werk und seine Teile sind urheberrechtlich geschützt. Jede Nutzung in anderen als den gesetzlich zugelassenen Fällen bedarf der vorherigen schriftlichen Einwilligung des Verlags. Hinweis zu § 52 a UrhG: Weder das Werk noch seine Teile dürfen ohne eine solche Einwilligung eingescannt und in ein Netzwerk eingestellt werden. Dies gilt auch für Intranets von Schulen und sonstigen Bildungseinrichtungen.

Fotomechanische oder andere Wiedergabeverfahren nur mit Genehmigung des Verlags.

Die Rechtschreibung der deutschen Texte folgt den Empfehlungen des Rates für Deutsche Rechtschreibung vom März 2006.

© Ernst Klett Verlag GmbH, Stuttgart 2006. Alle Rechte vorbehalten.
Internetadresse: www.klett.de

Redaktion: Peter Cole M.A., Monique Kunhar M.A.
Gestaltung: Marietta Heymann

Umschlaggestaltung: Christian Dekelver, Weinstadt
Reproduktion: Meyle + Müller, Medien-Management, Pforzheim
Druck: Aprinta, Wemding
Printed in Germany
ISBN-13 978-3-12-547240-2
ISBN-10 3-12-547240-7

Vorwort

Hallo und herzlich willkommen
bei LEARNING ENGLISH GREEN LINE NEW 4, Ausgabe Bayern!

Die vertraute Grundstruktur eures Englischbuchs mit **Units, Focus on, Revision, Extra Line** und nicht zu vergessen den wichtigen Nachschlageseiten am Ende, nämlich **Grammar, Vocabulary, Dictionary, Classroom phrases** und **Irregular verbs** ist gegenüber dem Vorjahr fast unverändert geblieben. Wo ihr die einzelnen Abschnitte findet, steht genau im Inhaltsverzeichnis.

Gleiches gilt auch für die **Skills pages** (einmal pro **Unit**) und auch für die **Revisions**, die wieder eine **Test yourself page** enthalten (Lösungen auf S. 186/187). Falls hier noch Fehler vorkommen, könnt ihr mit den **Doctor-G**-Übungen im **Workbook** selbstständig weiterarbeiten, alles wie bei Band 3. Doch auch in der 8. Klasse gibt es wieder einige Neuerungen:
1. Übungen zum Übertragen und Dolmetschen (**Mediation**) findet ihr jetzt direkt in den **Units**, nicht mehr als separaten Teil des Buches.

2. Das Vokabular enthält in der Mittelspalte verwandte Wörter aus dem Lateinischen und aus dem Französischen. So könnt ihr beim Vokabellernen Querverbindungen zwischen den Sprachen herstellen, das Erschließen und Behalten der Wörter wird leichter.

Worauf es in Klasse 8 besonders ankommt: Selbstständiges Lernen und das Anwenden von Lern- und Arbeitstechniken. Darüber hinaus geht es stärker um die Präsentation von Arbeitsergebnissen in der Klasse, z.B. durch ein Referat oder einen Arbeitsbericht. Mündlichkeit, d. h. das Sprechen auf Englisch, wird auch immer wichtiger. Hier gilt: Übung macht den Meister, und wenn ihr die vielfältigen Übungen in **Green Line NEW Bayern** nutzt, werdet ihr mit diesen neuen Anforderungen sicher gut zurechtkommen.

Weiterhin also viel Freude am Unterricht und viel Erfolg beim Lernen!

Zeichenerklärung

🟢1 Alle Texte und Übungen, die auf der Begleit-CD zum Schülerbuch aufgezeichnet sind, erkennst du an diesem grünen Zeichen. ■ Hier beginnt ein neuer Track auf der CD.

🔵1 Übungen mit diesem blauen Symbol verweisen auf die CD zum Hörverstehen. Die Hörtexte sind nicht im Schülerbuch abgedruckt.

👥 Übungen mit diesem Symbol kannst du am besten in Partnerarbeit lösen.

👥👥 Alle Übungen mit diesem Symbol könnt ihr gemeinsam in Gruppenarbeit lösen.

⟨ ⟩ Diese Klammern zeigen an, dass die Übung fakultativ ist.

G10 Dieses Symbol verweist auf den Grammatikteil.

Inhaltsverzeichnis

Units / Steps ⟨ ⟩ fakultativ	Lernschwerpunkte Techniken & Methoden (T); Hörverstehen (HV)	Strukturen	Seite
Unit 1	**Down under**	G1–G2	**8**
Intro	▸ Landeskundliche Besonderheiten in Australien HV ▸ Textsorte: *Road signs* ▸ Mündlicher Kurzvortrag		
Language A New neighbours	▸ Einwanderer in Australien ▸ Textsorten: Alltagsdialog, *Song: Van Diemen's Land* ▸ Diebstahl am Strand HV ▸ Höflich reagieren ▸ *Reporting*	▸ Indirect speech (revision)	10
Language B An experience in the outback	▸ Umgang mit Gefahren in der Wildnis ▸ Konditionalsätze kategorisieren T ▸ *Mediation:* Dolmetschen HV, Inhalt eines englischen Artikels wiedergeben	▸ Conditional, types I and II (revision) ▸ Conditional, type III, mixed forms	13
Text Rabbit-proof fence	▸ Auszüge aus einem Roman lesen und verstehen ▸ Eine Diskussion durchführen T ▸ Produktives Schreiben		16
Skills	▸ *Dealing with texts (film review)* T		19
Let's check	▸ Integration der Lernziele von *Unit 1*		20
Focus 1	**Focus on the Golden Age**		**22**
	▸ Leistungen der Renaissance in Westeuropa ▸ England unter der Herrschaft Elizabeths I ▸ Historische Persönlichkeiten kennen lernen HV ▸ *Discussion, Presentation, Role play*		
Unit 2	**On the southwestern coast** G3–G6		**24**
Intro	▸ Historische und gegenwärtige Bedeutung einer Region Großbritanniens ▸ Textsorte: illustrierte Landkarte ▸ Eine lokaltypische Geschichte verstehen HV ▸ *Project: A map of your area*		
Skills	▸ *Using an English-German dictionary* T		26
Language A Paradise on earth	▸ Ein ökologisches Projekt in Cornwall ▸ Textsorte: Sachtext	▸ The passive (revision) ▸ The passive: present and past progressive	27
Language B Two men in a boat	▸ Probleme bei einer Segeltour ▸ Eine internationale Rettungsaktion HV ▸ Redemittel für Alltagssituationen zusammenstellen T ▸ *Role play* ▸ Weitere Wortbildungsregeln T	▸ Verbs with two objects ▸ Personal passive	29

Inhaltsverzeichnis

Units / Steps ⟨ ⟩ fakultativ	Lernschwerpunkte Techniken & Methoden (T); Hörverstehen (HV)	Strukturen	Seite
Text The ghost of St Dominic	▶ Eine Geistergeschichte lesen und verstehen ▶ Systematischer Umgang mit einem Text (Leerstellen füllen, Meinungen äußern, Szenen aufführen) T ▶ *Song: Smugglers* ▶ *Mediation:* Inhalt einer deutschen Piratenlegende wiedergeben		32
Let's check	▶ Integration der Lernziele von *Focus 1/Unit 2*		37
⟨Revision 1⟩	▶ Wiederholung Bände 1–3: Wortschatz		38
	▶ *Test yourself page*	▶ Use of *to do* ▶ *Relative clauses*	39
	▶ Unitübergreifende Wiederholung Band 4: Strukturen, Wortschatz, Redemittel	▶ The passive ▶ Conditional, types I–III	40
Unit 3 Intro	**Young people in Scotland** G7–G11 ▶ Landeskundliche Informationen über Schottland ▶ Die Lebensweise junger Leute HV ▶ Über vorgefasste Meinungen diskutieren		**42**
Language A Please, Dad!	▶ Ein Konflikt zwischen Vater und Tochter ▶ Redemittel zum Argumentieren ▶ Strukturen systematisieren und Regeln finden T	▶ Definite and indefinite article	44
Language B It makes me so angry!	▶ Die eigene Meinung zu Missständen äußern ▶ Strukturen systematisieren und Regeln finden T ▶ *Mediation:* E-Mail nach deutschen Stichwörtern verfassen	▶ Singular and plural ▶ Adjectives as nouns ▶ Possessive pronouns	46
Skills	▶ *Preparing for your oral exam* T HV		49
Text The kiss	▶ Eine Geschichte lesen und verstehen ▶ Systematischer Umgang mit Texten *(characters, style, level of tension)* T ▶ Einen Schluss zur Geschichte schreiben ▶ *Formal and informal language* ▶ *Song: Why does it always rain on me?*		50
Let's check	▶ Integration der Lernziele von Unit 3		54
Focus 2	**Focus on the New World** ▶ Koloniengründung der ersten Siedler ▶ Alltagsschwierigkeiten in den Kolonien HV ▶ Textsorten: historische Zeitleiste, Tagebuch, Landkarte		**56**

five 5

Inhaltsverzeichnis

Units / Steps ⟨ ⟩ fakultativ	Lernschwerpunkte Techniken & Methoden (T); Hörverstehen (HV)	Strukturen	Seite
Unit 4 Intro	**New England** ▸ Historische und gegenwärtige Bedeutung ▸ Textsorten: Landkarte, Brief ▸ Gezielte Informationsentnahme aus Text- und Bildmaterial ▸ In einem amerikanischen Restaurant HV	G12–G13	58
Language A An e-mail from Susie	▸ Textsorte: E-Mail ▸ Weitere Wortbildungsregeln T ▸ Über Vorlieben und Abneigungen sprechen ▸ *Song: Unforgettable*	▸ Gerund as subject ▸ Gerunds after verbs, adjectives, prepositions	60
Language B The 1627 Pilgrim Village	▸ Leben der Kolonisten und der Eingeborenen, Besuch im Freilichtmuseum ▸ Textsorte: Infobroschüre ▸ Redemittel zur Bewältigung von Alltagssituationen ▸ *Mediation:* Dolmetschen, Wiedergabe eines deutschen Sachtextes	▸ Gerunds after certain expressions ▸ Infinitives	63
Skills	▸ *Giving a talk* T		67
Text The ransom	▸ Eine Detektivgeschichte lesen und verstehen ▸ Systematischer Umgang mit Texten *(characters, narrator, reader)* T ▸ *Speaking practice*		68
Let's check	▸ Integration der Lernziele von *Focus 2/Unit 4*		71
⟨Revision 2⟩	▸ Wiederholung Bände 1–2: Wortschatz, Register		72
	▸ *Test yourself page*	▸ Present perfect simple and progressive ▸ *since* and *for*	73
	▸ Unitübergreifende Wiederholung Band 4: Strukturen, Wortschatz, Redemittel	▸ Definite and indefinite article ▸ Gerund and infinitive	74
Unit 5 Intro	**Fame and fortune** ▸ Vor- und Nachteile eines Lebens als Star ▸ Textsorte: Ausschnitte aus Interviews HV	G14–G15	76
Language A The audition	▸ Persönlicher Bericht über ein *Casting* ▸ Unterschiedliche *points of view* herausfinden ▸ Weitere Funktionen des Adverbs erarbeiten	▸ Adverbs of comment and degree ▸ Position of adverbs	78
Language B After the audition	▸ Unterschiede zwischen *formal and informal language* HV ▸ Merkmale verschiedener Textsorten ▸ Einen formellen Brief schreiben ▸ *Mediation:* Übertrag englischer Hinweis- und Verbotstafeln		80
Skills	▸ Mit wesentlichen Unterschieden zwischen Sprachvarianten *(BE* und *AE)* umgehen T		83

Inhaltsverzeichnis

Units / Steps ⟨ ⟩ fakultativ	Lernschwerpunkte Techniken & Methoden (T); Hörverstehen (HV)	Strukturen	Seite
Text **A song project**	▶ Verschiedene Popsongs erarbeiten und über Inhalt, Wirkung, Hintergründe informieren ▶ Ein Projekt in arbeitsteiliger Gruppenarbeit durchführen T ▶ Unterschiedliche Informationsquellen selbstständig nutzen ▶ Präsentation von Arbeitsergebnissen T		84
Let's check	▶ Integration der Lernziele von Unit 5		89

Focus 3	**Focus on international contacts**		90
	▶ Bedeutung sprachlicher Kenntnisse ▶ Möglichkeiten zur Kontaktaufnahme mit ausländischen Partnern ▶ Sprachlich-soziale Konventionen in GB ▶ Sprachliches Verhalten optimieren ▶ Textsorten: Cartoons, Statistiken, Dialoge HV		

⟨Revision 3⟩	▶ Wiederholung Bände 1–3: Textarbeit		92
	▶ *Test yourself page*	▶ The passive ▶ Indirect speech	93
	▶ Unitübergreifende Wiederholung Band 3: Strukturen, Wortschatz, Redemittel	▶ Adverbs	94

⟨Extra Line⟩			96
▶ A Why the emu can't fly		Einsetzbar nach *Unit 1*	96
▶ B More about films		Einsetzbar nach *Unit 2*	97
▶ C Poetry pages (Nonets, Clerihews, Limericks, Rhyming words)		Einsetzbar nach *Unit 3*	98
▶ D An extract from Stephen King		Einsetzbar nach *Unit 4*	100
▶ E A workshop		Einsetzbar nach *Unit 5*	102
▶ F A sketch: Boogaloo		Einsetzbar nach *Unit 5*	103

Grammar	▶ Unitbegleitende Grammatik	**104**
Vocabulary	▶ Unitbegleitendes Vokabular	**123**
Dictionary	▶ Alphabetische Wortliste Englisch-Deutsch	**157**
⟨**Solutions**⟩	▶ Lösungen zu den *Test yourself pages*	**186**
Classroom phrases	▶ Redemittel für den Unterricht	**188**
Irregular verbs	▶ Liste der unregelmäßigen Verben	**190**

unit 1 intro
Down under

1 Talking about Australia

a) Tina Mayr went to Australia in the summer holidays and now she is giving a talk to her English class about her trip.

- What facts about Australia does she tell them?
- What else do you know about Australia?

b) She interviews Matt Donovan. Listen and find out:

- the good points about his job.
- if anyone can become a bridge climb leader.
- what things are the wrong way round in Australia.
  (Try to explain why. Then think of more examples.)

> G'day! That's how Australians say hello.

> This is the Australian flag. It shows a group of stars called the Southern Cross. It also has the British flag – that's because Australia was once a British colony.

> This fence in Western Australia is 1,800 km long. It was built to keep the rabbits in the east away from the farming land on the west coast.

> Australia is the hottest and driest continent so the outback can be really dusty. We were glad when there was a shower of rain. And it's quite a lonely place as not many people actually live out there – except the people who work on the huge sheep and cattle stations.

> I bought this postcard because I really love Australia's wildlife. There's the cute koala, but you'll also find some of the world's deadliest animals and plants. Each year more Australians are killed by poisonous spiders which live in the cities than by crocodiles or sharks.

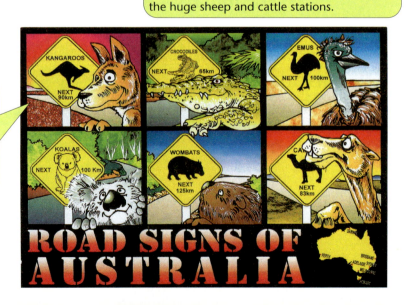

8 eight

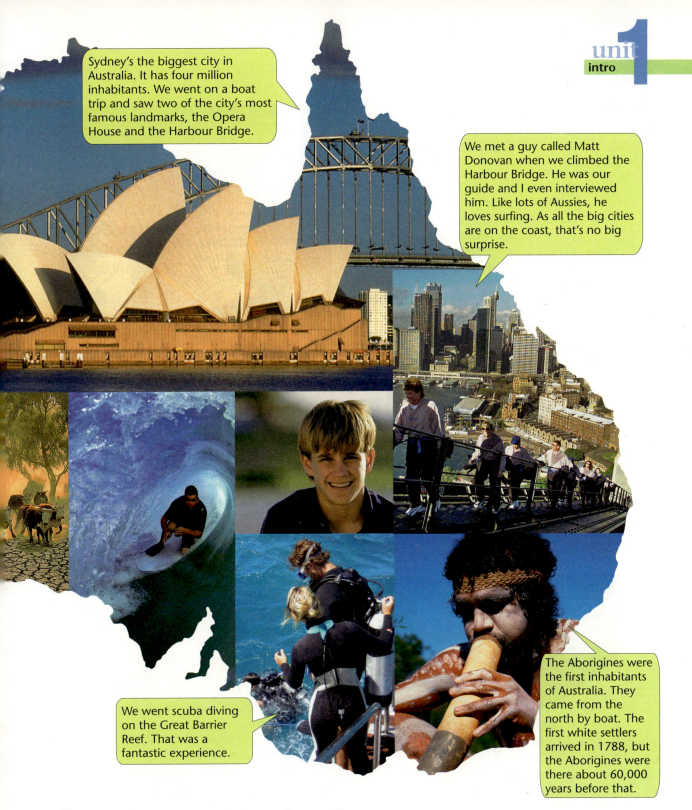

2 Speaking practice: Giving a short talk

Choose one of the aspects of Australia on the right. Use the information on these pages, the Internet, travel brochures etc. to prepare a short talk of at least two minutes.

history   Aboriginal culture
music   wildlife   sports

unit 1 language A

A New neighbours

Matt Donovan lives with his parents Jill and Bob and his sister Nicky in Rockdale, a suburb of Sydney.

Nicky: Here he is. We can put the steaks on the barbie at last!
Bob: Where have you been, Matt? You said you'd be back early today.
Matt: I know. Sorry I'm late. Actually, I've been back in the street for some time. I've been meeting our new neighbours.
Jill: Oh, at number 30? Has another family moved in there now?
Nicky: I told you earlier I'd seen a van outside the house, Mum.
Matt: Well, when I came past, a girl was fetching boxes from the van. So I asked her if she needed help and she said yes.
Nicky: Funny how different it was when I wanted you to help me this morning!
Bob: What are the people like, Matt?
Matt: They seem very friendly. They're Asians. Their name is Wang and the girl is called Lin.
Nicky: Great! Maybe she'll help me with my Japanese homework.
Matt: I doubt it – they're Chinese.

Jill: You see more and more Asian immigrants about these days. Er, not that I think it's a bad thing –
Bob: Of course it isn't! The countries of the Pacific Rim are our biggest trading partners.
Matt: Right. But I don't think the Wangs have only just arrived in Oz. They speak good English. And Lin's already a real Aussie – she told me she loved surfing and beach volleyball! So I asked her to come to the beach with me this weekend –
Nicky: You don't waste any time, do you?
Matt: Actually she said she wasn't sure when she'd be able to. You should see the chaos in their house!
Jill: Poor things! I'm sure they need a break. Run back, Matt, and tell them to come and have something to eat with us. Don't take no for an answer.
Matt: No worries! We'll be back in a few minutes.
Nicky: Yeah, but bring the whole family, Matt – not just the girl!

1 Australians

a) What do you learn about the Donovans and their lifestyle?

b) Why do you think Australia has a lot of immigrants from Asia?

2 Revision: Indirect speech

Find examples of indirect speech in the dialogue. Then say what was said in direct speech. (Be careful with the short forms!)

3 Lin

What did Matt say to his family when he reported what else Lin had said or asked?

She asked / said / told me / explained / mentioned / pointed out / …

Example: 1. "She wanted to know how long we had been living in the street."

1. How long has your family been living in the street?
2. I'm planning to paint my new room a funky colour.

3. My mother didn't speak any English before we came to Australia.
4. My father sometimes goes back to China on business.
5. Will I find it easy to make friends at the local school?
6. Can you give me any good surfing tips?
7. Have you ever won a surfing competition?
8. I don't think I'd like to live in the outback.

4 At the Donovans' house

Use indirect commands to report what was said while the Wangs were at the Donovans' house. Try to use each of the verbs once.

| invite | ask | want | advise | warn | tell |

1. **The Donovans to the Wangs:** Please call us by our first names, Jill and Bob.
   → The Donovans wanted the Wangs to call them by their first names.
2. **Nicky to her father:** Look after those steaks, Dad. Don't burn them!
3. **Jill to Matt:** Bring the chairs over here out of the sun.
4. **Bob to Nicky:** Can you get some more cold beers, please?
5. **Jill to Lin's mother:** You should join the local women's group and meet everyone.
6. **Nicky to Lin:** Could you teach me a few words of Chinese?
7. **Bob to the Wangs:** Come and use our pool as often as you like.
8. **The Wangs to the Donovans:** You must come and have a Chinese meal with us soon.

5 Listening: Trouble at Bondi Beach

Anja and Timo from Augsburg visited Bondi Beach one afternoon. They left their van in the car park at 2 pm. On their way down to the beach they met two girls in jogging gear. It was quite cold so there weren't many people on the beach. An Asian family were playing football. A young couple were listening to music on a big radio. A few people were surfing and some women were out in a rowing boat. Some rugby players were having a party and they invited Anja and Timo to join them. The two young Germans had a lot of fun until about 4 pm when they left the beach. But back at the car park, they found that their van had been

broken into and two leather jackets had been stolen! The police are now asking three people who were on the beach about what they were doing between 2 and 4 pm that afternoon.

Listen to what they tell the police. One of them is lying. Listen twice and then say who it is and how you know.

unit 1
language A

6 Everyday English: At the barbie

Work with a partner. Read out what Mr Donovan says and Mr Wang's three possible reactions. Then decide which is the most polite reaction.

1 G'day. I'm Bob Donovan.
A My name is Wang.
B I'm Mr Wang.
C Hi. My name's Lee Wang.

2 I'm glad you could come to our barbecue.
A Me, too.
B It was very kind of you to invite us.
C I hope there's enough food for all of us.

3 Would you like a drink?
A Thank you, Bob. Yes, I'd love a beer.
B Yes. A beer.
C Well, all right. I'll have a beer then.

4 Is your steak OK, Lee?
A Yes, it is. It's OK.
B It's just right, thanks.
C Er, it tastes quite good actually.

7 A song: Van Diemen's Land (U2)

Hold me now, oh hold me now
Till^1 this hour has gone around
And I'm gone on the rising tide^2
For to face^3 Van Diemen's Land

It's a bitter pill I swallow^4 here
To be rent^5 from one so dear
We fought for justice^6 and not for gain^7
But the magistrate^8 sent me away

Now kings will rule^9 and the poor will toil^{10}
And tear^{11} their hands as they tear the soil^{12}
But a day will come in this dawning^{13} age
When an honest^{14} man sees an honest wage^{15}

^{1}bis • ^{2}on the rising tide – mit der Flut • ^{3}gegenübertreten • ^{4}schlucken • ^{5}fortgerissen • ^{6}Gerechtigkeit • ^{7}Profit • ^{8}Friedensrichter • ^{9}herrschen • ^{10}sich abmühen • ^{11}zerreißen • ^{12}Erde • ^{13}anbrechend • ^{14}redlich • ^{15}Lohn

Words: Adam Clayton, Laurence Mullen, David Evans, Paul David Hewson

Listen to the song and look at the information on the right and the pictures below. Then write the story that you think the song tells.

The first European settlement in Australia was for convicts. The prisons in Britain had become so crowded that the government sent ships full of convicts to start a colony at Botany Bay (now Sydney) in 1788. The laws were cruel in those days. You could even be 'transported' if you stole some bread or protested against the government. The colony of Van Diemen's Land (now Tasmania) was founded in 1825.

B An experience in the outback

When Matt found a website that invited people to write about their experiences in the outback, he wrote this:

It wouldn't have happened if I'd thrown the boomerang correctly. But I didn't, and so it didn't come back to me. Instead it landed near a shed on the Queensland cattle station where I was staying with my cousin Jack. He laughed because I'd proved once again what a typical city boy I was, with no bush skills at all. And maybe if I'd grown up in the outback, I'd have had eyes for the snake. But the brown snake is brown – otherwise it wouldn't have got that name! – and it isn't easy to see it on the dry ground. Anyway, I had no idea of the danger I was in while I was running to pick up the boomerang until it was too late. By then the snake had raised itself from the ground and bitten my leg.

Jack reacted immediately. He recognized what kind of snake it was and shouted to me to lie down and keep completely still. Before he reached me he had already taken off his T-shirt and was tearing it into strips. He used the strips to make a pressure bandage, first over the two little scratches low down on my leg, then up over my knee to where my shorts finished. I don't really remember very much of the next few hours. I was in shock, and I was scared, too. I tried to lie very still while Jack fetched help.

Even with the bandage, if I'd moved, more of the poison could have got into my blood. From where I was I could see a fly that was caught in a spider's web on the side of the shed. I felt helpless like the fly. It was waiting for the spider to kill it. I was waiting for the poison to kill me. I already felt ill with fear. But at last Jack returned with my uncle in the car, and after they had made a splint for my leg with a piece of wood from the shed, I was taken back to the house. Some time after that the Flying Doctor arrived and I was transported to hospital by plane.

It might have ended very differently. If Jack hadn't known what to do that day, I probably wouldn't be alive now to tell this story. It was certainly a scary experience in the outback. If only I'd been able to throw that boomerang correctly!

1 Maybe it would have been different

a) Find the right endings for the sentences.

1. If the boomerang had come back, …
2. If the snake had been a different colour, …
3. If Jack hadn't told Matt to keep still, …
4. If Matt had been wearing long trousers instead of shorts, …
5. If Jack hadn't torn his T-shirt into strips, …
6. If they hadn't found the wood, …
7. If the Flying Doctor hadn't come, …

— it would have been easier to see.
— Matt wouldn't have got to hospital so fast.
— they would have made a splint from something else
— Matt might have run around in panic.
— Matt wouldn't have looked for it.
— he couldn't have made a bandage from it.
— his legs might have been protected.

b) Finish this sentence with your own ideas.
If Matt had died, …would/wouldn't have …

c) There is a new tense here that is called the conditional perfect. How is it formed?

unit 1
language B

2 More from the website

All these people wrote about experiences in the past. What did they write?

Example: 1. It would/might have jumped away if I had frightened it.

1. I hid while I was watching the little kangaroo. (It/jump away • I/frighten it)
2. Luckily we had water with us. (We/have nothing to drink • our situation/be even worse)
3. I shouted to him to put the gun down. (I/feel terrible • he/shoot the rabbits)
4. The pictures on the rock were thousands of years old. (I/not get lost • I/not see them)
5. The helicopter rescued us just in time. (Pilot/not see us • we/not escape from the fire)
6. Actually, the insect didn't taste too bad. (I/never eat it • my new friend/not offer it to me)

3 Different types of conditional sentences

a) There are three basic types of conditional sentences. Which one you use depends on the kind of condition you are talking about. Match the following conditional sentences with rules A–C. Then write down what tenses are used in the if-clause and the main clause.

1. If I go to Australia, I will see lots of kangaroos.   A — The condition hasn't been fulfilled. The speaker knows that something **cannot** happen **any more**.

2. If I had the money, I would fly to Sydney.   B — The condition can be fulfilled. The speaker thinks that something is **likely** to happen.

3. If I had been to Australia, I would have travelled in the outback.   C — The condition can't (or probably won't) be fulfilled. The speaker thinks that something is **impossible** or **unlikely** to happen.

b) Now look at the following sentences. How are they different from the three basic types?

1. If I hadn't been to Australia, I wouldn't know so much about it.
2. If I lived near Bondi Beach, I would have learnt how to surf.

c) Now make your own sentences for each type.

4 Life on the cattle station

Complete what Jack told Matt with the correct tenses.

1. If I lived in a city, I (**miss**) the wide open spaces out here.
2. If my parents hadn't taught me to ride, I (**not be able**) to help them on the station.
3. The cattle will escape if we (**not mend**) that fence over there right away.
4. If I hadn't learnt about snakes from the Aborigines, I (**not know**) what to do when that snake bit you.
5. There (**not be**) any water at all left in the river if it doesn't rain soon.
6. You know, a big kangaroo could hurt you badly if it (**decide**) to attack you.
7. There would be too many rabbits on the station if we (**not shoot**) some of them.
8. If the wind (**not change**) direction, our house would have been in the path of a terrible fire last year.
9. Our family would have been ruined if the station (**burn down**).

5 Mediation/Listening: A visitor from Germany

While Matt is staying with Jack at the cattle station, there is another visitor – Dirk from Germany. His English isn't very good, so Matt has to interpret.

a) Take over Matt's role. Before you listen to the dialogue, read the following texts in order to learn some useful new words.

Australia's unique wildlife
Until about 50 million years ago Australia was joined to the huge continent Gondwana, but it then became a separate continent and that has led to its unique wildlife. There are lots of living things on the Australian continent that can't be found anywhere else! In fact Australia, New Zealand and Tasmania are the only places in the world where you can find the group of animals that are called marsupials (they carry their babies in a pouch).

Australia

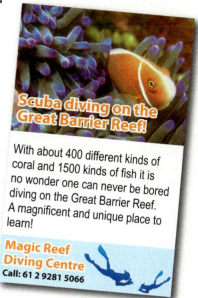

Scuba diving on the Great Barrier Reef!
With about 400 different kinds of coral and 1500 kinds of fish it is no wonder one can never be bored diving on the Great Barrier Reef. A magnificent and unique place to learn!

Magic Reef Diving Centre
Call: 61 2 9281 5066

b) Dirk would like to know what is in this newspaper article. What are the main facts in German?

Teenage friends watch in horror as surfer is torn apart by sharks

A teenage surfer was torn apart and eaten by two great white sharks off an Adelaide beach yesterday. Nick Peterson, 18, who was being pulled behind a boat, was attacked by the first shark as he fell from his board in full view of a crowded holiday beach. A second shark ate the rest of his body.

The attack left Mr Peterson's friends, who were in the boat, in deep shock. Fraser Bell, of the South Australia Sea Rescue Squadron, said that the four young men had been at sea for about 30 minutes when the attack occurred. "They were just boys having a good time. The weather was perfect and they were just doing what lads do." The great white shark is protected in Australian waters and as a result its numbers have increased in recent years. Sharks are becoming more of a danger and this raises the question of how to deal with them. If or when the two great white sharks responsible for yesterday's death are found, beach safety officers, conservationists and the South Australia Government will have to decide whether to kill them or leave them free. Some conservationists argue that as the ocean is their natural home they have as much right to be there as people.

c) Speaking practice: Discuss the following statement which was made after the attack.
"Sharks should not be killed just because they act naturally in their own environment."

Rabbit-proof fence

In 1931 the Australian government decided that it would be better for part-Aboriginal children if they were put in settlements and trained to be like Europeans. 'Rabbit-proof fence' is the true story of fourteen-year-old Molly and her two younger cousins, ten-year-old Gracie and eight-year-old Daisy, who in July of that year were taken from their mothers in the small village of Jigalong near the rabbit-proof fence in the north of Western Australia and transported more than a thousand miles south to the Moore River Native Settlement near Perth. The children there were treated badly, not even allowed to speak their own language. Anyone who tried to escape was brought back and beaten. But on their first day Molly persuaded Gracie and Daisy to run away with her and try to find their way home. These extracts describe some of their experiences.

■ On their second day they came into an area of bush that had been ruined by fire. In a few weeks' time, however, this black landscape would be brought back to life by the rain. It would be a green wilderness again, full of beautiful flowers and animals that are wonderfully and uniquely Australian. The three girls walked in silence over the next hill where they saw a very welcome sight. Two Aboriginal men were coming towards them on their way home from a hunting trip. Gracie and Daisy were so pleased to see them that they almost ran to meet them, but Molly held the girls back and whispered, "Wait." So the three girls waited until the men came closer. When they saw what the men had caught, they drooled – a kangaroo and two goannas. The girls were more interested in the bush tucker than in the two men.

"Where are you girls going?" asked the men.

"We are running away back home to Jigalong," replied Molly.

"Well, you girls want to be careful," advised the old man with white hair. "They got a policeman. He follow runaway girls and take 'em back to the settlement. He's a good tracker."

"We know that," replied Molly who was quite sure that the black tracker would not be able to follow their path because all their footprints would have been washed away by the rain.

The men gave them a piece of kangaroo and one of the goannas. They turned to walk away when the younger man remembered something.

"Here, you will need these," he said as he held up a box of matches.

The girls thanked them and said goodbye.

■ Everything was quiet. The sun was shining through the clouds and the raindrops on the leaves and spiders' webs sparkled like diamonds. The girls seemed very relaxed as they walked together.

The silence was broken suddenly by Molly. "Run under that big tree over there," she shouted. "Climb up and hide there. You too, Daisy. Come on." When she saw that it was difficult for them, she ran over to help them. She pushed them up into the branches and told them not to move.

Although they could not see any danger they did what she said without question, they trusted her with their lives. Hadn't she proved herself a good leader during the trek? So there they lay on the branches, and waited. At last they heard it. It was a plane, a plane that had been sent out to search for them. They listened while the plane circled above them, then it gave up and returned home.

After a few minutes Molly decided it was safe to climb down from the trees. Back on the ground they walked faster and stayed close to the trees in case they needed to hide again. No one noticed the change in the weather until they were caught in the showers. It was only then that they realized that the sun and blue sky had disappeared. There were only dark rain clouds. It seemed hopeless to try and find shelter; they were wet and the water was running off their hair. Just when they felt worst they heard familiar sounds. At that moment they realised just how much they had missed them and they became completely depressed.

It was the middle of the day and these were the sounds of chickens and dogs that reminded them of the stations at Jigalong but most of all these sounds brought back memories of the people they loved there. When they came closer, Molly pushed the other two towards the farmhouse.

"Go and ask for some food to eat. Hurry up. I'll wait here," she said.

Daisy and Gracie were happy to go because they were feeling very hungry. The last pieces of rabbit left from breakfast had all gone. They were welcomed by a little girl.

"My name is Susan" she said. "Mummy, there's two girls outside and they're all wet." Little Susan's mother came to the door and asked them, "Are you the runaways from the settlement?"

"Yes," they replied.

"Where's the other one? Go and tell her to come inside and dry herself while I make something to eat. It's all right, you won't be reported."

■ The woman, whose name was Mrs Flanagan, made thick meat sandwiches which the three girls devoured. These were followed by large pieces of cake and a cup of sweet tea. The girls watched while Mrs Flanagan filled bags with tea, sugar, meat, cake and bread. She took three large empty tins and said, "You will need these to boil your tea in. Have you all had enough to eat?"

"Yes, thank you," they said.

"Right then, I'll give you some dry clothes and warm coats."

She watched while the three girls disappeared into the bush. She had had a phone call from the settlement on Tuesday afternoon and had been asked to look out for three runaways and report if she saw them. "Those girls are too young to be out there," she said loudly to herself. "They don't know this part of the country. And the three of them with just dresses on. It's a wonder they haven't got colds, or worse. I'll have to report this for their own good before they get lost and die in the bush. It's my duty." Then she went inside to the telephone.

Mrs Flanagan was sure that she had done the right thing. Anyway, she told herself, those three girls would have no more success than the other runaways. When they reached the railway they would decide to sit and wait for the train, then they would be handed over to the police at the next station. They always get caught.

■ Mrs Flanagan was not the only person who knew about the girls. The whole state found out about them when an article appeared in the 'West Australian' on 11 August 1931. Reports came in from all around. But the girls trekked on, just a few days ahead of the search parties that were being organized by the police. They had been on the run for over a month. They had left the landscape of green fields and found themselves in a very different one of red earth. But the three girls were very much at home in this part of the country. Their traditional skills helped them to survive and to hide from their enemies. But scratches on their legs had become open sores.

"My legs hurt," cried Gracie. "I can't walk."

"My legs hurt, too," said Daisy.

"We can't hang around here all day, we gotta walk on," Molly told them. "I'll carry Daisy first, then it will be your turn, Gracie." It was very slow and difficult, but they always went on. Their simple meals were just like the ones they ate at home – especially when they managed to find birds, birds' eggs, rabbits and goannas. Although their sores hurt and they were in pain they never gave up.

One day when the sun was high in the blue sky, Daisy and Gracie heard an excited shout

from Molly who was walking ahead of them. "Here it is. I've found it. Come and look." She laughed and waved her arms. "I've found the rabbit-proof fence. This will take us all the way home to Jigalong."

"But how do you know that's it?" asked Daisy. She didn't notice anything special about this fence.

"This fence is straight, see," Molly explained. "And it's clear on each side of the fence." She should know. After all, her father helped to check and repair the fence and he told her all about it. Now it would help them find their way home. The girls were all very excited when they at last reached the rabbit-proof fence.

From when she was young Molly had learned that the fence was an important landmark for her people. It cut through the country from south to north. It was a typical reaction by the white people to a problem they had made themselves. As well as horses, cattle and sheep they had introduced rabbits to Australia, but now there were too many rabbits, and the fence that had been completed in 1907 to keep them in the east was useless because there were already rabbits on the western side.

For the three runaways, however, the fence was a symbol of love, home and safety.

Even after the girls had found the fence they still had almost five hundred miles to walk. Gracie did not go all the way back to Jigalong. When she found out that her mother had moved to another village she went there instead, and was caught and sent back to Moore River. However, Molly and Daisy completed their fantastic trek and reached Jigalong in October. Molly later married and had two daughters. One of them is Doris Pilkington, the author of 'Rabbit-proof fence'.

1 Comprehension

1. Why are children like Molly and her cousins sometimes called the "stolen generations"?
2. Why do the three girls run away?
3. What people do they meet on their way?
4. What problems do they have and how do they deal with them?
5. Why is the story called 'Rabbit-proof fence'?
6. Write down all the information about Molly from the text. Would you have gone with her if she had wanted you to run away with her? Use your notes to say why or why not.

2 Creative writing

Choose one of these writing tasks.

1. What could the article about the runaways in the 'West Australian' on 11 August 1931 have looked like?
2. Imagine Molly had written a diary. Choose one of the scenes from the text and write about it in her diary.

3 Word power

Use all these new words to tell a short story to your partner:

settlement • runaway • tracker • footprint • shelter • match • boomerang • to remind • landmark • boil • sore

4 Speaking practice: A discussion

Discuss these statements in class.

1. Mrs Flanagan was a cruel woman.
2. It was a good idea to take part-Aboriginal children away to special settlements.

Skills: Dealing with texts

Rabbit-proof fence (Australia 2002. 94 min.)

In Australia in 1931, the Chief Protector of Aboriginals Mr Neville (Kenneth Branagh) decides that all part-Aboriginal children should be sent to special schools, with the intention of marrying them to white people or training them to be servants. To Neville this is not cruel. He believes that "in spite of himself, the native must be helped". As a result of his decision Molly (Everlyn Sampi), Gracie (Laura Monaghan) and Daisy (Tianna Sansbury) are taken over a thousand miles away from their families. They run away, however, and although Neville sends a tracker to catch them, they manage to make the long trek home again.
In 'Rabbit-proof fence' Australian director Phillip Noyce presents a magnificent true-life story, which was first told in the book of the same name by Molly's daughter Doris Pilkington. We feel for the three girls in their terrible situation because the young actors who play the girls are brilliant, with Sampi especially good. Branagh is also in wonderful form as the quietly evil Neville. The Aboriginal music and the beautiful views of the Australian outback help to make this a film that will touch your heart. It is a cinema experience not to be missed.

1 A film review

a) Before you read:

1. What kind of information do you expect from a film review?

b) Things to think about while you read:

2. What is the difference between the two main parts of the text?
3. What are the characteristics of a film review that make it different from other types of text? (Subject? Form? Style? Tenses that are used? …?)
4. How does the author underline his opinion of the film? Look for examples.

c) After you have read:

5. What information does the text give you about the film? Is anything missing that you need to know?
6. Would you like to see the film? Say why or why not.
7. Now complete the grid below.

Text type	Film review
Who wrote it?	– Someone who saw the film, probably a journalist
For what purpose?	– To tell people …
Characteristics?	– …
Who is it aimed at?	– …
Where to find it?	– …

2 Writing tasks

a) Write a review of a film you have seen. Use the text above and your grid to help you.

Or:

b) Turn the review of 'Rabbit-proof fence' into a different type of text. It could be a letter, a poem, a newspaper article or any other kind that you want. First think about the characteristics of the text type you have chosen and make a grid for it like the one above.

unit 1 — let's check

1 Word power

a) Explain the link between these words.

1. city – suburb
2. silence – noise
3. sore – hurt
4. wet – shower
5. snake – poisonous
6. match – fire
7. hungry – drool
8. station – shed

b) Make six compounds with the correct pairs. Show the meaning in example sentences.

| rail | rain | foot | out | run | land |
| back | print | away | mark | drop | way |

c) Give the noun forms of these adjectives.

original • ill • different • dangerous • safe • alive • possible

2 Facts about Australia

Finish these sentences. Use your own words to give the correct reasons.

1. English is the main language that is spoken in Australia because …
2. Most Australians live on or near the coast because …
3. The British government started sending convicts to Australia because …
4. In the last thirty or forty years the population has been gradually changing because …
5. December and January are good months for the beach in Australia because …
6. The number of great white sharks is growing because …
7. The interesting thing about most of the wildlife in Australia is …

3 Mrs Flanagan's phone call

Read what Mrs Flanagan told Miss Evans, one of the staff at the Moore River settlement. Think what Miss Evans's questions were. Then write down how Miss Evans reported the conversation.

Start: I've just had a phone call from Mrs Flanagan. She told me … I asked her if … and she said …

> The three runaways are in this area. They've just left my house. (…) Yes, I made some sandwiches for them, and I gave them some food to take with them, too. (…) They seem to be OK, although they were very wet and hungry when they arrived here. (…) They're looking for the rabbit-proof fence. But they'll reach the railway first. If they sit and wait for the train, you'll be able to catch them there.

4 Instructions for an adventure trip

The day before an adventure trip into the bush, Nicky Donovan's teacher Mr Roussos gave the class some instructions. What did Nicky tell her parents about what Mr Roussos said? Use indirect commands and try to find a different verb to introduce each one.

Start: 1. He advised us …

1. You should wear suitable shoes.
2. You mustn't leave the group at any time.
3. You must always follow my instructions.
4. Don't forget to bring a water bottle.
5. Protect your head from the sun.
6. Don't do anything that could start a fire.

unit 1
let's check

5 If

Match the ideas and make sentences with the conditional
or conditional perfect. Start: If the Wangs …, they …

1. the Wangs / buy a house in a different street
2. Matt / not see Lin near the van
3. Lin / not love water sports
4. the Wangs / have a pool
5. Mrs Wang / not learn English

- 4 be able to swim in their own garden
- 3 not learn to surf
- 1 not become the Donovans' neighbours
- 5 find it hard to communicate
- 2 not offer to help with the boxes

6 What would you have done?

Explain why you would or wouldn't have done the same as this visitor to Australia.

Example: 1. I'd have said no, too. I wouldn't have wanted to eat kangaroo meat.
or: I'd have tried it. It might have tasted good.

1. "I could have had a kangaroo steak from the barbie, but I said no."
2. "Ugh! I found a spider in my motel room, so I grabbed it and threw it out of the window."
3. "I only had time to visit Sydney or Perth, and I chose Sydney."
4. "It was a beautiful beach, but I was worried about sharks, so I didn't go into the water."
5. "At the airport I saw someone who looked like Kylie Minogue, but I wasn't sure if it really was her, so I didn't ask for her autograph."

7 Mixed bag: News from Australia

Matt Donovan is writing an e-mail to a cousin in England. Put in the missing words.
(Sometimes more than one version is possible.)

  1 you hear about the terrible fires in the bush around Sydney in the 2 few weeks? Luckily we had a huge storm two days 3 , and that brought them to an end. But 4 the rain hadn't come, nobody knows what 5 have happened. Thousands of extra people had 6 helping the regular fire service, but even they could do 7 to control the fires. If 8 the wind hadn't been 9 strong! Lots of families 10 forced to leave their homes, and more 11 a hundred houses were burned down in a suburb not very 12 from where we live. The awful thing is that 13 fires can start naturally in the bush, it seems that some 14 these fires were started 15 purpose. 16 mean, what kind of person 17 do something like that?! At least this time 18 was killed. Anyway, we're getting 19 the end of the summer now. 20 March arrives, the season for fires 21 be past.

8 A cartoon

"I wasn't born here but I've adapted[1] to life in Australia quite well!"

[1] to adapt to something – sich an etwas anpassen

focus 1
Focus on the Golden Age

1 Listening: A talk show

Elizabeth I | Sir Francis Drake | Sir Walter Ralegh

These three people all played an important part in English history. Imagine they have been invited to a talk show in which the host interviews them about their lives and ideas.

First copy the grid into your exercise book. Then listen to what the people say and put in more information about them. Before you start find out what these words mean:

to rule   wealth   wealthy   Armada   to explore   fleet   Virgin Queen   to execute

Who?	Elizabeth I	Drake	Ralegh
Job?	Queen of England	Sailor/explorer/pirate	Explorer/colonist/writer
Lived when?	…	…	…
Why famous?	During her reign England became rich and powerful. …	… … …	… … …
Other details?	… … …	… … …	One of Elizabeth's favourites until he married. …

2 The Renaissance

In the 15th century things started to change in Europe. The Renaissance (about 1480–1630) followed the Middle Ages.

1. Look at the information on the next page and say what changes there were.

2. How are they connected with Elizabeth I, Drake and Ralegh and how did they influence life in Britain?

3. Why do you think the Elizabethan Age (the time when Elizabeth I was queen) is often called the Golden Age?

⟨3⟩ Speaking practice: A discussion

Discuss the lives of the three talk show guests and decide which one played the most important role in the Golden Age.

focus 1

Christopher Columbus discovered a new continent, America, when he tried to find a new route to India for the Spanish queen in 1492. Ships and navigation had been improved so people were able to explore regions that had been unknown before.

Gold and other valuable goods were found in the New World. Europeans started to colonize it, and there was a lot of competition between them, especially between Spain and England. People began to emigrate and settle in the New World. Many hoped to become wealthy, others wanted religious freedom.

While the Renaissance in Europe produced some of the finest works of art and architecture in history, in England literature played a more important role during this period. Drama was very popular, especially the plays of William Shakespeare (1564–1616), one of the greatest writers of all time.

Henry VIII, Elizabeth I's father, broke with the Catholic church and founded his own church in 1534 because the Pope would not allow him to get divorced. Henry married six times. Two of his wives were executed.

The Reformation started with people like Luther and Calvin, and Protestantism came to England some time later. Protestants believed that people should know the Bible better and live more strictly according to its moral values. They thought there was too much ceremony in the Catholic church.

The printing press was invented by Gutenberg in about 1450. Later, when Luther translated the Bible from Latin into German, mass copies of it could be printed. This was important for the Reformation, as one of its main ideas was that people should have the chance to read the Bible in their own language.

⟨4⟩ A project

a) Choose one of the pictures or texts on this page, find out more about the topic and give a short talk.

Or: **b)** Find out more about William Shakespeare. Then prepare an interview between him and the talk show host and act it out.

twenty-three **23**

Unit 2 intro — On the southwestern coast

1. Cornwall with its cliffs, coves and bays – an ideal place for wreckers, smugglers and pirates.

2. Land's End, the far western edge of the world.

3. Falmouth: Ellen MacArthur arrived here on February 8, 2005, after she had sailed round the world in record time.

4. The Eden Project, near St. Austell, attracts over a million visitors each year. The place was once a clay-pit.

5. Tintagel, the legendary birthplace of King Arthur.

6. Jamaica Inn – the setting for a famous novel about smugglers.

7. Devon produces a lot of cider, a drink made from apples.

8. A traditional cream tea: a pot of tea with scones, thick cream and jam.

9. Wild ponies live on Dartmoor and Exmoor.

10. Plymouth, the port from which Sir Francis Drake sailed against the Spanish Armada in 1588. The Pilgrims' ship the *Mayflower* left there for North America in 1620.

11. Towns on the south coast's 'English Riviera' are full of tourists in the summer. The mild climate helps palm trees to survive, thanks to the warm influence of the Gulf Stream.

12. England's "Jurassic Coast" – a fossil-hunter's paradise.

1 Listening: A story from Cornwall

Listen to the recording and then discuss with your partner what you have heard.

a) Talk about the situation (who is talking, what they are discussing, …).

b) Now listen again to the story that one of the people tells. Ask your partner to repeat it in his or her own words. Help him or her with details that are missing or wrong.

to emigrate auswandern
to immigrate einwandern

2 Project: A map of your area

Make a map of your area like the one of Devon and Cornwall on these pages.

Form groups and decide:
- what information you want to put on your map
- who is going to do what (draw the map, draw pictures, write texts, …)

Skills: Working with words

1 Surviving without a dictionary

Read the text on the next page. New words are marked in blue. Don't worry, you will be able to understand most of them without a dictionary.

a) Put them into the following groups as you go through the text, and guess their meaning.

1. Words that look similar to German words: medicine, plastic …
2. English words you sometimes see in a German context: label, display, …
3. Compounds of words you already know: greenhouse, building material, …
4. Words from a word family you already know: importance, …
5. Words you already know, but with a different meaning: rubber, …
6. Words whose meaning you can guess from the context (translate the rest of the sentence and replace the new word by a word that would fit in): to refer to, steel, …
7. Words you cannot put into any of these groups: …

b) What are the main facts that you learn about the Eden Project from the text?

2 Using a dictionary

a) The following questions may help you to find the translation that fits best in the context. Look up the words from exercise 1 whose meaning you could not guess or you aren't sure about. Use the list of abbreviations to make dictionary work easier.

1. What is 'label' in line 4?
Is it a noun or a verb?

> **label** ['leɪbl] I. s ❶ Etikett(e f), Schildchen, Label nt; (Anhänge)Zettel m ❷ Beschriftung, Aufschrift f; Kennzeichnung f ❸ (fig) Bezeichnung, Klassifikation f II. vt ❶ etikettieren ❷ beschriften, kennzeichnen; markieren ❸ (fig) bezeichnen, benennen, klassifizieren; **label·ing** s (Am), **labelling**

2. What is 'focus' in line 7?
Is it a noun or a verb? If it is a verb, does it take an object (transitive) or not (intransitive)?
What other words is it used with?
Has it got anything to do with photos?

> **fo·cus** ['fəʊkəs] <pl focuses, foci> [pl 'fəʊsaɪ] I. s ❶ (MATH OPT) Brennpunkt m ❷ (fig) Brennpunkt, Herd m, Zentrum nt; **in (out of)** ~ (un)scharf eingestellt; **bring into** ~ scharf einstellen II. vt ❶ (OPT PHOT) einstellen (on auf) ❷ (fig) konzentrieren (on auf); **focus group** s (in marketing) [ausgewählte] Test-

3. What is 'flush' in line 49? Is it a noun, a verb or an adjective? If it is a verb, does it take an object (transitive) or not (intransitive)? What other words is it used with?

> **flush¹** [flʌʃ] I. vi rot werden, rot anlaufen II. vt ❶ (aus-, durch)spülen ❷ (Gesicht) röten; ~ **out** (Dieb) aufstöbern, aufspüren III. s ❶ (Wasser)Guss m, Spülung f ❷ Auf-, Erblühen nt; Blüte f ❸ Erregung f, Aufwallen nt ❹ Röte f; **in the first ~ of victory** im ersten Siegestaumel
> **flush²** [flʌʃ] adj pred in gleicher Ebene; bündig; **be ~** gut bei Kasse sein
> **flush³** [flʌʃ] vt (Vögel) aufscheuchen
> **flush⁴** [flʌʃ] s (Poker) Flush m
> **flushed** [flʌʃt] adj rot; gerötet

b) Now you can do these tasks:
1. Replace 'referred to' in line 17 by another expression.
2. Draw something that is dome-shaped.
3. Give the name of a Mediterranean country.
4. What does a humid place contain much of?
5. Which of the Eden plants that are mentioned in the text can be used as food?
6. Which word in the text is a false friend?
7. What abbreviation should go with the verb 'to grow' as it is used in this text (line 52)?

2 unit
A language

🔟 A Paradise on earth

The Eden Project near St. Austell in Cornwall was opened in March 2001. It is a huge greenhouse that contains about 250,000 plants from around the world, with labels
5 to explain what each plant is used for today (food, clothing, building material, medicine etc). A display which is focused on the importance of plants to civilization shows what is left of a modern home when all
10 the products that are made from plants are removed – hardly anything.

Half a million visitors went to see the Eden Project as it was being built, and over a million people have visited the place each
15 year since then. It is now one of the most popular tourist attractions in Britain and has even been referred to as the 'eighth wonder of the world'.

Two 'biomes', huge dome-shaped
20 greenhouses of steel and clear plastic, are the main attraction of Eden. Plants that grow in a Mediterranean, Californian or South African environment, such as olives, citrus fruits, maize and cotton can be looked at in one
25 of the biomes. However, it is the Humid Tropical Biome that is most amazing. It is big enough to hold the Tower of London and contains some of the most interesting tropical plants, such as tropical
30 hardwoods, coffee, bananas, pineapples, rubber trees and of course cocoa. A third biome is being planned for the future.

The greater part of the Eden
35 Project was paid for by lottery money, but it also earns money from visitors. A lot of these visitors may have been attracted to Eden because part of the James Bond movie 'Die another day' with Pierce Brosnan
40 was filmed in the biomes.

The aim of the project is to teach the public about the natural world and to show how natural resources have to be looked after so that they can still be used in the future.
45 For example, the rainwater that falls on the biomes is used to water the plants and create the mist of the rainforest. Even the toilets are flushed with rainwater. Nothing is done that might damage the environment. In fact, most
50 of the rare plants were not taken from the wild, but were grown from seed.

Overcrowding is becoming a problem at Eden, so sometimes the gates have to be closed. More and more car parks are being
55 built, and some are so far away that visitors have to be transported by special buses.

twenty-seven **27**

language A

1 Right or wrong?

Four of the statements below are wrong. Correct the mistakes.

1. The Eden Project was completed in March 2001.
2. It has about 250,000 plants from the Southwest of England.
3. Most products that are used in a modern home are made from plants.
4. The Humid Tropical Biome contains plants that grow in a Mediterranean environment.
5. The Eden Project has been paid for by money from visitors.
6. If there are too many visitors, the gates have to be closed.

2 At the Eden Project

Read what a visitor said. Then turn it into a written report. Change the active progressive forms into passive ones (see the box below).

grammar

The present progressive: active and passive:
They **are closing** the gates. (active)
The gates **are being closed**. (passive)

Explain how the present progressive passive is formed.
What about the past progressive passive?

"The Eden Project isn't finished, you know. They're planning a new biome and they're building new car parks. I think they're designing a new visitor centre, too.
When I was there, everybody was busy. They were planting trees near the entrance and they were watering plants in the gardens. And in one of the biomes they were making a film! They were doing a lot of work, I can tell you. We were lucky to get in. A lot of people arrived just as they were shutting the gates!"

3 Tim Smit's dream

Tim Smit is a Dutch-British businessman. The Eden Project was his idea.

Complete what he says with the right prepositions:

> into • with • of • about • for • after • to • at

"Although Eden has been written **1** a lot, people forget that this place was originally an old clay-pit. When I first suggested what it could be turned **2**, I was laughed **3**. Of course, there were problems, but these were all dealt **4**. The huge building costs, for example, were paid **5** by lottery money. But Eden has to be looked **6** by a large staff and that's expensive. Our biomes contain a lot of plants that most people have never even heard **7**. I am often spoken **8** by people who are simply amazed by the place."

4 Talking about the environment

Complete this dialogue. Use passive forms.

1. We must protect our environment.
   – Yes, of course. …
   ➔ Yes, of course. Our environment **must be protected.**
2. They're doing little to save the rainforest. – I agree. Little …
3. They've damaged large areas of it. – Isn't it terrible that …!
4. Will they ever clean our beach up? – Hm, I don't know if …
5. Everyone's talking about the Eden Project. – I'm glad …
6. I haven't seen it. They didn't allow me in. – Why …?
7. Overcrowding! They were just closing the gates when I arrived! – Oh, I'm sorry …
8. I hear they paid for it with lottery money. – Yes, …
9. They should create more projects like that. – I agree. …

B Two men in a boat

Rob and Frank have been on a sailing trip in the Channel in Frank's sailing boat, the *Southern Star.* Now Rob is phoning his girlfriend.

Rob: Hello, Polly? Can you hear me, Polly? It's Rob here.
Polly: Rob! Are you all right? I was told there was a terrible storm in the Channel. I've been so worried. Where are you?
Rob: We're being towed to Cherbourg.
Polly: Towed to Cherbourg! What's happened?
Rob: Oh, Polly, I'm lucky to be alive. This trip has been a disaster!
Polly: Oh dear, but you were really looking forward to it!
Rob: Well, everything was fine at first, but then the wind changed and became stronger and stronger. It blew us right off course and we got completely lost.
Polly: But you told me Frank was an experienced sailor.
Rob: Well, I thought so, but I was wrong. This was his first longer trip, and on top of that we got into a real storm. You won't believe this, but Frank had never been shown what to do in an emergency like that.
Polly: Oh my God! And what did you do then?
Rob: To make matters worse, Frank got terribly seasick and I had to take over! But how could I? I've never been taught how to sail! The situation was hopeless. We nearly sank because there was so much water in the boat.
Polly: That's awful!
Rob: But that was nothing! While I was getting rid of the water, we were nearly hit by a passenger ferry. I had no idea where we were, Frank was completely useless, and I couldn't control the boat. I didn't know what to do, so I sent a mayday call, and half an hour later the coastguards came. We were thrown a rope which we tied to the boat, and now we're on our way to safety.
Polly: Thank God!
Rob: Right, well, I'd better stop now. I'm being offered some whisky!
Polly: Cheers, Rob! But listen, when are you coming back to Torquay? I miss you!
Rob: Soon, I hope, but I'm never going to go sailing again!

1 Speaking practice: What happened?

Put the pictures in the right order and tell the story.

unit 2 language B

2 The personal passive

a) Find passive sentences in the text that express the same thing as these active sentences.

b) Translate the passive sentences into German passive sentences. What do you notice?
This special type of passive is called the **personal passive.** Can you imagine why?

1. Someone told me there was a terrible storm in the Channel.
2. Nobody had ever shown Frank what to do in an emergency like that.
3. Nobody has ever taught me how to sail.
4. Someone threw us a rope.
5. Someone is offering me some whisky.

3 Say it another way

Change the sentences into the personal passive.
Example: Someone sold me a very old boat. → I was sold a very old boat.

1. Nobody has given us any instructions yet.
2. Someone is sending the coastguards a mayday call.
3. Somebody had lent me a jacket.
4. Nobody has ever told me a story like that.
5. The French people offered us some coffee.
6. My parents had promised me a huge surprise.
7. A friend showed me an interesting newspaper article.

4 In the news

Write out the story below, with the verbs in the passive or active. Be careful with the tenses.

Englishmen rescued by French coastguards

Two men **1 rescue** by French coastguards early on Saturday morning. They **2 set off** from Torquay in a small sailing boat on Friday and **3 blow** off course by a storm. The men **4 pick up** three miles off the French coast. The boat **5 tow** to Cherbourg, where the men **6 give** dry clothes and **7 take** to hospital. After they **8 treat** for shock, they **9 hand over** to the police because they **10 not be** able to prove their identity. One of the men **11 say** he was Frank Wilson from Exeter. "We **12 not want** to go to France," he said, "that's why we **13 not take** our passports." His partner, Robert Smith, added, "We **14 tell** that the weather would be OK." Marcel Bertaud, one of the French coastguards, said, "If we **15 send** a mayday call, we **16 act** as quickly as we can. There **17 be** no lights on board the boat, so it **18 cannot see** by other boats. In fact, it **19 nearly hit** by a ferry. The channel **20 be** very busy. Up to 400 ships **21 use** it each day."

5 Listening: The rescue operation

a) Listen and answer the questions.

1. What mistakes did Rob and Frank make?
2. Does Captain Carbonne come on board the *Southern Star?*
3. Why are they asked to pay money to the French coastguards?
4. Make a list of sailing do's and don'ts.

b) Speaking practice:
Rob and Frank have an argument about who should pay the € 200. One of you is Rob, the other is Frank. Prepare your roles. Then act out the argument and try to find a solution.

30 thirty

G6

6 Word power: Word building

a) Make nouns from these verbs.

call • clean • drive • drum • play • farm • teach • keep • lead • manage • ride • score • sing • smuggle • speak • swim • win

What did you have to add? Find the rule.

fight + ?	bake + ?	begin + ?
…	…	…

b) What do you have to add to make opposites for these words?

ability • able • to agree • to like • to pack • necessary

c) Make adjectives from these nouns:

beauty • help • home • hope • use • wonder

7 Everyday English: Organizing your speech

Look at the following phrases. Make a grid with the headings: *Phoning a friend, Giving a talk, Having an argument.* Then decide which phrases you can use for each situation and put them in the grid. Some of the phrases fit into more than one list.

Phoning a friend	Giving a talk	Having an argument
…	…	…

1. I don't think you're right!
2. Hi, this is Rob.
3. I'm going to start with …
4. I've got to tell you about …
5. This isn't getting us anywhere.
6. First of all, …
7. You won't believe it, but …
8. In my opinion, …
9. You'll never guess what happened.
10. Furthermore, …
11. I'd better stop now.
12. It's true that …, but …
13. On top of that, …
14. I'd like to talk to you about …
15. See you later.
16. Now I'd like to turn to …
17. I don't agree.
18. Don't forget that …
19. Well, maybe you're right.
20. Bye for now.
21. Finally, …

8 Speaking practice

Choose one of these activities. If you record your dialogue or talk, you can listen again to find out what was good or bad about it.

Role play:
Phone your friend. Talk about your weekend. Arrange your next meeting.

Role play:
You want to stay up late to watch something really special on TV. Your mum/dad won't allow you to watch it.

Short talk:
Give a short talk about the place where you live.

The ghost of St Dominic

For many years Jack Todd did not know he had any living relatives. But on his fifteenth birthday, in the year 1785, he was told to pack his bags and prepare for a long journey. He was sent from an orphanage in London to the far western edge of the world to live with his uncle in the village of St Dominic, on the wild and rocky north coast of Cornwall.

Jack's uncle, the Reverend Humphrey Bellows, was the vicar of St Dominic. He lived by himself in a fine house near the church. He was a generous man and Jack was given fine clothes and plenty to eat. He was expected to do little jobs around the house when his uncle was away in London or visiting the fishing villages along the coast. And he also helped his uncle in the church on Sundays. People came from far and wide to enjoy the Reverend Bellows' services and his excellent communion wine.

At first Jack was lonely. He missed his friends in the orphanage and he hardly ever saw his uncle. But he did not stay lonely for long. The housekeeper, Mrs Bebb, had a daughter called Rebecca, a beautiful girl with long blonde hair and green eyes. She was about Jack's age and she liked to tell him stories about Cornwall as they sat in front of the kitchen fire.

"You know, this is the most haunted part of England," she said. The ghosts of drowned sailors, fishermen and pirates haunt the beaches and caves from here to Penzance!" Her eyes shone like a cat's in the firelight.

"Huh!" said Jack. He did not believe in ghosts. "Drowned men go to the bottom of the sea. The fish eat them."

"You don't know anything, Jack Todd," she replied. "Hasn't your uncle told you about Captain Parfitt yet?"

Jack shook his head. "I hardly ever see my uncle."

Mrs Bebb put a bowl in front of him. "You shouldn't talk about him like that. You're a lucky young man, Jack. If your uncle hadn't brought you here, you'd still be in that nasty orphanage! He always helps people in trouble – even people like Pierre."

"Pierre's a French sailor," explained Rebecca. "You sometimes see him in the village."

"Too often! Usually it's in the Fisherman Inn and he's drunk!" added Mrs Bebb. "He should be in prison! He was nearly hanged for killing an excise man, but they couldn't prove it. Your uncle said it was an accident and that saved his life. But he's a bad man, that Pierre."

■ After Mrs Bebb had left, Rebecca went back to her story. "Captain Parfitt's ship hit the rocks just off our cove. That was in 1720. But it was no accident. There was a terrible storm and some wreckers made a fire on our beach so that ships would think it was a lighthouse. Parfitt thought he was sailing into a harbour. When the ship hit the rocks, the crew were washed into the sea and drowned. Captain Parfitt drowned, too, but they say he cursed the village of St Dominic with his last words. The next day the excise men came to our cove. They found the ship in pieces, but they didn't find any sign of the cargo of wine and tobacco. The wreckers had stolen and hidden it. Although the village was searched, nothing was ever found. But Parfitt's ghost still walks along the beach at midnight. They say anyone who looks into his empty eyes will lose his soul and …"

"A fine story!" said Jack. "But I'm sure my uncle doesn't believe it." –

"Oh yes, he does!" Rebecca cried. "He's seen the ghost himself! Now nobody from the village dares to go down to the cove at night!"

"Hah! Well, I'm not afraid to go down there!" said Jack. "And you must come with me – so I

can prove to you that there is no ghost."
"No, Jack!" Rebecca protested. "We can't. It's dangerous! And your uncle won't allow it."
85 Jack laughed. "My uncle always goes to bed early, so he'll never find out."
Rebecca opened her mouth to say something, but Jack interrupted her. "Listen, he wants me to take some bibles from the church up to the
90 Fisherman Inn tonight. Let's meet behind the inn, then we can go down to the cove together. And if you aren't waiting at the oak tree at 11 o'clock, I'll go down there by myself!"

■ Later that evening Jack set off for the
95 Fisherman Inn. The bibles had already been carefully packed into a box by his uncle, and he pulled them in one of the carts that were kept in the church. It was a dark night. The moon was hidden behind clouds and Jack was
100 glad that he met no one on the way.
When he arrived at the Fisherman Inn, the landlord, Tony Pengelly, was there to meet him. "Ah! there you are!" he cried and took the cart. "I'll sort things out with Mr Bellows
105 the usual way, eh?"
When he saw that Jack didn't understand, he went on quickly, "Ah yes – well, off you go, young man. It's late. You should be at home in bed!"
110 Of course, Jack didn't go home. He went straight to the oak tree. He was glad that Rebecca was waiting for him there, and soon they were on their way down the steep cliff path to the cove. Fog was coming in from the sea and Rebecca
115 held on to Jack's coat in the darkness.
"Watch out for ghosts," he whispered, "if you believe in them! I don't." He tried to laugh, but his voice was trembling a little.
Slowly they made their way down to the beach and looked around. The moon came out
120 briefly and they could see some rocks and the entrance to a cave. A rowing boat had been tied to one of the rocks, but otherwise the cove seemed empty.
Jack felt better. "There's nobody here," he said,
125 "unless old Parfitt's ghost appears. Anyway, it's getting foggy. We won't see anything now."
At that moment, they both froze. A dark figure was coming towards them through the fog. Rebecca was shaking. "Look, Jack. It's … the
130 ghost. It's Captain Parfitt."
"Quick, let's hide in here," said Jack. He pulled Rebecca into the cave behind them. "Don't move, we mustn't be seen."
Inside the cave they found shelter behind
135 some rocks. They heard a sound. Something was being pulled across the sand.
"I hate you, Jack Todd," hissed Rebecca. "I should never have listened to you!"
"Don't worry, Rebecca," whispered Jack. "We're
140 safe here." But his heart was beating fast.
Suddenly, a light appeared at the back of the cave and for a moment a narrow tunnel could be seen there. Could they escape down it? But the dark figure had already reached the entrance of
145 the cave and was pulling something behind it. Then from the tunnel came a strange creaking sound. A moment later a tall figure came past them from the back of the cave, but it was too dark to see it clearly. The two figures met at the
150 entrance of the cave. Rebecca and Jack heard men's voices, but they couldn't understand what was being said.
"It sounds like French," whispered Rebecca. Suddenly there were angry shouts and one of
155 the men grabbed the other and knocked him over. He hit his head against a rock and lay absolutely still. Then the other man started to pull his body away until he disappeared into the fog and there was silence again.
160

■ Rebecca and Jack had watched all this in horror and now they waited for a few minutes until they thought it was safe. Then they crept out from behind the rock and were making

their way out of the cave when suddenly they saw the man again. He was coming towards them out of the fog. But when he saw them, he ran away. All they heard after that was the sound of a boat that was being rowed out to sea.

Jack's heart was still beating fast. "I think your ghost was more frightened of us than we were of him," he said. "Now let's see what he's left behind."

He took a candle out of his pocket and lit it. Inside the cave they found a large chest, and behind it a cart. They opened the chest and looked inside. It was full of tins of tobacco and bottles of wine. Rebecca and Jack looked at each other. Without a word, they lifted the heavy chest onto the cart and stepped into the tunnel. Rebecca led the way with the candle, and Jack followed with the cart, until they stepped out at the other end – into the crypt of the Church of St Dominic.

The Reverend Bellows and the Frenchman, Pierre, were never seen again. The same is true of the ghost of Captain Parfitt. For some time a vicar from another area came to St Dominic to hold the church services, but now, ten years later, the village has a popular new vicar, the Reverend Jack Todd. He and his wife Rebecca live quite comfortably in the house near the church which he inherited from his uncle.

A week ago an orphanage in London was given a generous sum of money. Where it came from and who sent it is still a mystery.

1 Difficult questions

a) Some questions are left open at the end of the story. But if you read it carefully, you can explain everything that happened.

b) Is Jack a 'good' character? Give reasons for your opinion. Think of what decisions he makes and what you would have done in his situation.

2 Creative projects

a) Choose one of the scenes from the story. Think about how it can be performed. Then write a script for it. That means a dialogue with comments on how to act it out, as in the example (Ext. = exterior, Int. = interior). Perform it and record it on video or tape. Or:

b) Turn the text into a picture story. Divide it into scenes and draw pictures or take photos for each one. Put the dialogue for each scene into speech bubbles.

Outside Fisherman Inn, Ext./night

Jack arrives with a box in a cart. It is dark. Some people are talking and laughing inside.

Jack (shouts): Good evening, Mr Pengelly. My uncle has given me these bibles for you.

Tony Pengelly comes around the corner.

Pengelly: Ah! there you are!

He takes the cart.

Pengelly: I'll sort things out with Mr Bellows the usual way, eh?

Jack looks surprised.

Pengelly: Ah yes – well, off you go, young man. It's late. You should be at home in bed!

Jack: Er – Goodbye, Mr Pengelly.

Jack walks away quickly.

3 A song: Smugglers (The Men They Couldn't Hang)

The boat rides south of Ailsa Craig in the waning[1] of the light,
There's thirty men in Lendalfit to make our burden[2] light,
And there's thirty horse in Hazelholm, with the halters[3] on their heads,
All set this night upon your life, if wind and water speed[4].

Chorus: *Smugglers drink of the Frenchman's wine,
And the darkest night is the smuggler's time.
Away we ran from the excise man,
It's a smuggler's life for me, it's a smuggler's life for me.*

Oh, lass[5], you have a cosy[6] bed and cattle you have ten,
Can you not live a lawful[7] life and live with lawful men?
But must I use old homely[8] goods[9] while there's foreign[10] gear so fine,
Must I drink at the waterside, and France so full of wine?

Chorus

Though well I like to see you, Kate, with the baby on your knee,
My heart is now with the gallant[11] crew that plough[12] through the angry sea.
The bitter gale[13], the tightest[14] sail[15] and the sheltered[16] bay our goal,
It's the wayward[17] life, it's the smuggler's strife[18], it's the joy[19] of the smuggler's soul.

Chorus

And when at last the dawn[20] comes up and the cargo's safely stored[21],
Like sinless[22] saints[23] to church we'll go, God's mercy[24] to afford[25],
And it's champagne[26] fine for communion wine, and the parson[27] drinks it too
With a sly[28] wink[29] prays, "Forgive[30] these men, for they know not what they do."

Words: Henry Stephan Cush, Shanne Hasler, Philip Frederick Odgers, Paul Wayne Simmonds

[1]Nachlassen • [2]Bürde • [3]Halfter • [4]sausen • [5]Mädchen • [6]gemütlich • [7]gesetzestreu • [8]hausbacken • [9]Güter • [10]ausländisch • [11]tapfer • [12]pflügen • [13]Sturm • [14]stark gestrafft • [15]Segel • [16]geschützt • [17]unberechenbar • [18]Kampf • [19]Freude • [20]Morgendämmerung • [21]verstaut • [22]sündenfrei • [23]Heilige • [24]Gnade • [25]sich leisten • [26]Champagner • [27]Pfarrer • [28]verschmitzt • [29]Zwinkern • [30]vergeben

a) How is the smuggler's life described in the song? Give examples of the dangers and the attractions.

b) Which of the ideas in the song also appear in the story 'The Ghost of St Dominic'?

c) Who is Kate? What do you think her relationship is with the smuggler in the song?

4 Speaking practice: Smuggling today

Smuggling is still a problem today.
Do you know what is smuggled today and why? Why is it a problem?
What could be done about it? Discuss these questions in class.

5 Mediation: Ein legendärer Pirat

Can you tell an English visitor what the guide says about a famous pirate who sailed the Baltic and the North Sea in the Middle Ages?

tip

Look at each paragraph separately. Find the most important points in each paragraph. Don't try to translate the text. You don't need to keep to the sentence structure. Just give the basic facts in your own words. Use simple vocabulary to express the gist. Only give details if you understand them and think they are important. Many of the points in the text cannot be proved.

For German 'soll', 'man sagt', 'der Legende nach', 'angeblich' you can use phrases like 'People say/think', 'According to the legend' etc.

Moin, moin, meine Damen und Herren,

willkommen im Hamburger Hafen, wo wir heute eine kleine Rundfahrt beginnen wollen, die sich mit einem legendären Freibeuter befasst, der zum Ende des 13. Jahrhunderts Nord- und Ostsee in Angst und Schrecken versetzte.

Zu Ihrer Linken sehen Sie hier die etwa 1,50 m große Bronzestatue eines Mannes aus dem Mittelalter. Die Inschrift auf dem Sockel lautet: Gottes Freund und aller Welt Feind!

Es handelt sich um Claus Störtebeker, der seinen Namen daher haben soll, dass er seinen Becher in einem Zug leerte – oder hinunterstürzte. Seine Herkunft ist umstritten, die meisten glauben jedoch, dass er aus der Gegend um Verden stammte. Man sagt, er habe in seiner wilden Jugend in Hamburg ausgiebig gerauft und gezecht und sein ganzes Geld durchgebracht, bis er der Stadt verwiesen wurde.

Er war ein sehr tapferer Mann und wurde einer der berühmtesten norddeutschen Piraten. Er plünderte die Handelsschiffe der reichen Küstenstädte und soll einen Teil seiner Schätze mit den Armen geteilt haben, was ihm bei den einfachen Leuten Bewunderung eintrug, so dass er manchmal als Robin Hood der Meere bezeichnet wird. Zahlreiche Legenden ranken sich um seine Person, zum Beispiel, dass er angeblich aus Reue über seine Taten dem Dom zu Verden sieben Fenster gestiftet haben soll. Außerdem habe er, nachdem er endlich gefangen genommen worden war, einen riesigen Goldschatz geboten, um sein Leben zu retten, der bis heute nicht gefunden wurde. Doch es nützte ihm nichts. Zusammen mit seinen Kumpanen wurde er am 20. Oktober 1401 in Hamburg geköpft. Der Legende nach soll ihm noch ein letzter Wunsch gewährt worden sein: Jeder seiner Männer, an dem er kopflos noch vorbeischreiten könnte, würde am Leben bleiben. Elf soll Störtebeker noch geschafft haben …

Über 600 Jahre nach seinem Tod ist Claus Störtebeker den meisten Einwohnern unserer Stadt oder anderen Nachbarn an der Ostsee bestens bekannt und seine Schand- bzw. Heldentaten werden von Generation zu Generation weitergegeben.

6 Mediation/Speaking practice: Telling stories

Collect stories about smugglers, pirates and ghosts in German. Look up important words in a dictionary if necessary. Then tell the stories to each other in English.

let's check unit 2

1 Word power

a) Explain what these words mean:

crew   cargo   harbour   ferry   seasick

b) What do these people do?

sailor   wrecker   smuggler   pirate   landlord

c) Draw a picture to show what these words mean:

entrance   edge   bottom   top

d) Say what is made from:

cotton   steel   plastic
rubber   cocoa   wood

e) Use words or phrases you have learnt in this Unit to replace the words in **blue**.

1. We **got** my grandfather's house **after he died**.
2. I was lost in the forest. And **then** it started to rain, **too**!
3. These birds are **ones which you don't find very often**.
4. This key **is the right key for** the lock.
5. Nobody **is brave enough** to talk about the problem.

f) Put words from the boxes together to make as many new words as you can.

| air • birth • coast • green • hard • land • light • pass • pine • rain | apple • forest • guard • house • day • bow • lord • port • place • water • wood |

2 Getting the facts right

Put the words in the right order to make questions, and give the answers.

1. **What** • Sir Francis Drake • from • port • did • sail?
2. **What** • from • cider • made • is?
3. **What** • like • the southwestern coast • is • of • the • landscape?
4. **What** • lottery money • for • was • paid • Cornwall • in • attraction • by?
5. **What** • from • was • built • materials • it?

3 Personal passive: Verbs with two objects

a) Complete the sentences with the correct indirect object.

Jack   the orphanage   Tony Pengelly
the people who came to the church   Rebecca   the crew

1. In 1785, the Reverend Humphrey Bellows sent ? a letter in which he asked for Jack.
2. The next day, the owner of the orphanage gave ? instructions to pack his bag.
3. The Reverend Humphrey Bellows offered ? plenty of good food to eat.
4. He also served ? his excellent communion wine.
5. Mrs Bebb brought ? and ? some soup.
6. Rebecca told ? the story about Captain Parfitt, but he didn't believe a word.
7. Captain Parfitt had promised ? a safe journey.
8. Jack gave ? his uncle's cart.
9. Someone gave ? a generous sum of money.

b) Rewrite the sentences in the personal passive. Give the 'by-agent' if necessary.

thirty-seven 37

revision Books 1–3

The talking dog

One day, a guy sees a sign in front of a house: 'For sale: Talking dog'.
He rings the bell and the owner opens up. "Come in," he says. "The dog's in the back yard."
So the guy goes through to the back yard and finds a dumb-looking dog sitting there.
"You talk?" the guy asks.
"Sure do."
"Wow! So what's your story?"
The dog looks up and says, "Well, I found out a few years back that I had this gift of speech. I decided I wanted to help the government, so I told the CIA. They took me on, and in no time I was jetting around from country to country, sitting in rooms with world leaders and secret agents. Obviously I was a great asset because naturally nobody figured a dog was listening in. For eight years I was one of their most valuable spies. But in the end the job tired me out, and I decided to give it up, get myself a wife, have puppies and settle

Sure do.

down. So here I am now, just retired and enjoying life."
The guy is amazed. He goes back in and asks the owner what he wants for the dog.
"Ten dollars," the owner says.
"I don't believe this!" the guy says. "That dog's a marvel! Why on earth are you selling him so cheaply?"
"He's a liar, that's why. He never did any of that stuff!"

1 Word power: Words in context

a) Find these words in the text, and decide which of these meanings is correct in the context.

1. **sale**:
   • Auktion? • Schlussverkauf? • Verkauf?

2. to **figure**:
   • gestalten? • in Erscheinung treten? • glauben? • eine Ahnung haben? • eine Rolle spielen?

3. to **settle down**:
   • sich hinlegen? • sich häuslich niederlassen? • sich beruhigen? • sich eingewöhnen?

b) Find words or expressions in the text that mean …

1. gave me a job; 2. very soon; 3. clearly; 4. of course.

c) Look at the context, then explain the meaning of these words and expressions:

1. to jet around; 2. a secret agent; 3. to listen in; 4. a puppy; 5. a liar.

d) Find other new words in the text and work out their meaning. Then use a dictionary to check if you were right. Which one is a false friend?

2 Talking about the text

a) What makes the story funny? Do you like stories of this kind? Say why or why not.

b) Try to remember a story or joke you know – perhaps about an animal. Then tell it to a partner in English.

revision
test yourself

Test yourself!

3 People and places

a) Make negative sentences. Write down your answers, then turn to page 186 to check them.

1. Matt comes from Sydney. (✗ Melbourne)
2. The Wangs speak Chinese. (✗ Japanese)
3. Matt met Lin in the street. (✗ her parents)
4. The Donovans have got a swimming pool. (✗ tennis court)

b) On Lin's first day at the local school, the others asked her a lot of questions. This is what they found out:

What questions did they ask? Write them down, then turn to page 186 to check them.

Lin Wang
- Lives in Rockdale.
- Family comes from China.
- Came to Australia 10 years ago.
- Lived in Adelaide first.
- Moved because father got a better job in Sydney.
- Mother works, too (in an office).
- Family speaks Chinese at home.
- Likes: surfing; barbies; dancing.
- Hates: homework; museums; milk.

4 Questions with and without "do"

Write down the questions, then turn to page 186 to check them.

1. "I met one of your friends last night." – "Oh? Who ___ (meet)?"
2. "Something strange happened to us yesterday." – "Really? What ___ (happen)?"
3. "Do you like my Valentine's card?" – "Great! Who ___ (send) it?"
4. "I want to have a big party." – "Right. Who ___ (want) to invite?"
5. "We've got a great tennis team!" – "Who ___ (play) in it?"
6. "Have you got tea and coffee?" – "Yes. Which ___ (prefer)?"
7. "Both these pairs of shoes look nice!" – "OK, so which ones ___ (fit) best?"
8. "My sister's got a very good job." – "Really? What ___ (do)?"

5 Jack and the ghost

Use the information below to complete the sentences on the right with relative clauses. Write down your answers and note where contact clauses are possible. Then turn to page 186 to check.

a) A ghost appeared on the beach at night.
b) Jack is vicar of St Dominic now.
c) Her daughter was called Rebecca.
d) Jack and Rebecca would never forget that night!
e) Jack had never heard of his uncle.
f) Jack Todd was sent to St Dominic.
g) The vicar used an excellent red wine at his Sunday services.
h) There was wine and tobacco on the ship.
i) Rebecca told Jack stories about Cornwall.
j) Captain Parfitt's ship went down in a storm in 1720.

1. In 1785, Jack had news from an uncle ___ 2. St Dominic was the name of the village ___ 3. His uncle, the vicar, had a housekeeper ___ 4. Jack enjoyed the stories ___ 5. Rebecca knew about a captain ___ 6. Wreckers stole all the wine and tobacco ___ 7. After that, people were scared by the story of a ghost ___ 8. Years later, the people of St Dominic enjoyed the wine ___ 9. But in 1785, on a dark night ___, the vicar disappeared for ever! 10. The Reverend Todd is the name of the man ___

Example: 1. In 1785, Jack had news from an uncle **(who / that) he had never heard of.**

revision Units 1–2

6 Say it with "if"

a) Example: I was so tired, I didn't stay up to watch that film on TV.
→ If I **hadn't been** so tired, **I would have stayed up** to watch that film on TV.

1. Sorry I didn't send you a card from New York, but I didn't have your address.
2. We missed our flight because there was so much traffic on the way to the airport.
3. The holiday wasn't a success – the weather was really awful!
4. I never knew it was Judy's birthday, so of course I didn't buy her a present.
5. The accident was caused by a dog that ran onto the road.
6. Dad wasn't able to collect us from the party – so we had to walk home.

b) Which type of conditional sentence do you need here? Look at each situation carefully. In two cases you will need "mixed" forms (with Type 2 and Type 3).

1. I'm not going to order that DVD – it's so expensive!
2. Please come round here tonight so I can show you the photos Jack and I took in Queensland.
3. I hope I'll feel better tomorrow. I'd love to go outside again.
4. Bad luck you live so far away – so I can't visit you often!
5. Sorry I didn't go to that museum with you – I didn't feel well that day.
6. I'd like to get steaks for dinner on Sunday. Does your friend eat meat?
7. Sorry I can't go to Cornwall with you next weekend. I'm afraid I've got no time.
8. Hurry up! We don't want to miss our train.
9. We have a dog. So we weren't able to look after the Bradens' cat when they went away.
10. Those jeans didn't fit well, so I didn't buy them.
11. My parents never learnt German at school. So they can't help me with my German homework.
12. I'd like to go to Italy, but I can't speak Italian at all.
13. Luckily John wasn't badly injured in the crash, so he didn't have to go to hospital.
14. I hope I'll have time to go to the match with you on Saturday.
15. There aren't a lot of hotels here because the beach isn't good for surfing.

7 Word power: Phrasal verbs

Expressions with a verb + preposition or short adverb can be called "phrasal verbs". Find the right ones to complete these sentences.

1. Please ___ the TV ___ before you go to bed!
2. If a language isn't spoken any more, in the end it will ___ ___.
3. What does "asset" mean? – Let's ___ it ___ in the dictionary.
4. Are you cold? ___ your jacket ___, then!
5. It'll be a long journey. Let's try to ___ really early!
6. Do you think this red T-shirt will suit me? Perhaps I should ___ it ___.
7. Grandpa's dropped his keys. Can you ___ them ___, please?
8. Where does Sue live? – We can easily ___ ___.

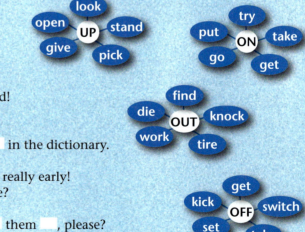

revision 1

Passivo!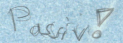

8 Using the passive

Put these sentences into the passive. Use the personal passive where possible.
Think carefully before you decide whether it seems necessary to use a "by-agent" or not.

1. Our neighbours are going to look after our cat when we go down to Cornwall.
2. Someone has given me this brochure about the Jurassic Coast.
3. People sometimes refer to the Eden Project as the "8th wonder of the world"!
4. Eden doesn't have enough car parks. When will they deal with this problem?
5. They showed us the place where they're going to build the new biome.
6. My uncle paid for the cream tea we had at "The Old Teapot" café in Torquay.
7. They're turning that big house on the cliffs into a hotel.
8. We visited St Dominic, but nobody told us any stories about ghosts there.
9. The local vicar disappeared in 1785, and nobody ever heard of him again.
10. When I was in Exeter, someone from Southwest Television was interviewing tourists outside the cathedral.
11. If you get to the hotel late in the evening, they'll probably only offer you sandwiches.

9 Passengers rescued from river ferry

Passengers on a river ferry at Dartmouth in Devon **1 have to** **2 rescue** by a coastguard crew yesterday afternoon. 23 passengers, two crew and fifteen cars **3 carry** across the River Dart in terrible weather when it suddenly **4 happen**: the chains[1] that **5 use** to pull the ferry across the river **6 break** by the strong wind and waves. Moments later, the boat **7 begin** to move down the river towards the open sea. After emergency calls **8 send** out by some of the passengers, coastguard crews **9 arrive** on the scene, and they **10 manage** **11 stop** the ferry just before it **12 reach** the sea.

The passengers **13 throw** ropes, then they **14 put** on a lifeboat[2] and **15 take** to safety. But yesterday evening coastguards **16 say** the cars **17 not take** off the ferry yet. They **18 explain** that this **19 cannot** **20 do** until the ferry **21 pull** back to its normal position again. "We **22 not know** yet when the cars **23 return** to their owners," a coastguard **24 tell** passengers. "We **25 be** sorry for the trouble that **26 cause** by all this."
Nobody **27 injure**, but at 6 pm yesterday two of the passengers **28 be** still at the local hospital, where they **29 treat** for shock.

[1][tʃeɪnz] – Ketten • [2]['laɪfbəʊt] – Rettungsboot

Complete the text of this newspaper article. Decide which forms are needed – active or passive. Be careful with the tenses and forms of the verbs.

10 Cartoon

What else might she say? Collect ideas and make sentences with **would have / could have / might have**. These ideas will start you off.

"You could have used the wood to build us a shelter. Then we would have ..." •
"We might have made a fire. Then maybe ..." •
"If you'd ..." / "If you hadn't ..."

"Any other man would have built a raft[3]!"   [3][rɑːft] – Floß

unit 3 intro: Young people in Scotland

1 One of the most popular shows at the Edinburgh Festival every summer is the Military Tattoo. However, the Festival is not just bagpipes and Scottish traditions, it is a big international celebration of all kinds of cultures.

2 At least it costs nothing to enjoy the beautiful scenery. The Scottish Highlands have the highest mountains in the UK.

3 If you are interested in wildlife, there are lots of interesting animals and birds you can look at. You would have to be very lucky to see the famous monster in Loch Ness!

4 Although whisky is produced in Scotland, the UK tax makes it more expensive there than in many other countries.

5 Over the years lots of immigrants have made their homes in Scotland, especially in its biggest city, Glasgow. So don't expect to meet only people with names that begin with 'Mac' (it means 'son of').

6 Kilts were originally worn only by men, in their own family tartan, while women wore long skirts. These days you don't see so many kilts except at special events – and of course in shops for tourists.

1 Typically Scottish?

a) Say which texts go with which pictures.

b) Now describe what you can see in photos A to G.

c) What else do you know about Scotland? Where did you get the information?

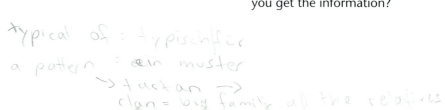

2 Listening: Three teenagers

a) First look at the information about Amir, Emma and Mark. Then listen to what they tell Florian Seiler, a German boy who is visiting Scotland with his family. While you listen, take notes about what they say.

Amir Hassan	Emma Campbell	Mark Slater
born in Glasgow • parents own corner shop • good at school • loves football • big Celtic fan	lives in Fort Augustus • southern end of Loch Ness • mother runs family bed and breakfast business • father is a mechanic • crazy about horses	originally from England • moved to Aberdeen last year • father works on oil rig • interested in Scottish history and traditions

b) Use your notes and the information in **a)** to talk about the three teenagers in Scotland. What is typically Scottish about their interests and lifestyle? Compare them with your own interests and lifestyle.

c) Now look at Donald McDonald. Some people might call him a typical Scotsman. What do you think? Why do people often have wrong ideas about other countries? What is the best way to get correct information?

Donald McDonald

Unit 3 language A

A Please, Dad!

Jody Morrison lives with her father in a flat in Livingston, a town west of Edinburgh. Their meal has been interrupted by a phone call from Jody's best friend, but now Jody is back at the table.

Dad: It'd be nice if we could have tea without any phone calls for a change! Look, the food on your plate is cold now. It was the same with the tea I made for you yesterday.

Jody: Oh, I don't mind cold food. And Morag wanted to discuss arrangements for Saturday.

Dad: Couldn't she have waited half an hour? She clearly wasn't in a hurry because you talked for such a long time! Anyway, arrangements for what?

Jody: Er – I was planning to tell you. You see, this is the Saturday when everyone's going to the Barrowland in Glasgow. There's a great rock concert, and it's only £10 a ticket, and –

Dad: Wait a minute. We've had this argument before. You're too young to be out and about alone in a big city late at night.

Jody: I'm not too young. I'll be fifteen in May. Anyway, I won't be alone. I'll be with Morag and Rory and Brad.

Dad: Who are Rory and Brad?

Jody: You know very well who Rory is. He's Morag's older brother. And Brad's an American from New York. He's at the school Rory goes to, and he's here because his father's with a local company. He's a software designer or something.

Dad: ■ It's quite a long way to Glasgow, you know. How do you think you're going to get there and back?

Jody: By car. Rory's already seventeen, and he passed his driving test last week. So –

Dad: I can't believe you think I'm going to let you set off along a busy motorway with some young idiot with a new driving licence in his pocket. No way!

Jody: It's not fair to call poor Rory an idiot when you hardly know him. And if the MacLeans didn't think he was a good driver, they wouldn't lend him the car, would they? See? You can't answer that!

Dad: Please don't use that tone, Jody.

Jody: Sorry. But it's not as if I hang out with the wrong kind of people or anything. And I usually do OK at school, don't I? So if I work hard five days a week, I think that at the weekend I should be allowed to have fun.

Dad: But I don't like the idea of you at a big rock concert. What if you get separated from the others? Safety is an important issue, especially for young girls. I'm sure that if you become a parent one day, you'll worry about the safety of your children, too.

Jody: You're probably right, but I hope I'll also remember what it was like to be young, and to want freedom. – Please, Dad! I've been looking forward to this so much.

1 Talking about the dialogue

a) What is the problem between Jody and her father? Make a list of the arguments they each use to underline their view.

b) Can you think of a solution to the problem? Use your own ideas to finish the dialogue.

44 forty-four

A language

2 Using the indefinite article (a/an)

a) Use these examples from the dialogue to explain the difference between English and German when you describe someone's nationality or job.
Brad's an American … – He's a software designer …

b) Look in the dialogue for phrases with 'such', 'quite' and 'half'. What do you notice about them?

3 The definite article (the)

a) Copy the grid below. Then complete it with more phrases from the dialogue.

examples of	no article	definite article
uncountable nouns	safety is an important issue	the safety of your children
institutions (college, church, …)	…	…
names of meals	…	…
means of transport	…	…
names of days and months	…	…

b) Look at the lists of examples with no article and with the definite article. Can you make a rule?

4 On the phone

Complete what Jody tells Morag on the phone. Choose from the nouns on the right. Use the same noun twice, once with the definite article and once without it.

life   love   time   bus
fashion   school   money

1. Dad always complains about ☺ I spend on the phone. But ☺ goes so fast when you talk to friends! *time*
2. There's a good article about ☺ in this week's 'Shout'. I really like ☺ in the shops at the moment. *fashion*
3. ☺ is a problem with me. I've already spent almost all ☺ I got for my birthday. *money*
4. I think there's too much pressure at ☺ we go to. I think we should have more fun at ☺. *school*
5. My aim in ☺ is to get an exciting job. I wouldn't like to live ☺ of most adults I know. *life*
6. I'll come over to your house by ☺. I'll get ☺ that leaves just after three o'clock. *bus*
7. You fall in ☺ with every new boy you meet! Tell me. Who's ☺ of your life now? *love*

5 Jody's e-mail to her mother

Put in the correct articles – definite and indefinite – but only where you need them.

Sorry I didn't send you **1** e-mail yesterday, but I was tired after all **2** fun on **3** Saturday evening. I didn't get out of **4** bed and have **5** breakfast until late, and then I had to learn about **6** history of Scotland in the Middle Ages for **7** test at **8** school today. We get tests once **9** month in **10** history – it's enough to give anyone **11** headache! Anyway, I wanted to tell you what **12** great time I had in Glasgow. In **13** end we went by **14** train – Dad's idea. We got **15** early train so we wouldn't be in **16** hurry. In fact we arrived **17** hour and **18** half before **19** concert – but that was good because otherwise we wouldn't have been so close to **20** stage with such **21** good view. And **22** music was brilliant – I hadn't realized how much more exciting **23** music is when it's live. It was funny because one band had **24** drummer who looked just like Brad, Rory's friend from **25** United States who was with us. As **26** result, a girl asked for Brad's autograph after **27** concert. He loved that. He says it's cool to be **28** pop star with **29** lots of fans!

G7, 8

forty-five **45**

unit 3 language B

🔴 19 **B It makes me so angry!**

STEAMPOT

A big 'Hi' to all you young Scots who are listening out there. Yes, it's me again, Coleen Murdoch, with **Steampot**, the show where you can let off steam about things that have made you angry. What has made you boil this week? Call and tell us your story now!

Emma: My family have a bed and breakfast place, and last week we had an Englishwoman who complained about everything. Really stupid things, like the stairs were noisy, the furniture in her room was too old, the information we gave her about the area wasn't what she needed, the police weren't as friendly as in England. But what really made me mad was when she said the people here speak with a funny accent. Anyway, the good news is that she's left now. But on her last morning she was so rude at breakfast that I thought I'd give her a reason to complain. So I put lots of extra salt in her porridge. Well, everyone has their breaking point, don't they? And I wanted revenge!

STEAMPOT

■ **Amir:** I overheard two guys in a café who were complaining about the homeless in Glasgow, and saying that they should be kicked out of the city. They thought the British should make it a crime to sleep in the street. Well, I didn't say anything because you can't make people like that change their minds. But I found it very hard to stay silent. I think we should do a lot more to help the disadvantaged in our society. I'm sure it wouldn't be too hard to raise the money. Most people – not just the rich – could pay a bit more tax. Those two guys, for example – I'm sure it wouldn't hurt them at all.

■ **Morag:** I was on my way to see a friend of mine here in Livingston the other day. And while I was waiting at a bus stop a woman ordered me to pick up an empty crisps bag on the ground. It wasn't mine, but she just assumed I was the one who'd dropped it. I mean, why didn't she say anything to the man in front of me in the queue? The bag could just as easily have been his. No, it was just another example of how older people are always ready to blame kids. They always think everything is our fault, not theirs. It makes me so angry!

1 Your reactions

a)
1. Was Emma's revenge too much?
2. Should Amir have said something?
3. Is Morag right about older people?

b) Imagine you call the show to let off steam. What would your story be?

B language

2 Singular and plural

a) Look at the nouns (and verbs that go with them) in Emma's story and think what they would be in German. Then copy this grid and complete it.

noun	plural form only + plural verb	singular form only + singular verb	singular form + plural verb	plural form + singular verb
stairs	X			

b) Check the information in **G9** on page 113–115. Then complete what an American guest says to the Campbells with the correct verb forms.

1. Look – do you think my new tartan trousers (**suit**) me? suit
2. I can understand why the Scottish people (**feel**) so proud of their beautiful country. feel
3. I think the best advice for tourists (**come**) comes from local people, not from guide books.
4. I think Highland cattle (**look**) great with their long hair! look
5. You have a wonderful home – that lovely old furniture (**have**) so much character. has
6. The information about Loch Ness in our guide book (**seem**) to be quite good. seems
7. I notice that the police in Scotland (**not carry**) guns. don't carry
8. The news (**be**) good – sunshine all day tomorrow. is
9. I don't want to hike quite so far. Ten miles (**sound**) like an awfully long way to me! sounds

3 Adjectives as nouns

a) Find examples in Amir's story where adjectives are used as nouns. What do they describe?

b) Use these adjectives to complete the descriptions from a TV and radio guide:
blind • poor • homeless • English • famous • rich ✔ • nervous • young • disabled

1. **Different worlds:** a look at the different lifestyles of the **rich** and the poor.
2. **Kidshop:** Saturday morning entertainment for the young.
3. **Life on the street:** the problems of the homeless
4. **Wheelchairs welcome:** holidays for the disabled
5. **Startalk:** more interviews with the famous
6. **Through the eyes of a dog:** a report on how guide dogs for the blind are trained.
7. **Our southern neighbours:** A group of Scots discuss the English
8. **Night of Horror:** not a film for the nervous

c) Which of these phrases can be replaced by 'the' and an adjective? Explain why. Find the best way to translate the phrases into German. What do you notice?

disadvantaged people • a crazy person • the old man • dead people • a Welsh girl • able-bodied people • some rich people • two sick people • a stupid person • French people

4 Possessive pronouns

Emma is helping with the breakfast. Complete what her mother says with the correct pronouns.

mine   yours   his   hers   ours   theirs

Germans seem to like coffee with their breakfast. I must say, I prefer tea with **mine**. That orange juice is for the French family. The Seilers have already got 1 . Ah, that porridge I forgot is ready! Well done, Emma! It was a good idea of 2 to microwave it.

No, that's not Mrs Seiler's plate. 3 is the one with no egg. Florian likes bacon, so that one is 4 . At last! All the guests have got their breakfast. Now we can have 5 . Your father? He got up hours ago. He's gone fishing with a friend of 6 .

G9–11

language B

5 Mediation: Florian's e-mail

Back in Germany, Florian wants to write an e-mail in English to his new friend Mark in Aberdeen. Follow the instructions below and write the e-mail for Florian. Compare versions with a partner.

→ Sag Mark, dass eure Rückreise schwierig war – kurz nach der Forth-Brücke Panne mit Mietwagen gehabt – Auto von einem Mechaniker namens MacAlister (wie in seinem Witz!!) repariert – viel Zeit gekostet – Flug verpasst.
→ Erzähl, dass ihr drei Stunden auf nächsten Flug warten musstet – Sandwiches und Getränke zum Mittagessen gekauft – Picknick gemacht – ein Desaster – Vater kippte Orangensaft um – landete voll auf Mutters weißer Hose – Mutter schrie lauthals.

The Forth Bridge, near Edinburgh

→ Erzähl, wie alle Leute geguckt haben – hoffentlich denken Schotten nicht, dass Deutsche immer so laut sind!
→ Sag ihm, dass bei Ankunft in München Probleme nicht vorbei – Koffer von allen Fluggästen da – nur eure nicht – noch in Schottland!
→ Sag ihm, dass du auch gern dort geblieben wärst – morgen musst du wieder in die Schule!

6 Mediation: *Do* and *make*

a) Read the joke below. Then tell it to your partner in German. What verbs did you use for the expressions with 'do'?

Jimmy and Bobby work as gardeners. They've got a lot to do today, but they're sitting in the greenhouse with their feet up when their boss comes in.
"What are you doing, Jimmy?" he asks.
Jimmy looks embarrassed. "Er – nothing, sir."
Their boss is angry. He turns to Bobby.
"And what are you doing, Bobby?"
"I'm helping Jimmy, sir."

b) Look at these expressions and discuss the difference in meaning between them. What would you say in German? Use a dictionary where you need to.

c) Put these German phrases with 'machen' into English and make two lists – expressions with 'do' and expressions with 'make'. Then choose three phrases from each group and write your own sentences with them.

1. What are you doing?
2. What are you making? 3. What do you do?
4. How do you do? 5. How are you doing?
6. We've made it! 7. That won't do!

tip
'Do' is the correct word to use about work or obligation. 'Make' often expresses the idea of a result or product. There are no clear rules, so it is best to learn the whole expression.

| Hausaufgaben • das Frühstück • Geld • Geschäfte • ein Projekt • Lärm • eine Arbeit • einen Anruf • Vorschläge • Einkäufe • einen Unterschied • Fehler • ein Experiment • nichts • das Beste daraus • 200 Stundenkilometer | machen |

Skills: Preparing for your oral exam

In your oral exam you either take part in a dialogue (which you can practise on this page) or give a short talk (see the Skills page in Unit 4).

1 How to deal with vocabulary problems

It is important to keep talking and not use any German. If you don't know a word, paraphrase it. Practise with these words you might need to talk about a trip to another country.

Unterkunft • anstrengend • faulenzen • Grenze • eindrucksvoll • Vorurteil • gepflegt • sich täuschen • Umrechnungskurs •

2 Dialogues

a) First read the dialogue without the **blue** phrases. Then read it again with the phrases and say what their function is.

Edinburgh Festival

Hazel: I'm not going to be here next week.
Emma: **Oh?** Where are you going to be?
Hazel: My aunt in Edinburgh has invited us to stay during the festival. **Great, huh?**
Emma: **You lucky thing!** I've never been to the festival. It's a busy time of year for us.
Hazel: It's not much fun for you, **is it?**
Emma: **I know, but** I can't change it.
Hazel: **Hey, wait a minute.** Your parents are busy with the guests. Not you. **Right?**
Emma: **Well,** I sometimes help, but –
Hazel: **Exactly.** You don't have to. So you could come to Edinburgh with us.
Emma: **Hey, are you serious?!** I'd love to.
Hazel: **Great!** My aunt has got lots of space and I'm sure she wouldn't mind.

b) Make dialogues for these pictures with a partner. First think of the following things:

- Decide who is going to play which role.
- Look carefully at the situation and identify with your role. (Thoughts? Reactions?)
- Collect ideas and key words you can use.
- Use phrases that show your partner that you are listening to him or her.

3 Listening: The piece of chewing gum

a) You are going to hear another phone call to the radio show 'Steampot'. The caller is Jody Morrison. Before you listen, look at the heading and imagine what Jody is complaining about. Collect ideas.

b) Now listen. Take notes so you can explain what Jody's problem is and how Coleen reacts.

c) Your own view: Say what you think about chewing gum and people who use it.

Unit 3 text

22 The kiss (by Rosie Rushton)

I shouldn't have done it. I wouldn't have done it if I'd known what would happen. But I thought they'd kill me if I didn't do it.

1 Before you read the whole story, comment on these first three sentences. Why do you think the author starts the story like this? What do you think the story might be about?

It happened yesterday, but it started weeks before. I've always been the odd one out at school. My face is lopsided, my skin's a strange colour and my top lip is almost invisible – that's because my big sister played with matches when she was three and my buggy caught fire with me in it. I don't play sport because the skin on my feet is all funny and even when I'm laughing my face doesn't look happy. I can't do many expressions. It doesn't mean I don't feel things.

It was the middle of last term when they started. Spike and his gang, I mean. At first they just called me names – Ugly Face, No Lip – and grabbed my books and threw them over the wall. Maybe it would have stayed like that. If only I'd been thick, or not at school that day, maybe none of this would have happened.

It was Science with Mr Conway. What he does is, he grabs one of you and uses you as an assistant in experiments. It was my turn that day: I'd been dumb enough to get an A for my last assignment and so he chose me. Anyway, he'd just started and he struck a match, some stuff caught fire and I screamed. Well, actually I did more than that – I shouted and ran out of the room. The thing is, I can't remember the fire in the buggy, but Dad thinks my body does. I see a flame and alarm bells ring. I never even go near a barbecue. You have to admit – old Conners didn't make a scene. Just told me later he was sorry and he hadn't been thinking. But from that minute, Spike and his gang had me just where they wanted me. On the way home that afternoon they stopped me and Karl pulled out a box of matches. Luke and Adam pushed me against a fence and Spike grabbed the matches from Karl, struck one and held it up to my face.

"See this?" he sneered, while he waved the flame near my right eye. "I'm gonna burn off your eyelashes with this."

You wouldn't think one little match could make you feel hot all over but it did.

"Well?" Spike went on. "Yes or no?"

"Wh…wh..what d'ya mean?" My heart was beating in my ears so loudly that I could hardly hear my own voice.

"Burn – or do what we say?" said Karl.

I didn't reply. I felt sick.

"More!" Spike ordered Karl.

I fought. I promise you I did. I turned my head, I kicked with my feet, I even tried to pull my arm round and knock the matches from Karl's hand. But when the flame of the fourth match touched the eyelashes of my left eye, I screamed. Over and over.

"OK, OK, I'll do anything – stop it – please."

"I think," Spike said, "we've got a result."

■ And that's how it started. At first it was cigarettes, then they wanted booze as well. The first few times I didn't steal from shops – I took cigarettes from Mum's bag and a bottle of whisky from the drinks cupboard. But in the end I had to use shops because Spike wanted stuff we never had at home. I went to Mr Patel's at the corner of our street. And all the time I felt sick and the words 'Thief, thief' were going round in my head. Then last week, just when I was going out of the shop with cigarettes, Mr Patel shouted "Hey you!" and I ran down the street, round the corner and was sick all down my trouser leg.

80 I didn't sleep that night and the next morning I was sick again and Mum kept me at home. At first, the doctor said it was a 'virus'. Then he decided it was all in my mind, and I was just unhappy. He asked all 85 those dumb questions – "Anything wrong?" (Like, you want a list?) and "You can always talk about your problems, you know." (Oh sure, and then wait for Spike's revenge.) Anyway, I was away from school for three 90 weeks and when I went back, there was this new girl in my class.
The moment I saw her, I knew what all those love songs were about. Shelby, her name was. Is. She'd come to our town from Montana, 95 which is in America – because her father was working on some project at the college.
"Hi," she said to me that first morning at break. Just like that. "Hi." It may be nothing special to you, but you probably look normal. 100 Most people look away when they first meet me, or they offer me seats and smile sweetly to prove how good they are with the disabled. Shelby didn't do anything like that. She just spoke to me like I was normal.
105 "Hi," I replied.
"Are you better?" she asked.
"Better than what, exactly?" I grinned.
And she laughed. Not the awful embarrassed laugh at my lopsided lips, but a real, throw 110 back your head kind of laugh.
"That's cool," she said.
And that's how we started. Sounds good, doesn't it – 'we'. I'd never been part of a 'we' before. It was just mates, of course; nothing 115 more, but it was nice. At lunch times we hung out and talked and it was cool.
Until Spike and his gang noticed us.
"We've got a job for you, Ugly Face," Spike said at lunch time last Wednesday. "Adam 120 is having a party and we need booze. So get it." He was looking not at me, but at Shelby, whose eyes were getting wider. "Or else."
"Chris," Shelby asked after the gang had gone, "what was that guy talking about?"
125 "Him?" I shrugged. "Oh, my dad sells booze and he lets my mates have …"
"Chris Matthews, I'm not a fool," she said. "They want you to steal it, right?"

"What do you think I am?" I replied.
"A thief? Well, thanks very much!" 130
And with that, I marched off.
She didn't look at me for the rest of the day. Or the next day.
"Got the booze?" Spike asked at lunch break.
"No," I said flatly. "I'm not getting any 135 more."
They couldn't do much about it right then, but they got me after school. They held me on the ground and they kicked me and then struck a match and burned the ends of my 140 hair.
That's when I went crazy. I screamed and shouted "Help" over and over until Adam put his hand over my mouth.
"Wait!" Spike's tone made the other two stop 145 what they were doing to me. "Got an idea."
I was fighting for breath.
"You like Shelby, right?" Spike said.
"She's OK," I answered. There was blood on my lip and I was in pain. 150
"This is what you're going to do," Spike said. "Kiss her."
"What?" The idea had been in my mind for days, but the reality was hopeless. I can't even do the kiss shape in the mirror. 155
"Tomorrow. After school, behind the sports pavilion," Spike ordered. "Be there or die."
Even bullies like him don't kill people. I knew that. But I wasn't quite ready to prove it.
"Shelby," I said the next morning. "I need to 160 talk to you."
"To say what?" she asked. "How good you are at stealing stuff?"
"No," I answered quickly. "I'll never do that again as long as I live." 165
"You mean it?"
"Sure," I said. "It was dumb. It's just that when you look like a freak …"
"You don't look like a freak and if you want to feel sorry for yourself, I'm not hanging 170 around," she said. "Now what did you want?"
So I told her.
"And you, Chris Matthews, want me to kiss you just because they told you to? Well, thank you for nothing!" 175
She turned and walked off. I ran after her.
"It's not that – well, I mean it is that, but

it's not like I don't want to. I want to a lot but …"
"You do?"
I nodded sadly. "It's no good anyway. I can't do it. I don't know how."
"Right," she said. "Be there."

■ If only I hadn't been such a coward, if only I'd told someone … all the 'if onlys' in the world won't change a thing.
At four o'clock, we got to the sports pavilion. Spike and the gang were there – and also about fifty other kids.
"So what are you all staring at?" Shelby shouted. "We're not going to do anything."
"Do it or die," Spike ordered.
"By fire," added Adam.
"Slowly," sneered Karl. That's when I saw the fireworks in Spike's pocket – the ones called Flame Thrower that explode and shoot out blue and yellow flames.
"I'll do it," I said quickly.

"No," protested Shelby. "Stand up for yourself. What are you? A wimp?"
I stopped. I knew I was a wimp, but I loved Shelby and I wanted her to admire me.
But by then, Spike had stuck a firework in the ground next to my foot. Karl struck a match. "Kiss!" shouted Spike, "Or we light it."
"Kiss, kiss, kiss," the crowd of kids shouted.
My heart beat wildly. I leaned towards Shelby and tried to make my lips the right shape. I knew from the loud laughs that I was not doing it very well.
I've lived the next bit over and over in my mind. I saw Shelby's eyes wide with horror, and I guessed it was because of my ugly face so close to hers. But then, out of the corner of my eye I saw that Karl had lit the firework.
"Move!" Shelby shouted.
She pushed me to one side and put out her hand towards the firework.
"Noooo!" I screamed.
But it was too late.

2 The story

a) Look again at Exercise 1 and compare your expectations with what actually happened.

b) Who are the three main characters in the story? Give a short description of each.

c) What problems does Chris have? Talk about the effect they have on him and on other people.

d) The diagram shows how the level of tension goes up and down. What points in the story do the numbers stand for? Write short notes.

1. Chris is angry with himself (lines 1–3);
2. First problems with the gang (lines 15–19).
3. …   Go on.

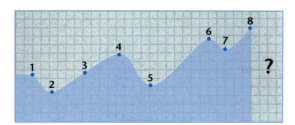

3 Creative writing

a) The end of the story is missing. Collect ideas about how it could end.

b) What style of language does the author use, and why? What are the characteristics of this style? Give typical examples from the story.

c) Write your own ending. Try to write your text in the same kind of style.

4 Speaking practice: A discussion

"All bullies are cowards." – Do you agree with this view?

5 Word power

Which words in these phrases from the story make the language especially informal?
What words could you use to make the style more formal?

1. If only I'd been thick (line 20)
2. alarm bells ring (line 34)
3. they wanted booze as well (line 66)
4. Spike wanted stuff we never had at home (line 71)
5. Oh sure, and then wait for Spike's revenge (line 88)
6. It was just mates, of course (line 114)
7. we hung out and talked and it was cool (line 116)
8. they got me after school (line 138)
9. I knew I was a wimp (line 201)

◉26 6 A song: Why does it always rain on me? (Travis)

I can't sleep tonight
Everybody saying everything's all right
Still I can't close[1] my eyes
I'm seeing a tunnel at the end of all these lights

Sunny days
Where have you gone?
I get the strangest feeling you belong[2]
Why does it always rain on me?
Is it because I lied when I was seventeen?
Why does it always rain on me?
Even when the sun is shining
I can't avoid[3] the lightning[4]

I can't stand myself
I'm being held up by invisible men
Still life on a shelf when
I got my mind on something else

Sunny days …

Oh, where did the blue sky go?
And why is it raining so?
It's so cold
I can't sleep tonight

Everybody saying everything's all right
Still I can't close my eyes
I'm seeing a tunnel at the end of all these lights

Sunny days …

Oh, where did the blue sky go?
Oh, and why is it raining so?
It's so cold
Why does it always rain on me?

Words: Francis Healy

[1]schließen • [2]hier etwa: das schlechte Wetter gehört dazu • [3]meiden • [4]Blitz

a) What kind of feelings are expressed in the song? Can you identify with them?

b) Talk about the images in the song. What do the 'weather' phrases stand for? What can you say about the line 'I'm seeing a tunnel at the end of all these lights'?

c) How does the music help to stress the important words?

> Travis is a band from Glasgow, with Fran Healy on vocals and guitar, Dougie Payne on bass, Andy Dunlop on guitar and Neil Primrose on drums. Healy, Payne and Dunlop met at the Glasgow School of Art. The band's first album in 1997 went straight into the Top 10, while their second in 1999 went to Number 1 and helped to inspire a new style of acoustic rock music.

fifty-three **53**

unit 3

let's check

1 A names quiz

Find the correct names.

1. What is the part of Scotland with the highest mountains called?
2. What is the name of the largest city in Scotland?
3. Where does Scottish oil come from?
4. What do you call the musical instrument that is traditionally played in Scotland?
5. Where do tourists go to look for a monster?
6. Which river reaches the sea just north of Edinburgh?

2 Word power

a) Give definitions of these words.

> to overhear • queue • to blame • term • disadvantaged • to assume

b) Give the opposite of these words and phrases.

> beautiful • to borrow • to drop • polite • hero • to shake your head

c) Complete the words missing from these sentences.

1. Don't worry, I'm sure you'll p___ the test.
2. I'd hate to be a prisoner and lose my f___.
3. Nobody said a word – everybody was s___.
4. I can't stop and talk because I'm in a h___.
5. I really a___ the way he's overcome so many problems.
6. The only f___ in the room was a table.

3 A letter to Germany

Use these notes to start a letter from a Scottish boy to a German boy. Decide where you need to put in extra words, especially the definite and indefinite article, and how to organize the ideas into paragraphs.
Go on and think of your own final paragraph to finish the letter.

- Dear Thomas • found your name and address on 'Links' page of magazine I was reading
- thought interesting to have German as new friend
- my name Cameron • fifteen • live in Highlands in town called Fort William • quite small place but lot of tourists • summer and winter • Ben Nevis near here highest mountain in United Kingdom
- although not such difficult one to climb as some others in area • have been to top few times myself
- come from quite big family • two brothers and sister • father hotel manager • mother teacher • but glad to say not at school I go to • favourite subject at school art
- interested in nature, too • sometimes paint pictures of local scenes or wildlife • last year sold three to souvenir shop in town centre • got £15/picture!

let's check

4 Taking part in a dialogue

Work with a partner. One of you is **A** and the other is **B**. Read your notes. Then discuss where you could spend a week in Scotland together. Explain your view, but also listen to and answer your partner's arguments.

A: Edinburgh
- easy to get to by air
- beautiful city
- things to do in all kinds of weather (important in Scotland!)
- lots of culture
- shopping
- evening entertainment

B: Fort Augustus
- fantastic scenery
- complete change from everyday life
- discover the 'real' Scotland
- meet local people in B&B places
- chance to look for Nessie!

Edinburgh

Fort Augustus

5 Mixed bag: Greyfriars Bobby

Complete the text with the missing words.

In about 1850 **1** man called John Gray arrived **2** Edinburgh. Because he was **3** to find work as a gardener as he **4** hoped, he had to look for another source **5** income. He was lucky. He got a job with the police (who **6** looking for somebody **7** could help to keep the streets safe **8** night). Every night John walked through the **9** of the city with his little dog Bobby. They **10** always together. There could not **11** been a closer pair **12** friends. However, **13** some years, John became ill and **14** the 15th February 1858 he died. His **15** was put in a grave in Greyfriars Churchyard.

At the churchyard there was a keeper **16** job was to keep the gates locked and **17** to allow anybody in. (In those days **18** dead were sometimes stolen from their graves.) When the keeper first **19** Bobby he didn't know whose dog it was. He couldn't understand why Bobby was in such **20** hurry to get into the churchyard. But **21** Bobby managed to get through the gates and

lay down on John's grave, it was clear that the dog was **22**. The keeper chased Bobby away a few **23**, but it was no good. He came back **24** and again. In the end the keeper gave **25** and let him stay. Soon this news **26** the main topic of conversation all around the city. Everybody heard **27** the little dog that could not **28** separated from his friend even **29** death. The only time that Bobby ever **30** the grave was to go and get his dinner every day. While John had been **31**, he and Bobby had often eaten at the Coffee House. All the people who worked **32** knew Bobby. He was a friend of **33**, so they were happy to feed him for nothing. Everyone wanted to do **34** best for him. Someone even gave **35** a dish with the words 'Bobby's Dinner Dish' on it. Bobby lived next to John's grave **36** fourteen years until his own **37** on the 14th January 1872. His dinner dish can still be seen at **38** Museum of Edinburgh, and **39** is a statue of him in the street near Greyfriars Churchyard.

focus 2 Focus on the New World

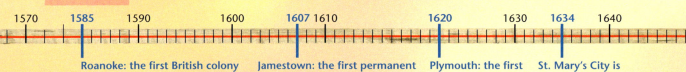

1570　**1585**　1590　　1600　　**1607** 1610　　　1620　　1630　**1634**　1640

Roanoke: the first British colony is founded by Sir Walter Ralegh, but it is not permanent.

Jamestown: the first permanent colony is set up by the Virginia Company of London.

Plymouth: the first Puritan colony is founded by the Pilgrims.

St. Mary's City is founded. Catholics are free to practice their religion in Maryland.

1 Life in the early colonies

May 16th, 1638
Mother died exactly two months ago today. Life since then has been terrible. I've been begging in the streets of London, because without Mother we had nothing to eat and I was starving. But this evening I met a rich lord at the 'Angel' pub. He's offered to take me to America with him. He needs servants to help him build a big house and work on his land. If I work for him, he will provide me with food, clothes, tools and shelter. I'll be free when I'm 21, and he'll give me some land of my own. It sounds very exciting. It's such a long way to America – and it's very dangerous. But what do I have to lose?

July 28th, 1638
We've arrived in Maryland – but what a terrible journey! Most of the passengers on our ship were sick the whole time. Once we were caught in a huge storm and I was sure we were going to die. We all prayed for our souls. Although our ship was seriously damaged, the crew managed to repair it, so we finally made it. Some Catholics came with us. They say they'll be treated better here in Maryland than they were in England. I like it here – everything is so different from London! The plants and animals, the climate, and of course the Natives.

September 4th, 1638
I've been here for five weeks now. I'm glad I'm still well. So many people have become ill since we got here. The work on the farm land is very hard. In the evenings we read the Bible, and those who can read and write teach the others. A lot of people have come to the New World because they weren't allowed to practice their religion in England. My master is very strict, but at least we get enough to eat, as the settlers have learned from the Natives how to grow corn.

November 6th, 1638
The winter is going to be very cold. Some of the people who came on the ship with me have already died of disease, but it will get worse in the winter. We haven't got much food, the cabins are dirty (we share them with the pigs), and the doctor here has no medicines to treat people who are ill. When those that are already weak get a fever, they are unlikely to survive.

December 26th, 1638
Our first Christmas away from England! I had dinner with the Smiths. I gave their two little boys some wooden toys I had made. They were really happy! I talked to Gwen for a while after church. She's a nice girl. When I get my own piece of land I'm going to marry her.

January 22nd, 1639
Mrs Miller, the wife of one of the men I work with, had a baby last night. The little girl was dead when the morning came. It's so sad, but only half the children who are born here are able to survive. I hope Gwen and I will have lots of healthy children one day.

a) Read the extracts from the diary and talk about the boy's experiences.

b) What were the reasons why people left Britain? How could they get to America? What was life like for the early settlers? What was better/worse than in Britain?

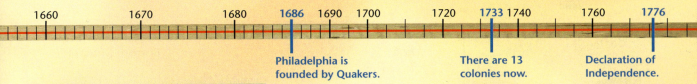

1660   1670   1680   1686 1690   1700   1720   1733 1740   1760   1776

Philadelphia is founded by Quakers.

There are 13 colonies now.

Declaration of Independence.

The 13 colonies

2 British colonies in America

a) Use the map, the time line and the diary to collect information about the early colonies. Then make a quiz for your partner. Close your books and answer each other's questions. Here are some ideas: When was … founded?/Which colony had a border with …?/Which was the first …?/Who …?/Why…?/When…?

b) Try to find out what the stars and stripes on the US flag stand for.

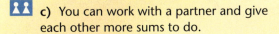

3 Listening: Shopping in the settlement

When you bought goods in a storehouse in the days of the early settlers, prices were added together with the help of a counter board because paper was very expensive then.

a) Make your own counter board and use some coins as counters.

b) Listen to find out how it works. Then do these sums: 21 + 7, 34 + 12, 154 + 49

c) You can work with a partner and give each other more sums to do.

Unit 4 intro — New England

Boston

221 Faywood Avenue
Boston, MA 02128

Hi, Susie!

I thought I'd better write you a letter this time – instead of an e-mail! – so I can send you a few things that may interest you about Boston and the surrounding area.

It took me a while to get used to Boston. It's the biggest city in New England (although actually it's not so much bigger than Baltimore) and I felt a bit lost here at first. But I've made some nice friends now at my new school, and I think I'll really start to feel at home here soon. Boston is one of the oldest cities in the US. It was founded in 1630 – so of course there are lots of old buildings. (But it isn't all history! Dad and I went to the Museum of Bad Art last week. It was so funny – some of the paintings were unbelievably bad!) There are lots of students here in Boston – that's because of all the colleges and universities in this area (there are 50 at least!). The most famous one is Harvard – the first American university – which is in a part of Boston that's called Cambridge. (Lots of places around here have English names. No wonder it's called New England!)

Last weekend we went to Cape Cod (where the Pilgrims first landed). On the way back we visited Plymouth (where they decided to settle). 'Plimoth Plantation' was absolutely great!

Well, you'll find out more from the stuff I'm enclosing. I'm looking forward to your next e-mail. (It was great you gave me your address. There are so many strange people in these chatrooms, you can't be too careful …) And tell me something about your hometown. Where exactly is Barre? Somewhere in Vermont, I see from the address, but where?? I couldn't find it anywhere on the map.

Bye for now,
Kate xxx

P.S. I'm also enclosing an Indian dreamcatcher I got for you at Cape Cod. Hang it up over your bed – and it'll chase all your bad dreams away, and maybe the good ones will come true!

Harvard

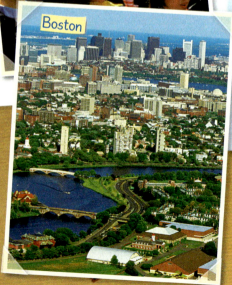

Boston

intro

1 Kate and Susie

Look at all the material on these two pages and find out all you can about:

- Kate and Susie.
- Boston and New England.

Is there anything else you already knew? Find the places that are mentioned here on the map at the back of the book.

2 Listening: At the Lobster Pot in Plymouth

Kate and her parents are in Plymouth.

a) Listen, and take notes about …
→ what's on the menu.
→ what each of them decides to eat and what kind of dish it is.
→ how they like it/what problems come up.

b) Talk about kinds of food you like or don't like. Have you had any interesting experiences at restaurants – perhaps on holiday? Are there any specialties you would (or wouldn't!) want to order?

Unit 4 language A

3 A An e-mail from Susie

Rock of Ages Quarry, Barre

State House, Montpelier

Farm in Vermont

Hi there, Kate!

Thanks for your letter. I really enjoyed reading it – and loved looking at all the things! The dreamcatcher is cute! I'm not afraid of having bad dreams now! Yeah, I guess leaving all your friends in Baltimore wasn't easy. But Boston sounds great!

I can't really imagine moving to a big city. I'm so used to being in a small town. I have to admit I like living in Vermont. And my parents have never thought of going anywhere else anyway. They don't mind staying here in Barre.

Barre (you pronounce it "Barry") is famous for having the largest granite quarries in the world. (The steps of the Capitol in Washington are made out of granite from our Rock of Ages Quarry.) And it's very near Montpelier (pronounced "Mont-PEEL-yer"), the state capital of Vermont. As capital cities go, Montpelier is kind of small – with a population of under 9,000 – so it's the smallest state capital in the US. It's pretty cute, though. Our State House is a grand white building that looks a bit like the White House – but with a gold dome!

Vermont (from the French 'les monts verts') is also often called the Green Mountain State. The Green Mountains are great, especially if you're interested in hiking or mountain biking. And they're fantastic for skiing (the winters here are pretty long). I'm really crazy about skiing! A lot of the kids around here are good at skiing or snowboarding. Some of them start doing winter sports when they're in kindergarten.

One of my friends had a cousin from Germany here last summer. He kept telling her that Vermont reminded him of Bavaria! (Where is Bavaria? Do you know?) More next time. I'm looking forward to getting your next mail.

Susie

P.S. Why don't we meet some time? Let me know if you feel like visiting us here in Vermont! (If you ever get tired of being in the city …) Mom suggests waiting till September (because of the fall leaves! They're really spectacular!).

A language

1 Is that right?

If you find anything wrong here, put it right.

1. Susie enjoyed reading Kate's letter, and she would like to live in Boston, too.
2. Although they're used to living in a small town, Susie's parents are actually thinking of moving somewhere else soon.
3. Montpelier is famous for being the smallest of all U.S. state capitals.
4. Susie likes skiing, but she says she's more interested in mountain biking.
5. She started snowboarding when she was in kindergarten.
6. She is looking forward to seeing Kate in Boston, and suggests going there in August.

2 Gerunds

a) All the -ing forms in the box are gerunds. Try to explain what a gerund is – and how it works.

Skiing is great. I love skiing. Is Susie good at skiing?	Baseball is great. I love baseball. Are you good at baseball?

b) Find more examples in the text and put them into two groups:

verb + gerund	verb/adjective/etc. + preposition + gerund
…	…

c) Talk in groups – or with a partner – about what you enjoy doing – and why. Write down a few ideas before you start. (You might think about drama, music, sports, books, entertainment, etc.)

Example: I'm very interested in music, and I love playing the piano. But I don't like playing in front of an audience because I get so nervous! – Well, I love football. I enjoy watching it on TV, of course. But I'm even more interested in playing myself because I love doing sports!

3 On vacation in New England

Complete what these people say – with suitable gerunds, and prepositions where they are needed.

go   do   experience   try   look   drive   stop   sit

see   explain   wonder   come   hunt

1. "What do you feel like **1** today? Are you interested **2** to one of the museums here in Boston?" – "OK, then. I suggest **3** the Computer Museum. Look at this brochure! It says they've got an enormous 'Walk-Through Computer' there, with a 250-foot keyboard! I'd really enjoy **4** a walk through that!"
2. "I'm tired **5** in the car, Dad! How much further are you thinking **6** today?" – "I don't mind **7** soon, honey. Just another hour or so on the road, I'd say. Then we can start **8** for a place to stay."
3. "Wow! The colors of the trees are unbelievable! I'd been looking forward **9** to New England in the fall for ages. But I never imagined **10** anything as spectacular as this! Why do they call it 'Indian Summer'?" – "Well, the Indians always liked **11** bears at this time of year. And when the leaves on the trees turned bright red like this, they started **12** why. They thought the color must come from the blood of the bears they'd killed. The Indians were good **13** natural events with stories and legends like that."

4 Say it with gerunds

Gerund constructions are very often used – in everyday spoken English, and in written texts, too. Use expressions with gerunds to change these sentences. (But make sure that the meaning stays the same!)

1. Would you like to go to the Green Mountains for the day?
→ Would you **be interested in** going to the Green Mts. for the day?
2. Sorry, but I really can't ski at all – I'm hopeless!
3. We can leave early – I've nothing against that.
4. It'll be great to see you!
5. Susie learned to ski when she was only four.
6. I don't really want to go up the mountain again!
7. I've got an idea – let's go to the café for a hot drink.
8. Good idea! We can wait there till the snow stops.
9. On my first day on skis I fell down a lot.
10. When it's foggy, I'm always worried I'll lose my way!

- be interested in …? ✔
- be afraid of …
- look forward to …
- don't mind …
- be no good at …
- stop …
- feel like …
- start …
- suggest …
- keep …

5 Word power: Building new words

a) Look at these new words – how they are formed and what they mean.
(Look carefully at the spelling of the new words. Can you work out a rule?)

- An **enjoyable** holiday ➜ That's a holiday that you enjoy (have enjoyed/will enjoy).
- An **unbelievable** story ➜ That's a story you really can't believe!
- An **unforgettable** adventure ➜ That's an adventure you will never forget.

1. A glass that you can't break ➜ That's an **unbreakable** glass.
2. An anorak you can wash
3. A question you can't answer
4. A dog that can't be controlled
5. Someone you find easy to like
6. An experience people can't imagine
7. A shot that can't be stopped
8. A bottle you can return to the shop

b) The endings **–ful**, **–less**, **–y** and **–ing** can also be used to form adjectives. Use definitions or think of ways to explain the meaning of these:

1. A helpful map ➜ That's a map that helps you to find the right way or route.
2. A useless pen
3. An uneventful day
4. An understanding friend
5. A hopeless situation
6. A relaxing weekend
7. A headless monster
8. A painful experience
9. Smelly socks
10. A milky drink
11. A meaningless song
12. A rainy day
13. Meaty sausages

6 A song: Unforgettable (Natalie Cole/Nat King Cole)

Unforgettable, that's what you are
Unforgettable though[1] near or far
Like a song of love that clings to me
How the thought[2] of you does things to me
Never before has someone been more …

Unforgettable in every way
And for evermore[3], that's how you'll stay
That's why, darling[4], it's incredible[5]
That someone so unforgettable
Thinks that I am unforgettable, too

[1] egal, ob • [2] Gedanke • [3] auf immer und ewig • [4] Liebling • [5] unglaublich

Talk about an unforgettable experience.

Words: Irving Gordon

B The 1627 Pilgrim Village

Welcome to Plimoth Plantation: The living history experience

"Welcome to the town! How do you fare? Are you just passing through? Or mayhaps you are desiring to settle in this wilderness?"

This is the kind of greeting you can expect to hear when you arrive in the 1627 Pilgrim Village, a re-creation of Plymouth Colony, a small town which was built by English colonists. These Pilgrims were the first English people to settle in New England.

Instead of speaking modern American English, the role players in the village talk to each other – and to all the visitors – in the language of Shakespeare's England! It's important for you to remember that – for them – the year is still 1627. Just seven years after the 'Mayflower' arrived from England.

Don't worry, you won't be the only visitors to feel surprised by this at first. You'll soon discover that it's no use trying to talk to the role players about life in the 21st century. It's no good mentioning things like phones – or even bathrooms! They won't have any idea what you're talking about.

The role players here in the village have all taken on the names, opinions and life histories of people who actually lived in the colony in 1627. By talking to them and asking them questions, you will hear their stories – and it will be easier for you to imagine those difficult times they went through after they arrived on the 'Mayflower'.

Apart from talking to the visitors, the 'Pilgrims' have work to do. Don't be shy! The colonists want you to walk around their village and step into their houses to see what they are doing. It can be fascinating for visitors to watch the women at work by the fire and to see the pots and pans they use for cooking their food. See how a duck or a fish is cooked – without using gas or electricity, of course! It will also be interesting for you to talk to the men as they work in the gardens and fields. They have had to learn how to build and repair houses and fences, how to grow crops, work with timber, look after animals, and so on.

It's worth spending at least two hours in the 1627 Pilgrim Village – or more if you can manage it. It will be an unforgettable experience!

Unit 4 language B

1 About the Pilgrim Village

Use information from the text to answer these questions that visitors sometimes ask.

1. Did any English people settle in New England before the Pilgrims?
2. Why do the role players at the village speak such a strange kind of English?
3. How can you find out about the real Pilgrims who came on the 'Mayflower'?
4. What jobs do the role players have apart from answering visitors' questions?

2 Looking at grammar: Gerund constructions

a) Find examples of gerund constructions in the text. Put them into two groups.

b) Now translate the expressions you have found into German. What kinds of constructions do you use?

after certain expressions with 'it is …'	after certain prepositions
…	…
…	…

3 Early days

Only half the Pilgrims who came on the 'Mayflower' managed to survive the first winter in America. All the others died. Put the sentences together to find out more.

1. A lot of the Pilgrims arrived in the 'New World' without …
2. They didn't have the right tools at all for …
3. Some of the women had never learnt to do anything apart from …
4. At first they didn't want to eat strange foods, in spite of …
5. The English wanted to eat lamb instead of …
6. In the end the Wampanoag Indians helped them by …

- looking after a family.
- seeing that the food they had brought with them was running out.
- giving them food and showing them how to grow corn.
- building a colony in the wilderness.
- having any experience of farming, hunting or fishing.
- trying new tastes like wild duck, turkey and lobster.

Now translate the sentences into German to show you've understood the gerund constructions.

4 Looking at grammar: Infinitive constructions

a) There are also some new infinitive constructions with 'to' in the text. Find three in lines 4–23 and write them down. Translate them into German.

b) Now put these sentences together with the help of infinitive constructions.

1. Visitors should get into conversation with the role players. That's important.
2. Are you surprised they speak 17th century English? You won't be the first person!
3. The 'colonists' will answer your questions about life in 1627. That won't be difficult.

The Mayflower

4. The Pilgrims came to America for religious reasons. They weren't the only people that did this.
5. They had to start a new life in the New World. This wasn't easy.

5 Hobbamock's Homesite

Apart from the Pilgrim Village, visitors to Plimoth Plantation can also see Hobbamock's Homesite, where they can find out about the way of life of the Wampanoag people. Use infinitive or gerund constructions to complete the text.

As of course you know, the Native Americans were the first people **(live)** on this continent. When you visit Hobbamock's Homesite, it's important for you **(remember)** that the people you meet there are Native People. They would like you **(realize)** that they are NOT role players! It's nice for them **(talk)** to you about their past, but the things they want **(tell)** you are always told from a modern perspective. A lot of visitors do not quite know what **(expect)** when they come here, especially if they have just been to the Pilgrim Village.
Watch the Wampanoag while they work and see how they cook. Keep **(ask)** questions! The staff want you **(talk)** to them and **(say)** so if you would like them **(repeat)** things or **(explain)** anything you don't understand. **(Look)** at Hobbamock's Homesite won't take as long as **(see)** everything at the Pilgrim Village. Here there are only two houses **(visit)**. But it's certainly worth **(plan) (spend)** at least an hour here. Allow yourself plenty of time **(ask)** the Native People about all the things you would like **(know)**. But we ask you **(be)** careful about certain things. For example, although the Native staff members look forward **(answer)** your questions about the history and culture of their People, **(talk)** about their own lives and personal experiences is something they naturally do not feel like **(do)** with visitors.

> Welcome to Hobbamock's Homesite. I am Wampanoag, and my people have lived here in New England for over twelve thousand years.

6 Everyday English: Acting and reacting

a) Find pairs of phrases that go together.

1. I don't know what to do tonight.
2. Do you feel like watching a DVD?
3. Do you want me to help you?
4. Sorry for shouting at you just now!
5. When do you want us to come? At seven?
6. Can't you ever listen to what I say without interrupting?
7. Hurry up! I'm tired of waiting!
8. Do you mind shutting the window?

a) Fine! We look forward to seeing you then!
b) How about going to the movies?
c) Please stop complaining! I'm nearly ready.
d) No, it's OK – but thanks for offering!
e) Great idea! Let's watch the James Bond film I bought last week.
f) Of course not – it's getting a bit cold now.
g) Forget it! It's not the end of the world.
h) Sorry. I thought you'd finished.

b) Make more dialogues with a partner. Think what you might want to say in these situations. Some of the phrases in **a)** may help you. Otherwise use your own ideas.

1. You missed your bus – so you've arrived late.
2. Your sister's music is on loud – and you're trying to do your homework.
3. A friend is moving house next Saturday. There'll be a lot of work to do.
4. You're wondering who you want to invite to your birthday party.
5. One of your friends has come round for the evening.
6. You are planning a trip to a museum at the weekend.

G12 (3c–4), G13

7 Mediation: Wampanoag and Pilgrims

Maria from Hof is at Hobbamock's Homesite with her parents. Listen to what Russell Hinton, a staff member, tells them. Later, Maria's parents ask her to explain some of the things they didn't quite understand. What does Maria say? (Listen again if you need to.)

The Pilgrims' first Thanksgiving

Mutter: Was war noch mal die Bedeutung des Wortes Wampanoag? Das hab' ich nicht ganz mitgekriegt. *Maria:* …
Vater: Russell hat etwas von Krankheiten erzählt. Sind die Pilger auf der Reise krank geworden, oder wie war das? *Maria:* …
Mutter: Ach so! Dann ging's ja um 'trouble': Probleme also. Haben denn die Engländer alles bestimmen wollen? *Maria:* …
Vater: Wahrscheinlich kamen die Ureinwohner den Engländern schon seltsam vor, oder? *Maria:* …
Mutter: Aber schön, dass sie das erste Erntedankfest zusammen gefeiert haben. War das die Idee der Indianer? *Maria:* …
Vater: Was haben sie denn beim Fest alles gegessen? Fisch und Kartoffeln hab' ich verstanden. *Maria:* …
Mutter: Ah! Und wie feiern die Amerikaner heute ihren Danktag? *Maria:* …

8 Mediation: Covered Bridges

Diane's cousin Max is visiting from Germany. He has a guide book of New England. She sees this page and ask a lot of questions. How does Max explain?

"Hey, that's about our Covered Bridges! New England is famous for them. Does it explain why we call them 'kissing bridges'?"
"I've no idea when they were built. Does it say?"
"Funny, I often thought, 'Why build a bridge with a roof?'"
"The Cornish-Windsor Bridge? I've never seen that one. What's so special about it?"

Niemals oben ohne

Covered Bridges, überdachte Brücken, gelten als historische Wahrzeichen und beliebte Fotomotive Neuenglands, besonders wenn zur Herbstlaubfärbung leuchtend bunte Blätter die Brücken umrahmen. Seit jeher wurden sie – ein wenig romantisch verklärt – manchmal *kissing bridges* genannt, konnten sich doch Liebespaare wunderbar abgeschirmt von der Öffentlichkeit schnell und verstohlen einen Kuss geben. Überdachte Brücken verbergen sich abseits der Hauptstraßen, sind größtenteils einspurig, aber in aller Regel für den Autoverkehr zugelassen. Sie stammen zumeist aus der zweiten Hälfte des 19. Jahrhunderts. Einige wenige erhaltene Exemplare datieren auf die erste Hälfte zurück. Auch zu Beginn des 20. Jahrhunderts wurden noch *Covered Bridges* gebaut.
Für die Errichtung dieser speziellen Brücken sprechen mehrere Gründe: Zum einen erhöht das Dach die Haltbarkeit der witterungsanfälligen Holzkonstruktion in erheblichem Maß, zum anderen konnten Pferde ohne Scheu einen reißenden Fluss überqueren. Sicherlich wurden durch die imposante Erscheinung der Brücken auch die Mautforderungen erleichtert, z. B. an der längsten überdachten Brücke Neuenglands, der *Cornish-Windsor Bridge.*

Skills: Giving a talk

1 Choosing a topic

Choose a subject that has something to do with New England. Here are three ideas. You can work in groups.

1. Interesting things to see and do in Boston
2. New England's wildlife
3. Vermont – the Green Mountain State

2 Collecting ideas and information

How about starting with a mind map (with all the interesting aspects you can think of?) Or brainstorming for ideas?

How – and where – can you get more information? Who (in your group) is going to look for what?

3 Getting information from texts

a) Make printouts or photocopies of texts that seem important.

- Skim texts first. (Look at headings, pictures, beginnings and ends of paragraphs.) Then decide which ones you can use!
- Scan the texts you have chosen. Look for key words and mark them. Then make notes.

b) Don't try to translate a German text word for word! Just use the most interesting information – and say it in English in your own words.

tip

Understanding difficult texts
First try to guess the meaning of new words …
➡ by looking at the context
➡ by remembering words from the same family
➡ from words you know in German (or French)
If you can't guess, use a dictionary for help.

Mark the key words in a German text.
Then put the main ideas into notes in English.
Use a dictionary where necessary.

4 Getting ready – and giving your talk

- Write notes that you can use during your talk.
- Keep your audience interested! Bring things for them to look at (photos? maps? …?) or listen to.
- Get your audience involved! How can you do this?

- Practice your talk at home first – alone (in front of a mirror), or with your friends, or in front of your family.
- Check the time. Make sure your talk isn't too long!
- When you give the talk, speak loudly – and not too fast.

5 Presentation techniques

- Visual elements (pictures, diagrams, key words etc.) will make your talk clearer and more interesting. Use transparencies or a laptop and video projector. Remember: it is easier for your audience to follow when they can see what you mean as well as hearing about it.
- Make sure that all visual elements are large enough for everyone to see. Use colors systematically (to make things clearer, not simply for decoration).
- You might like to prepare a handout, to give your audience background information, and to underline the main points of your talk.

woodchuck

platypus

Which of these animals lives in New England? Yes, right, it's the woodchuck. But who can answer this question: How much wood would a woodchuck chuck if a woodchuck could chuck wood?

The ransom

It was a Wednesday afternoon, sometime around 4.30 p.m., I guess, when the kid first came up to my office. 'McGill', it says on the door. 'J. McGill. Private Detective'. Not a bad job. A tough one at times, I admit, but that's the way I like it. It was a beautiful October day, I remember, and the maple trees down on Commercial Street were blood red against the deep blue sky. From up in my office on the fourth floor, I can see right over Boston Harbour to Charlestown Bridge. But on that afternoon, like most days, I had pulled down the blinds, so the sunlight was coming through in stripes.

"You've got to help me, Mr. McGill! You –"
"Now wait a minute!" The kid was scared. I noticed that the moment he burst into my office. "Keep cool, kid. Let's start at the beginning, OK? What's your name, then?"
"Wainwright. Nelson Wainwright. You know my brother Steve, right?"
"Oh? Steve Wainwright? Yeah, I remember him, sure." So Nelson here was the younger of the Wainwright brothers. Their father owned the Wainwright Corporation. Rich, stinking rich. I knew Steve from a few years back, when we'd played baseball together. Since then, Steve had left Boston and now lived in L.A., as far as I knew.
I looked at the kid in front of me. How old would he be? Twenty, twenty-one maybe? "OK, Nelson, so what's wrong? Something wrong at home? You left home or something?" The kid was carrying a small suitcase, I noticed.
"No, Mr. McGill. It's not that. It's my girlfriend, Mr. McGill. She –"
"Call me Butch. Everybody else does. – So, what's this about your girlfriend?"
"She's been kidnapped! And the kidnappers are demanding a ransom of half a million dollars! I've got to hand over the money by tomorrow night. They –"
"Wait a minute, Nelson. You say your girlfriend has been kidnapped? And you have to pay the kidnappers? Now, that sounds kind of strange. Why don't the kidnappers try to get the money from her parents?"
"Gloria doesn't have any parents. They died years ago. And they weren't exactly rich."
Unlike the Wainwrights, I thought.
"OK, I understand," I said. "Now tell me, when did this happen?"
"Last night. Gloria told me she was going out with some friends and would call me when she got back to her apartment. But she never did! And this morning I got this phone call from the kidnappers."
"And you don't have any idea who these kidnappers might be?"
"No, Butch. All I know is they're going to kill Gloria if they don't get their money. I've got to make sure they get it. I've got to get Gloria back alive!"
He put the small suitcase down on a chair. "The money's in there. Keep it for me, Butch, till tomorrow. I – "
"You what? You're telling me there's half a million dollars in that suitcase? Are you crazy? Where did you get the money, kid?"
"Out of my father's safe. My parents are away just now – but they may be back at any time! I can't risk being found with the money in my room at home. My father would go crazy if he knew I'd taken it! He doesn't like Gloria. Help me, Butch, please!"
"Who is this girl, Nelson? Gloria who?"
"Hammersmith. That's her name. She –"
"You needn't tell me. Gloria Hammersmith, the model, right? Wasn't she Tony Cavori's

girl at one time? From 'Cavori's Pizzeria' over on Hanover Street, just a few blocks away from here?"

"Yeah. The jerk! But that's past history. She's my girl now. We're practically engaged."

It all seemed kind of strange to me. If it was old Wainwright's money these guys were after, why not kidnap the boy? But this girl Gloria … it made no sense. On the other hand, here was the kid with the money, and he was obviously sick with worry about his girl, so I agreed to help. He said he'd come back the next day to pick up the money and talk about handing it over to the kidnappers. When he'd gone, I picked up the phone. I had some calls to make.

■ Early Thursday evening, Nelson was back. Before I gave him the suitcase, we talked. The kidnappers had called again and told him where to come with the money. I suggested going with him, or following at a safe distance, but he didn't like the idea.

"No, Butch! They told me to come alone. I don't want to risk anything. There may be three or four of them – it might be a gang!"

"But – "

"No!" Nelson's eyes flashed in anger. "It's best for me to do this alone. If anything goes wrong, Gloria's life'll be in danger. You know that!"

"But at least promise me one thing," I warned him. "Make sure it's a direct exchange – the money for Gloria. Got it? If you give them the money without getting Gloria back, they'll keep coming back for more. Don't forget that, kid. OK?"

"I won't mess it up," he answered. He took the suitcase and left.

That night, at eleven or so, Nelson rang me from his home. The kid was in a panic. Something had obviously gone wrong.

"We can't talk on the phone," I told him. "You stay right where you are. I'll be there in ten minutes."

I knew where he lived. It was up on Beacon Hill, where all the million-dollar houses are. I got in my car and drove down towards Causeway Street, under the I-93 expressway and along Stanford Street until I came to Beacon Hill. The Wainwrights' place was in a quiet cobbled street where there were old-fashioned gas lamps outside the houses. The door of their house had a brass knocker. Very English! Nelson opened the door and I went inside. He was alone.

"Where's Gloria?" I said. "What happened?"

"I went to the place," he began. "It was a phone booth on a street corner. But then they called me and sent me off to another place."

"What? So you never saw Gloria? You never met anyone?" It didn't sound good.

"No. And I had to leave the money there. They said if I didn't, they'd – "

"But that's just what I warned you not to do, kid!" I shouted. I was angry now.

"I know that!" he said. "But they said they needed time to get away. They promised to phone again tomorrow evening at 8 and tell me where I could pick Gloria up."

"And you think they'll still make that phone call? Well, let's hope they do, kid," I said. "I'll come back tomorrow evening and we'll see what happens."

■ On Friday evening I was back on Beacon Hill. Nelson's parents still hadn't returned. We waited a couple of hours, but the phone didn't ring. Not that it surprised me. The kid was getting more and more nervous. Me, too, because my plan had gone wrong. In the end I had to tell him.

"Nelson," I said. "There's something you don't know. I – er – I still have the money."
"What d'you mean?"
"The money in that suitcase – I changed it."
"Changed it? What? I don't get this," he said.
"It's quite simple," I said. "I didn't want you and your family to lose all that money – so I changed the bills for forged ones. I have my contacts, you know."
"You did what?" he shouted. "You filled the suitcase with forged bills?"
"It was good stuff, Nelson. Not perfect, but good enough. I thought the kidnappers wouldn't notice it until they'd let Gloria go. I thought it would be a direct exchange."
The kid was furious.
"You know what that means? You've killed Gloria! You've killed her!"
He raised his fist and came over to where I was sitting, his face twisted with anger. Then the doorbell rang.
"Gloria?" He rushed out into the hall. I listened as he opened the door.
"Sergeant Kelly, State Police," I heard a man's voice say. "Are you Mr. Nelson Wainwright?"
"That's right. But Gloria …? Have you …?"
"Miss Gloria Hammersmith was arrested an hour ago at Logan International Airport. She and her friend were trying to buy tickets to Honolulu – with forged bills. We understand you or your father may be able to help us with our inquiries."
"Friend? What friend?" Nelson asked.
"Someone by the name of Cavori. Antonio Cavori. You know the guy at all?"

1 Looking at the story

a) The events of the story happen over a period of four days. Sum up what happens on each of these days. Start like this: Tuesday: In the evening Gloria …

b) How does McGill treat Nelson? Find examples in the text to show it.

c) What do you think of the characters and the way they act?

d) The story is written in the first person. How much does the narrator know? How much does he tell the reader?

2 Speaking practice: A new job

a) What kinds of job can you give to a private detective?

b) With a partner, act out a dialogue between the people in the picture. Use your role card to prepare your part.

Butch McGill
Find out
- who the lady is,
- what her problem is,
- what she wants you to do.

What other information do you need to do the job?

What questions do you need to ask?

Faye Delacroix
- has three daughters; youngest daughter is 16.
- is worried about her; she has fallen into "bad company".
- wants McGill to follow her.

If necessary, invent more facts about your daughter to answer McGill's questions.

let's check

1 Word power

a) Which words from the right go together in some way with the words on the left? When you have found the pairs, explain how they are connected or use them in example sentences.

1. story
2. maple
3. fashion
4. Vermont
5. police
6. snowboarding
7. engaged
8. electricity
9. transparency

a) skiing
b) gas
c) Green Mountains
d) leaf
e) married
f) narrator
g) arrest
h) presentation
i) model

b) Which words have the same basic meaning, only stronger (just as hot is stronger than warm)?

1. interesting – f■■■■■■■■■ fascinating
2. easy to remember – un■■■■■■■■■ unforgettable
3. to ask for – to d■■■■■ demand
4. angry – f■■■■■■ furious
5. local dish – sp■■■■■■■ specialty
6. worth seeing – sp■■■■■■■■ spectacular
7. to be worried – to be in a p■■■■ panic
8. to be keen on – to be c■■■ a■■■■ crazy about

2 Airport situations

Use gerund constructions to describe the people in the pictures. Choose from these verbs:

| be afraid of | dream about | feel like | look forward to | be tired of |

3 C-Test: 'Leaf peepers' in New England

Copy the text into your exercise book – and complete it. Each blank (■) stands for one letter.

Fall is the time when the 'leaf peepers' come to New England. That's t■■ name th■■ is gi■■■ to tour■■■■ who wa■■ to s■■ the fam■■■ fall lea■■■. The aut■■■ colors i■ Europe ca■'t be comp■■■■ with Ind■■■ Summer i■ Vermont, N■■ Hampshire o■ Maine, wh■■■ thick for■■■■ cover ab■■■ 85 per■■■■ of t■■ land. T■■ oaks, map■■■ and ot■■■ great tr■■■ in th■ northern sta■■■ are alw■■■ the fi■■■ to tu■■ red, yel■■■ and bri■■■ orange.

Th■■ begins i■ late Sept■■■■■■ and ea■■■ October, a■ soon a■ the da■■ get sho■■■■ and t■■ nights col■■■. (The sout■■■■ states o■ Connecticut, Massac■■■■■■■ and Rh■■■ Island exper■■■■■■ their Ind■■■ Summer t■■ or th■■■ weeks la■■■.) The col■■■ are unbeli■■■■■■■! So, i■ you pl■■ to vi■■■ New Eng■■■■ then, reme■■■■ to bo■■ your vaca■■■■ early! The leaf peepers will be everywhere!

seventy-one **71**

revision Books 1–3

1 Speaking practice: Using suitable language

a) Read what these people say in different situations, and decide whether the language they use is suitable or not. If not, explain why and suggest what they could say instead.

1. *Boy to girl at teenagers' party:*
   I would like to ask if you would be kind enough to dance with me.
2. *Woman to girl in street:*
   Hey, pick up that rubbish you just dropped on the ground!
3. *Man in tourist office:*
   Hi, what kind of stuff can I do with my kids in this town?
4. *Customer at fruit stall:* Give me six apples.
5. *Customer in restaurant to waiter:*
   Please allow me to point out that there is no menu on my table.
6. *One passenger to another on train:*
   Excuse me. Would you mind if I opened the window?
7. *Girl who has just hit woman with backpack:*
   Oh, I'm terribly sorry. I hope I haven't hurt you.

b) Make short dialogues for the situations in **a)** and use suitable language for the contexts.

2 Word power: Watch out!

a) It is easy to make mistakes with some pairs of words in English. Choose the correct pairs to complete the sentences and put the words in the right place.

> remember – remind • borrow – lend •
> carry – wear • boil – cook • lonely – alone •
> hard – hardly • embarrassed – embarrassing

1. Although I sometimes like to be ___, I think I'd feel ___ if I never saw anyone.
2. Do you find it ___ to have a conversation with someone you ___ know?
3. Will you ___ to send him a birthday card, or should I ___ you nearer the time?
4. If you ___ me your computer game for the weekend, you can ___ my skateboard.
5. Without electricity or gas in the house we couldn't ___ a meal or even ___ water for a cup of tea.
6. In ___ situations my face always goes red, so then I feel even more ___!
7. I don't want to ___ these clothes any longer. I'm going to put them in a plastic bag and ___ them to the charity shop.

b) Make sentences with these 'false friends' to show that you can use them correctly.

> to become • note • meaning • brave •
> gymnasium • to overhear •
> brief • to blame • mist • actually •

3 Word power: Adjectives and nouns

Which of the adjectives below can be used with all the nouns in each group on the right? Do you use the same adjectives for all these nouns in German, too?

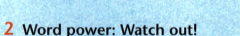

| serious | heavy | poor | hard | strong | bad |

1. traffic • rain • heart • suitcase
2. winter • facts • work • drink
3. mistake • luck • cold • language
4. crime • expression • problem • accident
5. coffee • arms • character • accent
6. harvest • area • grades • service

revision 2

Test yourself!

4 Girls and boys in Scotland

a) An American boy and a girl from New Zealand meet in a ticket queue at the Edinburgh Festival. Complete what they say with 'since' or 'for'. Write down your answers and then turn to page 186 to check them.

Girl: I've been away from home **1** about a month now. And I've been in the UK **2** the tenth of July.
Boy: Oh, I've been travelling around **3** a bit longer than that, although I've only been in Edinburgh **4** last Saturday.
Girl: I've wanted to see the Tattoo **5** I saw it years ago on TV. My parents have been living in New Zealand **6** 1970, but both their families were originally from Scotland.
Boy: Family histories are interesting, aren't they? **7** the last year or so my sister has been collecting facts about our family in the US.

b) Read what a girl from Glasgow tells her friend in an e-mail. Put the verbs into the correct tense and form (simple or progressive), and choose between 'since' and 'for'. Write down your answers and then check them on page 186.

People I don't know don't usually notice me, but **1 since/for** last Saturday everyone **2 look** at me! Saturday was the day of Cindy's party. Cindy and I **3 know** each other **4 since/for** our first day at school together, and we're best friends. "I'm going to invite Dan, too," she said when she first told me about the party. "Don't worry. I won't tell him you **5 be** in love with him **6 since/for** months. But I **7 try 8 since/for** ages to think of a way to bring you together, and I think this is the answer!" Of course I wanted to make Dan notice me at the party, so I decided to follow Cindy's example. The thing is,

9 since/for I was small, I **10 have** really boring brown hair, but I've never been brave enough to do anything about it. But Cindy **11 change** the colour of her hair regularly **12 since/for** at least a year, and she always gets the guys she wants. Anyway, on Saturday morning I bought some stuff to turn me into a beautiful blonde. But something went wrong and – oh, my God! – suddenly my hair was green! At least Dan **13 not see** me **14 since/for** then – you don't think I went to the party, do you?! – but **15 since/for** the last five days I **16 go** crazy because I can't get rid of this awful green …

5 Visitors to the 1627 Pilgrim Village

Complete what pairs of visitors say with 'some' or 'any', or their compounds with '-one/-thing/-where'. Then check your answers on page 186.

1. "Have you talked to **1** in the village yet?" – "Yes. I spoke to a woman, but she used **2** very strange expressions!"
2. "We can go into **3** house we like." – "Are you sure? We don't want to interrupt **4** 's work."
3. "What are you eating? **5** duck from that woman's pot?" – "Yes. I've never tasted **6** so delicious!"
4. "When I showed a Pilgrim my cellphone, he didn't have **7** idea what it was." – "Of course not. That's **8** that hadn't been invented in 1627!"
5. "What happens when **9** wants to use the bathroom?" – "Good question. I haven't seen a bathroom **10** in the village. Let's ask **11** ! There must be one for the visitors **12** ."

revision 2 Units 3–4

6 News from Susie in Barre

Put in definite or indefinite articles where necessary.

"I had **1** great time in Acadia National Park last week. We go there once **2** year, usually in **3** July. It takes us **4** few hours to get from Barre to **5** Atlantic coast by **6** car, but it's really worth it because it's **7** such **8** beautiful area. It became **9** national park in 1916, and that makes it older than any other national park in **10** US east of **11** Mississippi. We always camp because it makes us feel **12** lot closer to **13** nature. I just love lying in my tent at **14** night. And being near **15** wildlife in Acadia is **16** unforgettable experience. When we were out in **17** little boat on **18** Thursday we suddenly saw **19** huge whale next to us. Another visitor in **20** boat – he was **21** Frenchman, I think – was so excited that he quickly stood up with his camera, and as **22** result almost fell in **23** water! But **24** whale wasn't in **25** hurry. It swam around for **26** half **27** hour before it left again. So there was **28** lots of **29** time to take photos. It made me think what **30** great job that must be – to be **31** wildlife photographer, I mean – although I'm not sure that **32** animals are always as helpful as that whale!"

7 Visiting other countries

a) Complete the sentences with the pairs of verbs on the right. Choose the correct form for the second verb in each pair: infinitive or gerund.

> hope / see • want / be • imagine / lie •
> expect / find • enjoy / visit • risk / miss

1. I love art, so wherever I am, I **enjoy** ⬚ galleries.
2. I'm crazy about nature, so I always ⬚ interesting wildlife.
3. I look for restaurants where I can ⬚ local specialties.
4. I'm a very active person – I can't ⬚ on a beach all day.
5. I take a guidebook, so I don't ⬚ important sights.
6. I learn how to say 'Please' and 'Thank you' in the local language because I ⬚ polite.

b) Use gerund constructions to put these ideas into English.

1. Ich gehe gern auf Reisen.
2. Ich freue mich immer darauf, etwas Neues zu erleben.
3. Ich finde es uninteressant, jeden Tag in einem Reisebus zu sitzen.
4. Wie wäre es, wenn wir an dem Austausch teilnehmen würden?
5. Du lernst ein Land am besten kennen, indem du bei einer Familie wohnst.

c) Kate and her new friends are discussing what to do with a group of German exchange students who are coming to Boston. Complete what they say with gerunds and your own ideas for a program of interesting activities in New England. (If necessary, look again at Unit 4.) Example: 1. How about **organizing** a welcome party? / **going** to Cape Cod?

1. How about …?
2. I think they'd enjoy …
3. I suggest …
4. It's definitely worth …
5. They're probably looking forward to …
6. What do you think of …?
7. I'm sure they'd be interested in …
8. They can't go home again without …

| look around | take them to | visit | have a look at |
| show them | go to | try | organize a trip to | see | … |

8 Scotland's national poet

Infinitive with 'to' or gerund? Complete this guidebook text with the correct forms.

Robert Burns
1759–1796

ALLOWAY

Alloway is famous for **(be)** the birthplace of Scotland's national poet Robert Burns. So if you are keen on **(learn)** about Scottish culture, it might be interesting for you **(visit)** this little village in the southwest of the country. **(Drive)** through the area will also give you the chance **(see)** the lovely landscape which helped **(inspire)** Burns **(write)** many of his famous poems. Apart from **(write)** his own poems Burns also collected old Scottish songs – he was one of the first people **(realize)** the importance of **(do)** this for future generations – and one of these songs, 'Auld Lang Syne', is sung at New Year everywhere in the English-speaking world. Of course if you really want **(understand)** the importance of Burns to Scottish people, it is worth **(arrange) (be)** in Scotland on January 25th. This is Burns Night, the great man's birthday, when celebrations are held **(remember)** him. Every year people all over the country look forward to **(sit)** down together **(enjoy) (listen)** to Burns' words while they eat 'haggis'. Don't be nervous about **(try)** this traditional dish of sheep's offal[1] that is boiled in a bag. It is the only thing **(eat)** on Burns Night. The highlight of the evening is the **(play)** of bagpipes while the haggis is carried to the table!

[1] [ɒfl] – Innereien

9 Word power: New words

Test each other or the rest of the class on new words from Units 3 and 4.

a) Write down definitions of ten useful words. Your partner has to guess the words.

b) Make a list of ten words with difficult spelling. You say the words (remember to check the pronunciation first!), and your partner has to spell them.

10 Mixed bag

Jody's father has just arrived home from work.

Father: ¹ you have a good day ² school, Jody?

Jody: ³ morning was OK, but in the ⁴ we had a Maths test, and Maths ⁵ never been my best ⁶ .

Father: Oh, ⁷ expect you've done ⁸ than you think. – Is that letter for ⁹ ?

Jody: Yes, ¹⁰ you are. ¹¹ ever writes to me. – Hey, what's the ¹² , Dad? Bad news?

Father: No, I'm just in shock! Actually, the news ¹³ very good. An old uncle of ¹⁴ died a few months ¹⁵ , and –

Jody: ¹⁶ is that good? Didn't you like ¹⁷ ?

Father: To tell the truth, I ¹⁸ really know him. He ¹⁹ in Australia. Anyway, he didn't have ²⁰ children, so he left instructions for his money to ²¹ shared between his other relatives – ²² I've got £20,000!

Jody: Wow, you're one of ²³ rich now!

Father: It's fantastic, ²⁴ it?

Jody: If it ²⁵ my money, I'd go ²⁶ holiday with it!

Father: But it isn't ²⁷ ! And I'm not ²⁸ to spend it all at ²⁹ . – But a holiday ³⁰ be nice. What do you ³¹ of visiting America, Jody?

Jody: Wow, Dad! Great idea!

intro
5 Fame and fortune

Will Smith

» I don't know what my calling is, but I want to be here for a bigger reason. I strive to be like the greatest people who have ever lived. «

» If it was something that I really committed myself to, I don't think there's anything that could stop me becoming President of the United States. «

» Money and success don't change people; they merely amplify what is already there. «

Avril Lavigne

» Why should I care what other people think of me? I am who I am. And who I wanna be. «

» I'm just coming out and I'm going to clearly be myself – I write what I feel, I never worry what others think. «

» I don't want to be compared to Britney, Ashlee, Hilary or Lindsay. I want to be compared to me. «

1 Stars

a) Describe what you can see in the pictures.

b) What do you know about the stars on this double page? Find out more about them from magazines or the Internet.

c) Read what each of them says, and compare their attitudes towards life, their jobs and themselves. What kind of people are they?

d) What do you think about what they say? Be prepared to talk to a partner or to the class for one minute.

2 Listening: Interviews with actors

The actors below were interviewed by the BBC. Listen to some of the things they said. Try to follow the gist, but don't worry if you can't understand everything. Then say what they were talking about.

1. Will Smith: a) … b) …
2. Renée Zellweger: …
3. Rowan Atkinson: …
4. Orlando Bloom: a) … b) …
5. Jennifer Lopez: a) … b) …

5 unit intro

Orlando Bloom

» I mean, I have a great job. I get to dress up and become somebody else, especially when it's somebody like Legolas, who's this super-cool kind of otherworldly elf. It's, like, I'm lucky, man, so why would I not appreciate that? «

» The girls have got a bit excited. I spoke to my agent and she says she's wading through the fan mail. We've got bags of it. Whatever happens in life is fine – just trust in that. «

Robbie Williams

» I have to be careful what I ask for in life, 'cause I always seem to get it! The good thing is, I've got a purpose now, whereas before my purpose was to go out and party. «

» I'm not a musician, I'm an entertainer. «

» I'm rich beyond my wildest dreams. «

» I like listening to good music – and I can't stop playing my album. «

3 Your turn

Would you like to be a star? Why or why not? Talk about the advantages and disadvantages of fame and fortune.

Reneé Zellweger   Rowan Atkinson   Jennifer Lopez

seventy-seven 77

A The audition

People often use the Internet to tell others about their experiences. Here's an example.

One day I'd really love to see my name up in bright lights. I mean, who wouldn't? I can sing, and I've always been pretty good at dancing, so maybe my mom is right. She's
5 absolutely convinced that I'm going to be a star. But sometimes she can be really pushy. Like last year, when she put me in to audition for a Broadway musical. Apparently they were looking for teenage performers. Anyway,
10 we had to travel up to New York City and, frankly, it was one of the worst experiences of my life. A hundred hopeful kids and their ambitious parents were there. Nothing happened for ages until the director suddenly
15 came in and shouted, "We don't have much time. Who wants to go first?"
When nobody answered, Mom started pushing me onto the stage. Obviously, that was quite embarrassing!
20 "Name?" shouted the director.
Normally I'm not particularly shy, but up there, in front of all the others, I was utterly terrified. My legs turned to jelly and I thought I had lost my voice completely.
25 In fact I had to say my name three times before he understood and found it on his list. Then I had to introduce my song. But the piano accompaniment was a bit strange, so unfortunately I missed my first few notes. I
30 even forgot the words at one point. I don't remember much else except that my knees were knocking together and the lights blinded me as I walked off the stage.

Hardly anybody clapped.
"Next please!" shouted the director. That was 35 all.
Mom was more encouraging, of course.
"That was fine, Billy!" she said when I finally sat down next to her. I just wanted to go straight home, but Mom wouldn't leave until 40 we'd heard all the other kids.
"Well, honey, the others weren't very good!" she said at the end.
The director didn't call me back. Mom was furious, but actually I wasn't surprised at all. 45
Mom says I get too nervous. I need to show more confidence because that's what they're mainly looking for. Maybe she's right. I've had a few auditions since then, and I really think I get a little better each time. Hopefully 50 someone will spot my talent one day and give me a break.

1 A look at the text

a) Sum up in three sentences what the text is about.

b) What can you say about the characters and their individual points of view?

narrator	mother	director
…	…	…
…	…	…

2 Word power: New adverbs

a) Look at these adverbs in the text. How do they change the meaning of their sentences?

1. apparently (line 8)
2. frankly (line 11)
3. normally (line 21)
4. unfortunately (line 29)
5. hopefully (line 50)

b) Use each adverb to write a new sentence.

A language

3 Embarrassing!

Singer Rikki Baker is telling a friend about an audition she had with a rock band. Add a suitable adverb of comment to each of her statements:

| obviously | hopefully | of course | unfortunately | frankly | apparently | actually | in fact |

1. I overslept and arrived two hours late!
2. The guys were mad at me for having to wait so long.
3. They were expecting me to be really good.
4. I *am* pretty good, but I was lousy that day.
5. They said they'd let me know, but I knew they didn't want me.
6. The whole thing was a complete disaster.
7. It was my most embarrassing experience ever.
8. I'll be luckier with my next audition.

4 What adverbs refer to

a) Make a list of all the adverbs of comment in the text. Put in what they refer to and what their position in the sentence is.

b) Now look at the adverbs of degree in the text and say what they refer to. To find out more about their position look at **G15**.

adverb of comment
maybe ➡ whole sentence (front position)
apparently ➡ …
…

adverb of degree
pretty ➡ adjective: good
absolutely ➡ …
…

5 What Rikki's friends say about her

Put the word order right. Think carefully about the position of the adverbs and adverbials.

1. unhappy • obviously • was • after • Rikki • really • that lousy audition.
2. she • unfortunately • sing • very • that day • didn't • well.
3. that band • actually • never • have taken • anyway • her • would.
4. is • her voice • right for • I don't think • frankly • a rock band • quite.
5. try to • she • get into • instead • maybe • a musical • should.
6. this afternoon • apparently • on Broadway • she's got • an audition.
7. this time • better • will • hopefully • she • perform.
8. I'm • convinced • she's going • absolutely • a star • one day • to be.

6 Pictures of Robbie

Try to improve this text by adding suitable adverbs or adjectives. You can change the structure of the sentences if you want.

I'm a photographer. I'm one of the best. You can see my work in the Mirror. I take pictures of pop stars. Last week I was waiting outside Robbie Williams's house. At 10 o'clock he came out. I was standing in a good position, so I took some pictures. Robbie looked funny. But it was him! I sent the pictures to my newspaper. They didn't want them. They said, "We've got lots of pictures of Robbie Williams like that." I made inquiries. Robbie Williams wears a mask and the same clothes when he sees photographers outside his house so they get the same photo every time! He thinks it's funny. I don't.

5 unit language B

B After the audition

How'd it go? Well, frankly, Mrs Denker, the whole thing was a joke! Billy never got a fair chance. Do you know, it took us hours to get to the place, and then we had to hang around forever before the director even showed up! (…) Right! Of course there were far too many kids there. And they didn't have a running order, can you believe that? So if I hadn't kind of pushed Billy forward, we'd never've got off the ground! (…) I always thought serious auditions were, like, done in front of the casting people only, with all the others outside. Not this one. Oh no, Billy had to get right up in front of all those people and sing his song. OK, so he was a little nervous – I can understand that – and OK, he wasn't exactly fantastic – but he sure was better than most of the other kids. And did the director thank him? No way! Not a word of encouragement from the jerk! And no callback since. (…) Yeah, I think you're right, Mrs Denker. I ought to write and complain.

Music Theater International
221 Broadway
New York, NY 10115

135 South Warren Street
Trenton, NJ 08608
March 23

Dear Sir or Madam,

On March 10 my son William auditioned for a part in the musical "Flash".
I wish to complain about the disgraceful way in which this audition was organized, as I do not feel that my son was given a fair chance. After a long journey to reach the theater, we were kept waiting for a considerable time before the director even arrived. An unnecessarily large number of young people had been invited to audition and apparently no running order had been set. This meant that had I not persuaded my son to go on first, things might never have got started.
I always believed that serious auditions did not require a performance in front of all the other candidates. However, this is exactly what happened. My son was understandably nervous and did not perform as well as he can. That the director did not even thank him or say an encouraging word afterwards was completely unprofessional.
I believe my son compared very favorably with the best of the others, so I was both surprised and disappointed that he did not receive a callback.

Yours sincerely,

Natalie Simons

Natalie Simons

1 Two texts

a) Read the two texts and explain the situation (who is communicating with whom and why, what their relationship might be, etc.).

b) What do you think Mrs Denker said on the telephone? Fill in the gaps.

2 Formal or informal language

Write down words or phrases in the spoken text that are replaced by others in the written text. Make two lists and compare them.

Informal	Formal
– The whole thing was a joke.	– The disgraceful way in which this audition was organized …
– Billy never got a fair chance.	…
– It took us hours to get to the place …	…
…	

B language

3 A question of style

Look at the list below and decide what is typical of formal or informal style. Give examples from the text.

1. being exact
2. short forms
3. long sentences with subordinate clauses
4. passive verb forms
5. exaggeration
6. feedback phrases
7. words of more than two syllables
8. words of Latin or French origin

4 Writing a formal letter

a) Billy went to an open air concert over the weekend. It was a disaster! He blames the people who organized it and wants to write a letter of complaint. Read his notes and imagine what he told his friends.

b) Write the letter. The expressions on the right and the box on page 152 will help you.

arrived Friday afternoon • no room for tent on campsite • campsite cost extra money • only two bathrooms for 100 people • water a mile away • ground rocky • next to expressway • sound lousy • only bad fast food • top act cancelled • heavy rain the next day • campsite flooded • cellphone broken • no help • tow cars out of the mud • want money back

Helpful expressions
- to provide somebody with something
- to charge somebody a sum of money
- suitable
- low quality
- service
- to prevent something from happening
- damage
- to repair
- refund

5 Mediation: What does it mean?

Where might you see these notices and warnings? Explain what they mean in German. Use a dictionary if necessary.

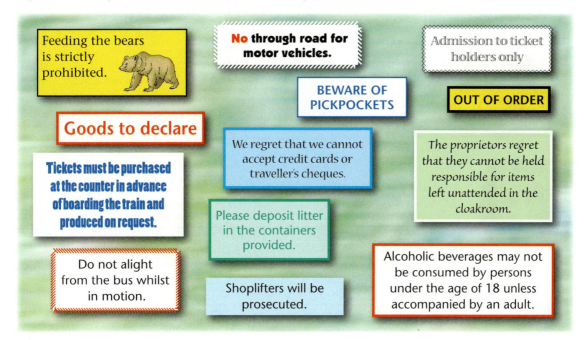

Skills: American and British English

Posted by	Topic
sven.mielke e-mail	Hi everyone, I'm learning English in school (or is it at school?) and my teacher says we shouldn't mix American English and British English when we write. My problem is I'm not sure what the difference is. Can anybody help?
elfinpower e-mail	Hey, that's not an easy question to answer! I'm from England and we British often use American expressions. But we are aware of the differences between American and British English. Even the grammar can be slightly different. For example, Americans say things like "I already did that" and "I just had lunch" whereas we British would usually say "I've already done that" and "I've just had lunch". They say "in school" and "on the weekend" when we would say "at school" and "at the weekend". And they never say "haven't got". It's always "don't have". Using "gotten" as the past participle of "to get" (as in "She's gotten better") is definitely American.
tony.blackwell e-mail	Hi, I'm American and, as I see it, it's mainly a vocabulary thing. The Brits use a whole lot of different words – like holiday, sweets, mobile and so on, instead of vacation, candy and cellphone. It can get quite funny. In Britain if you say you like someone's pants, you get a funny look because they call them trousers and they think you're talking about their underpants! In the US the subway is an underground railway. In Britain you use a subway to cross under the street. There are lots of other examples. Too many to mention here. But there are lists on the Internet.
IT_freak e-mail	Hi, Sven. Spelling might be difficult for you because some words that end in -our and -re in British English are spelled differently in American English, e. g. color, humor, center. Of course, if you're writing with a PC, it's easy. Just use the spell checker and set it to either American or British English.
witch_of_oz e-mail	I speak Australian English. It may seem like British English at first, but some of it is similar to American English. My husband Bob is from England, however, and I've noticed that differences in pronunciation can cause misunderstandings. Like when we were in the US and Bob tried to order a glass of water. At first nobody understood his funny English "waw-tuh", so he had to change it to a more American "wah-da". But don't worry! Most of the time speakers of different Englishes understand each other quite well.

1 Differences between American and British English

English is spoken all over the world, but it isn't the same everywhere. You already know the main differences between American and British English. You can find more in the texts on page 82 from an Internet forum on the English language.

a) Make a grid for each of the four areas of language (1. spelling, 2. ...) in which the differences are found and give as many examples as you can.

b) What do you think of Sven's problem? How do you and your teachers deal with it?

c) What about German? Is it different in different parts of the world? Do you think this is a problem?

	AE	BE
1. Spelling	center	centre
	...	...
	...	...

2 Blacky's vacation

Listen to this American English text. What would be different if it were in British English? Then listen to the British English version to check.

Last fall, our neighbors, a retired principal and his wife, went on vacation and asked us to look after their dog. So while they were traveling around China, good old Blacky stayed with us. When Dad was watching his favorite soccer program on TV at a quarter after seven, Blacky lay on the sofa with him. When Mom was preparing fries in the kitchen, Blacky sat on the floor and waited for a cookie. When I came back from school and opened the door of our apartment, he jumped up at me and we went for a walk. On the weekend, when I wasn't in school, we sometimes took a cab downtown to one of the large parks. One day we even watched some students from my grade who were practicing a kind of dance for a theater audition. I really loved those afternoons with Blacky.

3 Misunderstandings and surprising facts

a) Listen and talk about the texts:
Explain the misunderstandings in the first two texts.
Say how Americans, British and German people use their knives and forks differently (to scoop [sku:p] = schaufeln, schöpfen).

b) Do you know more cultural differences or misunderstandings between people from different countries?
What do you think about them?
Can they be a problem?
What can you do about it?

What people consider good manners is different everywhere in the world.

A song project

1 Miss California

Listen to the song, read the words and talk about it in class. The tip box will help you.

tip

How to deal with songs	Music
What you present depends on how much you can find out.	♪ What kind of music is it? ♪ What instruments are used? ♪ What does it sound like? ♪ Can you describe the rhythm? ♪ What feelings are created by the music? ♪ What is the structure of the song (verses, chorus)?
Don't worry if you can't explain everything. Songs are like poems. They can often be interpreted in different ways.	
First look at all the information you have got. If something is missing that could help you to understand the song better, try to find it out. The Internet is probably the best source of information for you.	**Words** ♪ Do the words tell a story? ♪ What is the point of view? ♪ What is the setting (when and where a story takes place)? ♪ What feelings are expressed by the words? ♪ Is there a message? ♪ Is there anything special about the language? ♪ What words/names are unknown?

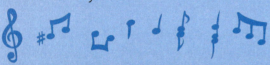

The following points may be worth looking at:

Background information	
♪ Who are the singer(s)/the band? ♪ Who wrote the words/the music? ♪ When was the song written? ♪ Was it a success?	If there's something you don't understand and you can't find an answer, use the information you have to make your own interpretation.

2 The project

1. Divide into groups of 4–5 people and choose one of the other three songs to work on. More than one group can work on the same song if necessary.

2. Your group can choose between two ways of presenting the result of your work:
a) You do an oral presentation (see the Skills pages in Units 3 and 4) on your song in front of the class. Or:
b) You design a booklet or poster about the song and put it on exhibition in the classroom.

3. Listen to the songs in class. Then start working in groups. The tip boxes after each song will help you. You will need to look things up in a dictionary and/or on the Internet.

4. After each song has been presented in class, talk about all four songs. What do you like or dislike about them? Compare what ideas are presented in the songs and how this is done. Link the songs to the unit title.

text

A Miss California (Dante Thomas featuring Pras)

Uh I mean, I'm just sitting right here
(California) Checking out this young lady right here,
Baby you're hot (That's where I saw her)
I mean, you sexy, oh my god (I learned to love her)
Let me ask you one question: Where you from anyway

Chorus:
She's Miss California, hottest thing in West L.A.
House down by the water, sails her yacht across the bay
Drives a Maranello, Hollywood's her favorite scene
Loves to be surrounded with superstars that know her name

She's a rich girl from the top of the food chain
Love and material things
Kinda lonely, till I met her at the Grammys
Ten mill on a diamond ring
She invites me to spend a day on the jet skis
At first it didn't mean a thing
Then she told me I'm the one that she searched for
It was hard to believe

Chorus

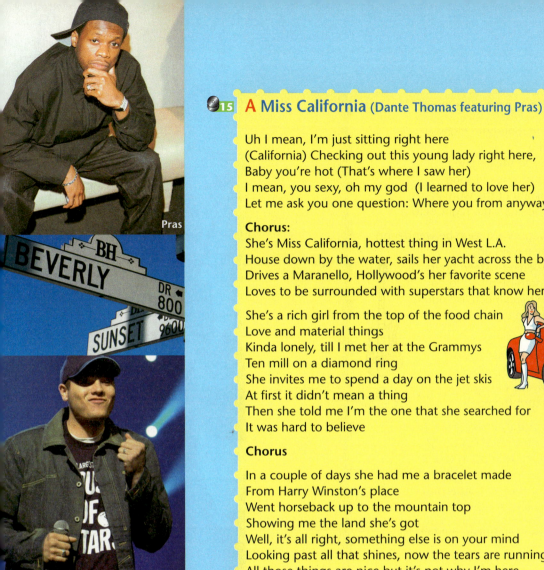

In a couple of days she had me a bracelet made
From Harry Winston's place
Went horseback up to the mountain top
Showing me the land she's got
Well, it's all right, something else is on your mind
Looking past all that shines, now the tears are running too
All those things are nice but it's not why I'm here
I will wipe away your tears simply by just loving you

Chorus (2x)

And there you have it
I mean, she just love the way I do my bling bling
From the ghetto to Beverly Hills, baby
Now I want everybody on the dancefloor to just shake it
I mean, I want you to get down 'cos we hot tonight, baby
We on fire – now tell these cats where you from

Chorus (2x)

Como estas senorita, yeah we got pretty Pras up in here
We got Dante up in here and it's on like that
That's right, that's right
Now all you cats that's talking that jebreezy[1]
Please stop it, man, we can't take it no more
Now tell them cats where you from, baby, c'mon, let 'em know

Chorus (2x)   [1]jebreezy: to shoot the breeze – belangloses Zeug daherreden

Words: Rasheem Sharif Pugh, Vada J Nobles

Unit 5 text

B Turn the page (Metallica)

On a long and lonesome highway
East of Omaha
You can listen to the engine
Moaning out its one old song
You can think about the woman
Or the girl you knew the night before

But your thoughts will soon be wandering
The way they always do
When you're riding sixteen hours
And there's nothing much to do
And you don't feel much like riding
You just wish the trip was through

Chorus:
Here I am on the road again
There I am up on the stage
Here I go playing star again
There I go – turn the page

So you walk into this restaurant
All strung out from the road
And you feel the eyes upon you
As you're shaking off the cold
You pretend it doesn't bother you
But you just want to explode

Most times you can't hear 'em talk
Other times you can
All the same old clichés:
Is it woman, is it man?
And you always seem outnumbered
You don't dare make a stand
Make your stand

Chorus

Out there in the spotlight
You're a million miles away
Every ounce of energy
You try and give away
As the sweat pours out your body
Like the music that you play

Later in the evening
You lie awake in bed
With the echoes of the amplifiers
Ringing in your head
You smoke the day's last cigarette,
Remembering what she said
What she said   **Chorus (2x)**

Words: Bob Seger

tip
This song works on different levels: events on the one hand and feelings on the other.

The pictures can help you to understand what the song is about. Be careful when you look up unknown words. Don't forget to look at the context!

Some things are left open to interpretation. Who could "she" be?

Metallica

C Candle in the wind (Elton John)

Goodbye Norma Jean
Though I never knew you at all
You had the grace to hold yourself
While those around you crawled
They crawled out of the woodwork
And they whispered into your brain
They set you on the treadmill
And they made you change your name

Chorus:
And it seems to me you lived your life
Like a candle in the wind
Never knowing who to cling to
When the rain set in
And I would have liked to know you
But I was just a kid
Your candle burned out long before
Your legend ever did

Loneliness was tough
The toughest role you ever played
Hollywood created a superstar
And pain was the price you paid
Even when you died
Oh the press still hounded you
All the papers had to say
Was that Marilyn was found in the nude

Chorus

Goodbye Norma Jean
Though I never knew you at all
You had the grace to hold yourself
While those around you crawled
Goodbye Norma Jean
From the young man in the 22nd row
Who sees you as something more than sexual
More than just our Marilyn Monroe

Chorus   Words: Bernie Taupin

tip
The names in this song are important. Find out first who it is about.
Then collect facts that explain what is in the song.
Be careful when you look up unknown words. Don't forget to look at the context!
Interpret the meaning of the title.

Unit 5 text

D Sk8er Boi (Avril Lavigne)

He was a boy
She was a girl
Can I make it any more obvious?
He was a punk
She did ballet
What more can I say?
He wanted her
She'd never tell
Secretly she wanted him as well
But all of her friends
Stuck up their nose
They had a problem with his baggy clothes

Chorus: He was a skater boy
She said see you later, boy
He wasn't good enough for her
She had a pretty face
But her head was up in space
She needed to come back down to earth

Five years from now
She sits at home
Feeding the baby, she's all alone
She turns on TV
Guess who she sees?
Skater boy rockin up MTV
She calls up her friends
They already know
And they've all got tickets to see his show
She tags along
Stands in the crowd
Looks up at the man that she turned down

Chorus: He was a skater boy
She said see you later, boy
He wasn't good enough for her
Now he's a superstar
Slamming on his guitar
Does your pretty face see what he's worth?

Sorry, girl, but you missed out
Well, tough luck, that boy's mine now
We are more than just good friends
This is how the story ends
Too bad that you couldn't see,
See the man that boy could be
There is more than meets the eye
I see the soul that is inside

He's just a boy
And I'm just a girl
Can I make it any more obvious?
We are in love
Haven't you heard
How we rock each other's world?

Chorus: I'm with the skater boy
I said see you later, boy
I'll be back stage after the show
I'll be at the studio
Singing the song we wrote
About a girl you used to know

Words: Scott David Alspach, Lauren Christy, Graham Edwards, Avril Ramona Lavigne

> **tip**
> Look at the structure of the song and the different points of view that you find in it.
> This song tells a very clear story, but it is also about attitudes.

Avril Lavigne

let's check

1 Adverb positions

Add the adverbs to the sentences.

1. I saw this advertisement in the newspaper. **(yesterday)**
2. I don't read it. **(usually)**
3. But I was waiting for Dad to get ready. **(that morning)**
4. They were looking for people who wanted to act in a film about Elvis Presley. **(apparently)**
5. I showed it to my friends in the drama group. **(of course)**
6. They all agreed that I should go to the audition because I can sing and dance. **(immediately) (beautifully)**
7. And I had wanted to be in a film. **(always)**

8. I was nervous. **(terribly)**
9. But I decided to go there. **(in the end)**
10. I didn't get the main part. **(unfortunately)**
11. But I got a small one. **(instead)**
12. That wasn't so bad! **(after all)**

2 Formal or informal language?

Decide which of these expressions are more likely to be used in formal than in informal language. Say why.

1. the man to whom I had given the letter – the guy I gave the letter to
2. to give back – to return
3. ages ago – ten years ago
4. refund – money that you get back
5. We'll get you what you need. – We will provide you with what is necessary.
6. lousy – of low quality
7. to arrive – to show up
8. It was kind of cool. – I quite liked it.
9. It was particularly long. – It went on for miles and miles.
10. in the end – finally
11. disadvantage – bad point
12. We were charged $5. – We had to pay $5.
13. in my opinion – I think
14. He was mad. – He was angry.

3 C-Test: Looking back

When I was a child I wanted to become a movie star. I liked dres■■■■ up i■ front o■ the mir■■■ and act■■■ out ro■■■ from mov■■■ which I h■■ seen. Appar■■■■■ my perfo■■■■■■ wasn't s■ bad, bec■■■■ my par■■■■ always encou■■■■■ me. Th■■ clearly appre■■■■■■ what I w■■ doing a■■ that hel■■■ me. Alth■■■■■ it requ■■■■■ quite a l■■ of confi■■■■■■ to st■■■ up o■ the st■■■, the fi■■■ time I w■■ invited t■ an audi■■■■■ I actually wa■■■ a bit ner■■■■■. The cas■■■■■ people h■■ set u■ a run■■■■ order f■■ the candi■■■■■ and th■■ called u■ in indivi■■■■■■■. I was su■■ that I wo■■■ be a suc■■■■■ after t■■ hard wo■■ I had do■■. I was conv■■■■■■ they wo■■■ soon sp■■ my tal■■■ and gi■■ me encour■■■■■■■■. With th■■ attitude not■■■■ could g■ wrong, co■■■ it? I wan■■■ to gi■■ them t■■ best sh■■ they h■■ ever se■■. And luc■■■■ it wor■■■. After■■■■■ the dire■■■■ offered m■ my fi■■■ role! Si■■■ then I ha■■ even man■■■■■ to bec■■■ quite fam■■■■. You s■■, you ju■■ have t■ bel■■■■ in your■■■■ and ke■■ working. It's important never to give up.

focus 3
Focus on international contacts

1 Aliens – just like us?

"You're not from around here, are you?"

a) How might the alien in the cartoon react? Suggest what it might say or do.

b) If you were sitting by yourself in a café in England, would people know where you came from? Why or why not?

c) Work in groups. Think what opportunities there are for contacts with people from other countries. Make a grid.

who?	where?	how?	why?
…	…	…	…

2 Facts and figures

a) Look at Diagram 1. What can you say about the number of German students who study abroad? Would you like to study abroad? Why or why not?

b) Look at Diagram 2. What does it tell you? Do the numbers surprise you? When and where do you use foreign languages? What do you think are the most important reasons for learning foreign languages?

German students abroad
— Students abroad per 1000 students at German colleges

Foreign language use in Europe
■ 1st foreign language ■ 2nd foreign language
(Holiday abroad, Audiovisual media, Work (spoken), Print media, Friends, Internet, Work (written))

3 Get in touch

LANGUAGE HOLIDAYS IN THE UK
☑ Stay with a qualified teacher and family with interests similar to your own.
☑ Live by the sea, in the country or in the city.
☑ Tell us your needs (who you are, when/where you would like to stay, why you need English, etc.) and we'll organize the rest.
☎ 00441092 217285
✉ Jules Dashworth, Kendall Farm, Exeter, Devon EX12 6PB

Wanted: E-pal in Germany
Hi, my name's Mike. I'm 15 and I live in Brisbane, Australia, where the sunshine never stops. I'm looking for an e-pal (guy/girl) in Germany, so drop me a line and tell me about yourself and what life's like 'up there' in good old Deutschland (where my grandma comes from). ☺ ☺ ☺
Contact: mike@roo.au

Work 'n' Play the American Way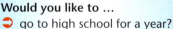
Would you like to …
➲ go to high school for a year?
➲ take part in an exchange program?
➲ be an au pair?
➲ work at a summer camp?
Write to us for our free brochure and enclose a short profile of yourself and your interests.
Tel. 0221/1626-089
Email: workplay@learn.de

a) Read the three advertisements, then say which one you find most interesting and why.

b) Write a reply to the advertisement you have chosen.

90 ninety

4 'Playtime' for Fluffy

a) Describe the situation in the cartoon and explain the joke.

b) If you were in Fluffy's position, what would you say to the others in the classroom?

Fluffy's first and last day as an exchange student.

5 Saying the right thing

a) If you stay with an English family, it is useful to know what phrases to use in certain situations. Saying the right thing will help you to be accepted more easily. Look at the list and think of situations in which you can use these phrases.

Greeting people
How d'you do? (Answer: How d'you do?/ Pleased to meet you.) Nice to see you again.

Saying no tactfully
No, thanks. I'm afraid not.

Apologising
I'm sorry, (but) …/I'm afraid …

Sounding positive/less direct/softer
unhappy ➡ not too pleased
not … ➡ not exactly …
rather (a) …/quite (a) …
a little …/a bit …

Using question tags
You are, aren't you? It wasn't, was it?

Asking politely
Would you mind … -ing? (Answer: Not at all/Of course not.) Perhaps you could …? May I …?

Offering
Can I offer you …/Would you like …/ How about …?

Accepting politely
Oh, yes, please. I'd love to/one.
Mmm. That sounds good!

Correcting
Actually, … That can't be right, surely.

Changing the subject
By the way, … Anyway, …

b) Steffen Bauer has just arrived at the Barkers' house. This is his first visit to England. Listen to the way he reacts to what they say to him. Use the list to think of better ways to react and act the dialogue out again with a partner.

1. *Mr Barker:* How do you do, Stephen? …
2. *Mr Barker:* Oh, sorry. Well, did you have a nice journey, Steffen? …
3. *Mr Barker:* Anyway, I hope you like it here. I mean, Bolton isn't exactly as big as Munich. …
4. *Philip:* And your football team is a bit more famous than Bolton's, isn't it? …
5. *Mr Barker:* Oops, I forgot about tea. Well, could you eat an Indian, Steffen? …
6. *Philip:* Dad means an Indian takeaway, Steffen. Do you like curry? …
7. *Mr Barker:* Well, if hot food isn't your cup of tea, how about pizza? …
8. *Mr Barker:* OK, I'll order some pizzas. …
9. *Philip:* You look thirsty, Steffen? Here, have a glass of water. …
10. *Philip:* Mineral water? That stuff they sell in bottles? Sorry, but we usually drink tap water here. It's perfectly OK. Or would you like a cola? …

c) A year later, Steffen comes back to England to stay with a different family. Listen and discuss how well he reacts this time. Which family would you prefer to stay with and why?

revision Books 1–3

Stopover in Sacramento

A man was flying from Seattle to San Francisco. Unexpectedly, the plane stopped in Sacramento along the way. The flight attendant explained that there would be a
5 delay, and the passengers were told that if they wanted to get off the aircraft, the plane would re-board in 50 minutes.
Everybody got off the plane except one gentleman who was blind.
10 The man noticed him as he walked by and could tell the gentleman was blind because he was accompanied by a Seeing Eye dog that had been lying quietly underneath the seats in front of him throughout the entire flight.
15 He could also tell that he had flown this very flight before because the pilot approached him, and calling him by name, said,

"Brad, we're in Sacramento for almost an hour. Do you want to get off and stretch your legs?" The blind man replied, "No thanks, 20 but I'm sure my dog would like to stretch his legs."
All the people in the gate area came to a complete standstill when they looked up and saw the pilot walk off the plane with a 25 Seeing Eye dog! The pilot was even wearing sunglasses.
People scattered. They not only tried to change planes, they were trying to change airlines, too! 30

1 Understanding the text

a) Find these words in the text, and decide which of these meanings is correct in the context.

1. **delay:** Aufschub? • Verspätung? • Stockung? • Aufenthalt?
2. **to tell:** erzählen? • sagen? • mitteilen? • erkennen? • unterscheiden? • befehlen?
3. **gate:** Tor? • Pforte? • Zugang? • Ausgang? • Schranke?
4. **to change:** sich umziehen? • austauschen? • wechseln? • umwandeln? • verändern? • umsteigen?

b) Find words or expressions in the text that mean …

1. during the journey; 2. plane; 3. came up to him; 4. walk around a bit; 5. moved away in different directions.

c) Explain in your own words:
1. unexpectedly
2. flight attendant
3. to re-board
4. a Seeing Eye dog
5. this very flight
6. to come to a standstill

d) Find examples of indirect speech in the text, and change them into direct speech. Then find examples of direct speech, and express them indirectly.

e) Find the two examples of the passive in the text. Explain why there is a 'by-agent' in one case, but not in the other.
(To check: What happens if you try to put the sentences into the active?)

2 Interpreting the text

a) Explain the misunderstanding. How could it have been avoided?

b) Imagine a conversation between two of the people in the gate area.
Write the dialogue and act it out.

Test yourself!

3 Bad news

Put these sentences into the passive. Only use a 'by-agent' where it is absolutely necessary. Write down your answers, then turn to page 187 to check them.

1. Someone has stolen my bike!
2. Stormy weather hit the South-East of England yesterday.
3. Did the wind blow many trees down?
4. They can't repair our TV set – it's too old.
5. If someone had recognized the thieves, the police would have arrested them sooner.
6. People will never forget the terrible damage that the storm did.
7. Bad driving causes a lot of road accidents.
8. Rabbits have destroyed all the young crops in these fields.
9. If we don't pay the ransom, the kidnappers may hurt the child – or they might even kill her.
10. Sharks sometimes attack swimmers and surfers. That's why some people think we should kill these sharks.

4 Jody and her dad

First read the dialogue between Jody and her dad. Then write down what Jody tells Morag later about their conversation and what was decided. Use indirect speech – with the reporting verbs that are given. Turn to page 187 to check your answers.

1. *Jody:* I've been looking forward to this concert so much, Dad! Morag and the others will be so disappointed if I can't go with them. **tell/say**
2. *Dad:* I understand how you're feeling, Jody. But Rory isn't an experienced driver yet – and none of us knows what the weather's going to be like at the weekend. It may be foggy again. There was a bad accident in the fog on that motorway only a week or two ago. **tell/say/add/say/remember**
3. *Jody:* Yes, Dad, I haven't forgotten. But how will Rory ever become an experienced driver if he never gets the chance to use the car at night? **admit/ask**
4. *Dad:* I'm only thinking of your safety, Jody. Please try to understand my position, too. **explain/want**
5. *Jody:* Well, what do you suggest? Do you expect me to stay at home while Morag and the others go without me? **ask/wonder**
6. *Dad:* Hm! I have a suggestion. Go by train, all of you! What do you think of the idea? **say/advise/ask**
7. *Jody:* I'm not sure. I've no idea what times the trains are on Saturday. **say/tell**
8. *Dad:* Well, get the timetable, Jody. I'm sure there'll be a good connection. **tell/say**
9. *Jody:* OK, I'll discuss the train times with Morag and we'll go by train. Thanks, Dad, for letting me go! **tell/thank**
10. *Dad:* I'm glad you're happy about it now. If you let me know what the train ticket costs, I'll give you the money, OK? **say/tell**

revision
Up to Unit 5

5 Different types of adverbs and adverbials

a) Organize the adverbs and adverbials on the right in groups:

1. Manner (how?)
2. Time (when?)
3. Place (where?)
4. Frequency (how often?)
5. Degree (how much?)
6. Comment

> slowly • of course • three years ago • to New York • very • always • absolutely • actually • fast • well • sometimes • at the airport • next week • perhaps • quite • pretty • at 8.30 • at the station • unfortunately

b) Now write a story and use as many of these adverbs and adverbials as you can. Be careful with the word order.

6 Butch remembers

Put in the adverbs and adverbials – in the position you think is best.

1. Nelson came to see me. **(last October/in my office)**
2. I knew his brother Steve. **(well/already/of course/quite)**
3. We had played baseball together. **(often/before he left Boston)**
4. Nelson's girlfriend had been kidnapped. **(the evening before/apparently)**
5. The kid was worried. **(obviously/terribly)**
6. I thought the situation was strange. **(pretty/frankly)**
7. Nelson had taken half a million dollars. **(at his parents' house/just/from the safe)**
8. I agreed to keep the money until he came back. **(carefully/in the end/the next day)**
9. Nelson was back. **(the next evening/in my office/at six o'clock)**
10. When I suggested going with him, his eyes flashed. **(angrily/later that evening/to the meeting place)**
11. I wasn't surprised when Nelson came back without Gloria. **(home/really/actually)**
12. My plan had gone wrong, but the police arrived and told us that Gloria and Cavori had been arrested. **(at the airport/luckily/completely/suddenly)**

7 Danger: Salt-water crocodiles

Complete the text with infinitive or gerund constructions.

Record numbers of salt-water crocodiles[1] have forced Kakadu National Park `1 close` its swimming holes[2]. Until 30 years ago, `2 hunt` crocodiles was allowed in Australia. But then the government decided `3 make` a law `4 protect` them from `5 die` out. Since then, their numbers have kept `6 grow` – from about 3,000 in the Northern Territory in the 1970s to 70,000 or more today! It is important for visitors to Kakadu `7 be` protected from these dangerous animals. But it is also right for the crocodiles `8 be allowed` `9 live` there in their natural environment. Kakadu's crocodiles are a big tourist attraction; visitors look forward to `10 see` them and enjoy `11 go` out in boats in areas where they expect them `12 be` in the water. But `13 swim` in the park has become very dangerous. In 2002 a German woman went `14 swim` in a natural pool without `15 realize` the danger; in fact, instead of `16 warn` her not `17 use` the pool, a tour guide had told her it was safe for her `18 swim` there. She was attacked and killed by a crocodile – not the only person `19 die` in this terrible way. There is a lot of discussion in the Territory about how `20 control` the 'salties'. A plan `21 allow` tourists `22 hunt` them in certain areas has been unpopular with local people who feel it is worth `23 protect` them. Clearly, `24 find` a solution to the problem is not going `25 be` easy.

[1] ['sɔːltˌwɔːtə 'krɒkədaɪl] – Leistenkrokodil
[2] ['swɪmɪŋ ˌhəʊl] – Tümpel, in dem man schwimmen kann

revision 3

8 Saying the right thing

What would you say in these situations?
Listen and choose the best reaction.
Then say why you chose it.

tip
- Is the reaction polite/rude? • Is it tactful?
- Does it sound positive? • Is it too direct?

1. **Somebody invites you for a meal, but you've already made other plans.**
   - A No. I can't tonight. I want to do something else.
   - B I'd love to, but I'm afraid I can't manage tonight.
   - C No. You can invite me another time.

2. **Your host offers you some more pizza. You don't like the pizza, but you don't want to hurt their feelings.**
   - A No. That's enough pizza, thank you.
   - B No thanks. I'm afraid I really can't.
   - C More of that pizza? No thanks.

3. **You're eating a very nice soup in a restaurant. The waiter asks if it's all right.**
   - A Yes, thank you. It's delicious.
   - B Yes. I quite like it.
   - C Thank you. It's all right.

4. **Your fork is dirty. You want to ask for a clean one.**
   - A Waiter! Bring me a clean fork at once.
   - B Could you bring me a clean fork, please?
   - C I don't like eating with a dirty fork.

5. **Your English friends are planning a holiday in Germany. You want to see them.**
   - A Great! You must come and visit us.
   - B You can come and visit us if you want to.
   - C Oh yes? Maybe we can meet.

9 Mixed bag: Is there a monster or not?

Complete the text. Be careful! Sometimes there is nothing missing.

Would ¹ such ² lot of tourists come to ³ Loch Ness if there weren't so many stories ⁴ a monster in ⁵ lake? Probably ⁶ ! Although ⁷ first tales date ⁸ the 6th century, the modern legend of ⁹ Nessie did ¹⁰ start until the 1930s, when a road was ¹¹ along the edge of ¹² water. One of ¹³ Britain's daily newspapers sent Marmaduke Wetherell (who was ¹⁴ big game¹ hunter) ¹⁵ look for the monster. Two days ¹⁶ , he reported that he ¹⁷ found ¹⁸ footprints of quite ¹⁹ large animal near ²⁰ loch. ²¹ , when these footprints ²² examined, it ²³ discovered that the foot of a hippopotamus² had ²⁴ used ²⁵ make them! (Wetherell ²⁶ brought it back ²⁷ Africa.) ²⁸ 1934, the ²⁹ famous monster photograph of all appeared. (It had been ³⁰ by a man ³¹ was ³² doctor.) It seemed ³³ show the shape ³⁴ a huge sea snake ³⁵ was just ³⁶ up out of ³⁷ water! In 1994, Wetherell's son finally admitted that Wetherell and the doctor ³⁸ faked³ the photo together all those years ³⁹ ! ⁴⁰ , they were not the only ones ⁴¹ fake photos of Nessie. During ⁴² 1970s, at ⁴³ twenty other photos ⁴⁴ produced! But no ⁴⁵ monster has ⁴⁶ been actually found in ⁴⁷ dark, deep water of ⁴⁸ Loch Ness.

¹big game ['bɪg geɪm] – Großwild • ²hippopotamus [ˌhɪpə'pɒtəməs] – Nilpferd • ³to fake [feɪk] – fälschen

ninety-five **95**

extra line

A Why the emu can't fly (after Unit 1)

A story from the Wongutha people of Western Australia.

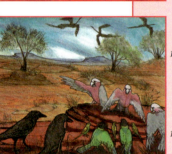

At the beginning of time, emus could fly. They were the biggest birds in the air and could fly higher and faster than anyone else, and they felt pleased with themselves. At first all the birds and animals in the bush lived peacefully, but then the emus became more and more boastful and nastier and meaner too, so the other birds grew tired of them. When the emus started flying straight at the little birds, flapping their huge, dusty wings to bully and frighten them, the little birds lost the will to sing and the land became quiet. The people and animals noticed this change and were sad, too.

The little birds asked the eagles to help them against the bullying emus, but the emus were too big and strong for the eagles. So they asked the animals to help, but there was nothing they could do. Then the little birds turned to the pink and grey galahs. The galahs said they should wait for the emus to lay eggs and crack them while they weren't watching, but this didn't work because the emus were too clever. Finally the small birds went to the Wongutha men, who told them to wait for their head man under the mulga tree. He would tell them what to do.

"I'll help you," said the head man, when he finally arrived. "Wait in the trees to see what happens." And he began to sing a song, an old song handed down to special Wongutha men. When they heard the singing, the emus flew in from every direction to listen. The old man finished his song and disappeared into the bush, while the emus stood there not knowing what to do. That night the bush was quiet and something strange happened to the emus as they ran around in the moonlight. In the morning they stretched and flapped their wings, but these had become small and stumpy, and the emus found that they could not fly! Then they remembered the words of the old man's song, which said, "You boastful emus, you won't ever fly again." And they understood its meaning. And the other birds were happy now. They had the sky to themselves, and the bush was filled with bird songs again.

1 Working with the text

a) The story
1. Say why and how the emus were punished.
2. Find out about the Aboriginal beliefs that lie behind this kind of story.

b) The language
1. Explain the meaning:
   to grow tired of (l. 10), to lose the will to sing (l. 14), to turn to (l. 24), head man (l. 32).
2. The story is told in simple style. Choose four suitable sentences and rewrite them in more formal style.

c) Creative writing
1. Write a dialogue between the emus and the head man. OR:
2. Write a story that tells how one of the other animals or birds that are mentioned in the unit was created.

B More about films (after Unit 2)

1 Some questions

First look at the questions. Then watch a scene from a film and answer them.

- Who are the people in the film?
- Where are they?
- What are they doing?
- How do they feel?
- What is the film about? (Guess!)
- What do you like about the film?

The people in a film are the **characters**. The place where they are is the **setting**. The **action** is what happens in the film. The **plot** is the story that the film tells.

Now work in groups. Watch another scene, take notes and find out as much as you can about the characters, the setting, the action and the plot. Talk about your notes in class and say what you think about the film.

2 Let's work with films

Use a video to do these exercises.

a) Play one or more scenes from a film without sound. What can you see in the pictures? How many characters are there? What are they saying?

b) Now play only the sound of a film. What is happening? What are the characters doing?

c) Play part of a scene and stop it. What are the characters going to do or say next?

d) Look at a freeze frame from a film. Who are the characters? What are they doing?

e) Dubbing: Make your own dialogue for a cartoon. Act it out and record it.

3 Let's be actors

Work in groups. Choose one of these settings and write a short scene with characters from Green Line New. Act it out and record it on video. Make a film poster for your film.

1. On the bus
2. In the shop
3. In the park
4. At a party

4 Your own film project

What is special about your school? Make a short video film in English about your school, your class, the pupils and the teachers.

ninety-seven **97**

C Poetry pages (after Unit 3)

1 Nonets

A nonet has nine lines.
The first line has nine syllables, the second line eight syllables, the third line seven syllables etc. until line nine, which finishes with one syllable:

line 1: 9 syllables
line 2: 8 syllables
line 3: 7 syllables
line 4: 6 syllables
line 5: 5 syllables
line 6: 4 syllables
line 7: 3 syllables
line 8: 2 syllables
line 9: 1 syllable

School
I wish we didn't have to stay here.
The only good part is lunchtime,
eating and playing handball
instead of doing maths.
I don't like history
or geography.
I can't wait
for the
bell.

It can be about anything and doesn't have to rhyme.
Now write your own nonet!

2 Clerihews

A clerihew is a funny poem about a certain person or character. The form was invented by and is named after Edmund Clerihew Bentley (1875–1956). You can write one about your parents, your teachers, your best friend, your pet, rock or movie stars, cartoon characters or anyone else you can think of.

Clerihews have just a few simple rules:

1. They are four lines long.

2. The first and second lines rhyme with each other, and the third and fourth lines rhyme with each other (rhyme pattern AABB).

3. The first line names a person, and the second line ends with something that rhymes with the name of the person.

4. A clerihew should be funny.

What is said in the poem is more important than the rhythm (the pattern of stressed and unstressed syllables).

Try to write a clerihew.

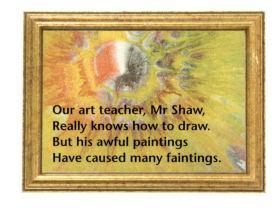

Our art teacher, Mr Shaw,
Really knows how to draw.
But his awful paintings
Have caused many faintings.

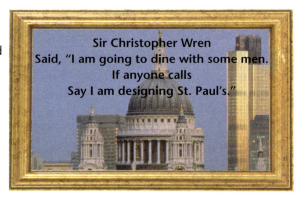

Sir Christopher Wren
Said, "I am going to dine with some men.
If anyone calls
Say I am designing St. Paul's."

3 Limericks

A limerick is a funny little poem that contains five lines. It has a very special rhythm and rhyme pattern. The most famous author of limericks was Edward Lear (1812–1888). He wrote more than 200 of them.

Rhyme pattern: The last words of the first, second, and fifth lines all rhyme with each other. And the last words of the third and fourth lines rhyme with each other (AABBA).

Rhythm pattern: The first, second, and fifth lines all have this rhythm pattern:

da DUM da da DUM da da DUM
("da" stands for an unstressed syllable and "DUM" for a stressed one).
There are three beats (DUMs):

"There ónce was a yóung boy named Jím"

The third and fourth lines have a different rhythm pattern: da DUM da da DUM
There are only two beats (DUMs):

"He féll off a trée".

You can practise the rhythm of limericks by clapping your hands. Then write your own limerick.

> There once was a fellow named Tim (A)
> Whose dad never taught him to swim. (A)
> He fell off a dock (B)
> And sank like a rock. (B)
> And that was the end of him. (A)

> There was an old man from Peru
> Who dreamed he was eating his shoe.
> He awoke in the night
> With a terrible fright
> And found it was perfectly true.

> There once was a young girl named Jill
> Who was scared by the sight of a drill.
> She brushed every day
> So her dentist would say,
> "Your teeth are so perfect; no bill."

4 Rhyming words

If you want to write verses that rhyme, it helps a lot to look for rhyming words before you start. Why don't you do this with a partner? Use the dictionary at the back of the book. It's also a good Word power exercise. Here are some lists that you can go on with by yourselves.

[ɪə]	[uː]	[aɪn]	[eɪt]	[iː t]	[æd]	[əʊ]	[aɪk]
appear	blue	fine	create	complete	add	although	bike
beer	barbecue	line	date	feet	bad	blow	hike
cheer	canoe	mine	gate	greet	Brad	go	like
ear	do	nine	late	meet	glad	grow	Mike
fear	kangaroo	pine	mate	Pete	mad	Joe	strike
gear	new	shine	plate	street	sad	know	unlike
hear	shoe	wine	skate	sweet		no	
here	Sue		slate	treat		show	
near	true		wait			snow	
tear	view					so	
year	zoo					throw	

D An extract from Stephen King (after Unit 4)

Stephen King, the "King of Horror", is one of today's most popular writers. His stories combine elements of psychological thrillers, ghost stories, science fiction and detective mysteries. Most of them are set in New England, often in the fictional town of Castle Rock, Maine. A number of his works have been turned into Hollywood movies with famous actors such as Jack Nicholson, Tom Hanks and Morgan Freeman.

This is an extract from *The body*, a Stephen King short story which was turned into the successful Hollywood movie *Stand by me*.

The story begins on a hot late summer afternoon in 1960, when Gordie, the narrator, was a teenager. He and his friends Chris and Teddy are playing cards in the treehouse they have built themselves and use as a clubhouse. Suddenly they are interrupted by the arrival of Vern, another friend.

"You ran all the way from your place?" Chris asked unbelievingly. "Man, you're crazy." Vern's house was two miles down Grand Street. "It must be ninety out there."
"This is worth it," Vern said. "Holy Jeezum. You won't believe this. Sincerely." He slapped his sweaty forehead to show us how sincere he was.
"Okay, what?" Chris asked.
"Can you guys camp out tonight?" Vern was looking at us earnestly, excitedly. His eyes looked like raisins pushed into dark circles of sweat. "I mean, if you tell your folks we're gonna tent out in my back field?"
"Yeah, I guess so," Chris said, picking up his new hand and looking at it. "But my dad's on a mean streak. Drinkin, y'know."
"You got to, man," Vern said. "Sincerely. You won't believe this. Can you, Gordie?"
"Probably."

I was able to do most stuff like that – in fact, I'd been like the Invisible Boy that whole summer. In April my older brother, Dennis, had been killed in a Jeep accident. That was at Fort Benning, Georgia, where he was in Basic. He and another guy were on their way to the PX and an Army truck hit them broadside. Dennis was killed instantly and his passenger had been in a coma ever since. Dennis would have been twenty-two later that week. I'd already picked out a birthday card for him at Dahlie's over in Castle Green.

I cried when I heard, and I cried more at the funeral, and I couldn't believe that Dennis was gone, that anyone that used to knuckle my head or scare me with a rubber spider until I cried or give me a kiss when I fell down and scraped both knees bloody and whisper in my ear, "Now stop cryin, ya baby!" – that a person who had touched me could be dead. It hurt me and it scared me that he could be dead … but it seemed to have taken all the heart out of my parents. For me, Dennis was hardly more than an acquaintance. He was ten years older than me, and he had his own friends and classmates. We ate at the same table for a lot of years, and sometimes he was my friend and sometimes my tormentor, but mostly he was, you know, just a guy. When he died he'd been gone for a year. We didn't even look alike. It took me a long time after that summer to realize that most of the tears I cried were for my mom and dad. Fat lot of good it did them, or me.

"So what are you pissing and moaning about, Vern-O?" Teddy asked.

Vern Tessio said: "You guys want to go see a dead body?"
Everybody stopped.

We'd all heard about it on the radio, of course. The radio, a Philco with a cracked case, played all the time. We kept it tuned to WALM in Lewiston, which churned out super-hits and boss oldies. When the news came on we usually switched some mental dial over to Mute. The news was a lot of happy horseshit about politics. But we had all listened to the Ray Brower story a little more closely, because he was a kid our age.

He was from Chamberlain, a town forty miles or so east of Castle Rock. Three days before Vern came busting into the clubhouse after a two-mile run up Grand Street, Ray Brower had gone out with one of his mother's pots to pick blueberries. When dark came and he still wasn't back, the Browers called the county sheriff and a search started – first just around the kid's house and then spreading to the surrounding towns of Motton and Durham and Pownal. Everybody got into the act. But three days later the kid was still missing. You could tell, hearing about it on the radio, that they were never going to find that poor sucker alive. He might have gotten smothered in a gravel pit slide or drowned in a brook, and ten years from now some hunter would find his bones. They were already dragging the ponds in Chamberlain, and the Motton Reservoir.

Nothing like that could happen in southwestern Maine today; most of the area has become suburbanized, and the bedroom communities surrounding Portland and Lewiston have spread out like the tentacles of a giant squid. The woods are still there, and they get heavier as you work your way west toward the White Mountains, but these days if you can keep your head long enough to walk five miles in one consistent direction, you're certain to cross two-lane blacktop. But in 1960 the whole area between Chamberlain and Castle Rock was undeveloped. In those days it was still possible to walk into the woods and lose your direction there and die there.

1 Looking at the story

a) What is Vern so excited about?

b) What information can you find in this extract about

- the narrator of the story?
- Chris, Teddy and Vern?
- Ray Brower?
- the area in which the story is set?

c) Later the four boys set off into the woods to try and find the dead body Vern has heard about. Why do you think they are so fascinated by death? Look at the text, and think of your own feelings too.

d) What would happen to the boys in the rest of the story if you were the author? (Perhaps you have seen the movie. If you have, tell your partner about it.)

Scenes from the movie *Stand by me*

extra line

E A theatre workshop (after Unit 5)

Before you start, warm up your body and do some stretching. Your sports teacher can show you how.

Body language
1. Walking:
   a) Bend your knees a little bit, so you are smaller. Then walk like this, as slowly as you can: Put your weight on one foot, then put your other foot forward, put it on the ground and put your weight on it. Then put the other foot slowly forward.
   b) Tiptoe – so you are taller – very fast with very small steps. This can be done with music, or somebody can clap their hands. When the music or the clapping stops, freeze your position. Now try to express these feelings by walking: You're happy. You're unhappy. You're angry. You're frightened.
2. Work with a partner. One of you closes their eyes and is blind. Your partner helps you to walk around the room without speaking.
3. Work in groups of two or three. One of you is a statue. The others must put the body of the statue in position.
4. Now the whole group are statues. When the music begins, you start walking around, dancing, etc.. When it stops, freeze again.
5. Do a pantomime: You eat a banana. You drink tea. You are an animal, and the others must guess what it is.
6. This looks like a pencil case. But only you know that it is a hamster/an ice cream/a knife etc. Use it so as to show the others what it really is.
7. Work in small groups. Think of a compound word and act it out. The others must guess the word.

Sound practice
1. Practise each of these sounds: [ɑː], [æ], [ɜː], [iː], [ɔː], [uː] together. Then add different consonants, for example p [pɑː], [pæ], [pɜː] etc. Repeat these syllables to a special rhythm, for example [pɑː pɑː pæpæpæ] etc.
2. Now use the syllables like real words in a sentence and express different feelings with them: You talk to somebody you like. You are surprised. You are angry at somebody. You are frightened.

Acting
1. Now use the dialogue "Hello." – "Hi." to express different feelings.
2. Look at the picture. Position actors in the room to imitate the scene in the picture. Then guess what is going to happen next and act out this scene, too. Find other pictures and work with them.
3. Act out dialogues from your English book.
4. You can also use a text that is not a dialogue (a poem for example) and act it out.

F A sketch: Boogaloo (after Unit 5)

Setting
A studio where a TV commercial for "Boogaloo" chewing gum is being made.

Characters
Bob
Simon
Nicole
The director
Guests at a disco
Barman
Band leader and band
Two camera operators
The light operator

A TV studio. No lights. We can't see anything.
Director: OK, the disco scene! Actors get ready! Is the band ready?
Band leader: Ready!
5 **Director:** Cameras ready?
Cameras: Ready!
Director: OK – Action! Lights! *(Nothing happens.)* Lights!! *(Nothing happens.)* Lights!!!
10 **Lights:** Sorry!
The lights go on. We see a disco. The actors are dancing and the band is playing. Bob and Simon are standing at the bar. They are watching the dancers.
15 **Bob:** Hey, Simon, who's that beautiful girl over there?
Simon: Which girl do you mean?
Bob: The girl with the red hair. She's gorgeous!
Simon: Oh, that girl. That's Nicola –
20 **Director:** Nicole! Not Nicola – Nicole! Cut!
Simon: Nicola – Nicole: what's the difference?
Director: The script says 'Nicole'. So you say Nicole, OK?
Simon: OK.
25 **Director:** OK! From the beginning. Cameras! Action!
Bob: Hey, Simon, who's that beautiful girl over there?
Simon: Which girl do you mean?
30 **Bob:** The girl with the red hair. She's gorgeous!
Simon: Oh, that girl. That's – er– Nicole.
Bob: I must meet her. Can you help me, Simon?
Simon: Hey, Nicole! Nicole! Come over here
35 and have a cola with us.
Nicole comes over to the two boys at the bar.
Simon: *(to the barman)* Three colas, please. *(To Nicole)* This is my friend Bob. Bob – Nicole.
Nicole smiles at Bob. The barman brings the
40 *drinks.*
Director: Cut!
Simon: Oh, no! What's the matter now?

Director: Everything is fine. But now I want a close-up of Nicole and Bob. Camera one on Nicole, camera two on Bob – OK, cameras? 45
Cameras: OK!
Director: OK! Cameras! Action!
Nicole: *(takes her cola)* Thanks, Simon. Cheers, Bob!
Director: No, no, no! Cut! Louder, Nicola! 50
Simon: Nicole.
Director: Nicola – Nicole. What's the difference? Speak up, Nicole, please. And smile. Smile! OK?
Nicole: OK. 55
Director: OK! Cameras! Action!
Nicole: *(takes her cola, smiles at Simon)* Thanks, Simon! *(She smiles at Bob.)* Cheers, Bob!
Bob: Cheers, Nicole!
The music changes. Now the band is playing a 60
slow number. They look at each other.
Bob: Nicole – do you want to dance?
Nicole: Oh, yes.
They dance together.
Director: Cut! Hey, you two – closer! This is 65
your big chance, Bob! You must dance closer and whisper in her ear.
Bob: All right.
Director: OK. From Bob's line. Cameras! Action! 70
Bob: Nicole – do you want to dance?
Nicole: Oh, yes.
Director: Cut! Nicole: You do want to dance. You want to dance with Bob. You like Bob. He looks nice. So you say, "Oh! YES!" 75
Nicole: Oh! YES!
Director: OK. Cameras! Action!
Bob: Nicole – do you want to dance?
Nicole: Oh! YES!
They dance close together. Bob whispers in 80
Nicole's ear. But suddenly she sniffs and makes a face. She leaves his arms.
Bob: What's the matter, Nicole?

Grammar

In jeder Unit gibt es wieder Verweise auf die mit **G1**, **G2** etc. durchnummerierten Grammatikkapitel, in denen du wie gewohnt Regeln und Beispiele zum neuen Grammatikstoff findest.

Die Seitenangabe rechts neben der Überschrift zeigt dir, auf welcher Seite der Stoff in der Unit eingeführt wird.

Wo ein ❗ steht, musst du wieder besonders aufpassen.

Der Grammatikteil fasst die Regeln zusammen, die du aus dem Unterricht kennst. Er kann dir auch beim selbstständigen Lernen zu Hause helfen, z.B. wenn du für eine Schulaufgabe übst oder wenn du etwas nicht verstanden hast und noch einmal wiederholen möchtest. Im Folgenden findest du eine Liste der grammatischen Begriffe aus diesem Buch.

Die Angabe **G**… zeigt, wo du im Grammatikteil zu dem Begriff etwas findest.

Grammatical terms

Englisch	Englisches Beispiel	Deutsch
adjective		Adjektiv
adjectives after verbs	He **looks good** in his new coat.	Adjektiv nach Verben
adjectives as nouns **G10**	The **rich** are lucky.	Adjektiv als Nomen
adverb/adverbial G14–15		Adverb/adverbiale Bestimmung
~ of degree **G15**	It's **very** late.	Gradadverb
~ of comment **G14**	**Of course** I like her.	kommentierendes Adverb
~ of frequency	I **always** get up early.	~ der Häufigkeit
~ of manner	**quickly, easily, in a friendly way** etc.	~ der Art und Weise
~ of place	They play **in the park**.	~ des Ortes
~ of time	We're going to meet **at ten o'clock**.	~ der Zeit
article		Artikel
definite article **G8**	**The** movie was scary.	bestimmter Artikel
indefinite article **G7**	He's such **a** nice guy.	unbestimmter Artikel
auxiliary	to be, to do, to have	Hilfsverb
modal auxiliary	can, may, might, must, need, should	modales Hilfsverb
substitutes for modal auxiliaries	to be able to, to be allowed to, to have to	Ersatzformen für modale Hilfsverben
comparative	old**er**, **more** beautiful etc.	Komparativ, 1. Steigerungsform
conditional sentence G2		Bedingungssatz
conditional sentence type I	If they **leave**, we**'ll go** with them.	
conditional sentence type II	If I **were** you, I **wouldn't complain**.	
conditional sentence type III	If I **had seen** the snake, I **would have run** away.	
connective	**and, or, because, when** etc.	Konjunktion/Bindewort
contact clause	That's the film **I like best**.	Relativsatz ohne Relativpronomen
defining relative clause	Tom was the boy **who phoned me**.	notwendiger Relativsatz
future		Futur
going-to future	We're **going to** have fun.	*going-to*-Futur
will future	It **will** be a big hit.	*will*-Futur
gerund G12	**Swimming** is fun.	Gerundium (Verb als Nomen)
	I'm tired of **waiting**.	
	He went away without **looking** back.	

Englisch	Englisches Beispiel	Deutsch
if and when	**If** it rains, we'll go to the cinema. **When** Mum comes, she'll cook for us.	konditionales 'wenn' temporales 'wenn'
indirect speech G1	He told me he **was** sorry.	indirekte Rede
infinitive constructions G13	We were the last **to arrive** at the party.	Infinitivkonstruktionen
noun G9	The **police** are at the door.	Nomen/Substantiv
object	Jenny is buying **a pen**.	Objekt
one, prop-word	I like the **green one** better than the **red one**.	Stützwort *one*
passive voice G3–6 progressive forms in the passive **G4** verbs with prepositions in the passive **G5** verbs with two objects in the passive **G6**	A new school **is being built**. It's **paid for** by the state. We **were given** instructions.	Passiv Verlaufsformen des Passivs Passiv bei Verben mit Präpositionen Passiv bei Verben mit zwei Objekten
past participle	**walked, done, eaten** etc.	Partizip Perfekt
past perfect past perfect passive past perfect progressive past perfect simple	 One of the windows **had been broken**. They **had been singing** for over an hour. He **had** already **left** when I arrived.	Plusquamperfekt Plusquamperfekt im Passiv Verlaufsform des Plusquamperfekts einfaches Plusquamperfekt
past tense past progressive simple past	 We **were dancing** when Kim came in. I **went** to a party last night.	Vergangenheit, Präteritum Verlaufsform der Vergangenheit einfache Vergangenheit
possessive determiner	**my, your, his, her** etc.	Possessivbegleiter/besitzanzeigendes Fürwort
possessive pronoun G11	**mine, yours, his, ours** etc.	Possessivpronomen
present perfect present perfect progressive present perfect with 'for' and 'since'	We **haven't done** it yet. I**'ve been watching** the birds for a long time. I**'ve been living** in London **since** 2005.	Perfekt Verlaufsform des Perfekts Perfekt mit 'seit'
present tense present progressive simple present	 Look, he**'s playing** football. I often **go** to school by bus.	Präsens/Gegenwart Verlaufsform des Präsens einfaches Präsens
pronoun object pronoun personal pronoun possessive pronoun **G11** reflexive pronoun relative pronoun	 **me, him, us** etc. **he, she, it, we** etc. **mine, yours, his, ours** etc. **myself, yourself, himself, herself, ourselves, yourselves** etc. **who/which/that/whose/whom**	Pronomen Personalpronomen im Objektfall Personalpronomen Possessivpronomen Reflexivpronomen Relativpronomen
reported speech	= indirect speech	indirekte Rede
sentence with comparison	Tim is **nicer than** his sister. He's **not as old as** Tom.	Vergleich im Satz
subject	**The book** is on the table.	Subjekt/Satzgegenstand
superlative	old**est**, the **most** difficult	Superlativ/2. Steigerungsform
word order G14		Wortstellung

unit 1

G1 Revision: Indirect speech — Wiederholung: Indirekte Rede
page 10

Du kennst schon die Unterschiede zwischen direkter und indirekter Rede und weißt, was man verändern muss, wenn man direkte in indirekte Rede „überträgt". Zur Erinnerung sind hier noch einmal die wichtigsten Dinge zusammengefasst.

Direct speech

Matt	Lin
"Hi. I **can** help you with those boxes."	"Oh, thank you. That**'s** very nice of you."
"**Have** you **been living** in Australia long?" "What **do** you **do** in your free time?"	"Yes, we **came** five years ago." "Well, I **love** surfing."
"Well, **come** to the beach with me at the weekend. **Tell me** when you're free."	"Hm, yes, perhaps. But I**'m** not sure if I**'ll have** time."

Die direkte Rede gibt wörtlich wieder, was jemand sagt. Wenn man weitergeben möchte, was jemand gesagt hat, verwendet man die indirekte Rede. Wenn man dies zu einem späteren Zeitpunkt berichtet, benutzt man einen Einleitungssatz im *simple past* (z. B. *She said* …).

Indirect speech

Matt
I talked to Lin, our new neighbour, this afternoon. I said that I **could** help her. She thanked me and thought that that **was** very nice of me.
Indirekte Fragen (indirect questions) I asked her **whether** they **had been living** in Australia long. She said that they **had come** five years ago. I wanted to know **what** she **did** in her free time. She told me that she **loved** surfing.
Indirekte Aufforderungssätze (indirect commands) I invited her **to come** to the beach with me at the weekend and asked her **to tell me** when she was free.
She answered that she **wasn't** sure if she **would have** time.

▸ Wenn das Verb im Einleitungssatz im *simple past* oder im *past perfect* steht (*I said, she had told me* etc.), werden die Verbformen in der indirekten Rede gegenüber denen in der direkten Rede um eine Zeitstufe in die Vergangenheit zurückversetzt (*can* ➔ *could*, *will* ➔ *would*, *is* ➔ *was*, *have been living* ➔ *had been living* etc.).

▸ Verben im *past perfect* sowie die Verbformen *could, would, should* und *might* bleiben in der indirekten Rede unverändert.

▸ Wird in der direkten Rede eine Frage ohne Fragewort verwendet (*Have you been* …?), so wird der Nebensatz der indirekten Rede durch *if* oder *whether* eingeleitet (… *whether they had been* …).

▸ Steht in der direkten Rede ein Fragewort (*What do you think?*), so wird dies in der indirekten Rede beibehalten (*He asked her what she thought.*).

▸ Aufforderungssätze werden in der indirekten Rede meist durch einen Infinitiv mit *to* wiedergegeben (*Come to the beach.* ➔ *He invited her to come to the beach.*).

G2 Conditional sentences Bedingungssätze

page 13

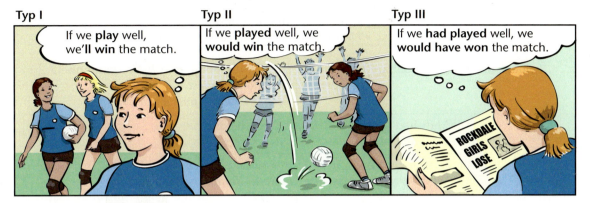

Ein Bedingungssatz besteht aus einem *if*-Satz *(if-clause)* und einem Hauptsatz *(main clause)*. Der *if*-Satz beschreibt eine Bedingung, und der Hauptsatz drückt aus, was passieren wird oder passieren könnte, wenn diese Bedingung erfüllt wird. Man unterscheidet drei Typen von Bedingungssätzen:

Typ I
Dieser Typ von Bedingungssätzen ist dir schon bekannt. Der Sprecher hält die Bedingung für realistisch. Sie scheint erfüllbar zu sein.

if-clause: **erfüllbare Bedingung** *simple present*	*main clause:* **Folge für die Zukunft** *will future*
If we **go** to Australia next year,	we'**ll stay** in Sydney for a week.
If we **don't save** enough money this year,	we **won't be able** to go.

Neben dem *will future* werden im Hauptsatz häufig auch die modalen Hilfsverben *can, must, needn't* usw. oder der Imperativ verwendet:
If you go to Australia, you **mustn't forget** to take your camera.
If you go to Australia, **remember** to take your camera.

Typ II
Auch diesen zweiten Typ kennst du schon. Man verwendet ihn, wenn man daran zweifelt, dass die Bedingung erfüllbar ist, oder wenn man genau weiß, dass sie nicht erfüllt werden kann.

if-clause: **nur theoretisch oder gar nicht erfüllbare Bedingung** *simple past*	*main clause:* **Folge für die Gegenwart oder die Zukunft** *conditional (would + infinitive)*
If I **lived** in Australia,	I **would go** surfing as often as possible.
If Lin **didn't speak** English,	she **wouldn't like living** in Sydney.
If I **were** Lin,	I **would invite** Matt to a Chinese meal.

Im Hauptsatz können außer dem *conditional* auch *could* oder *might + infinitive* verwendet werden: *If a big kangaroo attacked you, it **could hurt** you badly. – It **might** even **kill** you.*

Typ III

Bei diesem Bedingungssatz weiß der Sprecher, dass die Bedingung nicht mehr erfüllt werden kann, weil es sich um eine Situation handelt, die in der Vergangenheit liegt und vorbei ist. *(If Matt **had seen** the snake … ➜ He didn't see it.)*

if-clause: **nicht mehr erfüllbare Bedingung** *past perfect*	*main clause:* **Folge für die Vergangenheit** *conditional perfect* *(would + have + past participle)*
If Matt **had seen** the snake, *Wenn Matt die Schlange gesehen hätte,*	he **would have run** away. *wäre er weggerannt.*
If the snake **hadn't been** scared, *Wenn die Schlange sich nicht erschrocken hätte,*	it **wouldn't have bitten** him. *hätte sie ihn nicht gebissen.*
If Jack **hadn't found** his uncle, *Wenn Jack seinen Onkel nicht gefunden hätte,*	they **couldn't have taken** Matt back to the house. *hätten sie Matt nicht zum Haus bringen können.*
If the Flying Doctor **hadn't come**, *Wenn der 'Flying Doctor' nicht gekommen wäre,*	Matt **might have died**. *wäre Matt vielleicht gestorben.*

▸ Im *if*-Satz steht das *past perfect*, im Hauptsatz das *conditional perfect* (would + have + past participle) oder *could/might + have + past partciple*.
▸ Im Deutschen entspricht dem *past perfect* in Bedingungssätzen eine Konjunktivform: gesehen hätte, erschrocken hätte, gefunden hätte, gekommen wäre.

Mischformen

Darüber hinaus sind auch die folgenden Verbindungen von Verbformen recht häufig:

a) **Typ-III-Bedingung + Typ-II-Folge**

if-clause: **nicht mehr erfüllbare Bedingung** *past perfect*	*main clause:* **Folge immer noch wirksam** *conditional (would + infinitive)*
If the snake **hadn't bitten** him, *Wenn die Schlange ihn nicht gebissen hätte,*	Matt **wouldn't be** in hospital now. *wäre Matt jetzt nicht im Krankenhaus.*

b) **Typ-II-Bedingung + Typ-III-Folge**

if-clause: **nur theoretische Bedingung** *past tense*	*main clause:* **Folge für die Vergangenheit** *conditional perfect (would + have + past participle)*
If she **didn't speak** English so well, *Wenn sie nicht so gut Englisch spräche,*	she **wouldn't have found** a job so quickly. *hätte sie nicht so schnell eine Stelle gefunden.*

❗ Bei den Kurzformen musst du aufpassen:
'd kann die Kurzform von **had** und von **would** sein.
Der Zusammenhang macht dir klar, um welche Form es sich handelt.
I'd have phoned if I'd known your mobile number. =
*I **would** have phoned if I **had** known …*

unit 2

G3 Revision: The passive voice — Wiederholung: Passiv — page 27

Du kennst schon die meisten Formen des Passivs und weißt, wie sie verwendet werden. Passivsätze findet man häufig in Zeitungsberichten oder in historischen Texten. In ihnen steht die Handlung selbst im Mittelpunkt und nicht derjenige, der etwas tut. Hier, zur Erinnerung, noch einmal eine Zusammenstellung der dir bekannten Passivformen:

passive verb forms (simple forms)	
simple present: am/is/are + past participle	Eden **is visited** by lots of people every day.
simple past: was/were + past participle	It **was opened** in 2001.
present perfect: have/has been + past participle	Millions of visitors **have been attracted** by it since then.
past perfect: had been + past participle	After a James Bond movie **had been filmed** there, Eden became even more popular.
future: will be + past participle / going to be + past participle	A third biome **will be built** sometime in the future. A lot of other interesting plants **are going to be put in** there.
Infinitive: be + past participle	More **should be done** for the environment. The natural world **has to be protected**.

G4 The progressive forms of the passive — Die Verlaufsformen des Passivs — page 27

Neben den dir schon vertrauten *simple forms* des Passivs gibt es zwei *progressive forms*.

passive verb forms (progressive forms)		
present progressive: am/is/are being + past participle	At the moment a new car park **is being built**. Lots of other things **are being planned**.	… wird (gerade) … gebaut. … werden (gerade) geplant.
past progressive: was/were being + past participle	Thousands of people came to look at the Eden Project while it **was being built**. When I was there, some new tropical trees **were** just **being planted**.	… während es gebaut wurde./… während es im Bau war. … wurden … gerade gepflanzt.

- Für die Verwendung der Zeitformen des Passivs gelten die gleichen Regeln wie für die aktiven Verbformen.
- Das *present pogressive* beschreibt Vorgänge, die im Moment gerade ablaufen und noch nicht abgeschlossen sind.
- Das *past progressive* beschreibt Vorgänge, die in der Vergangenheit abliefen und noch nicht abgeschlossen waren.

G5 Verbs with prepositions in passive sentences
Das Passiv bei Verben mit Präpositionen

page 27

	subject	verb + preposition	object
active:	Britain's National Lottery	paid for	most of the Eden Project.

	subject	verb + preposition	by-agent
passive:	Most of the Eden Project	was paid for	by Britain's National Lottery.

- Wie du schon weißt, wird das Objekt des Aktivsatzes (hier: Präpositionalobjekt) zum Subjekt des Passivsatzes, und das Subjekt des Aktivsatzes wird zum **by-agent**.
- Verb und Präposition bilden im Englischen eine enge Verbindung und werden (anders als im Deutschen) auch im Passivsatz nicht getrennt.
- Bei der Übersetzung ins Deutsche werden häufig Sätze mit ‚man' verwendet:

*New ways to protect the environment **are being looked for**.* **Nach** neuen Methoden die Umwelt zu schützen **wird gesucht**./**Man sucht nach** neuen Methoden …

*These problems **must be dealt with** soon.* **Man muss sich** bald **mit** diesen Problemen **befassen**.

G6 Verbs with two objects in passive sentences
Das Passiv bei Verben mit zwei Objekten

page 29

- Viele englische Verben werden (ganz ähnlich wie ihre deutschen Entsprechungen) mit zwei Objekten, einem direkten und einem indirekten, verwendet. Zu ihnen gehören: *give, lend, offer, promise, send, show* usw. Vergleiche: *I've lent **him my mobile**.* – Ich habe **ihm mein Handy** geliehen.
- Nach dem direkten Objekt wird mit ‚Wen oder was?' gefragt, nach dem indirekten mit ‚Wem oder was?'
- Will man das indirekte Objekt besonders betonen oder ist es länger als das direkte, stellt man es zusammen mit der Präposition *to* ans Ende des Satzes:
*I gave him **the book**.* → *I gave the book **to him** (and not to his sister).*
*The guide showed the castle **to a group of young people from Britain**.*

! Bei den Verben *describe, explain, introduce, mention, say* und *suggest* muss man das indirekte Objekt immer mit *to* verwenden:
*Please explain the problem **to me**.* (Niemals: *Please explain ~~me the problem.~~*)

Es gibt zwei Möglichkeiten, Sätze, die Verben mit **zwei Objekten** enthalten, ins Passiv zu setzen.

		indirect object (Person)	direct object (Sache)
active:	We showed	our guests	the rooms.

passive: **Our guests** were shown the rooms.   **The rooms** were shown to our guests.
        subject   subject

! Bei Passivsätzen mit den Verben *describe, explain, introduce, mention, say* und *suggest* ist nur die zweite Möglichkeit richtig:
*The situation was explained **to us**.* (Niemals: *~~We were explained~~ the situation.*)

grammar
unit 2/3

passive 1 (personal passive)	passive 2
I was sent a brochure with a lot of useful information. *Mir wurde eine Broschüre … geschickt./ Man/Jemand hat mir eine Broschüre … geschickt.*	A brochure with a lot of useful information **was sent to** every person in the group.
We were given all the necessary instructions. *Man gab uns alle notwendigen Anweisungen.*	All the necessary instructions **were given to** the people who wanted to take part in the sailing course.

- Hier entspricht das Subjekt des Passivsatzes dem indirekten Objekt des Aktivsatzes.
- Da dies in den meisten Fällen eine Person ist, wird diese Passivkonstruktion auch als **persönliches Passiv** bezeichnet.
- Bei der Übersetzung ins Deutsche werden häufig Sätze mit ‚man' oder ‚jemand' verwendet.
- Diese Passivkonstruktion ist die gebräuchlichere der beiden Möglichkeiten.

- Hier entspricht das Subjekt des Passivsatzes dem direkten Objekt des Aktivsatzes (meist eine Sache).
- Das indirekte Objekt (meist eine Person) wird mit *to* angeschlossen.
- Diese Konstruktion ist weniger gebräuchlich. Sie wird vorwiegend dann verwendet, wenn das indirekte Objekt besonders lang ist oder betont werden soll (**every person in the group**.)

unit 3

G7 The indefinite article — Der unbestimmte Artikel
page 44

Der unbestimmte Artikel
Im Englischen wird der unbestimmte Artikel *a/an* meistens genauso verwendet wie in den deutschen Entsprechungen. Nur in einigen wenigen Fällen unterscheidet sich der Gebrauch:

1. Nationalitätsangaben und Berufsbezeichnungen

*Brad is **an American**. … ist **Amerikaner**.*
*Emma's father works as **a mechanic**. … arbeitet als **Mechaniker**.*

- Bei Berufsbezeichnungen und Nationalitätsangaben steht im Englischen der unbestimmte Artikel (meist nach *is* oder *as*).

2. Zeit- und Mengenangaben

*The Hassans' shop is open 24 hours **a day**.*
*… 24 Stunden **am** Tag …*
*These apples are 85p **a pound**.*
*… **pro/je/das** Pfund.*

- In der Bedeutung ‚pro' steht der unbestimmte Artikel vor Zeit- und Mengenangaben.

3. Wörter wie *half, quite, rather, such*

*It took me **half an** hour to do the exercise.*
*… **eine halbe** Stunde …*
*That was **quite/rather a** long time.*
*… **eine ziemlich** lange Zeit.*
*It was **such a** difficult problem.*
*… **ein so** schwieriges Problem.*

- Im Gegensatz zum Deutschen wird der unbestimmte Artikel im Englischen hier nachgestellt.

4. Bestimmte englische Redewendungen

*Sorry, I can't talk. I'm in **a hurry**. … in **Eile**.*
*I've got **a headache**. … **Kopfschmerzen**.*
*We got to Glasgow in **an hour and a half**.*
*… **anderthalb Stunden**.*

- Hier steht im Deutschen kein Artikel.

G8 The definite article Der bestimmte Artikel

page 44

Der bestimmte Artikel

"I like music."

"I don't like the music they're playing today."

- Der bestimmte Artikel *the* zeigt an, dass Personen oder Dinge näher bestimmt sind. Der Artikel steht nicht, wenn von Personen oder Dingen ganz allgemein gesprochen wird.
- Im Englischen gibt es für bestimmte Gruppen von Nomen Regeln, die dir sagen, wann der bestimmte Artikel verwendet wird. Diese sind im Folgenden aufgelistet. Beachte die Unterschiede zum Deutschen!

1. Stoffbezeichnungen, abstrakte (unzählbare) Begriffe, Verkehrsmittel, Monate, Wochentage und Mahlzeiten

ohne Artikel	mit Artikel
a) I like Italian **food**.	**The Italian food we had last night** was delicious.
b) We can learn a lot from **history**. … aus **der** *Geschichte* …	I'm especially interested in **the history of Scotland**.
c) We can go to Edinburgh by **train**. … mit **dem** *Zug* …	**The train to Edinburgh** leaves at 6.30.
d) **January** and **February** are usually the coldest months of the year. **Der Januar** und **der Februar** …	But **the January of 2003** wasn't very cold.
e) What do you usually do on **Saturday**? … am Samstag?	She'll never forget **the Saturday she met the famous drummer**.
f) We often watch TV after **tea**. … nach **dem** Abendessen …	**The tea Jody made yesterday** was very nice.

- Werden diese Begriffe ganz allgemein verwendet, dann steht kein Artikel.
- Werden diese Nomen durch eine Orts- oder Zeitangabe, einen Relativsatz oder eine Präpositionalphrase näher bestimmt, so steht der bestimmte Artikel.

! **Ausnahme:** *Next/Last January/Saturday* steht ohne Artikel.

2. Institutionen

ohne Artikel	mit Artikel
School in the UK starts later than in Germany. **Die** *Schule* …	**The school** Amir goes to is very modern. There are computers in every classroom.
We don't go to **church** every Sunday. … *in* **die** *Kirche*.	**The church** in Castle Road was built in the 19th century.

▶ Wenn man an den Zweck der Institution denkt (Schule: Unterricht, Kirche: Gottesdienst, Krankenhaus: Behandlung usw.), steht kein Artikel.
▶ Wenn eine bestimmte Schule oder Kirche (das Gebäude) gemeint ist, steht der Artikel.

3. Personennamen

ohne Artikel	mit Artikel
Poor Rory had a bad headache last night. **Der arme Rory** …	Are **the Slaters** and **the Hassans** neighbours? … **(die) Slaters** *und* **(die) Hassans** …
Mr Penrose often took **little Mark** to kindergarten. … **den kleinen Mark** …	

▶ Anders als im Deutschen werden Personennamen im Singular auch dann im Englischen **ohne Artikel** gebraucht, wenn ihnen ein Adjektiv vorausgeht.
▶ Familiennamen im Plural stehen im Englischen immer **mit** dem bestimmten **Artikel**, im Deutschen kann man ihn weglassen.

G9 Nouns for groups, collective nouns and abstract nouns *page 46*
Gruppenbezeichnungen, Sammelbegriffe und abstrakte Nomen

Gruppenbezeichnungen, Sammelbegriffe und abstrakte Nomen werden im Englischen häufig anders wahrgenommen als im Deutschen und daher anders verwendet. So hängt z.B. die Form des zugehörigen Verbs davon ab, ob die Bedeutung eines Ausdrucks stärker singularisch oder pluralisch aufgefasst wird.

1. Gruppenbezeichnungen mit singularischer oder pluralischer Bedeutung

▶ Hier ist die Gruppe als Ganzes gemeint. Wie im Deutschen wird hier die Familie, die Mannschaft als Einheit gesehen. Verben und Pronomen stehen im **Singular**:	▶ Hier wird betont, was die einzelnen Mitglieder der Gruppe tun, nicht die Gruppe als Ganzes. Verben und Pronomen stehen im **Plural**:
The McDonald **family has** lived in Scotland for over 800 years. **It is** one of the oldest in the country.	My **family** always **try** to get together at Christmas. But **we don't** always manage it.
Our **team isn't** doing very well this season. Perhaps **it needs** a new manager.	Just look at the way the **team are** playing today. **They don't** seem to know what to do.

▶ Auch bei den Gruppenbezeichnungen *audience, class, club, crowd, crew, government* usw. sind beide Betrachtungsweisen möglich.

2. Gruppenbezeichnungen mit ausschließlich pluralischer Bedeutung

The Scottish **people are** a proud **people**. **They are** proud of **their** beautiful country.	*Das schottische **Volk ist** ein stolzes **Volk**. **Es ist** stolz auf **sein** schönes Land.*
Highland cattle look really wild with their long hair.	*Das **Hochlandvieh sieht** wirklich wild aus mit **seinem** langen Fell.*
The **police are** at the door. **They want** to talk to you.	*Die **Polizei ist** an der Tür. **Sie will** mit dir reden.*

▶ *People* (Leute, Menschen oder Volk), *cattle* und *police* werden immer als Gruppe gesehen. Sie stehen deshalb immer mit den Pluralformen von Verben und Pronomen.

▶ Wenn man die einzelnen Polizisten meint, verwendet man *police officer*.

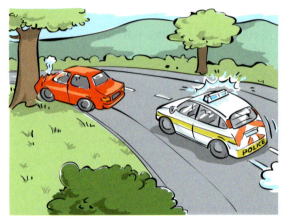

The police are arriving.   *There are two police officers at the door.*

3. Sammelbegriffe und Paarwörter mit pluralischer Bedeutung

The **clothes** they sell at that shop **are** really beautiful. You should have a look at **them**.	*Die **Kleidung** … **ist** wirklich schön. Du solltest **sie** mal anschauen.*
The **stairs are** over there.	*Die **Treppe ist** da drüben.*
Your new **trousers** really **suit** you. Where did you buy **them**?	*Deine neue **Hose steht** dir wirklich gut. Wo hast du **sie** gekauft?*
Where **are** my **glasses**? **They** must be somewhere.	*Wo **ist** meine **Brille**? **Sie muss** irgendwo sein.*

▶ *Clothes* und *stairs* werden – anders als ihre deutschen Entsprechungen – nur im Plural verwendet.

▶ Paarwörter wie *trousers, jeans, glasses* usw. bezeichnen Dinge, die aus zwei Teilen bestehen (z.B. zwei Hosenbeinen). Deshalb werden sie im Englischen nur im Plural verwendet.

▶ Wenn man von mehreren Hosen, Brillen usw. spricht, verwendet man *pairs of*: *Brad owns at least five different **pairs of** sunglasses.* = Brad besitzt mindestens fünf verschiedene Sonnenbrillen.

4. Nomen mit Pluralendung mit singularischer Bedeutung

Maths is my best subject at school. I like **it** very much.	*Mathematik ist ...*
The **news is** on. Let's listen to **it**.	*Die Nachrichten laufen. Hören wir sie an.*
The United States is one of the richest countries in the world. But **it isn't** as big as China.	*Die Vereinigten Staaten sind ... Aber sie ...*
Ten thousand **pounds is** a lot of money.	*... ist / sind eine Menge Geld.*
700 **miles sounds** too much for one day.	*... klingt ...*

▶ Viele Nomen oder auch Ländernamen haben zwar die Pluralendung *-s*, werden aber als eine Einheit gesehen und deshalb wie eine Singularform verwendet.

▶ Auch bei Geldbeträgen, Zeiträumen und Entfernungsangaben steht das Verb trotz der Pluralendung *-s* meist im Singular.

5. Sammelbegriffe und abstrakte Nomen mit singularischer Bedeutung

Furniture

Two pieces of furniture

The new **furniture** they bought **looks** very nice. But **it** must have been expensive.	*Die neuen Möbel ... sehen ... Sie müssen ...*
The **advice** we got from the travel agent's **wasn't** useful at all.	*Die Ratschläge ... waren nicht ...*
The **information** they gave us at the Information Centre **was** far better. **It was** really helpful.	*Die Informationen ... waren ... Sie waren ...*

▶ Sammelbegriffe wie *furniture* und abstrakte Nomen wie *advice, information* usw. werden im Englischen als Einheit aufgefasst und stehen immer mit Verben und Pronomen im Singular.

▶ Will man sich auf einzelne Elemente aus der Einheit beziehen, muss man sie durch Umschreibungen zählbar machen:
We bought **two pieces** of furniture. (... zwei Möbelstücke.)
That's an interesting **piece** of information. (... eine interessante Information.)

G10 Adjectives used as nouns — Das Adjektiv als Nomen *page 46*

Im Englischen können Adjektive – anders als im Deutschen – nur in bestimmten Fällen als Nomen verwendet werden.

the + adjective	adjective + noun
The homeless find life hardest in the winter. **Obdachlose/Die Obdachlosen** …	We saw a group of **homeless people**. They were sitting round a fire. … *eine Gruppe von* **Obdachlosen** …
They're collecting for **the blind**. … *für* **Blinde/die Blinden**.	A **blind man** was waiting at the traffic lights with his dog. *Ein* **Blinder**…
▸ Wenn ein Adjektiv als Nomen gebraucht wird, bezieht es sich auf die Gesamtheit einer Gruppe von Menschen (*the rich* = die Reichen allgemein, alle Reichen). ▸ Obwohl die Adjektive keine Pluralendung haben, werden sie wie Pluralformen verwendet und stehen mit Verben und Pronomen im Plural.	▸ Wenn man von einzelnen Personen oder bestimmten Gruppen spricht, muss das Adjektiv durch ein Nomen wie *person, man, woman, people* oder das Stützwort *one/ones* ergänzt werden. ▸ Ein auf ein Nomen im Singular bezogenes Adjektiv kann nicht allein stehen: *die Kleine* = *the* **little girl**

G11 The possessive pronouns — Die Possessivpronomen *page 46*

Du kennst schon die Possessivbegleiter *(possessive determiners)* **my, your, his, her** usw. Daneben gibt es auch noch die Possessivpronomen *(possessive pronouns)*.

	Possessivbegleiter + Nomen		Possessivpronomen	
Is that	**my mobile?**	Oh no, it's	**mine.**	
Is this	**your pen?**	I don't think it's	**yours.**	
He can't find	**his shoes.**	Look, these must be	**his.**	
Is this	**her pullover?**	No, it can't be.	**Hers**	is green.
These are	**our posters.**	And those are	**ours,**	too.
Are these	**your photos?**	I must say,	**yours**	are nicer than ours.
Those are	**their bikes.**	No, they aren't.	**Theirs**	are in the garage.

▸ Possessivbegleiter stehen immer vor einem Nomen:
That is **my** *mobile.* (*Das ist* **mein** *Handy.*)
▸ Possessivpronomen verwendest du, wenn das Nomen bekannt ist und du es nicht wiederholen möchtest:
Is that your mobile? – No, it's **mine.** (*Nein, es ist* **meins.**)
▸ Die Possessivpronomen können auch zusammen mit *of* verwendet werden:
He is a friend **of ours.** = *He is one of our friends.* (*Er ist ein Freund von uns.*)

❗ *Ein Freund von mir* = *a friend of* **mine.** Niemals: ~~a friend of me.~~

unit 4

G12 The gerund — Das Gerundium *page 60*

Das *gerund* wird gebildet aus dem Infinitiv ohne *to* + *-ing*:

play + ing ➡ playing   swim + ing ➡ swi**mm**ing   live + ing ➡ liv**ing**

Das *gerund* ist eine Verbform, die dem Nomen sehr ähnlich ist. Im Satz kann das *gerund* verschiedene Funktionen haben.

1. Das *gerund* als Subjekt des Satzes

Subjekt		Verb	Subjektergänzung	
Swimming		has always been	my favorite sport.	*Schwimmen …*
Playing	basketball	can be	fun, too.	*Basketballspielen …*
Skiing	in the USA	is	fantastic.	*Skifahren …*

- Das *gerund* kann wie ein Nomen Subjekt des Satzes sein.
  Vergleiche: *Football is fun. Biking is fun.*
- Es kann allein stehen *(swimming)*, zusammen mit einem Nomen verwendet werden *(playing basketball)* und auch eine adverbiale Bestimmung bei sich haben *(skiing in the USA)*.

2. Das *gerund* als Objekt nach bestimmten Verben

I love skiing.

I hate doing tests.

Subjekt	Verb	Objekt		
Susie	enjoys	reading	books.	*… liest sehr gerne …*
Jim	doesn't like	living	in Vermont.	*… lebt nicht gerne …*
I	can't stand	being	alone.	*… kann das Alleinsein nicht ausstehen.*

- Das *gerund* steht oft als Objekt nach Verben, die Vorliebe oder Abneigung ausdrücken *(to like, to love, to enjoy, to dislike, to hate, can't stand)*.
- Weitere Verben, nach denen das *gerund* verwendet wird, sind: **to avoid, to finish, to imagine, to keep, (not) to mind, to prefer, to start, to stop, to suggest.**
- Eine Reihe von Verben kann – praktisch ohne Bedeutungsunterschied – mit dem *gerund* oder mit dem Infinitiv verwendet werden, z.B. **to start, to like, to dislike, to love, to hate** und **to prefer**: *It* **started snowing** *early last year.* = *It* **started to snow** *early last year.*

! Nach **would like** ist jedoch nur der Infinitiv möglich:
Where would you like to go on vacation? I'd like to go to the Green Mountains.

grammar unit 4

3. Das *gerund* nach Präpositionen

a) Verb + Präposition + *gerund*

	Verb + Präposition	*gerund*		
We	dream of	going	to America.	… träumen davon, … zu fahren.
I	look forward to	hearing	from you.	… freue mich darauf, … zu hören.

▶ Weitere Verben mit Präposition, die mit dem ***gerund*** gebraucht werden, sind:
to complain about, to talk about, to think of, to worry about.

b) Adjektiv oder Nomen + Präposition + *gerund*

	Adjektiv oder Nomen + Präposition	*gerund*		
Are you	interested in	hiking?		… interessiert daran, wandern zu gehen?
I don't like	the idea of	walking	home alone.	… den Gedanken …, allein heimzulaufen.

▶ Weitere Verbindungen von Adjektiv + Präposition, die mit dem ***gerund*** gebraucht werden, sind: *to be afraid of, to be bad/good at, to be crazy about, to be famous for, to be fantastic/ideal for, to be keen on, to be tired of, to be/get used to.*

▶ Weitere Verbindungen von Nomen + Präposition, die mit dem ***gerund*** gebraucht werden, sind: *a chance of, in danger of, a way of.*
Chance und ***way*** können aber auch mit dem ***to-infinitive*** stehen:
*They gave me **a chance to talk** about my problems.*

! Bei *to look forward to* und *to be/get used to* ist das *to* nicht Teil des Infinitivs, sondern eine Präposition, auf die das ***gerund*** folgt: *Kate **has got used to** living in Boston. She's **looking forward to** getting Susie's next e-mail.*

c) Präposition + *gerund* als Teil einer adverbialen Bestimmung   page 63

	Präposition	*gerund*		
He walked past me	without	saying	a word.	… ohne ein Wort zu sagen.
She learned a lot	by	working	for the company in the holidays.	… indem sie … arbeitete.

▶ Zusammen mit den Präpositionen *apart from, by, for, instead of, in spite of* und *without* sind ***gerunds*** Teil einer adverbialen Bestimmung und werden im Deutschen mit einer Infinitivkonstruktion mit ‚zu' oder einem adverbialen Nebensatz wiedergegeben.

4. Das *gerund* nach bestimmten Wendungen

page 63

"It's no use waiting here. There won't be another bus for an hour."

	gerund		
It's no good/use	phoning.	There isn't anyone at home.	*Es nützt nichts/hat keinen Zweck …*
It isn't worth	calling	a taxi.	*Es lohnt sich nicht …*
How/what about	walking?		*Wie wär's, wenn …?*

▶ Nach den Wendungen *it's no good, it's no use, it's (not) worth, how/what about …?* steht immer das *gerund*.

G13 The infinitive with *to*   Der Infinitiv mit *to*

page 63

Du kennst schon viele Verwendungsweisen des Infinitivs mit *to*.
Hier findest du zur Erinnerung noch einmal eine Zusammenstellung.

		to-infinitive	
a) after certain verbs			
I	decided	to buy	a history book.
b) after verb + object			
My teacher	wants me	to learn	about American history.
c) to express an intention (Absicht)			
We went to Plimoth Plantation	(in order)	to find out	how the Pilgrims lived.
d) after question words			
I didn't know	what	to expect	there.
e) after nouns			
Plimoth Plantation is the	place	to go	if you're interested in history.
f) after adjectives			
It isn't	easy	to understand	the role players' English.

> Down in their hearts, wise men know this truth: the only way to help yourself is to help others.

Elbert Hubbard
(US author 1856–1915)

g) after *the first, the last, the only ...*

		to-infinitive	
The Native Americans were	the first (people)	to settle	in America.
Was Columbus really	the first (person)	to sail	across the Atlantic?
People from England were not	the only immigrants	to look for	a better life.
The Pilgrims were not	the last (people)	to come	for religious reasons.

- Nach *the first, the last* und *the only* kann der Infinitiv mit *to* stehen.
- *The first* und *the last* können mit oder ohne Nomen gebraucht werden.
  Nach *the only* muss jedoch ein Nomen (*immigrants*) oder das Stützwort *one/ones* stehen.
- Anstelle des Infinitivs kann auch (wie im Deutschen) ein Relativsatz gebraucht werden:
  *The Pilgrims were **the first English people to settle** in New England.* =
  *The Pilgrims were **the first English people that/who settled** in New England.*

h) after *adjective/noun + for + noun/pronoun*

	Adjektiv/Nomen	*for* + Nomen/Pronomen	*to-infinitive*	
It was often	difficult	for immigrants	to leave	their homes.
It's	impossible	for us	not to think	of the future.
There wasn't enough	room	for everyone	to sleep.	
There's no	need	for you	to worry.	

- Der Infinitiv mit *to* steht häufig nach *it is/it was* + Adjektiv + *for* + Nomen oder Pronomen (Objekt).
- Der Infinitiv mit *to* kann auch nach Nomen + *for* + Nomen/Pronomen stehen.
- Diese Konstruktion kann im Deutschen nicht immer mit einem Infinitiv wiedergegeben werden. Häufig verwendet man stattdessen einen dass-Satz:
  *It was **usual for the ships to take** more than six weeks.* =
  *Es war üblich, **dass die Schiffe** mehr als sechs Wochen **brauchten**.*

unit 5

G14 The position of adverbs and adverbials
Die Stellung von Adverbien und adverbialen Bestimmungen

page 78

Hier findest du noch einmal eine Zusammenstellung von Adverbien und adverbialen Bestimmungen mit Regeln und Beispielen für ihre Stellung im Satz.

Front position: vor dem Subjekt

Mid position: entweder zwischen Subjekt und Vollverb oder hinter *to be* (als Vollverb) oder zwischen Hilfsverb und Vollverb

End position: hinter dem Vollverb und (falls vorhanden) dem Objekt

	Front position	Subjekt	Hilfsverb / to be	Mid position	Vollverb	Objekt / Subjektergänzung	End position
1.		Billy			sang	his song	**nervously.**
		He		**quietly**	left	the stage.	
2.		His mom	was		singing	a song	**in the car.**
		They			went		**to New York.**
3.		Rikki			wants	to visit us	**tomorrow.**
		She			hopes	to arrive	**by 5 o'clock.**
4.	In Vermont	it		**often**	snows		in the winter.
	At night	it	is	**sometimes**		very cold.	
		Susie	has	**always**	liked	skiing.	
5.	**Frankly,**	this film	isn't			very good.	
		We	could		watch	a DVD,	**of course.**

Die Adverbien und adverbialen Bestimmungen in der Tabelle oben bilden fünf Gruppen:

▸ **1. Adverbien der Art und Weise**
(adverbs/adverbials of manner) stehen meist in *end position*, manchmal in *mid position*, wenn sie weniger wichtig sind als der Rest des Satzes.
Examples: brilliantly, slowly, excitedly, brightly.

▸ **2. Adverbien des Ortes/der Richtung**
(adverbs/adverbials of place/direction) stehen meist in *end position*. Zur Betonung können sie auch in *front position* stehen.
Examples: to Hollywood, in Camden, everywhere, over there, on top, at the gym.

▸ **3. Adverbien der Zeit**
(adverbs/adverbials of time) stehen meist in *end position.* Zur Betonung können sie auch in *front position* stehen.
Examples: yesterday, today, tomorrow, now, by 5 o'clock, for two days, since Monday.

▸ **4. Adverbien der Häufigkeit**
(adverbs/adverbials of frequency) stehen in der Regel in *mid position*.
Examples: often, never, always, sometimes, usually, ever.

▸ **5. Kommentierende Adverbien**
(adverbs/adverbials of comment) drücken aus, was der Sprecher über den Inhalt des Satzes denkt. Zu ihnen gehören *actually, apparently, obviously, unfortunately* und *of course*. Da sie häufig eine Art Einleitungsgedanken darstellen, stehen sie meistens in *front position*.
Manchmal können sie – als Nachgedanke – auch in *end position* stehen.
Apparently, obviously und *probably* können auch in *mid position* stehen:
They **obviously** liked the performance.

grammar
unit 5

❗ **Zur Erinnerung:** Wenn Adverbien der Zeit und Adverbien des Ortes am Satzende stehen, dann gilt:
ORT vor ZEIT *(PLACE before TIME)*
Let's meet **at the cinema** *this afternoon.*

P vor T oder O vor Z, genauso wie im Alphabet!

Im Deutschen ist die Stellung solcher Adverbien meist umgekehrt:
Ich werde **um 5 Uhr** dort sein.

Trifft auf die **adverbs of place and time** noch ein **adverb of manner,** dann gilt: **MPT**

             Manner   Place   Time
Rikki sang **brilliantly** *at the concert* *on Tuesday.*

G15 Adverbs of degree Gradadverbien   *page 79*

Gradadverbien *(adverbs/adverbials of degree)* werden verwendet, um ein anderes Wort (ein Adjektiv, ein Verb oder ein Adverb) zu verstärken oder um es abzuschwächen. Zu ihnen gehören von Adjektiven abgeleitete Adverbien wie *absolutely*, *completely* und *really* sowie endungslose Formen wie *pretty*, *quite* und *very*.

- Gradadverbien stehen in der Regel direkt vor dem Wort, das sie verstärken oder abschwächen: *He was **utterly** terrified.*
- Viele verstärkende Adverbien können auch in **end position** stehen:
  *The situation has changed **completely**.*
- Es gibt aber auch eine Reihe von Gradadverbien, die in der Regel in **end position**, stehen, z.B. *a bit, a lot, at all, very much: I'd like to thank you **very much**.*
  *I don't mind **at all**.*

❗ **Besonderheit der Stellung bei** *enough*
Es wird nachgestellt, außer wenn es als Mengenangabe für ein Nomen gebraucht wird.
*Billy's performance wasn't good **enough**.*
*He didn't play well **enough**.*
*He didn't have **enough** experience.*

Nowadays, parents don't show enough commitment.

vocabulary

Aufbau des Vokabulars

Im *Vocabulary*-Teil sind die Vokabeln dieses Bandes in der Reihenfolge ihres Vorkommens aufgelistet und erklärt. **Fett gedruckte Wörter** kommen häufig vor, so dass du sie verstehen und verwenden können musst. Normal gedruckte Wörter sind zur Behandlung bestimmter Themen und Texte notwendig. Die mittlere Spalte enthält folgende Dinge: Bilder, Beispiel- oder Erklärungssätze und Hinweise auf Besonderheiten.

Neu in diesem Band sind Verweise auf verwandte Wörter in Französisch oder Latein. Die rechte Spalte enthält deutsche Übersetzungen oder Erklärungen. Außerdem gibt es im *Vocabulary* wieder Lerntipps, nützliche Zusammenstellungen und Übungen. Im Anschluss findest du wieder einen alphabetisch geordneten *Dictionary*-Teil, in dem du die Wörter aller Bände noch einmal nachschlagen kannst.

Abkürzungen und Zeichen

pl.	= Plural	*fml*	= formell (förmlich)	=	entspricht	
sg.	= Singular	*infml*	= informell	≠	entspricht nicht	
sb	= somebody	*e.g.*	= zum Beispiel	!	Achtung!	
sth	= something	•	Wort, das im Deutschen	*f*	= feminin/weiblich	
jmdm	= jemandem		sehr ähnlich ist oder leicht aus	*m*	= maskulin/männlich	
jmdn	= jemanden		bereits bekannten Bestandteilen	*n*	= neutrum/sächlich	
jmds	= jemandes		erschlossen werden kann			
etw.	= etwas	*	unregelmäßiges Verb		French/Latin: Dieses	
AE	= Amerikanisches Englisch		(siehe S. 190-191)		Zeichen zeigt dir verwandte Wörter in Französisch und	
		↔	ist das Gegenteil von		Latein.	
BE	= Britisches Englisch	→	ist verwandt mit			

Lautschrift

Hier seht ihr noch einmal die Erklärung der Zeichen, die in der Lautschrift verwendet werden:

Konsonanten		**Vokale**		**Doppellaute**	
[ŋ]	morni**ng**	[ɑ:]	f**a**ther	[aɪ]	**I**, m**y**
[r]	**r**ed	[ʌ]	b**u**t	[aʊ]	n**ow**, h**ou**se
[s]	**s**thi**s**	[e]	p**e**n	[eə]	th**ere**, p**air**
[z]	i**s**	[ə]	**a** sist**er**	[eɪ]	n**a**me, th**ey**
[ʒ]	televi**si**on	[ɜ:]	g**ir**l	[ɪə]	h**ere**, id**ea**
[dʒ]	pa**ge**	[æ]	fl**a**t	[ɔɪ]	b**oy**
[ʃ]	**sh**e	[ɪ]	**i**t	[əʊ]	hell**o**
[tʃ]	lun**ch**	[i]	happ**y**	[ʊə]	s**ure**
[ð]	**th**e	[i:]	t**ea**cher, sh**e**		
[θ]	**th**anks	[ɒ]	g**o**t	**Zusätzliche Zeichen**	
[v]	**v**ideo	[ɔ:]	b**a**ll	[']	Hauptakzent auf der nachfolgenden Silbe
[w]	**w**ow, **o**ne	[ʊ]	b**oo**k		
		[u]	Jan**u**ary	[ˌ]	Nebenakzent auf der nachfolgenden Silbe
		[u:]	t**oo**, tw**o**		
				[‿]	Bindebogen zwischen zwei Wörtern

Alle anderen Zeichen werden genauso ausgesprochen, wie sie geschrieben werden, z. B. [b], [j], [l] usw.

vocabulary
unit 1

unit 1 Down under

In den ersten drei Bänden hast du schon viele nützliche Tipps kennen gelernt, die dir das Vokabellernen erleichtern.

Hier nochmals eine kleine Zusammenfassung zur Erinnerung:

- Nimm dir mehrmals am Tag kleine Lernportionen vor, die du dann jeweils für eine kurze Zeit (10 Minuten) bearbeitest.
- Lege eine Vokabeldatei an und gehe sie von Zeit zu Zeit von Anfang bis Ende durch.
- Stelle für jedes neue Wort so viele Zusammenhänge wie möglich her.
- Achte auf *false friends!*
- Gestalte das Lernen spannender, indem du mit anderen lernst oder Vokabellernspiele spielst.

In diesem Band neu in der Mittelspalte sind die Hinweise auf verwandte Wörter in der zweiten oder dritten Fremdsprache. Da ca. 40 % des englischen Wortschatzes romanischen Ursprungs sind, d. h. aus dem Lateinischen oder Französischen stammen, gibt es viele Verwandtschaftsbeziehungen, die auch beim Lernen durch Vernetzen helfen.

Intro

down under *(infml)* [ˌdaʊnˈʌndə]		*(Spitzname für Australien)*
1 G'day (= *Good day*) [gəˈdaɪ]	This is how Australians say hello.	Guten Tag *(australisch)*
the wrong way round [ðə ˌrɒŋ weɪ ˈraʊnd]	If you hold a text against a mirror, the letters and words will all be *the wrong way round*.	falsch herum
cross [krɒs]	Fr. *croix f*; Lat. *crux f*	Kreuz
• colony [ˈkɒləni]	Lat. *colonia f*	Kolonie
• continent [ˈkɒntɪnənt]	region – country – *continent*	Kontinent, Erdteil
outback [ˈaʊtbæk]	The wild, empty country away from Australia's towns and cities.	Outback *(australisches Hinterland)*
dusty [ˈdʌsti]	If you don't clean your room often enough, everything starts to get *dusty*.	staubig
shower [ˈʃaʊə]	1. The rain soon stopped – it was only a *shower*. 2. Did you have a bath or a *shower*?	Schauer; Dusche
quite a [ˈkwaɪt ə]	It's *quite a* way to the station. = It's quite far.	ein(e) ziemliche(-r/-s); ein(e) wirkliche(-r/-s)
lonely [ˈləʊnli]	I'm often alone, but I don't always feel *lonely*.	einsam
as [æz]		da; weil
station [ˈsteɪʃn]	There are huge sheep and cattle *stations* in Australia.	Farm *(in Australien)*
cute [kjuːt]		niedlich; süß
• koala [kəʊˈɑːlə]		Koala
• deadly [ˈdedli]	death → dead → *deadly*	tödlich
• plant [plɑːnt]	to plant → *plant*	Pflanze

vocabulary
unit 1

poisonous [ˈpɔɪznəs]	*Poisonous* snakes can be very dangerous.	giftig
• **crocodile** [ˈkrɒkədaɪl]		Krokodil
shark [ʃɑːk]		Hai
• **kangaroo** [ˌkæŋɡrˈuː]		Känguru
• **emu** [ˈiːmjuː]		Emu
• **wombat** [ˈwɒmbæt]		Wombat
• **camel** [ˈkæml]		Kamel
inhabitant [ɪnˈhæbɪtnt]	All the people who live in a place are its *inhabitants*. 🔍 Fr. habiter; Lat. habitare	Einwohner(in); Bewohner(in)
landmark [ˈlændmɑːk]	The Tower and Tower Bridge are two of London's most famous *landmarks*.	Wahrzeichen; Markstein
• **opera** [ˈɒprə]	concert – play – musical – *opera*	Oper
Aussie *(infml)* [ˈɒzi]		Australier(in)
scuba diving [ˈskuːbə ˌdaɪvɪŋ]		Tauchen *(mit Atemgerät)*
reef [riːf]		Riff
2 **Aborigine** [ˌæbəˈrɪdʒni]	The native people of Australia are called *Aborigines*. 🔍 Lat. ab + origo, originis f	Ureinwohner(in) Australiens
settler [ˈsetlə]	Sb who goes to a new country and makes their home there.	Siedler(in)

Interesting facts about Australia

Sydney Opera House
is considered by many to be one of the wonders of the modern world. It was designed by Jørn Utzon and opened in 1973.

Harbour Bridge
Sydney Harbour Bridge is one of Australia's best known and most photographed landmarks. It is the world's largest (but not longest) steel arch bridge with the top of the bridge standing 134 metres above the harbour. The Bridge celebrated its 70th birthday in March, 2002.

BBQ
Australians couldn't live without their "barbie". A typical BBQ has to consist of at least beer and steaks! The people in Australia have a barbie whenever they can, to meet friends and to get to know new people.

Suburbs
Australians like to own their own home. And for most Australians (roughly 80 per cent) that means owning their own home in the suburbs, because they are larger than most of the other suburbs in the world.

The wrong way round
A lot of things in Australia are exactly the opposite to the way they are in Europe. For example, Australians drive on the left hand side of the road, the north of Australia is warmer than the south and their summer is our winter.

Bondi Beach
is one of Australia's most famous beaches. It is a long sandy beach and very popular with surfers and beach volleyballers. Lots of cafés and restaurants can be found there. Swimmers are protected by shark nets and there are lifeguards who make them stay between the yellow and red flags for their safety.

Language A New neighbours

suburb [ˈsʌbɜːb]	Wimbledon is a *suburb* of London. 🔍 Lat. sub + urbs f	Vorort

vocabulary
unit 1

barbie *(infml)* ['bɑ:bi]		Grill(party)
barbecue ['bɑ:bɪkju:]	At a *barbecue* the food is grilled outside.	Grill(party)
van [væn]	car – pickup – *van* – truck	Lieferwagen; Transporter
•Japanese [ˌdʒæpnˈi:z]		japanisch; Japanisch
to doubt [daʊt]	If you *doubt* sth, you think it may not be true. 🔍 *Fr. douter; Lat. dubitare*	bezweifeln
•immigrant ['ɪmɪɡrənt]	Sb who has left their home country and come to live in another. 🔍 *Fr. immigrant m; Lat. immigrare*	Immigrant(in), Einwanderer; Einwanderin
about [əˈbaʊt]	If you see sb *about* (or around), you see them in the street, in your area etc.	herum; umher; hier in der Gegend
the Pacific Rim [ðə pəˌsɪfɪk 'rɪm]		Rand des Pazifik
to trade [treɪd]	When people, companies or countries *trade,* they buy, sell or exchange things.	Handel treiben
Oz *(infml)* [ɒz]		Oz (Spitzname für Australien)
•volleyball ['vɒlibɔ:l]	A popular team game.	Volleyball
to waste [weɪst]	to save ↔ to *waste*	verschwenden
Don't take no for an answer. [ˌdəʊnt teɪk 'nəʊ fərˌənˌɑ:ntsə]		Akzeptiere keine Widerrede.
No worries! [ˌnəʊ 'wʌriz]		Keine Sorge!
3 funky ['fʌŋki]	Young people usually like *'funky'* clothes more than their parents do.	irre
4 first name ['fɜ:st ˌneɪm]	Mr Donovan's *first name* is Bob.	Vorname
5 car park ['kɑ: ˌpɑ:k]	car → *car park*	Parkplatz; Parkhaus
couple ['kʌpl]	You can call a husband and wife a 'married *couple'.*	Paar
*to break in(to) [breɪkˌ'ɪn]	Sb has *broken into* the house. = The house has been *broken into.*	einbrechen (in)
7 •settlement ['setlmənt]	settler → *settlement*	Siedlung
convict ['kɒnvɪkt]	Sb who has been sent to prison.	Sträfling
prison ['prɪzn]	*prison* → prisoner → to take sb prisoner 🔍 *Fr. prison f*	Gefängnis
crowded ['kraʊdɪd]	crowd → *crowded*	überfüllt
law [lɔ:]	If you break the *law,* you may get into serious trouble.	Gesetz

Language B An experience in the outback

boomerang ['bu:mræŋ]		Bumerang
danger ['deɪndʒə]	*danger* → dangerous 🔍 *Fr. danger m*	Gefahr
*to bite [baɪt]	If a poisonous snake *bites* you, you may be very ill or even die.	beißen; stechen
*to tear [teə]	She hated the photo so much that she *tore* it into little pieces.	(zer)reißen
strip [strɪp]	In an emergency you can use a *strip* of material as a bandage.	Streifen

vocabulary
unit 1

pressure [ˈpreʃə]	If you have a lot of work to do in a short time, you may feel under *pressure*. 🔍 Fr. presser; Lat. premere: premo, pressi, pressum	Druck
scratch [skrætʃ]	Have you hurt yourself? – No, it's nothing, it's only a *scratch*.	Kratzer
• **shorts** *(pl.)* [ʃɔːts]	❗ Your *shorts* <u>are</u> nice. = Deine kurze Hose <u>ist</u> schön.	Shorts, kurze Hose
• **poison** [ˈpɔɪzn]	*poison* → poisonous 🔍 Fr. poison *m*	Gift
web [web]	A spider catches flies in its *web*.	(Spinnen-)Netz
splint [splɪnt]		Schiene
3 to **depend (on)** [dɪˈpend]	❗ Careful with the preposition: You can *depend* <u>on</u> me. 🔍 Fr. dépendre (de); Lat. de + pendere	abhängen (von); sich verlassen (auf)
• **condition** [kənˈdɪʃn]	❗ <u>On</u> one *condition* = <u>unter</u> einer Bedingung 🔍 Fr. condition *f*; Lat. condicio *f*	Kondition; Bedingung
to **fulfil** [fʊlˈfɪl]	❗ Careful with the spelling: full + fill = *fulfil (BE)*.	erfüllen
speaker [ˈspiːkə]	to speak → *speaker*	Sprecher(in)
*to **be likely (to)** [biː ˈlaɪkli]	❗ 'Likely/unlikely' are usually used with a 'to-infinitive': It isn't *likely* to rain. Matt is *likely* to be late.	wahrscheinlich sein
• **impossible** [ɪmˈpɒsəbl]	possibility → possible → *impossible* 🔍 Fr. impossible	unmöglich
*to **be unlikely (to)** [biː ʌnˈlaɪkli]		unwahrscheinlich sein
5 • to **interpret** [ɪnˈtɜːprɪt]	To explain what sb is saying in another language. 🔍 Fr. interpréter; Lat. interpretari	interpretieren; dolmetschen
unique [juːˈniːk]	Sth *unique* is the only one of its kind. 🔍 Fr. unique; Lat. unicus	einzig; einzigartig
marsupial [mɑːˈsuːpiəl]		Beuteltier
pouch [paʊtʃ]		Beutel
• **coral** [ˈkɒrəl]		Koralle
• **wonder** [ˈwʌndə]	You say "No *wonder!*" when you are not surprised about sth.	Wunder; Verwunderung
• **surfer** [ˈsɜːfə]		Surfer(in), Wellenreiter(in)
apart [əˈpɑːt]		auseinander; abseits
board [bɔːd]		Brett
attack [əˈtæk]	to attack → *attack*	Angriff; Anfall
squadron [ˈskwɒdrn]		Schwadron; Staffel
to **occur** [əˈkɜː]		sich ereignen; vorkommen
lad [læd]		Junge
to **increase** [ɪnˈkriːs]		zunehmen; vergrößern
in recent years [ɪn ˌriːsnt ˈjɪəz]		in den letzten Jahren
responsible [rɪsˈpɒntsəbl]		verantwortlich
conservationist [ˌkɒntsəˈveɪʃnɪst]		Umweltschützer(in)
to **argue** [ˈɑːɡjuː]		argumentieren; streiten
• **ocean** [ˈəʊʃn]		Ozean
right [raɪt]		Recht
to **act** [ækt]	The way you *act* is the way you behave.	handeln; sich verhalten

one hundred and twenty-seven 127

vocabulary
unit 1

environment [ɪnˈvaɪərnmənt]	Our *environment* is the world (or area) we live in.	Umwelt; Umgebung

Text   Rabbit-proof fence

-proof [pruːf]	water*proof* – fire*proof* – rabbit-*proof*	-sicher; -resistent
part [pɑːt]	A *part*-Aboriginal child might have a white father and an Aboriginal mother.	teils
• European [ˌjʊərəˈpiːən]	Europe → *European*	Europäer(in); europäisch
• extract [ˈekstrækt]	An *extract* from a book is just a small part of the story.	Extrakt; Auszug
	🔍 F. extrait **m**; Lat. extrahere: extraho, extraxi, extractum	
silence [ˈsaɪlənts]	They didn't speak as they walked. = They walked in *silence*.	Stille
	🔍 Fr. silence **m**; Lat. silentium **n**	
to drool [druːl]		sabbern
goanna [gəʊˈænə]		Waran
tucker *(infml)* [ˈtʌkə]		Proviant
• runaway [ˈrʌnəˌweɪ]	to run away → a *runaway*	Ausreißer(in)
tracker [ˈtrækə]		Fährtenleser(in)
footprint [ˈfʊtprɪnt]	foot → footstep → *footprint*	Fußabdruck
match [mætʃ]	It's difficult to make a fire without *matches*.	Streichholz
raindrop [ˈreɪndrɒp]	rain → rainbow → *raindrop*	Regentropfen
to sparkle [ˈspɑːkl]	*Diamonds* are stones that *sparkle* in all the colours of the rainbow when light shines on them.	glitzern; funkeln
diamond [ˈdaɪəmənd]		Diamant
trek [trek]	A very long walk, usually in the country.	Wanderung; anstrengender Marsch
to circle [ˈsɜːkl]	To move in a *circle*.	kreisen
hopeless [ˈhəʊpləs]	helpless – homeless – *hopeless*	hoffnungslos
shelter [ˈʃeltə]	If it rains heavily when you're outside, you have to look for *shelter*.	Obdach; Schutz(hütte)
depressed [dɪˈprest]	Very sad and disappointed with life.	deprimiert; bedrückt
to remind sb of sth/sb [rɪˈmaɪnd]	❗Notice the difference: I didn't <u>remember</u> Dad's birthday. Mum had to <u>remind</u> me.	(jmdn an etw./jmdn) erinnern
to devour [dɪˈvaʊə]		verschlingen
for their own good [fə ðər ˌəʊn ˈɡʊd]	I'm doing it *for their own good*. = I'm only doing it in order to help them.	zu ihrem Besten
duty [ˈdjuːti]	If sth is your *duty*, you feel you really must or should do it, even if it's hard to do.	Pflicht
railway [ˈreɪlweɪ]	You travel on it when you go by train.	Eisenbahn
to hand sth over [hænd ˈəʊvə]	If you *hand* sth *over* to sb, you give it to them.	etw. übergeben
report [rɪˈpɔːt]	to report → a *report*	Bericht
all around [ˌɔːl əˈraʊnd]	*all around* the world = everywhere in the world	überall; rundherum; rings umher
ahead of [əˈhed əv]	In front of.	vor

vocabulary
focus 1

search party ['sɜːtʃ ˌpɑːti]	to search → search party	Suchtrupp
on the run [ɒn ðə 'rʌn]	to run → runaway → on the run	auf der Flucht
sore [sɔː]	People who have to lie in bed all the time often get sores on their bodies.	wunde Stelle
after all [ˌɑːftər 'ɔːl]	My father knows how to help me when I'm ill. After all, he's a doctor!	schließlich; immerhin
• symbol ['sɪmbl]	A heart can be used as a symbol of love.	Symbol
1 • generation [ˌdʒenə'reɪʃn]	You think of your parents as the older generation.	Generation

Skills Dealing with texts

chief protector [ˌtʃiːf prə'tektə]		oberste(r) Beschützer(in)
• servant ['sɜːvnt]	to serve → servant	Bedienstete(r); Diener(in)
director [dɪ'rektə]	When a film is made, the director tells everyone what to do.	Direktor(in); Regisseur(in)
1 • characteristic [ˌkærəktə'rɪstɪk]	Sth that you recognize as typical of a person or thing.	typisches Merkmal
• to underline [ˌʌndə'laɪn]	under + line = to underline	unterstreichen

focus 1 Focus on the Golden Age

1 • golden ['gəʊldn]	gold → golden	golden
• talk show ['tɔːk ˌʃəʊ]		Talkshow
host [həʊst]	The host at a party is the person who has invited the guests.	Gastgeber(in); Talkmaster
to rule [ruːl]	In the past most European countries were ruled by kings and queens.	herrschen; regieren
wealth [welθ]	❗ Be careful with the pronunciation: The 'ea' in 'wealth' sounds the same as in 'health'.	Wohlstand; Reichtum
wealthy ['welθi]	wealth → wealthy	wohlhabend; reich
• Armada [ɑː'mɑːdə]	The 'Armada' was the Spanish fleet at the time of Queen Elizabeth II.	Armada (Name der spanischen Flotte)
to explore [ɪk'splɔː]	If you explore a place, you travel in it to find out what it is like.	erkunden; erforschen
fleet [fliːt]		Flotte
the Virgin Queen [ˌvɜːdʒɪn 'kwiːn]	Elizabeth I was called 'the Virgin Queen' because she never married.	die jungfräuliche Königin (Elizabeth I. wurde so genannt, weil sie nie heiratete.)
• to execute ['eksɪkjuːt]	To kill (in order to punish).	exekutieren; hinrichten
reign [reɪn]		Regierungszeit
• powerful ['paʊəfl]	power → powerful	stark; mächtig; leistungsfähig
sailor ['seɪlə]	to sail → sailor	Seemann, Matrose; Segler
• explorer [ɪk'splɔːrə]	to explore → explorer	Forscher; Forschungsreisender
• pirate ['paɪərət]	Pirates are sailors who attack other ships and steal things from them.	Pirat(in), Seeräuber(in)

vocabulary
focus 1

• writer [ˈraɪtə]	to write → writer	Schriftsteller
• Renaissance [rəˈneɪsnts]		Renaissance *(historisches Zeitalter: Wiedergeburt der klassischen Werte, Beginn der Moderne)*
• to **influence** [ˈɪnfluənts]	influence → to influence	beeinflussen
Elizabethan [ɪˌlɪzəˈbiːθn]		elisabethanisch
2 • navigation [ˌnævɪˈgeɪʃn]	You have to know about *navigation* in order to work out which way a ship should go.	Navigation; Orientierung
	🔍 Fr. *naviguer – navigation f;* Lat. *navis f – navigare – navigatio f*	
• unknown [ʌnˈnəʊn]	to know → unknown	unbekannt
goods *(pl.)* [gʊdz]	Useful things that can be moved and sold.	Güter; Waren
• to colonize [ˈkɒlənaɪz]	colony → colonist → to colonize	kolonisieren
• to emigrate [ˈemɪgreɪt]	To leave your own country in order to start a new life in another one.	emigrieren; auswandern
• to settle [ˈsetl]	to settle → settler → settlement	siedeln; sich niederlassen
freedom [ˈfriːdəm]	free → freedom	Freiheit
• architecture [ˈɑːkɪtektʃə]	If you study *architecture,* you learn how to plan and design buildings.	Architektur
• literature [ˈlɪtrətʃə]		Literatur

Die Montagsmaler

Hier kommt es nicht darauf an, schön zu malen, sondern flott zu zeichnen. Wer möglichst schnell etwas aufs Papier bringt, was seine Mitspieler auch erkennen können, der hat Erfolg.
Bevor es losgeht, sucht sich der Spielleiter Wörter aus der Vokabelliste aus. Aber denkt daran, dass es möglich sein muss, sie auch zu zeichnen. Jedes Wort wird auf einen eigenen kleinen Zettel geschrieben. Da der Spielleiter die Wörter kennt, darf er anschließend leider nicht mitmachen. Nun kommt abwechselnd aus jedem der zwei Teams ein anderer Maler an die Reihe. Beide Teams dürfen mitraten.
Das Team, das am Ende die meisten Punkte gesammelt hat, hat gewonnen.

• **Catholic** [ˈkæθlɪk]	*The Pope* is the head of the *Catholic* church.	Katholik(in)
the Pope [pəʊp]		der Papst
*to **get divorced** [ˌget dɪˈvɔːst]	to get married ↔ to get divorced	sich scheiden lassen
	🔍 Fr. *divorce m*	
• Reformation [ˌrefəˈmeɪʃn]		Reformation *(historische Periode der Trennung der protestantischen von der katholischen Kirche)*
Protestantism [ˈprɒtɪstntɪzm]		Protestantismus
• **Protestant** [ˈprɒtɪstnt]	Catholic ↔ Protestant	Protestant(in); protestantisch
• bible [ˈbaɪbl]	There are a lot of stories about religious people in the *Bible*.	Bibel
• strict [strɪkt]	The rules at our school are very *strict*.	streng; strikt
• moral [ˈmɒrl]		moralisch
• value [ˈvæljuː]	valuable → value	Wert

vocabulary
unit 2

ceremony [ˈserɪməni]		Zeremonie
• printing press [ˈprɪntɪŋ ˌpres]	This made it possible to produce a lot of copies of books.	Druckerpresse
• press [pres]		Presse
• to print [prɪnt]	to print → printer → printing press	drucken
• mass [mæs]	You can use the word 'mass' when a lot of people are influenced by sth (e. g. mass media).	Masse

unit 2 — On the southwestern coast

Vokabellernen mit Verstand I

- Warte nicht mit dem Lernen bis zum letzten Augenblick! Verteile die zu lernenden Vokabeln möglichst gleichmäßig auf die Zeit, die zur Verfügung steht.
- Vokabeln, die du dir nur schwer merken kannst, musst du dir möglichst oft vor Augen halten. Das kann ein Zettel an der Tür oder am Spiegel oder ein Lernplakat an der Wand sein.
- Auch kannst du diese „Problemfälle" in deinem Vokabelheft mit einem Markierstift hervorheben. Denn erst Markierungen lenken die Aufmerksamkeit und leiten das Auge.
- Und wenn du einzelne Wörter immer wieder falsch schreibst, hilft es, wenn du dir diese paar Wörter immer wieder hintereinander aufschreibst und die Buchstabenfolge laut vor dir hersagst.

Intro

cliff [klɪf]	A high area of land with a very steep side, usually near the sea.	Klippe; Kliff
cove [kəʊv]	A *cove* is a small *bay*.	kleine Bucht
bay [beɪ]		Bucht
wrecker [ˈrekə]		Strandräuber *(jmd, der Schiffe mit falschen Signalen an den Strand lockt, damit sie dort auflaufen, und sie dann plündert)*

edge [edʒ]	Don't put that bottle too near the *edge* of the table or it may fall off!	Rand; Kante
• **record** [ˈrekɔːd]	If you do sth in *record* time, nobody has ever done it as fast as that before.	Rekord
• **Eden** [ˈiːdn]	Everything was very beautiful in the legendary Garden of *Eden*.	(der Garten) Eden
clay-pit [ˈkleɪpɪt]		Lehmgrube
• **legendary** [ˈledʒəndri]	legend → legendary	legendär
birthplace [ˈbɜːθpleɪs]	The place where a person is born.	Geburtsort
inn [ɪn]	An old word for a small hotel or a pub where you can also stay the night.	Gasthaus; Herberge
cider [ˈsaɪdə]		Apfelwein

cream tea [ˌkriːm ˈtiː]		Cream Tea *(südwestenglische Spezialität: Tee mit süßen Brötchen, die mit sehr fester Sahne und Marmelade serviert werden)*
pot [pɒt]	If you want to drink more than one cup of tea, it's best to order a *pot*.	Kanne
scone [skɒn]		Scone *(eine Art süßes Brötchen)*
pilgrim [ˈpɪlgrɪm]	The people who came to America on the Mayflower were called the *Pilgrims* because they left Britain for religious reasons.	Pilger(in)
Riviera [ˌrɪviˈeərə]	The south coast of Devon and Cornwall is often called the 'English *Riviera*'.	Riviera *(Mittelmeerküste im Bereich Frankreich/Italien)*
• palm tree [ˈpɑːm ˌtriː]	A tree that grows in hot countries, often by the sea.	Palme
Jurassic [dʒʊəˈræsɪk]		aus dem Jura stammend
• **fossil** [ˈfɒsl]		Fossil
• **paradise** [ˈpærəˌdaɪs]	A lot of Australia's beaches are a surfer's *paradise*.	Paradies

Skills   Working with words

1	to **replace** (sth by/with sth) [rɪˈpleɪs]	If you break a window, it has to be *replaced*. 🔍 Fr. remplacer	ersetzen (etw. durch etw.)
	to **fit** (in) [ˌfɪt ˈɪn]	The right piece in a puzzle will *fit in* easily.	(hinein)passen
2	abbreviation [əˌbriːviˈeɪʃn]		Abkürzung
	transitive [ˈtrænsətɪv]		transitiv *(ein Objekt nach sich ziehend)*
	intransitive [ˌɪnˈtrænsətɪv]	transitive ↔ intransitive	intransitiv *(kein Objekt nach sich ziehend)*

Language A   Paradise on earth

greenhouse [ˈgriːnhaʊs]	Tomatoes are easier to grow in a *greenhouse* than outside.	Gewächshaus
to **contain** [kənˈteɪn]	Jam *contains* a lot of sugar. 🔍 Fr. contenir; Lat. continere	enthalten
label [ˈleɪbl]	A piece of paper on a bottle, box etc. that tells you about what it contains etc.	Etikett; Beschriftung
• medicine [ˈmedsn]	What your doctor may give you when you're ill.	Medizin
display [dɪˈspleɪ]	At a flower show you can see a wonderful *display* of flowers.	Vorführung; Ausstellung; Schaukasten; Anzeige
• to **focus** (on) [ˈfəʊkəs]	When you *focus* your eyes *on* sth, you concentrate on it and see it clearly.	sich konzentrieren (auf)
• importance [ɪmˈpɔːtnts]	important → importance 🔍 Fr. importance f	Bedeutung, Wichtigkeit

vocabulary
unit 2

• civilization [ˌsɪvlaɪˈzeɪʃn]	The Romans brought *civilization* to many parts of Europe. 🔍 *Fr. civilisation f; Lat. civilis*	Zivilisation
• to refer (to) [rɪˈfɜː]	If you *refer to* sb as a fool, you call them a fool.	(sich) beziehen (auf); sprechen (von)
biome [ˈbaɪəʊm]		Biom *(biologischer Lebensraum von Pflanzen und Tieren)*
dome-shaped [ˈdəʊmʃeɪpt]		kuppelförmig
steel [stiːl]	*Steel* is used to make things like bridges, cars, knives and forks etc.	Stahl
• plastic [ˈplæstɪk]	A material that is light and doesn't break easily.	Plastik, Kunststoff
• Mediterranean [ˌmedɪtrˈeɪniən]		mediterran, Mittelmeer-
• Californian [ˌkælɪˈfɔːniən]		kalifornisch
• olive [ˈɒlɪv]	A tree that grows in Mediterranean countries, and its fruit.	Olive; Ölbaum
• citrus fruit [ˈsɪtrəs ˌfruːt]	Oranges are a kind of *citrus fruit*.	Zitrusfrucht
maize [meɪz]	A tall plant that produces sweetcorn.	Mais
cotton [ˈkɒtn]	Shirts, T-shirts and sweatshirts are often made from *cotton*.	Baumwolle
humid [ˈhjuːmɪd]		feucht
• tropical [ˈtrɒpɪkl]	*Tropical* countries are in the hottest parts of the world.	tropisch
amazing [əˈmeɪzɪŋ]	amazed → amazement → *amazing*	erstaunlich
hardwood [ˈhɑːdwʊd]		Hartholz
pineapple [ˈpaɪnæpl]		Ananas
rubber [ˈrʌbə]	The wheels of cars and bikes would be very hard without this material.	Gummi; Kautschuk
cocoa [ˈkəʊkəʊ]	There would be no chocolate without *cocoa*.	Kakao
• lottery [ˈlɒtri]	If you buy a *lottery* ticket and the numbers you have chosen come up, you may win a lot of money.	Lotterie
• resource [rɪˈzɔːs]	It is important not to waste the world's *natural resources*.	Ressource
natural resource [ˌnætʃrl rɪˈzɔːs]		Bodenschatz
• rainwater [ˈreɪnˌwɔːtə]	rain – raindrop – rainbow – *rainwater*	Regenwasser
• to water [ˈwɔːtə]	If you don't *water* plants in dry weather, they may die.	bewässern, gießen
to create [kriˈeɪt]	to create → creative 🔍 *Fr. créer; Lat. creare: creatum*	(er)schaffen
mist [mɪst]	❗ A false friend. *Mist* is very thin fog or rain in very fine drops.	Nebel; Dunst
• rainforest [ˈreɪnˌfɒrɪst]	The world's tropical *rainforests* are important for our climate.	Regenwald
toilet [ˈtɔɪlɪt]	When you go to the *toilet*, remember to *flush* it before you leave!	Toilette
to flush [flʌʃ]		spülen; die Wasserspülung betätigen
• to damage [ˈdæmɪdʒ]	damage → to damage 🔍 *Fr. dommage m*	schaden, beschädigen

one hundred and thirty-three

vocabulary
unit 2

• **rare** [reə]	*Rare* animals and plants are not often seen.	rar, selten
the **wild** [waɪld]	wild → wilderness → the *wild*	Wildnis; freie Wildbahn
*to **grow** [grəʊ]	We *grow* vegetables in our garden.	züchten; ziehen
seed [si:d]	A lot of plants can be grown from *seed*.	Saat; Samen
overcrowding [ˌəʊvəˈkraʊdɪŋ]	crowd → crowded → *overcrowding*	Überfüllung
3 **entrance** [ˈentrənts]	The place – often a gate or door – where you go in.	Eingang; Eintritt
4 **Dutch** [dʌtʃ]	The *Dutch* come from Holland.	Niederländisch; niederländisch

Language B   Two men in a boat

the **Channel** [ðə ˈtʃænl]	The *Channel* (sometimes called the English Channel) is the sea that divides the south coast of England from the north coast of France.	Ärmelkanal *(Teil der Nordsee zwischen Großbritannien und Frankreich)*
to **tow** [təʊ]		abschleppen
course [kɔ:s]	If your boat is on *course*, you're going the right way, but if you're off *course*, you're heading in the wrong direction.	Kurs
	❗ Notice the difference: of course [əv] ≠ off course [ɒf]	
experienced [ɪkˈspɪəriəntst]	experience → to experience → *experienced*	erfahren
on top of that [ɒn ˌtɒp ˌəv ˈðæt]	top – on top of – *on top of that!*	obendrein; zusätzlich
to make matters worse [tə ˌmeɪk mætəz ˈwɜ:s]	You can say this in a difficult situation, when sth happens to make it even worse.	zu allem Überfluss; um es noch schlimmer zu machen
matter [ˈmætə]	An event or situation that has to be dealt with.	Angelegenheit; Frage
seasick [ˈsi:sɪk]	What you may feel if you're on a boat or ship in bad weather.	seekrank
*to **take over** [ˌteɪkˈəʊvə]	To start work or a job that another person doesn't or can't do any more.	übernehmen; ablösen
• *to **sink** [sɪŋk]	When a ship goes down, it *sinks*.	sinken
ferry [ˈferi]	A boat that takes passengers and cars across a river or a narrow bit of sea.	Fähre
• **mayday** [ˈmeɪdeɪ]		Mayday, SOS-Ruf
coastguard [ˈkəʊstgɑ:d]		Küstenwache
*I'd better = I had better [aɪd ˈbetə]	*I'd better* go. = It's best to go.	Ich sollte lieber …
Cheers! [tʃɪəz]	When people raise their glasses in Britain, they usually say *"Cheers!"* Young people in Britain often say *"Cheers!"* instead of *"Thanks!"* today.	Prost!
4 **passport** [ˈpɑ:spɔ:t]	A small book with your name, photo and other details to prove your identity.	(Reise-)Pass
7 • **in my opinion** [ɪn ˈmaɪ əˌpɪnjən]		meiner Meinung nach
furthermore [ˌfɜ:ðəˈmɔ:]	A formal word you can use to introduce another point that helps your argument.	überdies; außerdem

vocabulary
unit 2

Text   The ghost of St Dominic

orphanage [ˈɔːfnɪdʒ]		Waisenhaus
rocky [ˈrɒki]	rock → rocky	felsig
Reverend [ˈrevrnd]	The *vicar* of a (Church of England) church is officially called *'The Reverend …'* (e. g. *The Reverend* David Smith is the local *vicar*).	Pfarrer *(offizieller Titel des anglikanischen Pfarrers)*
vicar [ˈvɪkə]		Pfarrer
generous [ˈdʒenrəs]	A *generous* person likes to give things to others. Fr. généreux	großzügig
plenty [ˈplenti]	*plenty* of food = a lot of things to eat	eine Menge
along [əˈlɒŋ]	If you walk *along* a road, you walk towards one end of it.	entlang
service [ˈsɜːvɪs]	to serve → *service*	Gottesdienst
• excellent [ˈekslnt]	Very, very good or beautiful.	exzellent, hervorragend
• communion [kəˈmjuːniən]	community → *communion*	Kommunion
• housekeeper [ˈhaʊsˌkiːpə]	to keep + house → *housekeeper*	Haushälterin
haunted [ˈhɔːntɪd]	In *haunted* places there are ghosts.	Spuk-
to drown [draʊn]	Children who can't swim shouldn't play in deep water, or they might *drown*.	ertrinken; ertränken
fisherman, *pl.* fishermen [ˈfɪʃəmən]	fish → fishing → *fisherman*	Fischer
to haunt [hɔːnt]	to haunt → *haunted*	spuken in; heimsuchen
cave [keɪv]	A large open place in the side of a cliff or hill or under the ground. Lat. cavus	Höhle
bottom [ˈbɒtəm]	top ↔ *bottom*	Boden; Grund; unterer Teil
drunk [drʌŋk]	"No more wine, thanks. I don't want to get *drunk*."	betrunken
• to hang [hæŋ]	If you have killed a person, in some countries you may still be *hanged*.	hängen
excise man, *pl.* excise men [ˈeksaɪz ˌmæn]		Steuereintreiber
• crew [kruː]	The people who work on a ship or a plane.	Crew, Besatzung, Mannschaft
to curse [kɜːs]	Some people believe that if you *curse* a place, bad luck will come to it.	(ver)fluchen
cargo, *pl.* cargoes [ˈkɑːgəʊ]	The things (e. g. wine, fruit, coal) that a ship is carrying.	Ladung, Fracht
tobacco [təˈbækəʊ]	*Tobacco* smoke isn't good for your health.	Tabak
midnight [ˈmɪdnaɪt]	Twelve o'clock at night.	Mitternacht
to dare [deə]	Nobody *dares* to go. = Everyone is too frightened to go.	wagen
cart [kɑːt]	Years ago, *carts* were often pulled along by horses.	Karren
moon [muːn]		Mond
landlord [ˈlændlɔːd]	The man who looks after an inn or owns it, or the man who owns the house in which you live.	(Haus-)Wirt

to **sort** sth **out** [ˌsɔːtˈaʊt]	If you *sort* things *out*, you deal with sth or find a solution.	etw. klären; etw. erledigen

The big water mind map

Work in groups and add as many water-related words as you can.
Why not add pictures and make a wall poster for your classroom?

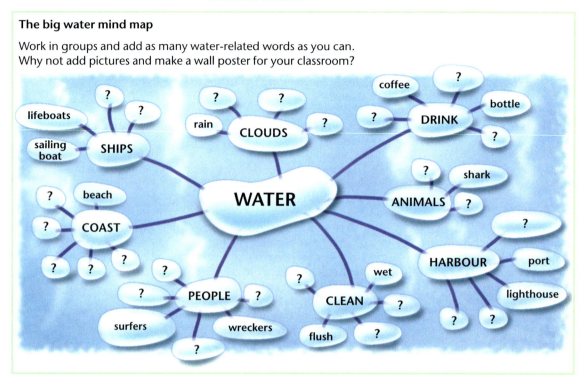

*to **make one's way to a place** [ˌmeɪk ˈweɪ]	They *made their way to* the beach. = They went to the beach.	sich an einen Ort begeben
unless [ənˈles]	You can't go on board the plane *unless* you show your passport first.	wenn nicht; es sei denn, (dass) …
*to **freeze** [friːz]		erstarren; gefrieren
to **hiss** [hɪs]		zischen
• **tunnel** [ˈtʌnl]	If you don't want to go across the Channel by ferry, you can go by train through the Channel *tunnel*.	Tunnel
to **creak** [kriːk]		knarren; quietschen
• **absolutely** [ˌæbsəˈluːtli]	Completely.	absolut; völlig
*to **light** [laɪt]	light → *to light*	anzünden; erhellen; beleuchten
chest [tʃest]		Kiste, Truhe
to **lift** [lɪft]		heben
to **step** [step]	step → footstep → *to step*	treten; steigen
*to **lead** [liːd]	If you *lead* the way, you walk in front.	führen
crypt [krɪpt]		Krypta, Gruft
Frenchman [ˈfrentʃmən]	A man from France is a *Frenchman,* and a woman from France is a Frenchwoman.	Franzose
to **inherit** [ɪnˈherɪt]	If you *inherit* money or a house, you get it from a person who has died and left it to you.	erben

vocabulary
unit 3

sum [sʌm]	Fifty thousand pounds is a large *sum* of money. 🔍 *Fr. somme f; Lat. summa f*	Summe; Betrag
2 exterior [ɪkˈstɪərɪə]	The *exterior* of a place or thing is the part that is outside, and the *interior* is inside.	Außenaufnahme
interior [ɪnˈtɪərɪə]		Innenaufnahme
bubble [ˈbʌbl]	If air is blown into water, it produces *bubbles*.	Blase
5 the Baltic [ˈbɔːltɪk]	Part of the German coast is on the *Baltic*.	Ostsee
• structure [ˈstrʌktʃə]	The way sth is built. 🔍 *Fr. structure f; Lat. structura f*	Struktur; Aufbau

unit 3 — Young people in Scotland

Vokabellernen mit Verstand II

- Wiederholen auf die immer gleiche Art ist langweilig und nicht besonders wirkungsvoll. Versuch es beim zweiten und dritten Mal lieber auf unterschiedliche Art und Weise.
- Dass eine Vokabelkartei auf dem Computer hilfreich ist, weißt du schon.
- Lege dir möglichst viele verschiedene Wortfelder in deinem Heft, auf dem Computer oder in einer Vokabelkartei an. Versuche jedes neue Wort diesen Wortfeldern zuzuordnen. Oder du stellst als Wiederholung alle *opposites* aus dieser Lektion zusammen. Oder alle Wörter mit gleicher oder ähnlicher Bedeutung. Oder alle Wörter, die zur gleichen Wortfamilie gehören, z. B. *sun, sunglasses, …* und dies müssen nicht immer Listen, sondern können auch *mind maps* oder Bilder sein.

Intro

Military Tattoo [ˌmɪlɪtri təˈtuː]		*Musikparade des Militärs*
bagpipes *pl.* [ˈbæɡpaɪps]	A Scottish instrument.	Dudelsack
• Scottish [ˈskɒtɪʃ]	From Scotland.	schottisch
the Highlands [ˈhaɪləndz]	A famous mountain region in Scotland.	
• whisky [ˈwɪski]	The best *whisky* is from Scotland.	Whisky
tax [tæks]	Money you must pay to the government, e. g. from what you earn.	Steuer
• kilt [kɪlt]	A kind of thick skirt that is traditionally worn by Scottish men.	Kilt; Schottenrock
tartan [ˈtɑːtn]	The kilts of different families are in tartans of different colours, e. g. with a red, blue or green background.	Schottenkaro *(bestimmtes Muster eines Clans; karierter Schottenstoff)*
2 corner shop [ˈkɔːnə ˌʃɒp]	corner → *corner shop*	Laden an der Ecke; Tante-Emma-Laden

Vocabulary
unit 3

• mechanic [məˈkænɪk]	Sb whose job is to repair cars etc.	(Kfz-)Mechaniker(in)
oil rig [ˈɔɪl rɪɡ]	There are a lot of *oil rigs* in the North Sea to get *oil* for the UK.	Bohrinsel
oil [ɔɪl]		Öl

Language A Please, Dad!

for a change [fər ə ˈtʃeɪndʒ]	to change → a change → *for a change*	zur Abwechslung
arrangement [əˈreɪndʒmənt]	A plan that you make for the future, sometimes with sb else.	Vereinbarung; Arrangement; Plan
in a hurry [ɪn ə ˈhʌri]	to hurry → to hurry up → *in a hurry*	in Eile
such [sʌtʃ]	It was *such* a good party that nobody wanted to go home.	solch
out and about [ˌaʊt ənd əˈbaʊt]	If you are *out and about,* you go to places where you can meet people.	unterwegs
• software [ˈsɒftweə]		Software (*Computerprogramme*)
• designer [dɪˈzaɪnə]	to design → *designer*	Designer(in); Entwickler(in)
• to pass [pɑːs]	When you have *passed* your driving test, you are allowed to drive a car alone.	bestehen; durchgehen
motorway (BE) [ˈməʊtəweɪ]	An extra wide road where cars can usually drive faster than on other roads.	Autobahn
• licence [ˈlaɪsnts]	If you have a *licence* to do sth, you are allowed to do sth.	Lizenz; Erlaubnis
• driving licence [ˈdraɪvɪŋ ˌlaɪsnts]	When you have passed your driving test, you are given a *driving licence*.	Führerschein
*to lend [lend]	to borrow ↔ to lend	(ver)leihen
• tone [təʊn]	Don't use that *tone!* = Don't speak to me like that!	Ton
• to separate [ˈsepreɪt]	❗ Careful with the pronunciation: separate (adj.) [ˈseprət] = getrennt *to separate* [ˈsepreɪt] = trennen	trennen
issue [ˈɪʃuː; ˈɪsjuː]	A subject or problem that is important and is often discussed.	Frage; Angelegenheit; Problem
2 • indefinite [ɪnˈdefɪnət]	definite ↔ *indefinite*	unbestimmt; indefinit
3 uncountable [ʌnˈkaʊntəbl]	'Bottle' is a countable noun, but 'milk' is *uncountable*: How much milk is there? – There are two bottles of milk.	unzählbar
• institution [ˌɪntstɪˈtjuːʃn]	Hospitals and schools are examples of *institutions*.	Institution; Einrichtung
5 • live [laɪv]	❗ Notice the difference in pronunciation: life [laɪf], but *live* [laɪv].	live

Language B It makes me so angry!

• Scot [skɒt]	Scotland → Scottish → *Scot*	Schotte; Schottin
*to let off steam [ˌlet ɒf ˈstiːm]	If you shout when you feel angry, it can help you to *let off steam*.	Dampf ablassen; seinem Ärger Luft machen
furniture (singular noun with plural meaning) [ˈfɜːnɪtʃə]	❗ The *furniture* is new. = Die Möbel sind neu.	Möbel

vocabulary
unit 3

porridge ['pɒrɪdʒ]	This dish is very popular at breakfast (with sugar and milk) in Scotland.	Haferbrei
• breaking point ['breɪkɪŋ ˌpɔɪnt]		Schmerzgrenze; kritischer Punkt
*to overhear [ˌəʊvə'hɪə]	! False friend: *to overhear* ≠ überhören	belauschen; zufällig mit anhören
• silent ['saɪlənt]	If you say nothing, you stay *silent*. silence → silent	still
• disadvantaged [ˌdɪsəd'vɑːntɪdʒd]	advantage → disadvantaged	benachteiligt
the other day [ðɪ ˌʌðə 'deɪ]	! False friend: *the other day* ≠ am anderen Tag	neulich
to assume [ə'sjuːm; ə'suːm]	If you *assume* sth, you think it is true although you don't really know. 🔍 Lat. *assumere*	annehmen; voraussetzen
queue [kjuː]	A line of people who are waiting, e. g. in a shop or at a bus stop.	(Warte-)Schlange
to blame [bleɪm]	Don't *blame* me! It's not my fault. ! False friend: *to blame* ≠ blamieren	verantwortlich machen; beschuldigen
2 • people ['piːpl]		Volk
3 • guide dog ['gaɪd ˌdɒg]	A dog that is trained to help blind people.	Blindenhund
6 • gardener ['gɑːdnə]	garden → gardener	Gärtner(in)
obligation [ˌɒblɪ'geɪʃn]		Verpflichtung

You'll make it!

Das englische Verb *to make* kann eine Menge unterschiedlicher Bedeutungen haben, je nachdem in welchem Kontext und mit welchen Präpositionen es verwendet wird. In den folgenden Sätzen findest du einige Beispiele. Ordne sie den passenden Bedeutungen aus dem Kasten zu.

1. What a lovely model house! Who made it?
2. The basketball coach says I am talented. I hope I'll make the school team.
3. I want to be a rock star and my father doesn't like the idea. But I know I'll make it!
4. I don't believe that story. I'm sure you've made it up!
5. If you don't work harder, you won't make the grade.
6. Mrs Winter made me do my homework all over again – only because she couldn't read it!

> to get into
> to be good enough
> to invent
> to build
> to tell sb to do sth
> to be successful (in one's job)

Skills   Preparing for your oral exam

oral ['ɔːrl]	An *oral exam* is a test in which you have to speak.	mündlich
• exam [ɪg'zæm]		Examen; Prüfung
either … or … ['aɪðə; 'iːðə … ɔː]	If you have to choose between two things, you must decide *either* on one *or* the other.	entweder … oder …
• vocabulary [vəʊ'kæbjəlri]	If you read a lot, you'll soon improve your *vocabulary*.	Vokabular; Wortschatz
1 to paraphrase ['pærəfreɪz]	To express in a different way, so the meaning stays the same.	paraphrasieren; umschreiben
2 • function [fʌŋkʃn]		Funktion

vocabulary
unit 3

• to **identify** (with) [aɪ'dentɪfaɪ]	identity → *to identify* (with)	(sich) identifizieren (mit)
3 **chewing gum** ['tʃuːɪŋ ˌɡʌm]	*Chewing gum* isn't allowed at our school.	Kaugummi

Text   The kiss

kiss [kɪs]	When they said goodbye, she gave him a *kiss*.	Kuss
lopsided [ˌlɒp'saɪdɪd]		schief; nach einer Seite hängend
• **lip** [lɪp]		Lippe
• **buggy** ['bʌɡi]		Buggy *(leichter Kinderwagen)*
• *to **catch fire** [ˌkætʃ 'faɪə]	fire → to set fire to sth → *to catch fire*	Feuer fangen
term [tɜːm]	In Britain, one of the three periods of time between the school holidays: the autumn *term*, the spring *term* and the summer *term*.	Trimester; Semester; Halbjahr
to **call sb names** [ˌkɔːl sʌmbɒdi 'neɪmz]	To use nasty words to describe sb.	beschimpfen
ugly ['ʌɡli]	beautiful ↔ *ugly*	hässlich
none of this ['nʌn əv ðɪs]	He told me a story, but *none of* it was true.	nichts davon
*to **strike** [straɪk]	matches → *to strike* a match	schlagen; anzünden *(ein Streichholz)*
• **The thing is** … [ðə ˌθɪŋ ˈɪz]	I'd like to buy her a present, but *the thing is,* I haven't got any money.	Die Sache ist die, …
• **flame** [fleɪm]	When you make a fire, *flames* go up and turn into smoke.	Flamme
• **alarm** [ə'lɑːm]	If *alarm* bells ring, you suddenly feel worried, frightened or in danger.	Alarm; Beunruhigung
eyelash ['aɪlæʃ]		Wimper
all over [ˌɔːl 'əʊvə]	If you feel hot *all over,* every part of your body feels hot.	überall
• to **knock** [nɒk]	to knock → to knock out → to knock over	stoßen; schlagen
over and over [ˌəʊvər ənd 'əʊvə]	Again and again.	immer wieder
• **cigarette** [ˌsɪɡ'ret]	I hate the smell of *cigarette* smoke!	Zigarette
booze *(infml)* [buːz]	Wine, beer, whisky etc. can also be called *booze*.	Alkohol
*to **be sick** [biː 'sɪk]	*I was sick.* = Ich musste mich übergeben.	sich übergeben
	❗ BE: *to be sick* = sich übergeben **AE:** *to be sick* = krank sein	
• **virus** ['vaɪərəs]	A lot of illnesses can be caused by *viruses*.	Virus
• **normal** ['nɔːml]	It's *normal* to feel tired after a long day.	normal
like [laɪk]		als ob
*to **be better** [biː 'betə]	I had a bad cold last week, but I*'m better* now.	sich besser fühlen; wieder gesund sein
• **laugh** [lɑːf]	to laugh → a *laugh*	Lachen
or else [els]	Otherwise. If you say *'Or else!'* to sb, you mean that sth bad will happen to them if they don't do what you want.	sonst; andernfalls
to **shrug** (one's shoulders) [ʃrʌɡ]	You can *shrug* your shoulders to show that you don't know or you aren't interested.	mit den Achseln/Schultern zucken
flatly ['flætli]		rundweg; kategorisch

• to **kiss** [kɪs]	a kiss → to kiss	küssen
shape [ʃeɪp]	A kiss *shape*:	Form
• **pavilion** [pəˈvɪljən]	A building near a sports field which is used by the players and by the people who come to watch the game.	Pavillon; Clubhaus
freak [fri:k]	If people think you're a *freak*, they find you very strange in some way, e. g. what you look like or what opinions you have.	Missgeburt; eigenartiger Mensch
to **nod** [nɒd]	to shake your head ↔ to nod	nicken
coward [ˈkaʊəd]	a hero ↔ a *coward*	Feigling
to **stare** [steə]	to see – to look at – to *stare* at	starren
firework [ˈfaɪəwɜ:k]	1. A firework: 2. fireworks:	Feuerwerkskörper; *Plural:* Feuerwerk
*to **stand up for oneself** [ˌstænd ˈʌp]	If you don't *stand up for yourself*, you will be more easily pushed around by bullies.	sich verteidigen
wimp *(infml)* [wɪmp]	Sb who is weak and too afraid to do things that might be difficult or dangerous.	Weichei; Schlappschwanz
to **admire** [ədˈmaɪə]	Everyone *admires* a hero. Fr. admirer; Lat. admirari	bewundern
*to **lean** [li:n]	You can *lean* towards sb, or you can *lean* your bike against a wall.	(sich) lehnen
out of the corner of my eye [aʊt əv ðə ˌkɔ:nər əv maɪ ˈaɪ]		aus dem Augenwinkel
2 • **effect** [ɪˈfekt]	A change or event that is the result of sth.	Effekt; Wirkung
tension [ˈtenʃn]	A nervous feeling that you get when you can't relax.	Spannung
6 • **image** [ˈɪmɪdʒ]	A word, phrase or picture that is used to describe or stand for an idea, e. g. in a book or film.	Bild; Image
vocals [ˈvəʊklz]	The part of a piece of music that is sung.	Gesang
• **album** [ˈælbəm]		Album
• to **inspire** [ɪnˈspaɪə]	To give the idea for sth (e. g. a poem or a song).	inspirieren; anregen
• **acoustic** [əˈku:stɪk]	1. an acoustic guitar: 1. 2. an electric guitar: 2.	akustisch

Let's check

5 • **income** [ˈɪnkʌm]		Einkommen
• **churchyard** [ˈtʃɜ:tʃjɑ:d]	The piece of land round a church where there are graves.	Kirchhof; Friedhof

> **Einige spielerische Möglichkeiten, Wortschatz zu üben:**
>
> ● Du nimmst einfach ein Quadrat mit 15×15 Kästchen und versteckst möglichst viele Wörter der Lektion oder eines Wortfelds darin, senkrecht, waagrecht, vorwärts und rückwärts geschrieben.
> ● Oder du nimmst 10 Wörter eines Wortfelds wie *Scotland*, zerlegst sie in Silben, ordnest sie alphabetisch und lässt deine Freunde diese Wörter suchen und zusammensetzen.
> ● Oder du stellst ihnen die Aufgabe, fünf Wörter aus der neuen Lektion zu benennen, wenn du ihnen alte Wörter nennst, auf die sich die neuen reimen, z. B. *name – blame, mean – lean* etc.

vocabulary
focus 2

focus 2 — Focus on the New World

Der Alphabet-Wettstreit

Vokabellernen kann im Wettstreit spannender sein!
Reihum müssen die Mitspieler zu einem Thema einen passenden Begriff aus der Vokabelliste finden. Dabei geht es bei jedem Begriff einen Buchstaben weiter im Alphabet. Der erste braucht also ein passendes Wort mit „A", der zweite mit „B" und so weiter. Wer kein Wort weiß, scheidet aus. Schnelligkeit zählt, und wer als letzter übrig bleibt, hat gewonnen!

•**permanent** [ˈpɜːmnənt]	A thing that is *permanent* lasts for a very long time or for ever. *Fr. permanent; Lat. permanere*	permanent; dauerhaft
*to **set up** [ˌsetˈʌp]	To start or found.	einrichten; aufbauen; gründen
Puritan [ˈpjʊərɪtn]	Some *Puritans* believed it was wrong to act, to dance or to play cards. *Fr. pur; Lat. purus*	Puritaner(in); puritanisch
•**religion** [rɪˈlɪdʒn]	*religion* → *religious* *Fr. religion f; Lat. religio f*	Religion
Quaker [ˈkweɪkə]		Quäker(in) *(Mitglied einer bestimmten christlichen Glaubensgemeinschaft)*
declaration [ˌdekləˈreɪʃn]	At the time of the *Declaration of Independence* the American colonists decided they wanted to break away from Britain and set up their own state.	Erklärung
independence [ˌɪndɪˈpendəns]	*depend* → *independent* → *independence* *Fr. indépendance f; Lat. de + pendere*	Unabhängigkeit
1 to **beg (for)** [beg]	! He was *begging for* money. He *begged* me to help him.	betteln (um); anflehen
to **starve** [stɑːv]	If you have nothing to eat, in the end you'll *starve*.	(ver)hungern
•**servant** [ˈsɜːvnt]	*to serve* → *service* → *servant*	Bedienstete(r); Diener(in)
to **provide sb with** [prəˈvaɪd]	We'll *provide* you *with* money. = We'll give you the money you need. *Lat. providere*	jmdn versorgen mit
*to **make it** [ˈmeɪkˌɪt]		es schaffen
master [ˈmɑːstə]		Herr; Meister
•**corn** [kɔːn]		Korn; Mais
disease [dɪˈziːz]	A lot of *diseases* can be caused by dirty water and bad food.	Krankheit
cabin [ˈkæbɪn]		Hütte
dirty [ˈdɜːti]		schmutzig
fever [ˈfiːvə]	If you get a high *fever*, it means your body is fighting against the illness.	Fieber

vocabulary
unit 4

• **wooden** ['wʊdn]	wood → *wooden*	hölzern
*to **have a baby** [ˌhæv ə 'beɪbi]	To bring a child into the world.	ein Kind bekommen
half, *pl* **halves** [hɑːf; hɑːvz]		(die) Hälfte
2 **border** ['bɔːdə]	The 'line' between one country or state and another.	Grenze
stripe [straɪp]	The US flag is called 'the stars and *stripes*': 	Streifen
3 **storehouse** ['stɔːhaʊs]	You can keep a lot of goods in a *storehouse*.	Lager; Speicher
price [praɪs]	❗ Notice the difference: *price* = what you must pay *prize* = what you can win	Preis
counter board ['kaʊntə ˌbɔːd]		Zählbrett; Rechenbrett
to **count** [kaʊnt]	How much money have we collected? – Let's *count* it, then we'll know. 🔍 Fr. compter; Lat. computare	zählen
board [bɔːd]	board → blackboard	Brett
paper ['peɪpə]	paper → newspaper	Papier
coin [kɔɪn]	*Coins* are the hard, round pieces of money.	Münze
counter ['kaʊntə]		Chip; Jeton; Spielfigur
sum [sʌm]	250–25? That's an easy *sum* to do.	Rechenaufgabe

unit 4 New England

Finde heraus, was für dich die beste Lernmethode ist, und nutze sie!

Ich lerne am besten Vokabeln, wenn ich
- sie aufschreibe
- sie auf Band aufnehme und anhöre
- meine eigenen Beispielsätze mache
- Reime mit ihnen mache
- sie in Listen oder *mind maps* gruppiere
- Bilder dazu male
- Gegensatzpaare oder Synonyme (Wörter mit gleicher oder ähnlicher Bedeutung) notiere
- schwierige Stellen und häufige Fehlerquellen farbig markiere
- …

Intro

to **surround** [sə'raʊnd]	The *surrounding* area is the area around a place.	umgeben
• **a while** [ə 'waɪl]	A little time.	eine Weile
*to **get used to** (+ *gerund*) [ˌget 'juːzt tə]	It takes time to *get used to* life in another country.	sich gewöhnen an

one hundred and forty-three **143**

vocabulary
unit 4

• **unbelievable** [ˌʌnbɪˈliːvəbl]	to believe → *unbelievable*	unglaublich
• **because of** [bɪˈkɒz əv]	We couldn't sleep *because of* the noise.	wegen
• **university** [ˌjuːnɪˈvɜːsəti]	Harvard is a very famous American *university*.	Universität
plantation [plænˈteɪʃn]		Plantage; Kolonie
to **enclose** [ɪnˈkləʊz]	If you *enclose* sth, you put it in with the letter you want to send.	beifügen
hometown [ˈhəʊmtaʊn]	home → *hometown*	Heimatstadt
dreamcatcher [ˈdriːmkætʃə]		Traumfänger *(indianisches verziertes Geflecht mit Federn, das böse Träume fernhalten soll)*
*to **hang up** [hæŋ ˈʌp]	You can *hang up* pictures or posters on the wall, and curtains at the window.	aufhängen
*to **come true** [ˌkʌm ˈtruː]	Wouldn't it be wonderful if our dreams always *came true?*	wahr werden; in Erfüllung gehen
2 **lobster** [ˈlɒbstə]		Hummer
• **specialty** *(AE)* [ˈspeʃlti]	A *specialty* (BE: speciality) of a place is a special product hat is always very good there.	Spezialität; Besonderheit

Language A   An e-mail from Susie

*to **be used to** *(+ gerund)* [biː ˈjuːzt tə]	to get used to → *to be used to*	gewöhnt sein an; gewohnt sein
• **granite** [ˈgrænɪt]	stone – rock – slate – *granite*	Granit
quarry [ˈkwɒri]	A place that is cut, often out of a mountain side, in order to get stone, slate, granite etc.	Steinbruch
kind of [ˈkaɪnd əv]	*AE:* A person who is described as '*kind of* strange' is a bit strange.	ziemlich
pretty [ˈprɪti]	Sth that is *pretty* good is really quite good.	ziemlich
• **State House** [ˈsteɪt ˌhaʊs]	*AE:* The building where the government of a state meets.	Regierungsgebäude
grand [grænd]		prächtig; großartig
dome [dəʊm]		Kuppel
*to **be crazy about** [biː ˈkreɪzi əbaʊt]	Sb who *is crazy about* sth likes it very, very much.	verrückt sein nach; abfahren auf
• **snowboarding** [ˈsnəʊbɔːdɪŋ]	Some people say *snowboarding* is a bit like surfing in the snow.	Snowboarden
Bavaria [bəˈveərɪə]	The biggest state in Germany.	Bayern
*to **feel like** *(+ gerund)* [ˈfiːl laɪk]	I'm off to the beach. Do you *feel like coming* with me?	Lust haben auf/zu
*to **be tired of** *(+ gerund)* [biː ˈtaɪəd]		es müde/leid sein/satt haben, etwas zu tun
till [tɪl]	Another word for 'until'.	bis
• **spectacular** [spekˈtækjələ]	The different colors of the leaves in the fall can make quite a *spectacular* show.	spektakulär
3 • **keyboard** [ˈkiːbɔːd]	You type on the *keyboard* of your computer.	Keyboard; Tastatur
Indian summer [ˌɪndɪən ˈsʌmə]	*AE:* A period of dry, warm weather in the fall, especially when the leaves on the trees change color.	Altweibersommer

vocabulary
unit 4

4 • to **ski** [ski:]	People who live in the Alps often learn to *ski* when they are very young.	Ski fahren
5 • **enjoyable** [ɪnˈdʒɔɪəbl]	to enjoy → *enjoyable*	angenehm; unterhaltsam
• **unforgettable** [ˌʌnfəˈgetəbl]	to forget → *unforgettable*	unvergesslich

Language B   The 1627 Pilgrim Village

to **fare** [feə]	"How do you *fare*?" = "How are you?" in modern English.	ergehen
mayhaps [ˈmeɪhæps]		vielleicht
to **desire** [dɪˈzaɪə]		begehren; wünschen
re-creation [ˌriːkriˈeɪʃn]		Wiedererschaffung
It's no use (+ *gerund*) [ɪts ˈnəʊ ˈjuːs]	*It's no use* arguing with him. He never admits he's wrong.	Es nützt nichts …
bathroom [ˈbɑːθrʊm]	! BE: *bathroom* = Badezimmer AE: *bathroom* = Toilette	Toilette (AE)
shy [ʃaɪ]	*Shy* people often feel nervous when they are together with other people.	schüchtern
• **fascinating** [ˈfæsɪneɪtɪŋ]	Very, very interesting.	faszinierend
pan [pæn]	Pans:	Pfanne; Kochtopf mit Stiel
• **gas**, *pl.* **gasses** [gæs]	Most people in Europe use either *gas* or *electricity* for cooking.	Gas
• **electricity** [ˌelɪkˈtrɪsəti]	electric → *electricity*	Elektrizität; Strom
crop [krɒp]	*Crops* are plants like wheat or potatoes that are grown in fields for food.	Feldfrucht; Ernte
timber [ˈtɪmbə]	Wood that is used for building houses and furniture.	(Bau-)Holz
*to **be worth** (+ *gerund*) [biː ˈwɜːθ]	*It's worth* buying really strong shoes for hiking.	(es) wert sein (zu)
3 *to **run out** [ˌrʌn ˈaʊt]	Time is *running out*. = There isn't much time left.	ausgehen
• to **farm** [fɑːm]	farm → farmer → farmyard → *to farm*	Landwirtschaft treiben
5 **homesite** [ˈhəʊmsaɪt]		Wohnstätte

Skills   Giving a talk

3 • **printout** [ˈprɪntaʊt]	printer → *printout*	Ausdruck
• **photocopy** [ˈfəʊtəʊˌkɒpi]	photo → photographer → *photocopy*	Fotokopie
4 *to **get (sb) involved** [ˌget ɪnˈvɒlvd]	If you *get* a person *involved* in sth, you make them take part.	sich (oder jmdn) beteiligen (an); sich engagieren (für); sich einlassen (auf)
5 • **presentation** [ˌprezn̩ˈteɪʃn]	A formal word for a talk.	Präsentation
technique [tekˈniːk]	! a *technique* = eine Methode *technology* = Technik, Technologie	Methode; Technik
• **visual** [ˈvɪʒuəl]	*Visual* elements in a talk are things like pictures, maps or *transparencies* that the audience can look at.	visuell; optisch
transparency [trænˈspærntsi]		Folie
video projector [ˌvɪdiəʊ prəʊˈdʒektə]		Beamer (Projektionsgerät)
• **systematic** [ˌsɪstəˈmætɪk]	system → *systematic*	systematisch; gezielt
woodchuck [ˈwʊdtʃʌk]		Waldmurmeltier

vocabulary
unit 4

platypus, *pl.* platypi [ˈplætɪpəs; ˈplætɪpaɪ]		Schnabeltier
chuck [tʃʌk]		werfen

Text The ransom

ransom [ˈræntsm]	Money that must be paid in order to set a prisoner free.	Lösegeld
• **private** [ˈpraɪvɪt]	A *private* detective works alone, not for the police, and will work for you if you pay.	privat

---

Useful discussion phrases

Wenn du jemanden in einem Gespräch unterbrechen möchtest:
Can I stop you there for a moment?
Excuse me for interrupting.

Wenn du deine Meinung sagen möchtest:
In my opinion …
The way I see things …
If you ask me, …

Wenn du die Meinung eines anderen einholen möchtest:
Do you (really) think that …
How do you feel about …?

Eine andere Meinung kommentieren:
Good point!
I get your point.
I see what you mean.

Einer anderen Meinung zustimmen:
Exactly!
That's (exactly) the way I feel.
I have to agree with Alan.

Einer anderen Meinung nicht zustimmen:
Up to a point I agree with you, but …
(I'm afraid) I can't/don't agree.
You don't really believe that, do you?

Einen Vorschlag machen:
We should …
Why don't you …?
How/what about …?
I suggest …

Nach einer Wiederholung fragen:
I didn't catch that. Could you repeat that, please?
I missed that. Could you say it again, please?

---

tough [tʌf]	A *tough* job is a hard one. *Tough* meat is difficult to bite.	hart; rau; zäh
maple [ˈmeɪpl]	A *maple* leaf:	Ahorn
blind [blaɪnd]	If you pull down the *blinds*, the room will get darker.	Jalousie; Sonnenblende
*to **burst** [bɜːst]	❗ 1. When sth *bursts*, it suddenly breaks open. 2. When you *burst* into a room, you go in very suddenly.	bersten; platzen
corporation [ˌkɔːprˈeɪʃn]		Unternehmen; Aktiengesellschaft *(AE)*
• stinking rich [ˌstɪŋkɪŋ ˈrɪtʃ]		stinkreich
• to **kidnap** [ˈkɪdnæp]	When a child is *kidnapped*, the *kidnappers* usually *demand* a ransom from the child's parents.	kidnappen; entführen
• **kidnapper** [ˈkɪdnæpə]		Kidnapper(in); Entführer(in)
to demand [dɪˈmɑːnd]	🔍 Fr. demander	fordern; verlangen
• **unlike** [ʌnˈlaɪk]	like ↔ unlike	anders als; im Gegensatz zu

vocabulary
unit 4

• safe [seɪf]	Can you really keep your money safe in a *safe*?	Safe; Tresor
• to risk [rɪsk]		riskieren
• model ['mɒdl]	A lot of young girls dream of working as a *model*.	Model; Modell
• block [blɒk]	An area of land (in a town) with streets on all sides.	(Häuser-)Block
• practical ['præktɪkl]	When you say *'practically'*, you mean 'almost', but not quite, or not exactly.	praktisch
engaged [ɪn'geɪdʒd]	in love – *engaged* – married	verlobt
*to make sense [ˌmeɪk 'sents]	If sth *makes sense*, you can understand it.	Sinn machen; einleuchten
sense [sents]	There's no *sense* in doing sth silly.	Sinn; Bedeutung
on the other hand [ɒn ði ˌʌðə ˌhænd]	When you say *'on the other hand'*, you mention another aspect of a situation.	andererseits
obvious ['ɒbviəs]	Easy to see or understand.	offensichtlich
*to be sick with worry [biː 'sɪk wɪð ˌwʌri]	To be very, very worried about sth.	krank vor Sorge sein
• worry ['wʌri]	*worry* → to worry → to be worried	Sorge
to flash [flæʃ]	When your eyes *flash*, they look extra bright because you are experiencing strong feelings.	blitzen; blinken
anger ['æŋgə]	*anger* → angry	Zorn; Wut
to mess sth up [ˌmes ˈʌp]	To do sth badly or wrong, or to make a mess of sth that was all right before.	etw. durcheinanderbringen; etw. vergeigen
expressway *(AE)* [ɪk'spreswei]	A wide road that is specially built for a lot of fast traffic.	Autobahn; Schnellstraße
• place [pleɪs]	Let's meet at my *place*. = Let's meet at my home (house or flat).	Heim; Haus
cobbled ['kɒbld]		mit Kopfsteinpflaster gepflastert
old-fashioned [ˌəʊld 'fæʃnd]	fashion → *old-fashioned*	altmodisch
• lamp [læmp]	There's a street *lamp* outside our house to light the way.	Lampe; Leuchte
brass [brɑːs]		Messing
• knocker ['nɒkə]		Türklopfer
phone booth *(AE)* ['fəʊn ˌbuːð]	A kind of shelter in the street with a telephone inside.	Telefonzelle
booth [buːð]	A *booth* can also be a stall, usually at a fair.	Bude; Stand
bill *(AE)* [bɪl]	The suitcase was full of *forged bills*.	Banknote; Geldschein
to forge [fɔːdʒ]		fälschen
furious ['fjʊəriəs]	Very, very angry. Fr. *furieux*; Lat. *furiosus*	wütend
fist [fɪst]		Faust
to twist [twɪst]	If sth is *twisted*, it moves into a strange shape.	verdrehen; verzerren
sergeant ['sɑːdʒnt]	A police officer.	Polizeimeister(in)
• to arrest [ə'rest]	The police caught the thieves and *arrested* them. Fr. *arrêter*	festnehmen; verhaften
inquiry [ɪn'kwaɪəri]	A question you ask in order to get information about sth.	Ermittlung; Nachforschung; Anfrage

vocabulary
unit 5

1 to **sum up** [ˌsʌmˈʌp]	If you *sum up* what happens in a story, you explain it in a few sentences.	zusammenfassen
narrator [neˈreɪtə]	The *narrator* of a story is the person who tells it. 🔍 Lat. *narrare*	Erzähler(in)

Let's check

3 to **peep** [piːp]		gucken; spähen

unit 5 — Fame and fortune

Englisch im Alltag

Achte auf alle englischen Wörter, die dir begegnen. Ob im Supermarkt, im Fernsehen, in Büchern, auf Werbeplakaten oder Schildern am Bahnhof, Flughafen etc.: Du wirst erstaunt sein, wie oft man im Alltag auf die englische Sprache stößt.
Deinen Sprachschatz erweiterst du, indem du dir ein schönes Heft oder Notizbuch kaufst, das speziell für solche Vokabeln da ist. Nimm es so oft wie möglich mit, vor allem, wenn du verreist. Aber Vorsicht! Schlage alles zur Sicherheit in einem Wörterbuch nach, denn manchmal begegnest du Wörtern, die es im Englischen gar nicht gibt oder die etwas völlig anderes bedeuten, z. B. *Handy, Smoking, Dressman, Oldtimer*.
Da du mit jedem Wort eine kleine Geschichte oder bestimmte besondere Umstände verbindest (zum Beispiel: „Ach ja! Dieses Wort habe ich am Bahnhof gesehen, im Kino gehört", etc.), wirst du es dir sehr leicht merken können!

Intro

fame [feɪm]	fame → *famous*	Ruhm
fortune [ˈfɔːtʃuːn]	🔍 Fr. *fortune* f; Lat. *fortuna* f	Vermögen; Reichtum; Schicksal; Glück
calling [ˈkɔːlɪŋ]		Berufung
*to **strive** [straɪv]	What you *strive* to be is what you want and try to be.	streben; sich bemühen
to **commit oneself to** [kəˈmɪt]		sich (jmdm/etw.) verschreiben/verpflichten/widmen; sich binden an
•**president** [ˈprezɪdnt]		Präsident(in)
mere [mɪə]	The story is a *mere* legend. = It's only a legend, not more.	bloß
to **amplify** [ˈæmplɪfaɪ]		verstärken
•to **care (about)**	If you *care about* sth, it's important to you.	sich kümmern (um); sich interessieren (für); wichtig nehmen
*to **get to do sth** [get]	Did you *get to see* Disneyland when you were in the USA?	die Möglichkeit haben, etw. zu tun

vocabulary
unit 5

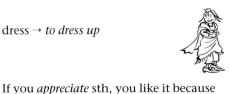

• to **dress up** [dres ˈʌp]	dress → to dress up	sich verkleiden
otherworldly [ˌʌðəˈwɜːldli]		aus einer anderen Welt
elf, *pl.* **elves** [elf]		Elbe; Elf(e)
like [laɪk]		irgendwie
to **appreciate** [əˈpriːʃieɪt]	If you *appreciate* sth, you like it because you recognize its positive characteristics.	schätzen; anerkennen
to **wade** [weɪd]		waten
• **mail** [meɪl]	mail → e-mail	Post
whereas [weərˈæz]	People can think for themselves, *whereas* a computer can't.	während; wohingegen
• to **party**	a party → to party	feiern
• **entertainer** [ˌentəˈteɪnə]	entertainment → entertainer	Entertainer(in); Unterhaltungskünstler(in)
beyond [biˈɒnd]		jenseits
1 **attitude** (to/towards) [ˈætɪtjuːd]	Your *attitude* to/towards life is the way you feel about it. 🔍 Fr. attitude *f*	Haltung; Einstellung
2 • **authentic** [ɔːˈθentɪk]	Real or realistic.	authentisch
3 • **disadvantage** [ˌdɪsədˈvɑːntɪdʒ]	advantage ↔ disadvantage	Nachteil

Language A   The audition

audition [ɔːˈdɪʃn]		Vorsprechen; Vorsingen; Vortanzen; Probespiel
to **convince** [kənˈvɪnts]	To make sb agree with you by giving them good arguments. 🔍 Fr. convaincre; Lat. convincere	überzeugen
pushy [ˈpʊʃi]	Try to get what you want – but don't be too *pushy*!	penetrant; aggressiv
to **audition** [ɔːˈdɪʃn]	audition → to audition	vorsprechen; vorsingen; vortanzen; vorspielen
apparently [əˈpærntli]	to appear → apparently 🔍 Fr. apparaître: apparement; Lat. apparere	anscheinend
• **teenage** [ˈtiːneɪdʒ]	Your *teenage* years are the time from age 13 to age 19.	jugendlich
• **performer** [pəˈfɔːmə]	to perform → performer	Darsteller(in); Schauspieler(in); Künstler(in)
frankly [ˈfræŋkli]	*Frankly*, … = To tell you the truth, …	ehrlich gesagt; offen gestanden
• **hopeful** [ˈhəʊpfl]	hopeless ↔ hopeful	hoffnungsvoll
ambitious [æmˈbɪʃəs]	An *ambitious* person wants to have success or to be rich and famous. 🔍 Fr. ambitieux; Lat. ambitiosus	ehrgeizig
utter [ˈʌtə]	If you are *utterly* terrified, you feel very, very scared.	äußerst; völlig
accompaniment [əˈkʌmpnɪmənt]		Begleitung
fortunately [ˈfɔːtʃnətli]	*fortunately* = luckily 🔍 Fr. fortune *f*; Lat. fortuna *f*	zum Glück
unfortunately [ˌʌnˈfɔːtʃnətli]	*Unfortunately*, … = It's a pity, but …	leider; unglücklicherweise
• **note** [nəʊt]	❗ – *notes* = einzelne Töne – music = Noten, Partituren	Note *(Musik)*; Ton

vocabulary
unit 5

• to **blind** [blaɪnd]	blind → to blind	blenden
to **encourage** [ɪnˈkʌrɪdʒ]	*Encouraging* words make you feel better and braver.	ermutigen; unterstützen
	Fr. encourager	
would not [ˈwʊd nɒt]	I wanted him to lend me his new CD, but he *wouldn't*.	weigerte(n) sich; wollte(n) nicht
confidence [ˈkɒnfɪdnts]	Sb who is shy doesn't have enough *confidence*.	Vertrauen; Zuversicht
	Fr. confiance f; Lat. confidentia f	
• **hopefully** [ˈhəʊpfli]	❗ I went on stage *hopefully* (= hoffnungsvoll). *Hopefully* I'll do well in the audition (= hoffentlich).	hoffentlich
to **spot** [spɒt]	*to spot* = to notice	entdecken; erkennen
• **talent** [ˈtælənt]	If you have *talent*, you are – or can become – very good at sth.	Talent
*to **give sb a break** [ˌgɪv əˈbreɪk]		jmdm eine Chance geben
1 • **individual** [ˌɪndɪˈvɪdʒuəl]	Each *individual* person is each separate person (not as part of a group).	individuell; einzeln
point of view [ˌpɔɪnt əv ˈvjuː]	Your *point of view* is your way of seeing things.	Standpunkt; Perspektive
	Fr. point de vue m	
3 **lousy** [ˈlaʊzi]	Really awful.	lausig
4 **degree** [dɪˈgriː]		Grad
mid [mɪd]	*mid position* = *hier:* Binnenstellung	mittel

Language B After the audition

• **forever** [fəˈrevə]	We won't live *forever*. We all have to die.	für immer; ewig
*to **show up** (infml) [ˌʃəʊ ˈʌp]	An informal expression for 'to appear' or 'to arrive'.	auftauchen
• **far** [fɑː]	It's *far* too expensive. = It's much too expensive.	bei weitem; weitaus
running order [ˈrʌnɪŋ ˌɔːdə]		Startreihenfolge
forward [ˈfɔːwəd]	If you go *forward*, you move towards the front.	vorwärts
• *to **get off the ground** [getˌɒf ðə ˈgraʊnd]	If we don't start soon, the project will never *get off the ground*.	in Gang kommen
• **casting** [ˈkɑːstɪŋ]	The job of choosing actors to play particular roles.	Casting; Rollenbesetzung
• **not exactly** [ˌnɒt ɪgˈzæktli]	It was*n't exactly* fantastic. = It wasn't very good.	nicht gerade
• **encouragement** [ɪnˈkʌrɪdʒmənt]	to encourage → encouragement	Ermutigung; Unterstützung
• **callback** [ˈkɔːlbæk]		Rückruf
Dear Sir or Madam [dɪə ˌsɜːr ɔː ˈmædəm]	This is sometimes written at the beginning of a formal letter.	Sehr geehrte Dame, sehr geehrter Herr
to **wish** [wɪʃ]	'I *wish* to' is a formal way of saying 'I want to'.	wünschen
disgraceful [dɪsˈgreɪsfl]		schändlich
*to **keep sb waiting** [ˌkiːp ˈweɪtɪŋ]	To make sb wait.	jmdn warten lassen
considerable [kənˈsɪdrəbl]	a *considerable* time = quite a long time	beträchtlich
	Fr. considérable; Lat. considerare	
• *to **set** [set]	If you *set* a time for sth, you decide on a time for it.	setzen; aufstellen

vocabulary
unit 5

• Had I not … *(fml)* [hæd]	*Had* I not … = If I hadn't …	Hätte ich nicht …
• *to **get (sth) started** [ˌget ˈstɑːtɪd]	to start → *to get started*	in Gang kommen; (etw.) in Gang bringen
to **require** [rɪˈkwaɪə]	If you *require* sth, it's necessary for you to have it.	benötigen; erfordern
• **performance** [pəˈfɔːmənts]	to perform → performer → *performance*	Aufführung; Vorstellung
• **candidate** [ˈkændɪdət]	Sb who is trying to get a position, e. g. a job, or taking part in a test of some kind.	Kandidat(in)
• **understandable** [ˌʌndəˈstændəbl]	to understand → *understandable*	verständlich
afterwards [ˈɑːftəwədz]	after → *afterwards*	danach; hinterher
• **professional** [prəˈfeʃnl]	A *professional* actor does acting as a job. If you do sth in a *professional* way, you do it very well.	professionell
• **unprofessional** [ˌʌnprəˈfeʃnl]	professional ↔ *unprofessional*	unprofessionell
favorable [ˈfeɪvrəbl]		günstig; positiv
both … and … [ˈbəʊθ … ænd]	The journey over the mountains was *both* long *and* difficult.	sowohl … als auch …
to **receive** [rɪˈsiːv]	A formal word for 'to get'. 🔍 Fr. *recevoir*; Lat. *recipere*	empfangen
Yours sincerely [ˌjɔːz sɪnˈsɪəli]	This can be used at the end of a formal letter.	Mit freundlichen Grüßen
1 **gap** [gæp]	There's a *gap* in the fence.	Lücke; Spalt; Abstand
3 **subordinate clause** [səˌbɔːdnət ˈklɔːz]		Nebensatz
exaggeration [ɪgˌzædʒrˈeɪʃn]	If you use *exaggeration,* you make a bad situation sound even worse, or a good one better than it really is. 🔍 Fr. *exagération f*	Übertreibung
syllable [ˈsɪləbl]		Silbe
4 • **open-air** [ˌəʊpnˈeə]	air → *open-air*	Freilicht-
• **complaint** [kəmˈpleɪnt]	to complain → *complaint*	Beschwerde
to **cancel** [ˈkæntsl]	One of the singers was ill, so the concert was *cancelled*.	absagen; stornieren
to **flood** [flʌd]	It rained so heavily that large areas of land were *flooded*.	überfluten; überschwemmen
to **charge sb a sum of money** [tʃɑːdʒ]	Although they *charged* us a large sum of money for the tickets, the *quality* of the performance was very low.	jmdm einen Geldbetrag in Rechnung stellen
• **quality** [ˈkwɒləti]		Qualität; Eigenschaft
to **prevent sth from happening/ sb from doing sth** [prɪˈvent]	The rain *prevented* us *from* finishing the match.	verhindern, dass etwas passiert/dass jmd etw. tut
refund [ˈriːfʌnd]		Rückerstattung

Skills   American and British English

• to **mix** [mɪks]	If you *mix* blue and yellow, you get green.	mixen; mischen
*to **be aware of** [biː əˈweə]	If you *are aware of* a fact, you know about it.	sich … bewusst sein
slight [slaɪt]	A *slight* difference between two things is a very small one.	leicht; gering

vocabulary
unit 5

How to write a formal letter

Hier findest du nützliche Ausdrücke und Redewendungen, die man zum Verfassen eines formalen Briefes benötigt.
Achte darauf, dass du dir erst im Klaren darüber sein musst, was du in dem Brief ausdrücken willst und an wen er gerichtet ist. Einen formalen Brief schreibt man z. B. Leuten, die man nicht kennt, bei der Arbeit, wenn man etwas bestellt, sich bewirbt oder sich beschweren will.

Aussehen eines formalen Briefes:
- auf weißem, sauberen DIN-A4-Papier
- möglichst nicht handgeschrieben
- sinngemäße Gliederung durch Absatzschaltungen
- Absender- und Empfängeradresse sowie Datum am entsprechenden Platz oberhalb des Textes
- Unterschrift unterhalb
- gegebenenfalls Hinweis auf Anlagen unter der Unterschrift: *Enclosure(s)*

Die richtige Anrede,
- wenn du nicht weißt, wer zuständig ist:
  Dear Sir or Madam,
- wenn du die Person zwar kennst, aber nicht befreundet bist:
  Dear Mr/Mrs/Ms …,
- wenn die Person ein Freund oder ein enger Arbeitskollege ist:
  Dear Frank,
- Nach der Anrede wird groß weitergeschrieben.

Bezug auf etwas nehmen
Thank you for your letter of March 5th.
I refer to your advertisement in the Times/your letter of 23rd March/your phone call today, …

Der Grund des Briefs
I am writing to inquire (mich erkundigen) *about/complain about …*

Nach etwas fragen
Could you please …?
I would be grateful (dankbar) *if you could …*

Einer Bitte zustimmen
I would be very happy to …

Schlechte Nachrichten überbringen
Unfortunately, …
I am afraid that …

Etwas dem Brief hinzufügen
I am enclosing …

Abschluss
Thank you for your help.
Please contact me again if I can help in any way/if there are any problems/if you have any questions.

Bezug zu zukünftigem Kontakt
I look forward to hearing from you soon/meeting you next Tuesday/seeing you next Thursday.

Der Schluss,
- wenn du jemanden nicht gut kennst:
  Yours sincerely, …
- wenn die Person ein Freund oder ein enger Arbeitskollege ist:
  Best wishes, …

---

*gotten (AE) ['gɒtn] — In American English people often say 'gotten' instead of 'got'. — bekommen; geworden *(past participle von 'to get' in AE)*

subway ['sʌbweɪ] — **!** BE: A path that goes under a busy road. AE: What British people call 'the underground'. — Unterführung *(BE)*; U-Bahn *(AE)*

- **underground** ['ʌndəgraʊnd] — unterirdisch
- **to cross** [krɒs] — cross → to cross
  A children's joke:
  Why did the chicken *cross* the road? – Because it wanted to get to the other side. — überqueren; kreuzen

vocabulary focus 3

spell checker ['spel ˌtʃekə]		Rechtschreibprüf-programm
• misunderstanding [ˌmɪsʌndəˈstændɪŋ]	to understand → misunderstanding	Missverständnis
3 to **consider** [kənˈsɪdə]	In Britain people *consider* it bad *manners* to take sth without saying 'thank you'.	betrachten; erwägen
manners *(pl.)* [ˈmænəz]		Manieren; Benehmen

Text A song project

1 • **rhythm** [ˈrɪðm]	A regular movement or beat (especially in music or poetry).	Rhythmus
• **verse** [vɜːs]	One of the parts that a poem or song is divided into.	Vers; Strophe
setting [ˈsetɪŋ]	What is the *setting* of the story? = Where and when does it take place?	Schauplatz; Rahmen
• **interpretation** [ɪnˌtɜːprɪˈteɪʃn]	An explanation of what sth means or may mean. to interpret → interpretation	Interpretation; Auslegung
booklet [ˈbʊklət]	book → booklet	Broschüre; Heft
2 to **feature** [ˈfiːtʃə]	This film *features* three of my favorite actors.	jmdn in einer Hauptrolle haben
chorus [ˈkɔːrəs]	The part of a song that is often sung again and again (between the different verses).	Refrain

focus 3 Focus on international contacts

1 **alien** [ˈeɪliən]		Fremde(r); Ausländer(in); Außerirdische(r)
opportunity [ˌɒpəˈtjuːnəti]	Another word for a chance. 🔍 Fr. *opportun*; Lat. *opportunus – opportunitas f*	Gelegenheit; Chance
2 **abroad** [əˈbrɔːd]	❗ They live *abroad* (= im Ausland). They went *abroad* (= ins Ausland).	im/ins Ausland
• to **surprise** [səˈpraɪz]	surprise → to surprise	überraschen
foreign [ˈfɒrɪn]	A lot of British schools teach French as the first *foreign* language.	ausländisch; fremd
3 *to **get in touch (with)** [ˌget ɪn ˈtʌtʃ]	To make contact (with).	in Verbindung treten (mit); kontaktieren
• **qualified** [ˈkwɒlɪfaɪd]	A *qualified* teacher has learnt how to teach at a special college.	qualifiziert
• **interest** [ˈɪntrəst]	interest → interesting → interested	Interesse
• **need** [niːd]	Your *needs* are what you need.	Bedürfnis; Erfordernis
e-pal [ˈiːˌpæl]	A friend you exchange e-mails with.	E-Mail-Brieffreund(in)
to **drop sb a line** [ˌdrɒp ə ˈlaɪn]		jmdm ein paar Zeilen schreiben
• **au pair** [ˌəʊˈpeə]	A girl (sometimes a boy) who works abroad, in a family, in order to learn their language.	Au-pair(-Mädchen)

vocabulary
focus 3

• **advertisement** [əd'vɜːtɪsmənt]	*Advertisements* sometimes persuade people to buy products they don't really need.	Anzeige; Werbespot
• **reply** [rɪ'plaɪ]	Another word for 'answer'.	Antwort
4 **fluffy** ['flʌfi]		flaumig; flauschig; flockig
5 • to **greet** [griːt]	In Britain or America people don't usually shake hands when they *greet* each other.	(be)grüßen
pleased [pliːzd]	happy – glad – *pleased*	erfreut; zufrieden
• to **accept** [ək'sept]	If you *accept* an invitation to a party, you say you'd like to come.	akzeptieren; annehmen
• **tactful** ['tæktfl]	When you're *tactful*, it means you try not to hurt other people's feelings.	taktvoll
to **apologise** [ə'pɒlədʒaɪz]	To say sorry.	sich entschuldigen
soft [sɒft]	hard ↔ *soft*	weich; sanft
rather ['rɑːðə]		ziemlich
a little [ə 'lɪtl]	*a little* = a bit	ein bisschen; ein wenig
*to be sb's **cup of tea** [ˌkʌp əv 'tiː]		jmds Fall sein
• **mineral water** ['mɪnrl ˌwɔːtə]	Some people think drinking *mineral water* is especially healthy, but others believe *tap water* is just as good.	Mineralwasser
tap water ['tæp ˌwɔːtə]		Leitungswasser
tap [tæp]		Wasserhahn
• **cola** ['kəʊlə]	A kind of lemonade that has become so popular that you can buy it all over the world.	Cola

Endungen von Nomen

Diese Tabelle enthält einige häufige Endungen, an denen du englische Nomen erkennst.
Findest du noch mehr Beispiele? Du kannst solche Listen für weitere Vor- oder Nachsilben anlegen und im Laufe der Zeit ergänzen.

-ness	-hood	-ship	-ion
blind**ness**	brother**hood**	friend**ship**	act**ion**
…	…	…	…

extra line

A Why the emu can't fly

pleased [pli:zd]	erfreut; zufrieden	*to lay [leɪ]	legen
peaceful ['pi:sfl]	friedlich	to crack [kræk]	zerbrechen; springen
boastful ['bəʊstfl]	prahlerisch	mulga ['mʊlgə]	Mulga (australische Baumart)
*to grow tired of sb/sth [ˌgrəʊ 'taɪəd]	jmds/einer Sache überdrüssig werden	to hand sth down to sb [ˌhænd 'daʊn]	etw. an jmdn weitergeben/überliefern
to flap one's wings [ˌflæp wʌnz 'wɪŋz]	mit den Flügeln schlagen	stumpy ['stʌmpi]	stummelig
will [wɪl]	Wille; Testament	1 belief [bɪ'li:f]	Glaube
eagle ['i:gl]	Adler	to create [kri'eɪt]	(er)schaffen
galah [gə'lɑ:]	Galah (australische Vogelart)		

B More about films

1 setting ['setɪŋ]	Schauplatz; Rahmen	2 freeze frame ['fri:z ˌfreɪm]	Standbild
plot [plɒt]	Handlung	to dub [dʌb]	synchronisieren

C Poetry page

poetry ['pəʊətri]	Lyrik	3 limerick ['lɪmrɪk]	Limerick (bestimmte Form eines fünfzeiligen Gedichts)
1 nonet [nəʊ'nət]	Nonett (bestimmte Form eines neunzeiligen Gedichts)		
syllable ['sɪləbl]	Silbe	beat [bi:t]	Schlag; Takt; Hebung
2 clerihew ['klerɪhju:]	Clerihew (bestimmte Form eines vierzeiligen Gedichts)	by clapping your hands [baɪ ˌklæpɪŋ jə 'hændz]	indem ihr in die Hände klatscht
		fellow ['feləʊ]	Bursche; Kerl
		dock [dɒk]	Dock
to name [neɪm]	benennen	*to awake [ə'weɪk]	erwachen; aufwachen
to rhyme [raɪm]	(sich) reimen	fright [fraɪt]	Schreck
rhyme [raɪm]	Reim	to brush [brʌʃ]	putzen
rhythm ['rɪðm]	Rhythmus	dentist ['dentɪst]	Zahnarzt; Zahnärztin
painting ['peɪntɪŋ]	Gemälde	bill [bɪl]	Rechnung
to dine [daɪn]	dinieren; zu Abend essen		

D An extract from Stephen King

to combine [kəm'baɪn]	kombinieren; verbinden	science fiction [ˌsaɪəns 'fɪkʃn]	Science-Fiction (Zukunftsdichtung)
psychological [ˌsaɪkl'ɒdʒɪkl]	psychologisch; psychisch	fictional ['fɪkʃnl]	fiktional; fiktiv
		Hollywood ['hɒliwʊd]	
thriller ['θrɪlə]	Thriller; spannender Krimi; Schauergeschichte	successful [sək'sesfl]	erfolgreich
		ninety ['naɪnti]	neunzig Grad Fahrenheit = ca. 32° Celsius

vocabulary
extra line

Holy Jeezum! (= Jesus) (infml) [ˌhəʊli ˈdʒiːzəm]	Heiliger Jesus!
to slap [slæp]	schlagen; einen Klaps geben
sweaty [ˈsweti]	verschwitzt
forehead [ˈfɒrɪd]	Stirn
sincere [sɪnˈsɪə]	aufrichtig
raisin [ˈreɪzn]	Rosine
folks (infml) [fəʊks]	Leute; Eltern
hand [hænd]	Blatt (beim Kartenspiel)
*to be on a mean streak [biːˌɒn ə ˌmiːn ˈstriːk]	schlecht drauf sein
Basic [ˈbeɪsɪk]	militärische Grundausbildung
PX [ˌpiːˈeks]	PX (Einkaufszentrum in der Kaserne)
army [ˈɑːmi]	Armee
instantly [ˈɪnstəntli]	sofort
coma [ˈkəʊmə]	Koma
funeral [ˈfjuːnrəl]	Beerdigung; Begräbnis
to knuckle [ˈnʌkl]	mit dem Knöchel zudrücken
to scrape [skreɪp]	kratzen; schürfen
acquaintance [əˈkweɪntnts]	Bekannte(r); Bekanntschaft
tormentor [tɔːˈmentə]	Peiniger(in)
alike [əˈlaɪk]	ähnlich
Fat lot of good it did them. [ˌfæt lɒt ˌəv ˈgʊd ɪt ˌdɪd ðəm]	Einen Dreck hat es ihnen genützt.
What are you pissing and moaning about? (infml) [ˌwɒt ə jə ˌpɪsɪŋ ənd ˈməʊnɪŋ əˌbaʊt]	Was machst du denn für ein Theater?
to crack [kræk]	zerbrechen; springen
case [keɪs]	Gehäuse
to tune [tjuːn]	einstellen; stimmen (ein Instrument)
to churn out [ˌtʃɜːnˈaʊt]	am laufenden Band produzieren
boss (infml) [bɒs]	cool
We switched some mental dial over to Mute. [wiː ˌswɪtʃt səm ˌmentl ˌdaɪəl ˌəʊvə tə ˈmjuːt]	Wir schalteten gedanklich ab.
happy horseshit (infml) [ˌhæpi ˈhɔːsʃɪt]	uninteressantes Zeug
to listen closely [ˌlɪsn ˈkləʊsli]	genau zuhören
to bust into [ˈbʌst ˌɪntə]	hereinplatzen in
county [ˈkaʊnti]	Landkreis
*to spread [spred]	(sich) verbreiten
the poor sucker [ˌpɔː ˈsʌkə]	das arme Schwein
to smother [ˈsmʌðə]	ersticken
gravel pit slide [ˈgrævl pɪt ˌslaɪd]	abrutschender Kies in einer Kiesgrube
brook [brʊk]	Bach
to drag the ponds [ˌdræg ðə ˈpɒndz]	die Teiche mit Netzen absuchen
reservoir [ˈrezəvwɑː]	Stausee
to suburbanize [səˈbɜːbnaɪz]	eingemeinden
bedroom community [ˌbedrʊm kəˈmjuːnəti]	Schlafstadt; reines Wohngebiet
tentacle [ˈtentəkl]	Tentakel; Fangarm
giant [dʒaɪənt]	riesig
squid [skwɪd]	Tintenfisch
consistent [kənˈsɪstnt]	konsistent, gleich bleibend
to cross [krɒs]	überqueren; kreuzen
two-lane [tuːˈleɪn]	zweispurig
blacktop [ˈblæktɒp]	Teerdecke
undeveloped [ˌʌndɪˈveləpt]	nicht entwickelt/erschlossen

E A theatre workshop

*to bend [bend]	beugen; biegen
weight [weɪt]	Gewicht
to tiptoe [ˈtɪptəʊ]	auf Zehenspitzen gehen
mime [maɪm]	Pantomime
syllable [ˈsɪləbl]	Silbe
to position [pəˈzɪʃn]	positionieren; aufstellen
to imitate [ˈɪmɪteɪt]	imitieren; nachahmen

F A sketch: Boogaloo

bar [bɑː]	Bar
gorgeous [ˈgɔːdʒəs]	hinreißend; wunderschön
close-up [ˈkləʊsʌp]	Nahaufnahme
*to speak up [ˌspiːkˈʌp]	lauter sprechen
to sniff [snɪf]	schnüffeln; schnuppern

dictionary

In dieser alphabetischen Liste ist das gesamte Vokabular von Green Line NEW Bayern I, II, III und IV enthalten, mit Ausnahme der nicht zum Lernwortschatz gehörenden Wörter aus Band I, II und III. Namen werden in gesonderten Listen nach dem Vokabular aufgeführt.
Die mit * gekennzeichneten Verben sind unregelmäßig (siehe S. 190). Die Wörter, deren Fundstellen in Spitzklammern stehen, gehören nicht zum aktiv zu beherrschenden Lernwortschatz.
Die Fundstellen verweisen auf den erstmalige Vorkommen der Wörter, z. B.
a(n) [ə; ən] ein(e) I kommt zum ersten Mal vor in Band I
address [əˈdres] Adresse II kommt zum ersten Mal vor in Band II
abroad [əˈbrɔːd] im/ins Ausland **IV F3, 90** kommt zum ersten Mal vor in Band IV, Focus 3, Seite 90
acquaintance [əˈkweɪntnts] Bekannte(r); Bekanntschaft ⟨IV EL, 100⟩ kommt zum ersten Mal vor in Band IV, Extra Line, Seite 100
F = Focus, U = Unit, EL = Extra Line

A

a(n) [ə; ən] ein(e) I
　a bit [ə ˈbɪt] ein bisschen I
　a few [ə ˈfjuː] einige, ein paar II
　a hundred [əˈhʌndrəd] hundert I
　a little [ə ˈlɪtl] ein bisschen IV F3, 91
　a lot of [ə ˈlɒt əv] viele, eine Menge I
　a pair of [ə ˈpeər əv] ein Paar I
　a week [ə ˈwiːk] pro Woche, in der Woche II
abbreviation [əˌbriːviˈeɪʃn] Abkürzung ⟨IV U2, 26⟩
able [ˈeɪbl] fähig, begabt II
　to be able to (do sth) [biː ˈeɪbl] fähig sein (zu); können; dürfen II
Aboriginal [ˌæbəˈrɪdʒnl] Ureinwohner(in) Australiens I
Aborigine [ˌæbəˈrɪdʒni] Ureinwohner(in) Australiens IV U1, 9
about [əˈbaʊt] ungefähr, circa, etwa II; herum; umher; hier in der Gegend IV U1, 10
　out and about [ˌaʊt ənd əˈbaʊt] unterwegs IV U3, 44
about [əˈbaʊt] über; wegen I
above [əˈbʌv] oben, über, oberhalb I
abroad [əˈbrɔːd] im/ins Ausland IV F3, 90
absolutely [ˌæbsəˈluːtli] absolut; völlig IV U2, 33
accent [ˈæksnt] Akzent II
to **accept** [əkˈsept] akzeptieren; annehmen IV F3, 91
accident [ˈæksɪdnt] Unfall II
accompaniment [əˈkʌmpnɪmənt] Begleitung ⟨IV U5, 78⟩
according to [əˈkɔːdɪŋ tə] laut, gemäß III
acoustic [əˈkuːstɪk] akustisch IV U3, 53
acquaintance [əˈkweɪntnts] Bekannte(r); Bekanntschaft ⟨IV EL, 100⟩
acrobat [ˈækrəbæt] Akrobat(in) II
across [əˈkrɒs] über, hinüber, quer durch/darüber II
*to get one's **act** together [ˌget wʌnz ˈækt təgeðə] sich am Riemen reißen III
to **act** [ækt] handeln; sich verhalten IV U1, 15
　to act something out [ˌækt sʌmθɪŋ ˈaʊt] etwas durchspielen I
action [ˈækʃn] Aktion, Handlung I

active [ˈæktɪv] aktiv; Aktiv III
activity [ækˈtɪvəti] Aktivität II
　activity centre [ækˈtɪvəti ˌsentə] Jugendzentrum II
actor [ˈæktə] Schauspieler(in) II
actually [ˈæktʃuəli] eigentlich; tatsächlich I
AD (= Anno Domini) [eɪˈdiː] nach Christus III
to **add** [æd] hinzufügen, addieren II
address [əˈdres] Adresse II
adjective [ˈædʒəktɪv] Adjektiv II
to **admire** [ədˈmaɪə] bewundern IV U3, 52
to **admit** [ədˈmɪt] zugeben III
adult [ˈædʌlt] Erwachsene(r) II
in **advance** [ɪn ədˈvɑːnts] im Voraus III
advantage [ədˈvɑːntɪdʒ] Vorteil III
adventure [ədˈventʃə] Abenteuer II
adverb [ˈædvɜːb] Adverb II
　adverb of manner [ˌædvɜːb əv ˈmænə] Adverb der Art und Weise II
advertisement [ədˈvɜːtɪsmənt] Anzeige; Werbespot IV F3, 90
advice [ədˈvaɪs] Rat III
to **advise (sb to do sth)** [ədˈvaɪz] (jmdm) raten III
*to be **afraid** (of) [biː əˈfreɪd] (sich) fürchten, Angst haben (vor) II
African [ˈæfrɪkən] afrikanisch; Afrikaner(in) I
after [ˈɑːftə] nach I
　after all [ˌɑːftər ˈɔːl] schließlich; immerhin IV U1, 18
after [ˈɑːftə] nachdem III
afternoon [ˌɑːftəˈnuːn] Nachmittag II
aftershave [ˈɑːftəʃeɪv] Aftershave, Rasierwasser III
afterwards [ˈɑːftəwədz] danach; hinterher IV U5, 80
again [əˈgen] wieder I
　again and again [əˈgen ənd əˈgen] immer wieder I
against [əˈgenst] gegen II
age [eɪdʒ] Alter; Zeitalter II
　for ages [fr ˈeɪdʒɪz] ewig lange III
　Middle Ages [ˌmɪdl ˈeɪdʒɪz] Mittelalter II
agent [ˈeɪdʒnt] Agent(in), Vertreter(in) II
　travel agent's [ˈtrævl ˌeɪdʒnts] Reisebüro II
ago [əˈgəʊ] vor (zeitlich) I

to **agree (with)** [əˈgriː] zustimmen, (mit jmdm) einer Meinung sein II
to **agree (on)** [əˈgriː] sich einigen (auf) II
ahead of [əˈhed əv] vor ⟨IV U1, 17⟩
aim [eɪm] Ziel II
to **aim at** [ˈeɪm ət] zielen auf, sich richten an III
air [eə] Luft I
airport [ˈeəpɔːt] Flughafen I
alarm [əˈlɑːm] Wecker III
alarm [əˈlɑːm] Alarm; Beunruhigung IV U3, 50
album [ˈælbəm] Album IV U3, 53
alien [ˈeɪliən] Fremde(r); Ausländer(in); Außerirdische(r) ⟨IV F3, 90⟩
alike [əˈlaɪk] ähnlich ⟨IV EL, 100⟩
*to be **alive** [biː əˈlaɪv] lebendig sein; leben I
all [ɔːl] alle(s); ganz I
　after all [ˌɑːftər ˈɔːl] schließlich; immerhin IV U1, 18
　all around [ˌɔːl əˈraʊnd] überall; rundherum; rings umher IV U1, 17
　all over [ˌɔːl ˈəʊvə] überall IV U3, 50
　all right [ˌɔːl ˈraɪt] in Ordnung; alles klar II
　all the time [ˌɔːl ðə ˈtaɪm] die ganze Zeit I
　at all [ət ˈɔːl] überhaupt II
　most of all [ˈməʊst əv ˌɔːl] am meisten II
allergic [æˈlɜːdʒɪk] allergisch II
bowling **alley** [ˈbəʊlɪŋ ˌæli] Bowlingbahn III
to **allow** [əˈlaʊ] erlauben, gestatten II
　to be allowed to (do sth) [biː əˈlaʊd] dürfen II
almost [ˈɔːlməʊst] fast, beinahe I
alone [əˈləʊn] alleine I
　to leave sb alone [ˌliːv əˈləʊn] jemanden in Ruhe lassen II
along [əˈlɒŋ] entlang IV U2, 32
alphabet [ˈælfəbet] Alphabet I
already [ɔːlˈredi] schon I
also [ˈɔːlsəʊ] auch I
although [ɔːlˈðəʊ] obwohl II
always [ˈɔːlweɪz] immer, ständig I
am [ˌeɪˈem] vormittags (Uhrzeit) I
amazed [əˈmeɪzd] erstaunt, verblüfft II
amazement [əˈmeɪzmənt] Erstaunen III
amazing [əˈmeɪzɪŋ] erstaunlich IV U2, 27
ambitious [æmˈbɪʃəs] ehrgeizig IV U5, 78

Dictionary

ambulance [ˈæmbjələnts] Krankenwagen III
American [əˈmerɪkən] amerikanisch; Amerikaner(in) I
    Native American [ˌneɪtɪv əˈmerɪkən] Ureinwohner(in) Amerikas, Indianer(in); indianisch II
to **amplify** [ˈæmplɪfaɪ] verstärken ⟨IV U5,76⟩
to **amuse** oneself [əˈmjuːz] sich amüsieren; sich die Zeit vertreiben III
and [ænd; ən(d)] und I
angel [ˈeɪndʒl] Engel III
anger [ˈæŋɡə] Zorn; Wut IV U4,69
angry [ˈæŋɡri] verärgert, böse I
animal [ˈænɪml] Tier I
annoyed [əˈnɔɪd] verärgert II
annoying [əˈnɔɪɪŋ] ärgerlich, lästig II
anorak [ˈænəræk] Anorak I
another [əˈnʌðə] noch ein(e); ein(e) andere(-r/-s) I
answer [ˈɑːntsə] Antwort I
    Don't take no for an answer. [ˌdəʊnt teɪk ˈnəʊ fər ən ˌɑːntsə] Akzeptiere keine Widerrede. ⟨IV U1,10⟩
to **answer** [ˈɑːntsə] (be)antworten I
any [ˈeni] irgendein(-e/-er); irgendwelche I
    not any better [ˌnɒt eni ˈbetə] (überhaupt) nicht besser II
    not any more [ˌnɒt eni ˈmɔː] nicht mehr II
anybody [ˈeniˌbɒdi] irgendjemand; jeder (beliebige) II
anyone [ˈeniwʌn] irgendjemand; jeder (beliebige) II
anything [ˈeniθɪŋ] irgendetwas II
anyway [ˈeniweɪ] jedenfalls, sowieso II
anywhere [ˈeniweə] irgendwo; überall (egal, wo) II
apart [əˈpɑːt] auseinander; abseits ⟨IV U1,15⟩
apart from [əˈpɑːt frəm] außer, abgesehen von I
apartment (AE) [əˈpɑːtmənt] Apartment, Wohnung I
to **apologise** [əˈpɒlədʒaɪz] sich entschuldigen IV F3,91
apparently [əˈpærntli] anscheinend IV U5,78
to **appear** [əˈpɪə] erscheinen III
appetite [ˈæpɪtaɪt] Appetit II
apple [ˈæpl] Apfel I
to **appreciate** [əˈpriːʃieɪt] schätzen; anerkennen IV U5,77
April [ˈeɪprl] April I
archaeology [ˌɑːkiˈɒlədʒi] Archäologie II
archery [ˈɑːtʃri] Bogenschießen II
architecture [ˈɑːkɪtektʃə] Architektur ⟨IV F1,23⟩
area [ˈeəriə] Areal; Fläche; Gebiet III
to **argue** [ˈɑːɡjuː] argumentieren; streiten ⟨IV U1,15⟩
argument [ˈɑːɡjəmənt] Argument; Streit II
arm [ɑːm] Arm I
army [ˈɑːmi] Armee ⟨IV EL,100⟩
around [əˈraʊnd] herum, umher I
all around [ˌɔːl əˈraʊnd] überall; rundherum; rings umher IV U1,17
to **hang around** [ˌhæŋ əˈraʊnd] herumhängen II
to **arrange** [əˈreɪndʒ] ausmachen; arrangieren III
arrangement [əˈreɪndʒmənt] Vereinbarung; Arrangement; Plan IV U3,44
to **arrest** [əˈrest] festnehmen; verhaften IV U4,70
arrival [əˈraɪvl] Ankunft III
to **arrive** (at) [əˈraɪv] ankommen I
arrow [ˈærəʊ] Pfeil II
art [ɑːt] Kunst II
    arts and crafts [ˌɑːts nd ˈkrɑːfts] Kunsthandwerk II
article [ˈɑːtɪkl] Artikel (in der Zeitung, etc.) I
as [æz; əz] als II
    as … as [æz; əz] so … wie … II
    as a result of [əz ə rɪˈzʌlt əv] infolge (von) III
    as far as [əz ˈfɑːr əz] bis III
    as soon as [əz ˈsuːn əz] sobald III
    as well [əz ˈwel] auch III
as [æz] da; weil IV U1,8
ash [æʃ] Asche III
Asian [ˈeɪʃn] asiatisch; Asiat(in) II
as if [əz ˈɪf] als ob III
to **ask** [ɑːsk] fragen I
    to ask (for) [ɑːsk] bitten (um) II
aspect [ˈæspekt] Aspekt II
Assembly [əˈsembli] Versammlung; Morgenappell I
assignment (AE) [əˈsaɪnmənt] Aufgabe II
assistant [əˈsɪstnt] Assistent(in) I
    shop assistant [ˈʃɒp əˌsɪstnt] Verkäufer(in) I
to **assume** [əˈsjuːm; əˈsuːm] annehmen; voraussetzen IV U3,46
at [æt; ət] in, auf, bei, an I
    at all [ət ˈɔːl] überhaupt II
    at first [ət ˈfɜːst] zuerst; zunächst II
    at home [ət ˈhəʊm] zu Hause I
    at last [ət ˈlɑːst] endlich I
    at least [ət ˈliːst] mindestens, wenigstens II
    at once [ət ˈwʌns] sofort, plötzlich I
    at the Burtons' [ət ðə ˈbɜːtnz] bei den Burtons II
    at the seaside [ət ðə ˈsiːsaɪd] am Meer I
athlete [ˈæθliːt] (Leicht-)Athlet(in) III
athletic [æθˈletɪk] athletisch II
Atishoo! [əˈtʃuː] Hatschi! II
attack [əˈtæk] Angriff; Anfall ⟨IV U1,15⟩
to **attack** [əˈtæk] angreifen I
attitude (to/towards) [ˈætɪtjuːd] Haltung; Einstellung II
to **attract** [əˈtrækt] anziehen III
attraction [əˈtrækʃn] Attraktion, Sehenswürdigkeit I
attractive [əˈtræktɪv] attraktiv III
audience [ˈɔːdiənts] Publikum III
audition [ɔːˈdɪʃn] Vorsprechen; Vorsingen; Vortanzen; Probespiel ⟨IV U5,78⟩
to **audition** [ɔːˈdɪʃn] vorsprechen; vorsingen; vortanzen; vorspielen ⟨IV U5,78⟩
August [ˈɔːɡəst] August I
aunt [ɑːnt] Tante I
au pair [ˌəʊˈpeə] Au-pair(-Mädchen) IV F3,90
Aussie (infml) [ˈɒzi] Australier(in) ⟨IV U1,9⟩
Australian [ˈɒstreɪliən] australisch; Australier(in) I
authentic [ɔːˈθentɪk] authentisch IV U5,76
author [ˈɔːθə] Autor(in) III
autograph [ˈɔːtəɡrɑːf] Autogramm II
autumn [ˈɔːtəm] Herbst II
an average of [ən ˈævrɪdʒ əv] durchschnittlich; im Durchschnitt III
average [ˈævrɪdʒ] durchschnittlich III
*to **awake** [əˈweɪk] erwachen; aufwachen ⟨IV EL,99⟩
*to **be aware of** [biː əˈweə] sich … bewusst sein IV U5,82
away [əˈweɪ] weg (von) I
    right away [raɪt əˈweɪ] sofort, gleich I
awful [ˈɔːfl] schrecklich, furchtbar III

B

baby [ˈbeɪbi] Baby, Säugling II
    to have a baby [ˌhæv ə ˈbeɪbi] ein Kind bekommen IV F2,56
back [bæk] Rücken I
back [bæk] Hinter-, rückwärtig II
back [bæk] zurück I
background [ˈbækɡraʊnd] Hintergrund II
backpack [ˈbækpæk] Rucksack III
backstage [bækˈsteɪdʒ] backstage, hinter der Bühne II
bacon [ˈbeɪkn] Schinkenspeck II
bad [bæd] schlecht I
    to be in a bad way [ɪn ə ˈbæd ˌweɪ] in schlechter Verfassung sein I
    to make matters worse [tə ˌmeɪk mætəz ˈwɜːs] zu allem Überfluss; um es noch schlimmer zu machen IV U2,29
bag [bæɡ] Tasche I; Sack II
    mixed bag [ˌmɪkst ˈbæɡ] buntes Allerlei I
    school bag [ˈskuːl bæɡ] Schultasche I
    sleeping bag [ˈsliːpɪŋ ˌbæɡ] Schlafsack III
bagpipes pl. [ˈbæɡpaɪps] Dudelsack IV U3,42
to **bake** [beɪk] backen III
ball [bɔːl] Ball I
    bowling ball [ˈbəʊlɪŋ ˌbɔːl] Bowlingkugel III
    golf ball [ˈɡɒlf ˌbɔːl] Golfball III
banana [bəˈnɑːnə] Banane III
band [bænd] Band, Kapelle II
bandage [ˈbændɪdʒ] Bandage; Verband III
bank [bæŋk] Bank II
bar [bɑː] Tafel; Riegel; Stück; Stange I; Bar ⟨IV EL,103⟩
barbecue [ˈbɑːbɪkjuː] Grill(party) IV U1,10
barbie (infml) [ˈbɑːbi] Grill(party) ⟨IV U1,10⟩
to **bark** (at) [bɑːk] (an)bellen I
barrel [ˈbærl] Fass, Tonne II
barrier [ˈbæriə] Barriere, Sperre III
baseball [ˈbeɪsbɔːl] Baseball I
    baseball bat [ˈbeɪsbɔːl ˌbæt] Baseballschläger III

dictionary D

baseball field ['beɪsbɔːl ˌfiːld] Baseballplatz III
basic ['beɪsɪk] grundlegend, Grund-, einfach II
Basic ['beɪsɪk] militärische Grundausbildung ⟨IV EL, 100⟩
basket ['bɑːskɪt] Korb, Körbchen I
basketball ['bɑːskɪtbɔːl] Basketball II
basketball court ['bɑːskɪtbɔːl ˌkɔːt] Basketballplatz III
bass [beɪs] Bass II
bat [bæt] Schläger (Tischtennis-, Baseball-); Fledermaus II
baseball bat ['beɪsbɔːl ˌbæt] Baseballschläger II
bath [bɑːθ] Bad I
bathroom ['bɑːθrʊm] Badezimmer I; Toilette (AE) IV U4, 63
battery ['bætri] Batterie, Akku II
battle ['bætl] Schlacht III
bay [beɪ] Bucht IV U2, 24
bazaar [bə'zɑː] Bazar II
BC (= before Christ) [biː'siː] vor Christus III
*to be [biː] sein I
  to be able to (do sth) [biː ˈeɪbl] fähig sein (zu); können; dürfen II
  to be afraid (of) [biː əˈfreɪd] (sich) fürchten, Angst haben (vor) II
  to be alive [biː əˈlaɪv] lebendig sein; leben I
  to be allowed to (do sth) [biː əˈlaʊd] dürfen II
  to be as hungry as a horse [əz ˌhʌŋɡri əz ə ˈhɔːs] einen Bärenhunger haben II
  to be aware of [biː əˈweə] sich … bewusst sein IV U5, 82
  to be better [biː ˈbetə] sich besser fühlen; wieder gesund sein IV U3, 51
  to be born [biː ˈbɔːn] geboren werden II
  to be called [biː ˈkɔːld] heißen, genannt werden II
  to be crazy about [biː ˈkreɪzi əˌbaʊt] verrückt sein nach; abfahren auf IV U4, 60
  to be fast [biː ˈfɑːst] vorgehen III
  to be frightened (of) [biː ˈfraɪtnd] Angst haben (vor) I
  to be going on [biː ˌɡəʊɪŋ ˈɒn] los sein II
  to be gone [biː ˈɡɒn] verschwunden sein II
  to be good at [biː ˈɡʊd ˌæt] gut sein in I
  to be hurt [biː ˈhɜːt] verletzt sein/werden I
  to be in a bad way [ɪn ə ˈbæd ˌweɪ] in schlechter Verfassung sein I
  to be in love (with) [ˌbiː ɪn ˈlʌv] verliebt sein (in) II
  to be interested in [biː ˈɪntrəstɪd ˌɪn] interessiert sein an, sich interessieren für I
  to be keen on [biː ˈkiːn ˌɒn] scharf sein auf, begeistert sein von II
  to be known as [biː ˈnəʊn ˌæz] bekannt sein als III
  to be late [biː ˈleɪt] zu spät dran sein, zu spät kommen I
  to be likely (to) [biː ˈlaɪkli] wahrscheinlich sein IV U1, 14
  to be located [biː ləʊˈkeɪtɪd] gelegen sein II
  to be lucky [biː ˈlʌki] Glück haben I
  to be made of [biː ˈmeɪd ˌɒv] hergestellt sein aus II
  to be married to [biː ˈmærɪd tə] verheiratet sein mit I
  to be on [biː ˈɒn] im Gange sein, laufen I
  to be on a mean streak [biː ɒn ə ˌmiːn ˈstriːk] schlecht drauf sein III
  to be on a team [ˌbiː ɒn ə ˈtiːm] Mitglied eines Teams sein III
  to be out of one's mind [biː ˌaʊt əv wʌnz ˈmaɪnd] verrückt sein III
  to be pleased [biː ˈpliːzd] erfreut sein III
  to be sb's cup of tea [ˌkʌp əv ˈtiː] jmds Fall sein ⟨IV F3, 91⟩
  to be scared [biː ˈskeəd] Angst haben, erschrocken sein I
  to be sick [biː ˈsɪk] sich übergeben IV U3, 50
  to be sick with worry [biː ˈsɪk wɪð ˌwʌri] krank vor Sorge sein ⟨IV U4, 69⟩
  to be stuck [biː ˈstʌk] stecken bleiben, festklemmen II
  to be surprised [biː səˈpraɪzd] überrascht sein I
  to be tired of (+ gerund) [biː ˈtaɪəd] es müde/leid sein/satt haben, etwas zu tun IV U4, 60
  to be trapped [biː ˈtræpt] in der Falle sitzen III
  to be unlikely (to) [biː ʌnˈlaɪkli] unwahrscheinlich sein IV U1, 14
  to be used to (+ gerund) [biː ˈjuːzt tə] gewöhnt sein an; gewohnt sein IV U4, 60
  to be worried [biː ˈwʌrid] besorgt, beunruhigt sein I
  to be worth (+ gerund) [biː ˈwɜːθ] (es) wert sein (zu) IV U4, 63
  to be wrong [biː ˈrɒŋ] Unrecht haben II
beach [biːtʃ] Strand I
bear [beə] Bär II
  black bear [ˌblæk ˈbeə] Schwarzbär II
  teddy bear [ˈtedi ˌbeə] Teddybär III
beat [biːt] Schlag; Takt; Hebung ⟨IV EL, 99⟩
*to beat [biːt] besiegen; schlagen I
beautiful [ˈbjuːtɪfl] wunderschön, hübsch I
because [bɪˈkɒz] weil I
  because of [bɪˈkɒz ˌəv] wegen IV U4, 58
*to become [bɪˈkʌm] werden II
bed [bed] Bett I
  bed and breakfast [ˌbed n ˈbrekfəst] Zimmer mit Frühstück I
bedroom [ˈbedrʊm] Schlafzimmer I
  bedroom community [ˌbedrʊm kəˈmjuːnəti] Schlafstadt; reines Wohngebiet ⟨IV EL, 101⟩
beef [biːf] Rindfleisch III
beer [bɪə] Bier II
before [bɪˈfɔː] vorher; zuvor; schon einmal II
before [bɪˈfɔː] vor I
before [bɪˈfɔː] bevor I
to beg (for) [beɡ] betteln (um); anflehen IV F2, 56
*to begin [bɪˈɡɪn] beginnen; anfangen III
beginning [bɪˈɡɪnɪŋ] Anfang, Beginn I
to behave [bɪˈheɪv] sich verhalten, sich benehmen II
behind [bɪˈhaɪnd] hinten; im Rückstand III
behind [bɪˈhaɪnd] hinter II
belief [bɪˈliːf] Glaube ⟨IV EL, 96⟩
to believe [bɪˈliːv] glauben II
bell [bel] Glocke II
below [bɪˈləʊ] unterhalb, unten I
*to bend [bend] beugen; biegen ⟨IV EL, 102⟩
  to bend over [ˌbend ˈəʊvə] sich vorbeugen II
best [best] beste(-r/-s) I
*to bet [bet] wetten III
better [ˈbetə] besser I
between [bɪˈtwiːn] zwischen II
  in between [ˌɪn bɪˈtwiːn] dazwischen II
beyond [bɪˈɒnd] jenseits IV U5, 77
bible [ˈbaɪbl] Bibel IV F1, 23
big [bɪɡ] groß; dick I
bike [baɪk] Fahrrad I
biking [ˈbaɪkɪŋ] Radfahren II
  mountain biking [ˈmaʊntɪn ˌbaɪkɪŋ] Mountainbikefahren II
bill (AE) [bɪl] Banknote; Geldschein IV U4, 70
bill [bɪl] Rechnung ⟨IV EL, 99⟩
biology [baɪˈɒlədʒi] Biologie II
biome [ˈbaɪəʊm] Biom (biologischer Lebensraum von Pflanzen und Tieren) ⟨IV U2, 27⟩
bird [bɜːd] Vogel I
biro [ˈbaɪərəʊ] Kugelschreiber, Kuli I
birthday [ˈbɜːθdeɪ] Geburtstag I
birthplace [ˈbɜːθpleɪs] Geburtsort IV U2, 24
biscuit [ˈbɪskɪt] Keks II
a bit [ə ˈbɪt] ein bisschen I
*to bite [baɪt] beißen; stechen IV U1, 13
bitter [ˈbɪtə] bitter II
black [blæk] schwarz I
  black bear [ˌblæk ˈbeə] Schwarzbär II
blackboard, board [ˈblækbɔːd; ˌbɔːd] Tafel I
blacktop [ˈblæktɒp] Teerdecke ⟨IV EL, 101⟩
to blame [bleɪm] verantwortlich machen; beschuldigen IV U3, 46
blanket [ˈblæŋkɪt] (Woll-)Decke II
bless you [ˈbles ju:] Gesundheit! II
blind [blaɪnd] Jalousie; Sonnenblende IV U4, 68
to blind [blaɪnd] blenden IV U5, 78
blind [blaɪnd] blind III
block [blɒk] (Häuser-)Block IV U4, 69
blonde [blɒnd] blond I
blood [blʌd] Blut III
blow [bləʊ] Hieb, Schlag III
*to blow [bləʊ] blasen III
  to blow a whistle [ˌbləʊ ə ˈwɪsl] auf einer Trillerpfeife pfeifen III
blue [bluː] blau I
blues [bluːz] Blues III
board [bɔːd] Brett ⟨IV U1, 15⟩; IV F2, 57
  board, blackboard [ˈblækbɔːd; ˌbɔːd] Tafel I
  counter board [ˈkaʊntə ˌbɔːd] Zählbrett; Rechenbrett ⟨IV F2, 57⟩

Dictionary

to **board** [bɔːd] an Bord gehen, besteigen II
boarding pass [ˈbɔːdɪŋ ˌpɑːs] Bordkarte II
boastful [ˈbəʊstfl] prahlerisch ⟨IV EL, 96⟩
boat [bəʊt] Boot, Schiff I
body [ˈbɒdi] Körper I
to **boil** [bɔɪl] kochen III
bone [bəʊn] Knochen III
book [bʊk] Buch; Heft I
    exercise book [ˈeksəsaɪz ˌbʊk] Übungsheft I
to **book** [bʊk] buchen, reservieren II
booklet [ˈbʊklət] Broschüre; Heft IV U5, 84
bookshop [ˈbʊkʃɒp] Buchhandlung I
boomerang [ˈbuːmræŋ] Bumerang ⟨IV U1, 13⟩
boot [buːt] Stiefel II
booth [buːð] Bude; Stand ⟨IV U4, 69⟩
    phone booth (AE) [ˈfəʊn ˌbuːð] Telefonzelle IV U4, 69
booze (infml) [buːz] Alkohol IV U3, 50
border [ˈbɔːdə] Grenze IV F2, 57
bored [bɔːd] gelangweilt II
boring [ˈbɔːrɪŋ] langweilig I
*to be **born** [biː ˈbɔːn] geboren werden II
to **borrow** [ˈbɒrəʊ] (sich) ausleihen III
boss [bɒs] Boss, Chef II
boss (infml) [bɒs] cool ⟨IV EL, 101⟩
both [bəʊθ] beide I
    both … and … [ˈbəʊθ … ænd] sowohl … als auch … IV U5, 80
bottle [ˈbɒtl] Flasche I
bottom [ˈbɒtəm] Boden; Grund; unterer Teil IV U2, 32
bow [bəʊ] Bogen II
bowl [bəʊl] Schale, Schälchen I
bowling alley [ˈbəʊlɪŋ ˌæli] Bowlingbahn III
    bowling ball [ˈbəʊlɪŋ ˌbɔːl] Bowlingkugel III
box [bɒks] Kiste, Schachtel; Kasten I
boy [bɔɪ] Junge I
boyfriend [ˈbɔɪfrend] Freund I
branch [brɑːntʃ] Zweig, Ast III
brass [brɑːs] Messing IV U4, 69
brave [breɪv] tapfer, mutig I
bread [bred] Brot II
break [breɪk] Pause; Bruch II
    to give sb a break [ˌgɪv əˈbreɪk] jmdm eine Chance geben ⟨IV U5, 78⟩
    to take a break [ˌteɪk ə ˈbreɪk] Pause machen II
*to **break** [breɪk] (zer)brechen; kaputtmachen II
    breaking point [ˈbreɪkɪŋ ˌpɔɪnt] Schmerzgrenze; kritischer Punkt ⟨IV U3, 46⟩
    to break in [breɪk ˈɪn] einlaufen; einreiten II
    to break in(to) [breɪk ˈɪn] einbrechen (in) IV U1, 11
breakfast [ˈbrekfəst] Frühstück I
    bed and breakfast [ˌbed n ˈbrekfəst] Zimmer mit Frühstück I
breath [breθ] Atem; Atemzug III
to **breathe** [briːð] atmen III
bridge [brɪdʒ] Brücke I
brief [briːf] kurz III

bright [braɪt] leuchtend, strahlend II
brilliant [ˈbrɪljənt] toll, prima; leuchtend I
*to **bring** [brɪŋ] bringen I
Made in **Britain** [ˌmeɪd ɪn ˈbrɪtn] Hergestellt in Großbritannien I
British [ˈbrɪtɪʃ] britisch I
Briton [ˈbrɪtn] Brite, Britin III
broad [brɔːd] breit II
brochure [ˈbrəʊʃə] Broschüre, Prospekt II
brook [brʊk] Bach ⟨IV EL, 101⟩
brother [ˈbrʌðə] Bruder I
brown [braʊn] braun I
to **brush** [brʌʃ] putzen ⟨IV EL, 99⟩
bubble [ˈbʌbl] Blase IV U2, 34
budgie [ˈbʌdʒi] Wellensittich I
buggy [ˈbʌgi] Buggy (leichter Kinderwagen) ⟨IV U3, 50⟩
*to **build** [bɪld] bauen III
building [ˈbɪldɪŋ] Gebäude I
bull's-eye [ˈbʊlsˌaɪ] Mittelpunkt der Zielscheibe II
bully [ˈbʊli] Rabauke, Rüpel, Tyrann II
*to give somebody the **bumps** [ˌgɪv ðə ˈbʌmps] jemanden hochwerfen und wieder auffangen I
to **bump** [bʌmp] (an)stoßen, stoßen I
bumpy [ˈbʌmpi] holprig II
bun [bʌn] Brötchen II
burger [ˈbɜːgə] Hamburger I
*to **burn** [bɜːn] (ver)brennen II
*to **burst** [bɜːst] bersten; platzen IV U4, 68
at the **Burtons'** [ət ðə ˈbɜːtnz] bei den Burtons II
bus [bʌs] Bus I
    by (bus) [baɪ] mit (dem Bus), per I
bush [bʊʃ] Busch, Strauch I
business [ˈbɪznɪs] Geschäft; Branche I
    on business [ɒn ˈbɪznɪs] geschäftlich I
to **bust** into [ˈbʌst ˌɪntə] hereinplatzen in ⟨IV EL, 101⟩
busy [ˈbɪzi] beschäftigt; belebt; voller Menschen I
but [bʌt; bət] aber I
butter [ˈbʌtə] Butter II
*to **buy** [baɪ] kaufen I
by [baɪ] von I; bei; an I; bis III
    by (bus) [baɪ] mit (dem Bus), per I
    by clapping your hands [baɪ ˌklæpɪŋ jə ˈhændz] indem ihr in die Hände klatscht ⟨IV EL, 99⟩
    by mistake [ˌbaɪ mɪˈsteɪk] versehentlich III
    by oneself [ˌbaɪ wʌnˈself] allein III
    by the way [ˌbaɪ ðə ˈweɪ] übrigens III
Bye! [baɪ] Tschüss! I

C

cabin [ˈkæbɪn] Hütte IV F2, 56
cable [ˈkeɪbl] Kabel III
cactus [ˈkæktəs] Kaktus III
café [ˈkæfeɪ] Café I
cake [keɪk] Kuchen I
calendar [ˈkæləndə] Kalender I
calf, pl. **calves** [kɑːf; kɑːvz] Kalb II
Californian [ˌkælɪˈfɔːniən] kalifornisch ⟨IV U2, 27⟩

call [kɔːl] Anruf I; Ruf III
to **call** [kɔːl] (an)rufen; Bescheid geben I; nennen II
    to be called [biː ˈkɔːld] heißen, genannt werden II
    to call sb names [ˌkɔːl sʌmbɒdi ˈneɪmz] beschimpfen IV U3, 50
callback [ˈkɔːlbæk] Rückruf ⟨IV U5, 80⟩
caller [ˈkɔːlə] Anrufer(in) I
calling [ˈkɔːlɪŋ] Berufung ⟨IV U5, 76⟩
camel [ˈkæml] Kamel ⟨IV U1, 8⟩
camera [ˈkæmrə] Kamera, Fotoapparat I
camp [kæmp] Camp; Lager III
to **camp** [kæmp] campen, zelten, kampieren II
campfire [ˈkæmpfaɪə] Lagerfeuer III
camping [ˈkæmpɪŋ] Camping, Zelten II
campsite [ˈkæmpsaɪt] Campingplatz, Zeltplatz III
can [kæn; kən] kann, können I
    can't [kɑːnt] nicht können I
to **cancel** [ˈkænsl] absagen; stornieren IV U5, 81
candidate [ˈkændɪdət] Kandidat(in) IV U5, 80
candle [ˈkændl] Kerze I
candy (AE) [ˈkændi] Süßigkeiten II
canoeing [kəˈnuːɪŋ] Kanufahren II
canyon [ˈkænjən] Canyon II
cap [kæp] Kappe, Mütze II
capital [ˈkæpɪtl] Hauptstadt I
captain [ˈkæptɪn] Kapitän; Mannschaftsführer(in) II
caption [ˈkæpʃn] Untertitel; Bildunterschrift III
car [kɑː] Auto I
    car park [ˈkɑː ˌpɑːk] Parkplatz; Parkhaus IV U1, 11
card [kɑːd] Karte I
    Valentine's card [ˈvæləntaɪnz ˌkɑːd] Valentinskarte III
to **care** (about) [keə] sich kümmern (um); sich interessieren (für); wichtig nehmen IV U5, 76
careful [ˈkeəfl] vorsichtig; sorgfältig II
caretaker (BE) [ˈkeəˌteɪkə] Hausmeister(in) III
cargo, pl. **cargoes** [ˈkɑːgəʊ] Ladung, Fracht IV U2, 32
Caribbean [ˌkærɪˈbiːən; kəˈrɪbiən] karibisch III
carnival [ˈkɑːnɪvl] Karneval III
to **carry** [ˈkæri] tragen I
cart [kɑːt] Karren IV U2, 33
carton [ˈkɑːtn] Karton (Verbundverpackung) III
cartoon [kɑːˈtuːn] Cartoon; Zeichentrickfilm I
case [keɪs] Gehäuse ⟨IV EL, 101⟩
    in case [ɪn ˈkeɪs] falls; für den Fall, dass … II
    pencil case [ˈpensl ˌkeɪs] Federmäppchen I
casting [ˈkɑːstɪŋ] Casting; Rollenbesetzung ⟨IV U5, 80⟩
castle [ˈkɑːsl] Schloss; Burg I
cat [kæt] Katze I

dictionary D

*to **catch** [kætʃ] fangen II
*to **catch fire** [ˌkætʃ ˈfaɪə] Feuer fangen IV U3, 50
Catholic [ˈkæθlɪk] Katholik(in) IV F1, 23
cattle (pl. only) [ˈkætl] (Rind-)Vieh II
   cattle drive [ˈkætl ˌdraɪv] Viehtrieb II
to **cause** [kɔːz] verursachen III
cave [keɪv] Höhle IV U2, 32
CD [siːˈdiː] CD I
   CD player [ˌsiːˈdiː ˌpleɪə] CD-Spieler I
   CD-ROM [ˌsiːdiːˈrɒm] CD-ROM III
ceiling [ˈsiːlɪŋ] (Zimmer-)Decke I
to **celebrate** [ˈseləbreɪt] feiern II
celebration [ˌseləˈbreɪʃn] Feier II
cellphone (AE) [ˈselfəʊn] Handy, Mobiltelefon III
Celtic [ˈkeltɪk; ˈseltɪk] keltisch II
centre [ˈsentə] Zentrum I
   activity centre [ækˈtɪvəti ˌsentə] Jugendzentrum II
   city centre [ˌsɪti ˈsentə] Stadtzentrum, Stadtmitte I
   shopping centre [ˈʃɒpɪŋ ˌsentə] Einkaufszentrum I
century [ˈsentʃri] Jahrhundert III
cereal [ˈsɪəriəl] Zerealie; Getreideprodukt (z. B. Cornflakes oder Müsli) III
ceremony [ˈserɪməni] Zeremonie ⟨IV F1, 23⟩
certain [ˈsɜːtn] bestimmt; sicher III
chair [tʃeə] Stuhl I
champion [ˈtʃæmpiən] Gewinner; Champion I
chance [tʃɑːnts] Chance, Möglichkeit, Gelegenheit II
change [tʃeɪndʒ] Wechsel, Änderung II
   for a change [fərˌə ˈtʃeɪndʒ] zur Abwechslung IV U3, 44
to **change** [tʃeɪndʒ] tauschen, wechseln; (sich) ändern I; umsteigen III
   to change sth into sth [tʃeɪndʒ] in … verwandeln II
   changing room [ˈtʃeɪndʒɪŋ ˌrʊm] Umkleideraum III
   to change one's mind [tʃeɪndʒ] seine Meinung ändern II
channel [ˈtʃænl] Kanal; Programm III
chaos [ˈkeɪɒs] Chaos; Durcheinander II
character [ˈkærəktə] Charakter, Figur II
characteristic [ˌkærəktəˈrɪstɪk] typisches Merkmal IV U1, 19
to **charge sb a sum of money** [tʃɑːdʒ] jmdm einen Geldbetrag in Rechnung stellen IV U5, 81
charity [ˈtʃærəti] Wohltätigkeitsverein; tätige Nächstenliebe II
to **chase** [tʃeɪs] verfolgen, jagen I
chatroom [ˈtʃætrʊm] Chatroom (Internetforum, wo man sich online unterhalten kann) III
cheap [tʃiːp] billig III
to **check** [tʃek] (über)prüfen; kontrollieren I
   Let's check! [lets ˈtʃek] Lass(t) uns überprüfen! I
   spell checker [ˈspel ˌtʃekə] Rechtschreibprüfprogramm ⟨IV U5, 82⟩

check-in [ˈtʃekɪn] Gepäckaufgabe II
cheer [tʃɪə] Jubel III
to **cheer** [tʃɪə] (zu)jubeln, anfeuern II
cheerleader [ˈtʃɪəˌliːdə] Cheerleader (Mädchen, das in einer Gruppe eine Sportmannschaft anfeuert) III
cheerleading [ˈtʃɪəliːdɪŋ] Cheerleading (Aktivitäten der Cheerleader) III
Cheers! [tʃɪəz] Prost! IV U2, 29
cheese [tʃiːz] Käse I
chest [tʃest] Kiste, Truhe IV U2, 34
chewing gum [ˈtʃuːɪŋ ˌɡʌm] Kaugummi IV U3, 49
chick [tʃɪk] Küken I
chicken [ˈtʃɪkɪn] Huhn, Hähnchen I
chief [tʃiːf] Häuptling II
   chief protector [ˌtʃiːf prəˈtektə] oberste(r) Beschützer(in) ⟨IV U1, 19⟩
child, pl. **children** [tʃaɪld; ˈtʃɪldrn] Kind I
Chinese [tʃaɪˈniːz] chinesisch; Chinese, Chinesin II
chip (AE) [tʃɪp] Kartoffelchip I
   chips pl. (BE) [tʃɪps] Pommes frites I
   fish and chips [ˌfɪʃ n̩ ˈtʃɪps] Fisch und Pommes frites I
chocolate [ˈtʃɒklət] Schokolade I
*to **choose** [tʃuːz] (aus)wählen I
chorus [ˈkɔːrəs] Refrain IV U5, 85
Christian [ˈkrɪstʃən] Christ(in) II
chuck [tʃʌk] werfen ⟨IV U4, 67⟩
church [tʃɜːtʃ] Kirche I
churchyard [ˈtʃɜːtʃjɑːd] Kirchhof; Friedhof IV U3, 55
to **churn out** [ˌtʃɜːn ˈaʊt] am laufenden Band produzieren ⟨IV EL, 101⟩
cider [ˈsaɪdə] Apfelwein ⟨IV U2, 24⟩
cigarette [ˌsɪɡrˈet] Zigarette IV U3, 50
cinema [ˈsɪnəmə] Kino I
circle [ˈsɜːkl] Kreis I
to **circle** [ˈsɜːkl] kreisen IV U1, 16
citrus fruit [ˈsɪtrəs ˌfruːt] Zitrusfrucht IV U2, 27
city [ˈsɪti] Stadt; Großstadt I
   city centre [ˌsɪti ˈsentə] Stadtzentrum, Stadtmitte I
civilization [ˌsɪvəlaɪˈzeɪʃn] Zivilisation IV U2, 27
to **clap** [klæp] klatschen I
   by clapping your hands [baɪ ˌklæpɪŋ jə ˈhændz] indem ihr in die Hände klatscht ⟨IV EL, 99⟩
class [klɑːs] Schulklasse, Klasse I; Kurs, Unterricht II
   in class [ɪn ˈklɑːs] in/vor der Klasse I
classroom [ˈklɑːsrʊm] Klassenzimmer I
clause [klɔːz] Satz (Teil eines Satzgefüges) II
   contact clause [ˈkɒntækt ˌklɔːz] Relativsatz ohne Relativpronomen II
   relative clause [ˌrelətɪv ˈklɔːz] Relativsatz II
   subordinate clause [səˌbɔːdnət ˈklɔːz] Nebensatz ⟨IV U5, 81⟩
clay-pit [ˈkleɪpɪt] Lehmgrube ⟨IV U2, 24⟩
to **clean** [kliːn] säubern, reinigen I
clean [kliːn] sauber III
cleaner [ˈkliːnə] Raumpfleger(in), Putzkraft III

clear [klɪə] klar II
clerihew [ˈklerɪhjuː] Clerihew (bestimmte Form eines vierzeiligen Gedichts) ⟨IV EL, 98⟩
clerk [klɑːk; klɜːrk] Angestellte(r) III
clever [ˈklevə] schlau, klug, intelligent II
cliff [klɪf] Klippe; Kliff IV U2, 24
climate [ˈklaɪmət] Klima III
to **climb** [klaɪm] klettern, (be)steigen II
*to **cling** (to) [klɪŋ] sich festhalten (an), sich festklammern (an) II
video **clip** [ˈvɪdiəʊ klɪp] Videoclip III
clock [klɒk] Uhr III
   o'clock [əˈklɒk] Uhr (Zeitangabe bei vollen Stunden) I
close [kləʊs] eng, knapp II
   close (to) [kləʊs] nahe (bei) III
   to listen closely [ˌlɪsn ˈkləʊsli] genau zuhören ⟨IV EL, 101⟩
closed [kləʊzd] geschlossen I
close-up [ˈkləʊsʌp] Nahaufnahme ⟨IV EL, 103⟩
clothes pl. [kləʊðz] Kleider, Kleidung I
clothing [ˈkləʊðɪŋ] Kleidung III
cloud [klaʊd] Wolke I
club [klʌb] Club, Verein II
   golf club [ˈɡɒlf ˌklʌb] Golfschläger III
   health club [ˈhelθ klʌb] Fitnessklub III
clue [kluː] Hinweis, Spur, Schlüssel II
CO [ˌkɒlrˈɑːdəʊ] Colorado (Abkürzung) II
coach [kəʊtʃ] Reisebus III; Trainer(in) III
coal [kəʊl] Kohle II
coast [kəʊst] Küste I
coastguard [ˈkəʊstɡɑːd] Küstenwache ⟨IV U2, 29⟩
coat [kəʊt] Mantel II
cobbled [ˈkɒbld] mit Kopfsteinpflaster gepflastert ⟨IV U4, 69⟩
cocoa [ˈkəʊkəʊ] Kakao IV U2, 27
coffee [ˈkɒfiː] Kaffee II
coffee bar [ˈkɒfiː ˌbɑː] Café III
coin [kɔɪn] Münze IV F2, 57
cola [ˈkəʊlə] Cola IV F3, 91
cold [kəʊld] Erkältung; Kälte III
cold [kəʊld] kalt I
collage [kɒˈlɑːʒ] Collage I
to **collect** [kəˈlekt] sammeln I
college [ˈkɒlɪdʒ] College; Institut II
colonist [ˈkɒlənɪst] Kolonist(in), Siedler(in) II
to **colonize** [ˈkɒlənaɪz] kolonisieren IV F1, 23
colony [ˈkɒləni] Kolonie IV U1, 8
colored (AE) [ˈkʌləd] bunt, farbig II
colour [ˈkʌlə] Farbe I
   What colour is/are … ? [ˌwɒt ˈkʌlər ɪz/ɑː] Welche Farbe hat/haben … ? I
coma [ˈkəʊmə] Koma ⟨IV EL, 100⟩
to **combine** [kəmˈbaɪn] kombinieren; verbinden ⟨IV EL, 100⟩
*to **come** [kʌm] kommen I
   Come on! [kʌm ˈɒn] Komm(t)! I
   to come in [kʌm ˈɪn] hereinkommen I
   to come true [ˌkʌm ˈtruː] wahr werden; in Erfüllung gehen IV U4, 58
comedy [ˈkɒmədi] Komödie III

dictionary

comfortable ['kʌmpftəbl] komfortabel; bequem III
comic ['kɒmɪk] Comic(heft) I
comma ['kɒmə] Komma II
command [kə'mɑːnd] Befehl III
comment ['kɒment] Kommentar III
commercial [kə'mɜːʃl] Werbespot III
to **commit** oneself to [kə'mɪt] sich (jmdm/ etw.) verschreiben/verpflichten/widmen; sich binden an IV U5, 76
to **communicate** [kə'mjuːnɪkeɪt] kommunizieren, sich verständigen III
communion [kə'mjuːniən] Kommunion ⟨IV U2, 32⟩
community [kə'mjuːnəti] Gemeinde; Gemeinschaft I
  bedroom community [ˌbedrʊm kə'mjuːnəti] Schlafstadt; reines Wohngebiet ⟨IV EL, 101⟩
company ['kʌmpəni] Gesellschaft; Firma; Kompanie II
comparative [kəm'pærətɪv] Komparativ II
to **compare** (with/to) [kəm'peə] vergleichen (mit) II
competition [ˌkɒmpə'tɪʃn] Wettbewerb, Turnier II
competitor [kəm'petɪtə] Teilnehmer(in); Mitbewerber(in) II
to **complain** [kəm'pleɪn] sich beschweren, sich beklagen II
complaint [kəm'pleɪnt] Beschwerde IV U5, 81
to **complete** [kəm'pliːt] vervollständigen II
complete [kəm'pliːt] vollständig III
compound ['kɒmpaʊnd] Kompositum (zusammengesetztes Wort) II
computer [kəm'pjuːtə] Computer I
to **concentrate** ['kɒntsntreɪt] (sich) konzentrieren III
concert ['kɒnsət] Konzert II
condition [kən'dɪʃn] Kondition; Bedingung IV U1, 14
conditional [kən'dɪʃnl] Konditional III
confidence ['kɒnfɪdnts] Vertrauen; Zuversicht IV U5, 78
conjunction [kən'dʒʌŋkʃn] Konjunktion III
to **connect** (to) [kə'nekt] verbinden (mit) I
to **conquer** ['kɒŋkə] erobern II
conservationist [ˌkɒntsə'veɪʃnɪst] Umweltschützer(in) ⟨IV U1, 15⟩
to **consider** [kən'sɪdə] betrachten; erwägen IV U5, 83
considerable [kən'sɪdrəbl] beträchtlich IV U5, 80
consistent [kən'sɪstnt] konsistent, gleich bleibend ⟨IV EL, 101⟩
contact ['kɒntækt] Kontakt II
  contact clause ['kɒntækt ˌklɔːz] Relativsatz ohne Relativpronomen II
to **contain** [kən'teɪn] enthalten IV U2, 27
context ['kɒntekst] Kontext, Zusammenhang II
continent ['kɒntɪnənt] Kontinent, Erdteil IV U1, 8
to **control** [kən'trəʊl] kontrollieren; beherrschen III

conversation [ˌkɒnvə'seɪʃn] Konversation, Gespräch II
convict ['kɒnvɪkt] Sträfling ⟨IV U1, 12⟩
to **convince** [kən'vɪnts] überzeugen IV U5, 78
to **cook** [kʊk] kochen II
cookie (AE) ['kʊki] Keks II
cool [kuːl] cool, prima II; kühl III
copy ['kɒpi] Kopie II
to **copy** ['kɒpi] abschreiben, kopieren I
coral ['kɒrəl] Koralle IV U1, 15
corn [kɔːn] Korn; Mais IV F2, 56
corner ['kɔːnə] Ecke III
  corner shop ['kɔːnə ˌʃɒp] Laden an der Ecke; Tante-Emma-Laden IV U3, 43
  out of the corner of my eye [aʊt ˌɒv ðə ˌkɔːnər ɒv maɪ 'aɪ] aus dem Augenwinkel ⟨IV U3, 52⟩
corporation [ˌkɔː pr'eɪʃn] Unternehmen; Aktiengesellschaft (AE) ⟨IV U4, 68⟩
to **correct** [kə'rekt] korrigieren, verbessern I
correct [kə'rekt] richtig, korrekt I
cost [kɒst] Preis; Kosten III
*to **cost** [kɒst] kosten III
costume ['kɒstjuːm] Kostüm II
cotton ['kɒtn] Baumwolle IV U2, 27
cougar ['kuːgə] Puma, Berglöwe II
could [kʊd] konnte(n) II; könnte(n) II
to **count** [kaʊnt] zählen IV F2, 57
  counter board ['kaʊntə ˌbɔːd] Zählbrett; Rechenbrett ⟨IV F2, 57⟩
  counter ['kaʊntə] Chip; Jeton; Spielfigur ⟨IV F2, 57⟩
country ['kʌntri] Land; ländliche Gegend, Landschaft I; Countrymusik III
county ['kaʊnti] Landkreis ⟨IV EL, 101⟩
couple ['kʌpl] Paar IV U1, 11
course [kɔːs] Gang II; Kurs IV U2, 29
  golf course ['gɒlf ˌkɔːs] Golfplatz III
  of course [əv 'kɔːs] natürlich, selbstverständlich I
basketball court ['bɑːskɪtbɔːl ˌkɔːt] Basketballplatz III
cousin ['kʌzn] Cousin, Cousine I
cove [kəʊv] kleine Bucht IV U2, 24
to **cover (up)** ['kʌvə] zudecken III
cow [kaʊ] Kuh I
coward [kaʊəd] Feigling IV U3, 52
cowboy ['kaʊbɔɪ] Cowboy, Rinderhirte II
to **crack** [kræk] zerbrechen; springen ⟨IV EL, 96⟩; ⟨IV EL, 101⟩
arts and crafts [ˌɑːts nd 'krɑːfts] Kunsthandwerk III
to **crash** [kræʃ] aufschlagen, gegen etwas krachen I
crash! [kræʃ] Krach! Bumm!; Zusammenstoß I
crazy ['kreɪzi] verrückt II
  to be crazy about [bi: 'kreɪzi əˌbaʊt] verrückt sein nach; abfahren auf IV U4, 60
to **creak** [kriːk] knarren; quietschen ⟨IV U2, 33⟩
cream [kriːm] Creme; Sahne I
  cream tea [ˌkriːm 'tiː] Cream Tea (südwestenglische Spezialität: Tee mit süßen Brötchen, die mit sehr fester Sahne und Marmelade serviert werden) ⟨IV U2, 24⟩
ice cream [aɪs 'kriːm] Eis, Eiscreme I
to **create** [kri'eɪt] (er)schaffen IV U2, 27; ⟨IV EL, 96⟩
creative [kri'eɪtɪv] kreativ III
*to **creep** [kriːp] schleichen; kriechen III
crew [kruː] Crew, Besatzung, Mannschaft IV U2, 32
crime [kraɪm] Verbrechen, Kriminalität II
crisp (BE) [krɪsp] Kartoffelchip I
crispy ['krɪspi] knusprig, kross III
crocodile ['krɒkədaɪl] Krokodil IV U1, 8
crop [krɒp] Feldfrucht; Ernte IV U4, 63
cross [krɒs] Kreuz IV U1, 8
to **cross** [krɒs] überqueren; kreuzen IV U5, 82; ⟨IV EL, 101⟩
crossword (puzzle) ['krɒswɜːd] Kreuzworträtsel II
crowd [kraʊd] Menschenmenge II
crowded ['kraʊdɪd] überfüllt IV U1, 12
cruel ['kruːəl] grausam II
crunchy ['krʌntʃi] knusprig; knackig III
to **cry** [kraɪ] schreien, rufen; weinen I
crypt [krɪpt] Krypta, Gruft ⟨IV U2, 34⟩
cultural ['kʌltʃrl] kulturell II
culture ['kʌltʃə] Kultur II
cup [kʌp] Tasse I; Pokal; Kelch III
  to be sb's cup of tea [ˌkʌp əv 'tiː] jmds Fall sein ⟨IV F3, 91⟩
cupboard ['kʌbəd] Küchenschrank, Schrank I
to **cure** [kjʊə] heilen; kurieren III
curry ['kʌri] Curry (Gewürz oder Gericht) II
to **curse** [kɜːs] fluchen III; (ver)fluchen IV U2, 32
curtain ['kɜːtn] Vorhang III
custom ['kʌstəm] Brauch, Sitte II
customer ['kʌstəmə] Kunde, Kundin I
short cut ['ʃɔːt kʌt] Abkürzung II
*to **cut** (off) [kʌt ˌɒf] (ab)schneiden II
cute [kjuːt] niedlich; süß IV U1, 8

D

dad [dæd] Papa I
daily ['deɪli] täglich II
damage ['dæmɪdʒ] Schaden III
to **damage** ['dæmɪdʒ] schaden, beschädigen IV U2, 27
damn [dæm] verdammt II
dance [dɑːnts] Tanz III
  square dance ['skweə ˌdɑːnts] Square Dance II
to **dance** [dɑːnts] tanzen II
danger ['deɪndʒə] Gefahr IV U1, 13
dangerous ['deɪndʒrəs] gefährlich I
Danish ['deɪnɪʃ] dänisch II
to **dare** [deə] wagen IV U2, 32
dark [dɑːk] dunkel I
darkness ['dɑːknəs] Dunkelheit II
date [deɪt] Datum I
to **date from** ['deɪt frəm] zurückgehen auf III
daughter ['dɔːtə] Tochter II
day [deɪ] Tag I
  every day [ˌevri 'deɪ] jeden Tag I
  G'day (= Good day) [gə'deɪ] Guten Tag

dictionary D

(australisch) ⟨IV U 1, 8⟩
  the day before yesterday [ðə ˌdeɪ bɪfɔː'jestədeɪ] vorgestern I
  the other day [ðiˌʌðə 'deɪ] neulich IV U 3, 46
  these days ['ðiːz ˌdeɪz] heutzutage II
dead [ded] tot I
deadly ['dedli] tödlich IV U 1, 8
deaf [def] gehörlos; schwerhörig III
*to deal with ['diːl wɪð] sich befassen/umgehen mit II
Oh **dear**! [ˈəʊ ˌdɪə] Oje! I
dear [dɪə] lieb I
  Dear Sir or Madam [dɪə ˌsɜːr_ɔː 'mædəm] Sehr geehrte Dame, sehr geehrter Herr IV U 5, 80
death [deθ] Tod III
December [dɪ'sembə] Dezember I
to decide [dɪ'saɪd] entscheiden II
decision [dɪ'sɪʒn] Entscheidung III
declaration [ˌdeklə'reɪʃn] Erklärung IV F 2, 57
decorated ['dekreɪtɪd] dekoriert, geschmückt II
decoration [ˌdek'reɪʃn] Dekoration II
deep [diːp] tief III
deer, pl. **deer** [dɪə] Hirsch, Reh; Rotwild II
definite ['defɪnət] definitiv, bestimmt, eindeutig II
definition [ˌdefɪ'nɪʃn] Definition; Festlegung II
degree [dɪ'griː] Grad ⟨IV U 5, 79⟩
delayed [dɪ'leɪd] verspätet, verzögert II
delicious [dɪ'lɪʃəs] köstlich II
to demand [dɪ'mɑːnd] fordern; verlangen IV U 4, 68
dentist ['dentɪst] Zahnarzt; Zahnärztin ⟨IV E L, 99⟩
department [dɪ'pɑːtmənt] Abteilung III
departure [dɪ'pɑːtʃə] Abflug, Abreise II
to depend (on) [dɪ'pend] abhängen (von); sich verlassen (auf) IV U 1, 14
depressed [dɪ'prest] deprimiert; bedrückt IV U 1, 17
derby ['dɜːbi] Derby III
to describe [dɪ'skraɪb] beschreiben II
description [dɪ'skrɪpʃn] Beschreibung II
to design [dɪ'zaɪn] entwerfen II
designer [dɪ'zaɪnə] Designer(in); Entwickler(in) IV U 3, 44
to desire [dɪ'zaɪə] begehren; wünschen ⟨IV U 4, 63⟩
desk [desk] Schreibtisch I
dessert [dɪ'zɜːt] Dessert, Nachspeise II
detail ['diːteɪl] Detail, Einzelheit II
detective [dɪ'tektɪv] Detektiv(in) III
device [dɪ'vaɪs] Gerät, Vorrichtung III
to devour [dɪ'vaʊə] verschlingen ⟨IV U 1, 17⟩
diagram ['daɪəgræm] Diagramm II
We switched some mental **dial** over to Mute. [wi: ˌswɪtʃt səm ˌmentl daɪəl ˌəʊvə tə 'mjuːt] Wir schalteten gedanklich ab. ⟨IV E L, 101⟩
dialect ['daɪəlekt] Dialekt I
dialogue ['daɪəlɒg] Dialog, Gespräch I
diamond ['daɪəmənd] Diamant ⟨IV U 1, 16⟩

diary ['daɪəri] Tagebuch; Terminkalender II
dictionary ['dɪkʃnri] Wörterbuch I
to die [daɪ] sterben II
difference ['dɪfrnts] Unterschied II
different ['dɪfrnt] anders, verschieden I
difficult ['dɪfɪklt] schwierig II
to dine [daɪn] dinieren; zu Abend essen ⟨IV E L, 98⟩
dinner ['dɪnə] Abendessen I
  to have dinner [hæv 'dɪnə] zu Abend essen I
dinosaur ['daɪnəsɔː] Dinosaurier III
dip [dɪp] Dip (cremige Sauce zum Einstippen) III
direct [dɪ'rekt] direkt II
  direct speech [dɪˌrekt 'spiːtʃ] direkte Rede III
direction [dɪ'rekʃn] Richtung III
director [dɪ'rektə] Direktor(in); Regisseur(in) IV U 1, 19
dirty ['dɜːti] schmutzig IV F 2, 56
disability [ˌdɪsə'bɪləti] Behinderung; Unfähigkeit III
disabled [dɪ'seɪbld] behindert III
disadvantage [ˌdɪsəd'vɑːntɪdʒ] Nachteil IV U 5, 77
disadvantaged [ˌdɪsəd'vɑːntɪdʒd] benachteiligt IV U 3, 46
to disagree [ˌdɪsə'griː] anderer Meinung sein; nicht einverstanden sein II
to disappear [ˌdɪsə'pɪə] verschwinden III
disappointed [ˌdɪsə'pɔɪntɪd] enttäuscht II
disaster [dɪ'zɑːstə] Desaster; Katastrophe III
disco ['dɪskəʊ] Disco, Diskothek III
to discover [dɪ'skʌvə] entdecken III
to discuss [dɪ'skʌs] diskutieren II
discussion [dɪ'skʌʃn] Diskussion II
disease [dɪ'ziːz] Krankheit IV F 2, 56
disgraceful [dɪs'greɪsfl] schändlich ⟨IV U 5, 80⟩
disguise [dɪs'gaɪz] Verkleidung II
  in disguise [ɪn dɪs'gaɪz] verkleidet II
dish [dɪʃ] Gericht, Speise II
dislike [dɪ'slaɪk] Abneigung I
display [dɪ'spleɪ] Vorführung; Ausstellung; Schaukasten; Anzeige IV U 2, 27
distance ['dɪstnts] Distanz, Entfernung III
to divide [dɪ'vaɪd] teilen II
*to get divorced [ˌget dɪ'vɔːst] sich scheiden lassen IV F 1, 23
dizzy ['dɪzi] schwindlig III
*to do [duː] tun, machen I
  Don't take no for an answer. [ˌdəʊnt teɪk 'nəʊ fərˌən_ɑːntsə] Akzeptiere keine Widerrede. ⟨IV U 1, 10⟩
  It's nothing to do with me. [ɪts ˌnʌθɪŋ tə ˌduː wɪð 'miː] Ich habe damit nichts zu tun. III
dock [dɒk] Dock ⟨IV E L, 99⟩
doctor ['dɒktə] Arzt, Ärztin II
documentary [ˌdɒkjə'mentri] Dokumentarfilm III
dog [dɒg] Hund I
  guide dog ['gaɪd ˌdɒg] Blindenhund IV U 3, 47

dollar ['dɒlə] Dollar (Währung) III
dome [dəʊm] Kuppel IV U 4, 60
dome-shaped ['dəʊmʃeɪpt] kuppelförmig ⟨IV U 2, 27⟩
door [dɔː] Tür I
double ['dʌbl] Doppel-, zweimal I
to doubt [daʊt] bezweifeln IV U 1, 10
down [daʊn] entlang; herunter, hinunter, nach unten I
  down under (infml) [ˌdaʊn 'ʌndə] (Spitzname für Australien) ⟨IV U 1, 8⟩
  the next size down [ðə ˌnekst saɪz 'daʊn] eine Größe kleiner III
downstairs [daʊn'steəz] (nach) unten; im Untergeschoss II
downtown (AE) [ˌdaʊn'taʊn] im Stadtzentrum I
to drag the ponds [ˌdræg ðə 'pɒndz] die Teiche mit Netzen absuchen ⟨IV E L, 101⟩
drama ['drɑːmə] Theater; Drama II
*to draw [drɔː] zeichnen I
drawer [drɔː] Schublade I
*to dream [driːm] träumen I
dreamcatcher ['driːmkætʃə] Traumfänger (indianisches verziertes Geflecht mit Federn, das böse Träume fernhalten soll) ⟨IV U 4, 58⟩
dress [dres] Kleid I
to dress up [dresˌ'ʌp] sich verkleiden IV U 5, 77
drill [drɪl] Bohrer, Bohrmaschine I
  electric drill [ɪˌlektrɪk 'drɪl] elektrische Bohrmaschine I
drink [drɪŋk] Getränk I
*to drink [drɪŋk] trinken I
drive [draɪv] Autofahrt III
  cattle drive ['kætlˌdraɪv] Viehtrieb II
driving licence ['draɪvɪŋˌlaɪsnts] Führerschein IV U 3, 44
*to drive [draɪv] fahren I
driver ['draɪvə] Fahrer(in) I
to drool [druːl] sabbern ⟨IV U 1, 16⟩
to drop [drɒp] fallen (lassen) II
  to drop sb a line [ˌdrɒp_ə 'laɪn] jmdm ein paar Zeilen schreiben ⟨IV F 3, 90⟩
to drown [draʊn] ertrinken; ertränken IV U 2, 32
drum [drʌm] Trommel, pl.: Schlagzeug II
drummer ['drʌmə] Schlagzeuger(in) II
drunk [drʌŋk] betrunken IV U 2, 32
to dry [draɪ] trocknen III
dry [draɪ] trocken III
to dub [dʌb] synchronisieren ⟨IV E L, 97⟩
duck [dʌk] Ente I
dumb [dʌm] dumm, doof III
during (+ noun) ['djʊərɪŋ] während (+ Nomen) III
dusty ['dʌsti] staubig IV U 1, 8
Dutch [dʌtʃ] Niederländisch; niederländisch IV U 2, 28
duty ['djuːti] Pflicht IV U 1, 17
DVD player [ˌdiːviːdiː 'pleɪə] DVD-Player III

E

each [iːtʃ] jede(-r/-s) I
each [iːtʃ] pro Person, pro Stück II

dictionary

each other [ˌiːtʃˈʌðə] sich gegenseitig II
eager [ˈiːgə] eifrig III
eagle [ˈiːgl] Adler ⟨IV EL, 96⟩
ear [ɪə] Ohr II
early [ˈɜːli] früh I
to earn [ɜːn] verdienen I
earring [ˈɪərɪŋ] Ohrring II
earth [ɜːθ] Erde II
east [iːst] Osten I
easy [ˈiːzi] einfach, leicht I
*to eat [iːt] essen I
economy [ɪˈkɒnəmi] Wirtschaft III
edge [edʒ] Rand; Kante IV U2, 24
education [edʒʊˈkeɪʃn] Erziehung, Bildung II
 Physical Education [ˌfɪzɪklˌedʒʊˈkeɪʃn] Sport (Schulfach) II
 Religious Education [rɪˌlɪdʒəsˌedʒʊˈkeɪʃn] Religionsunterricht II
effect [ɪˈfekt] Effekt; Wirkung IV U3, 52
egg [eg] Ei I
 fried egg [fraɪdˈeg] Spiegelei II
eight [eɪt] acht I
eighteen [eɪˈtiːn] achtzehn I
eighteenth [eɪˈtiːnθ] achtzehnte(-r/-s) I
eighth [eɪtθ] achte(-r/-s) I
eight-hundred-year-old [eɪt hʌndrəd ˈjɪərˌəʊld] achthundert Jahre alt I
eighty [ˈeɪti] achtzig I
either ... or ... [ˈaɪðə; ˈiːðə ... ɔː] entweder ... oder ... IV U3, 49
electric [ɪˈlektrɪk] elektrisch I
 electric drill [ɪˌlektrɪk ˈdrɪl] elektrische Bohrmaschine I
electricity [ˌelɪkˈtrɪsəti] Elektrizität; Strom IV U4, 63
element [ˈelɪmənt] Element III
elementary [elɪˈmentri] elementar, grundlegend II
 elementary school (AE) [elɪˈmentriˌskuːl] Grundschule II
elevator (AE) [ˈelɪveɪtə] Aufzug, Lift III
eleven [ɪˈlevn] elf I
eleventh [ɪˈlevnθ] elfte(-r/-s) I
elf, pl. elves [elf] Elbe; Elf(e) ⟨IV U5, 77⟩
Elizabethan [ɪˌlɪzəˈbiːθn] elisabethanisch ⟨IV F1, 22⟩
else [els] andere(-r/-s) I
 or else [els] sonst; andernfalls IV U3, 51
 what else [ˌwɒtˈels] was sonst/noch II
e-mail [ˈiːmeɪl] E-mail I
embarrassed [ɪmˈbærəst] verlegen III
embarrassing [ɪmˈbærəsɪŋ] peinlich III
emergency [ɪˈmɜːdʒntsi] Notfall, Notlage I
to emigrate [ˈemɪgreɪt] emigrieren; auswandern IV F1, 23
empire [ˈempaɪə] Reich; Kaiserreich III
empty [ˈempti] leer I
emu [ˈiːmjuː] Emu IV U1, 8
to enclose [ɪnˈkləʊz] beifügen IV U4, 58
to encourage [ɪnˈkʌrɪdʒ] ermutigen; unterstützen IV U5, 78
encouragement [ɪnˈkʌrɪdʒmənt] Ermutigung; Unterstützung IV U5, 80
end [end] Ende, Schluss I
 in the end [ɪn ðiːˈend] schließlich, zum Schluss I

to end [end] enden II
ending [ˈendɪŋ] Ende, Schluss (einer Geschichte) I
enemy [ˈenəmi] Feind(in) II
engaged [ɪnˈgeɪdʒd] besetzt, belegt I; verlobt IV U4, 69
engine [ˈendʒɪn] Motor I
English [ˈɪŋglɪʃ] englisch; Englisch I
 What's ... in English? [ˌwɒts ... ɪnˈɪŋglɪʃ] Was heißt ... auf Englisch? I
to enjoy [ɪnˈdʒɔɪ] genießen II
 to enjoy oneself [ɪnˈdʒɔɪ] Spaß haben; sich amüsieren III
enjoyable [ɪnˈdʒɔɪəbl] angenehm; unterhaltsam IV U4, 62
enough [ɪˈnʌf] genug, genügend I
entertainer [ˌentəˈteɪnə] Entertainer(in); Unterhaltungskünstler(in) IV U5, 77
entertainment [ˌentəˈteɪnmənt] Unterhaltung III
entrance [ˈentrəns] Eingang; Eintritt IV U2, 28
environment [ɪnˈvaɪərnmənt] Umwelt; Umgebung IV U1, 15
e-pal [ˈiːpæl] E-Mail-Brieffreund(in) ⟨IV F3, 90⟩
episode [ˈepɪsəʊd] Episode; Folge III
equal [ˈiːkwəl] Gleichgestellte(r); Gleichwertige(r); Ebenbürtige(r) III
er [ɜː] äh I
to escape [ɪˈskeɪp] flüchten, entkommen II
especially [ɪˈspeʃli] besonders, vor allem I
etc. [ɪtˈsetrə] usw., et cetera II
European [jʊərəˈpiːən] Europäer(in); europäisch IV U1, 16
even [ˈiːvn] sogar II
 even (+ comparative) [ˈiːvn] noch (+ Komparativ) II
 not even [ˌnɒtˈiːvn] nicht einmal II
even if [ˌiːvnˈɪf] auch wenn III
evening [ˈiːvnɪŋ] Abend I
event [ɪˈvent] Ereignis I
ever [ˈevə] jemals II
every [ˈevri] jede(-r/-s) I
 every day [ˌevriˈdeɪ] jeden Tag I
every [ˈevri] alle II
everybody [ˈevribɒdi] jeder; alle I
everyday [ˈevrideɪ] alltäglich III
everyone [ˈevriwʌn] jeder II
everything [ˈevriθɪŋ] alles II
everywhere [ˈevriweə] überall I
evil [ˈiːvl] böse, schlecht II
exactly [ɪgˈzæktli] genau II
 not exactly [ˌnɒt ɪgˈzæktli] nicht gerade IV U5, 80
exaggeration [ɪgˌzædʒəˈreɪʃn] Übertreibung IV U5, 81
exam [ɪgˈzæm] Examen; Prüfung IV U3, 49
to examine [ɪgˈzæmɪn] untersuchen, kontrollieren I
example [ɪgˈzɑːmpl] Beispiel I
 for example [fərɪgˈzɑːmpl] zum Beispiel I
excellent [ˈekslnt] exzellent, hervorragend IV U2, 32
except [ɪkˈsept] außer I
exchange [ɪksˈtʃeɪndʒ] Austausch III

excise man, pl. excise men [ˈeksaɪzˌmæn] Steuereintreiber ⟨IV U2, 32⟩
excited [ɪkˈsaɪtɪd] aufgeregt I
exciting [ɪkˈsaɪtɪŋ] spannend, aufregend I
Excuse me! [ɪkˈskjuːz mi] Entschuldigung! Entschuldigen Sie! I
to execute [ˈeksɪkjuːt] exekutieren; hinrichten IV F1, 22
exercise [ˈeksəsaɪz] Übung I
 exercise book [ˈeksəsaɪzˌbʊk] Übungsheft I
exhibition [ˌeksɪˈbɪʃn] Ausstellung; Vorführung II
to exist [ɪgˈzɪst] existieren III
to expect [ɪkˈspekt] erwarten II
expectation [ˌekspekˈteɪʃn] Erwartung III
expensive [ɪkˈspentsɪv] teuer II
experience [ɪkˈspɪəriəns] Erfahrung; Erlebnis II
to experience [ɪkˈspɪəriəns] erfahren, erleben II
experienced [ɪkˈspɪəriənst] erfahren IV U2, 29
experiment [ɪkˈsperɪmənt] Experiment, Versuch III
to explain [ɪkˈspleɪn] erklären, erläutern I
to explode [ɪkˈspləʊd] explodieren III
to explore [ɪkˈsplɔː] erkunden; erforschen IV F1, 22
explorer [ɪkˈsplɔːrə] Forscher; Forschungsreisender IV F1, 22
explosion [ɪkˈspləʊʒn] Explosion III
to express [ɪkˈspres] ausdrücken II
expression [ɪkˈspreʃn] Ausdruck III
expressway (AE) [ɪkˈspresweɪ] Autobahn; Schnellstraße ⟨IV U4, 69⟩
exterior [ɪkˈstɪəriə] Außenaufnahme IV U2, 34
extra [ˈekstrə] extra, besonders II
extract [ˈekstrækt] Extrakt; Auszug IV U1, 16
eye [aɪ] Auge I
 out of the corner of my eye [aʊt əv ðə ˌkɔːnər əv maɪˈaɪ] aus dem Augenwinkel ⟨IV U3, 52⟩
eyelash [ˈaɪlæʃ] Wimper IV U3, 50

F

face [feɪs] Gesicht I
fact [fækt] Fakt, Tatsache II
 in fact [ɪnˈfækt] tatsächlich; eigentlich III
factory [ˈfæktri] Fabrik; Werk III
to faint [feɪnt] ohnmächtig werden I
fair [feə] Messe, Jahrmarkt II
fair [feə] gerecht, fair I
fairy [ˈfeəri] Fee II
 fairy tale [ˈfeəriˌteɪl] Märchen II
fall [fɔːl] Sturz III
 falls (pl.) [fɔːlz] Wasserfall I
fall (AE) [fɔːl] Herbst II
*to fall (over) [fɔːlˈəʊvə] (hin)fallen; umfallen I
 to fall in love (with) [ˌfɔːl ɪnˈlʌv] sich verlieben (in) II
false [fɔːls] falsch I

dictionary D

fame [feɪm] Ruhm ⟨IV U5,76⟩
familiar [fəˈmɪliə] vertraut III
   to seem familiar [ˌsiːm fəˈmɪliə] bekannt vorkommen I
family [ˈfæmli] Familie I
famous [ˈfeɪməs] berühmt II
fan [fæn] Fan, Anhänger(in) II
to fancy [ˈfæntsi] angetan sein von III
fantastic [fænˈtæstɪk] fantastisch, großartig I
far [fɑː] weit I
   so far [ˌsəʊ ˈfɑː] bis jetzt II
far [fɑː] bei weitem; weitaus IV U5,80
   far more interesting [ˌfɑː mɔːr ˈɪntrəstɪŋ] weitaus interessanter I
to fare [feə] ergehen ⟨IV U4,63⟩
farm [fɑːm] Farm, Bauernhof I
to farm [fɑːm] Landwirtschaft treiben IV U4,64
farmer [ˈfɑːmə] Farmer, Landwirt(in) I
farmyard [ˈfɑːmjɑːd] Hof (auf einem Bauernhof) I
fascinating [ˈfæsɪneɪtɪŋ] faszinierend IV U4,63
fashion [ˈfæʃn] Mode III
fast [fɑːst] schnell I
   fast food restaurant [ˌfɑːst fuːd ˈrestrənt] Schnellrestaurant III
   to be fast [biˈfɑːst] vorgehen III
fat [fæt] Fett III
fat [fæt] fett, dick III
   Fat lot of good it did them. [ˌfæt lɒt əv ˈɡʊd ɪt ˌdɪd ðəm] Einen Dreck hat es ihnen genützt. ⟨IV EL,100⟩
father [ˈfɑːðə] Vater I
(my) fault [ˈmaɪ fɔːlt] (meine) Schuld III
favorable [ˈfeɪvrəbl] günstig; positiv ⟨IV U5,80⟩
favourite [ˈfeɪvrɪt] Lieblings- I
fax [fæks] Fax II
fear [fɪə] Angst, Furcht II
to feature [ˈfiːtʃə] jmdn in einer Hauptrolle haben IV U5,85
February [ˈfebruri] Februar I
***to feed** [fiːd] füttern I
feedback [ˈfiːdbæk] Feedback, Rückmeldung II
***to feel** [fiːl] (sich) fühlen I
   to feel like (+ gerund) [ˈfiːl laɪk] Lust haben auf/zu IV U4,60
   to feel sick [ˌfiːl ˈsɪk] Übelkeit verspüren; sich schlecht fühlen III
   to feel sorry for [fiːl ˈsɒri] Mitleid haben mit; bedauern III
feeling [ˈfiːlɪŋ] Gefühl II
fellow [ˈfeləʊ] Bursche; Kerl ⟨IV EL,99⟩
fence [fents] Zaun II
ferry [ˈferi] Fähre IV U2,29
festival [ˈfestɪvl] Festival, Fest II
to fetch [fetʃ] (ab)holen I
fever [ˈfiːvə] Fieber IV F2,56
few [fjuː] wenige III
   a few [əˈfjuː] einige, ein paar II
fictional [ˈfɪkʃnl] fiktional; fiktiv ⟨IV EL,100⟩
fiddle [ˈfɪdl] Geige II
field [fiːld] Feld; Acker I
   baseball field [ˈbeɪsbɔːl ˌfiːld] Baseballplatz III
   football field [ˈfʊtbɔːl ˌfiːld] Footballplatz III
   track and field [ˌtræk ənd ˈfiːld] Leichtathletik III
fifteen [fɪfˈtiːn] fünfzehn I
fifteenth [fɪfˈtiːnθ] fünfzehnte(-r/-s) I
fifth [fɪfθ] Fünftel III
fifth [fɪfθ] fünfte(-r/-s) I
fifty [ˈfɪfti] fünfzig I
***to fight** [faɪt] streiten, kämpfen I
figure [ˈfɪɡə] Figur, Gestalt; Ziffer II
to fill in [fɪlˈɪn] ausfüllen II
film [fɪlm] Film II
to film [fɪlm] filmen; drehen III
final [ˈfaɪnl] Finale II
finally [ˈfaɪnli] schließlich, endlich II
***to find** [faɪnd] finden I
   Find the odd word out! [ˌɒd wɜːd ˈaʊt] Finde das Wort, das nicht in die Gruppe passt! (Wortschatzübung) I
fine [faɪn] gut, in Ordnung; schön I
   I'm fine. [aɪm ˈfaɪn] Mir geht es gut. I
finger [ˈfɪŋɡə] Finger I
fingertip [ˈfɪŋɡətɪp] Fingerspitze II
to finish [ˈfɪnɪʃ] fertig machen; aufhören I
fire [faɪə] Feuer; Kamin; Ofen II
   to set fire to [set ˈfaɪə tə] in Brand stecken III
firework [ˈfaɪəwɜːk] Feuerwerkskörper; Plural: Feuerwerk IV U3,52
first [fɜːst] erste(-r/-s); zuerst I
   at first [ət ˈfɜːst] zuerst; zunächst II
   first name [ˈfɜːst ˌneɪm] Vorname IV U1,11
fish and chips [ˌfɪʃ ənˈtʃɪps] Fisch und Pommes frites I
fisherman, pl. **fishermen** [ˈfɪʃəmən] Fischer IV U2,32
fishing [ˈfɪʃɪŋ] Angeln, Fischen II
fist [fɪst] Faust IV U4,70
to fit (in) [ˌfɪtˈɪn] (hinein)passen IV U2,26
fit [fɪt] fit III
five [faɪv] fünf I
flag [flæɡ] Flagge I
flame [fleɪm] Flamme IV U3,50
to flap one's **wings** [ˌflæp wʌnz ˈwɪŋz] mit den Flügeln schlagen ⟨IV EL,96⟩
to flash [flæʃ] blitzen; blinken IV U4,69
flat [flæt] Wohnung I
flat [flæt] flach, platt III
flatly [ˈflætli] rundweg; kategorisch IV U3,51
flavor (AE) [ˈfleɪvə] Geschmack, Aroma III
fleet [fliːt] Flotte ⟨IV F1,22⟩
flight [flaɪt] Flug I
to flood [flʌd] überfluten; überschwemmen IV U5,81
floor [flɔː] Fußboden; Stockwerk I
flower [ˈflaʊə] Blume II
fluffy [ˈflʌfi] flaumig; flauschig; flockig ⟨IV F3,91⟩
to flush [flʌʃ] spülen; die Wasserspülung betätigen IV U2,27
fly [flaɪ] Fliege II
***to fly** [flaɪ] fliegen I
   to fly on [flaɪˈɒn] weiterfliegen I
focus [ˈfəʊkəs] Blickpunkt I
to focus (on) [ˈfəʊkəs] sich konzentrieren (auf) IV U2,27
fog [fɒɡ] Nebel II
foggy [ˈfɒɡi] neblig II
folder [ˈfəʊldə] Ordner, Mappe I
folks (infml) [fəʊks] Leute; Eltern ⟨IV EL,100⟩
to follow [ˈfɒləʊ] hinterhergehen; (be)folgen I
food [fuːd] Essen, Nahrung; Lebensmittel I
fool [fuːl] Narr, Dummkopf II
foot, pl. **feet** [fʊt; fiːt] Fuß I; Fuß (Längenmaß: 30,48 cm) III
football [ˈfʊtbɔːl] Fußball I
   football field [ˈfʊtbɔːl ˌfiːld] Footballplatz III
   football magazine [ˈfʊtbɔːl mæɡəˌziːn] Fußballzeitschrift I
footprint [ˈfʊtprɪnt] Fußabdruck ⟨IV U1,16⟩
footstep [ˈfʊtstep] Schritt III
for [fɔː] für I; wegen III; seit III
   for a change [fər ə ˈtʃeɪndʒ] zur Abwechslung IV U3,44
   for example [fər ɪɡˈzɑːmpl] zum Beispiel I
   for many years [fə ˌmeni ˈjɪəz] viele Jahre lang III
   for their own good [fə ðərˌəʊn ˈɡʊd] zu ihrem Besten IV U1,17
to force [fɔːs] zwingen III
forecast [ˈfɔːkɑːst] Vorhersage II
   weather forecast [ˈweðə ˌfɔːkɑːst] Wettervorhersage II
forehead [ˈfɒrɪd] Stirn ⟨IV EL,100⟩
foreign [ˈfɒrɪn] ausländisch; fremd IV F3,90
forest [ˈfɒrɪst] Wald I
forever [fəˈrevə] für immer; ewig IV U5,80
to forge [fɔːdʒ] fälschen ⟨IV U4,70⟩
***to forget** [fəˈɡet] vergessen I
fork [fɔːk] Gabel I; Gabelung II
form [fɔːm] Form I
   progressive form [prəʊˈɡresɪv] Verlaufsform III
to form [fɔːm] formen; bilden III
formal [ˈfɔːml] formal; formell; förmlich III
fortunately [ˈfɔːtʃnətli] zum Glück IV U5,78
fortune [ˈfɔːtʃuːn] Vermögen; Reichtum; Schicksal; Glück ⟨IV U5,76⟩
forty [ˈfɔːti] vierzig I
forum [ˈfɔːrəm] Forum III
forward [ˈfɔːwəd] vorwärts IV U5,80
fossil [ˈfɒsl] Fossil IV U2,25
to found [faʊnd] gründen III
four [fɔː] vier I
fourteen [fɔːˈtiːn] vierzehn I
fourteenth [fɔːˈtiːnθ] vierzehnte(-r/-s) I
fourth [fɔːθ] vierte(-r/-s) I
freeze frame [ˈfriːz ˌfreɪm] Standbild ⟨IV EL,97⟩
frankly [ˈfræŋkli] ehrlich gesagt; offen gestanden IV U5,78

Dictionary

freak [fri:k] Missgeburt; eigenartiger Mensch **IV U3, 51**
free [fri:] frei **I**; kostenlos **III**
freedom ['fri:dəm] Freiheit **IV F1, 23**
*to **freeze** [fri:z] erstarren; gefrieren ⟨**IV U2, 33**⟩
    freeze frame ['fri:z ˌfreɪm] Standbild ⟨**IV EL, 97**⟩
French [frentʃ] französisch; Französisch **I**
Frenchman ['frentʃmən] Franzose **IV U2, 34**
fresh [freʃ] frisch **I**
Friday ['fraɪdeɪ] Freitag **I**
fried [fraɪd] in der Pfanne gebraten **II**
    fried egg [ˌfraɪd ˈeg] Spiegelei **II**
friend [frend] Freund(in) **I**
    to make friends (with) [ˌmeɪk ˈfrendz] Freundschaft schließen (mit) **III**
friendly ['frendli] freundlich, nett **II**
fries *pl.* *(AE)* [fraɪz] Pommes frites **I**
fright [fraɪt] Schreck ⟨**IV EL, 99**⟩
to **frighten** ['fraɪtn] erschrecken, Angst machen **II**
*to be **frightened** (of) [bi: ˈfraɪtnd] Angst haben (vor) **I**
frog [frɒg] Frosch **I**
from [frɒm; frəm] aus, von **I**
    Where are you from? [ˌweər ə jə ˈfrɒm] Woher kommst du/kommt ihr/kommen Sie? **I**
    Where … from? [ˌweə … ˈfrɒm] Woher …? **I**
front [frʌnt] Vorderseite **II**
    in front of [ɪn ˈfrʌnt əv] vor, davor **I**
fruit [fru:t] Frucht **III**
fruit *(pl.)* [fru:t] Obst **II**
to **fulfil** [fʊlˈfɪl] erfüllen **IV U1, 14**
full [fʊl] voll **I**
fun [fʌn] Freude, Spaß **I**
    to make fun of [ˌmeɪk ˈfʌn əv] sich lustig machen über **III**
function ['fʌŋkʃn] Funktion **IV U3, 49**
funeral ['fju:nrəl] Beerdigung; Begräbnis ⟨**IV EL, 100**⟩
funky ['fʌŋki] irre **IV U1, 11**
funny ['fʌni] komisch, lustig **I**
furious ['fjʊəriəs] wütend **IV U4, 70**
furniture *(singular noun with plural meaning)* ['fɜ:nɪtʃə] Möbel **IV U3, 46**
furthermore [ˌfɜ:ðəˈmɔ:] überdies; außerdem **IV U2, 31**
future ['fju:tʃə] Zukunft **II**

G

galah [gəˈlɑ:] Galah *(australische Vogelart)* ⟨**IV EL, 96**⟩
gallery ['gæləri] Galerie **III**
game [geɪm] Spiel **I**
    game show ['geɪm ˌʃəʊ] Spielshow **III**
gang [gæŋ] Gang, Bande **II**
gangster ['gæŋkstə] Gangster, Verbrecher **I**
gap [gæp] Lücke; Spalt; Abstand **IV U5, 80**
garage ['gærɑ:ʒ] Garage **I**
garden ['gɑ:dn] Garten **I**
gardener ['gɑ:dnə] Gärtner(in) **IV U3, 48**
gas, *pl.* **gasses** [gæs] Gas **IV U4, 63**

gate [geɪt] Tor, Pforte **I**; Gate, Flugsteig, Ausgang **II**
gear [gɪə] Ausrüstung, Zeug **II**
general ['dʒenrl] allgemein **II**
generation [ˌdʒenəˈreɪʃn] Generation **IV U1, 18**
generous ['dʒenrəs] großzügig **IV U2, 32**
gentle ['dʒentl] sanft, liebenswürdig **II**
gentleman, *pl.* **gentlemen** ['dʒentlmən] Gentleman, (feiner) Herr **II**
    ladies and gentlemen [ˌleɪdiz n ˈdʒentlmən] meine Damen und Herren **II**
geography [dʒiˈɒgrəfi] Geographie, Erdkunde **I**
German ['dʒɜ:mən] deutsch; Deutsche(r); Deutsch **I**
gerund ['dʒernd] Gerundium **I**
*to **get** [get] (be)kommen; kriegen **I**; werden **II**
    Get well soon! [get ˌwel ˈsu:n] Gute Besserung! **III**
    I don't get it. [aɪ ˌdəʊnt ˈget ɪt] Das kapiere ich nicht. **III**
    to get divorced [ˌget dɪˈvɔ:st] sich scheiden lassen **IV F1, 23**
    to get into [getˈɪntə] in etwas hineingelangen **I**
    to get in touch (with) [ˌget ɪn ˈtʌtʃ] in Verbindung treten (mit); kontaktieren **IV F3, 90**
    to get (sb) involved (in) [ˌget ɪnˈvɒlvd] sich (oder jmdn) beteiligen (an); sich engagieren (für); sich einlassen (auf) **IV U4, 67**
    to get lost [get ˈlɒst] verloren gehen, sich verirren **I**
    to get married [get ˈmærɪd] heiraten **I**
    to get off (the bus) [getˈɒf] aussteigen (aus dem Bus) **I**
    to get off the ground [getˌɒf ðə ˈgraʊnd] in Gang kommen ⟨**IV U5, 80**⟩
    to get on (the bus) [getˈɒn] einsteigen (in den Bus) **I**
    to get one's act together [ˌget wʌnz ˈækt təgeðə] sich am Riemen reißen **III**
    to get rid of [get ˈrɪd əv] loswerden **II**
    to get (sth) started [ˌget ˈstɑ:tɪd] in Gang kommen; (etw.) in Gang bringen **IV U5, 80**
    to get the gist [ˌget ðə ˈdʒɪst] das Wesentliche erfassen **II**
    to get to do sth [get] die Möglichkeit haben, etw. zu tun ⟨**IV U5, 77**⟩
    to get to know [ˌget tə ˈnəʊ] kennen lernen **III**
    to get up [getˈʌp] aufstehen **I**
    to get used to (+ *gerund*) [ˌget ˈju:zt tə] sich gewöhnen an **IV U4, 58**
    to get wet [get ˈwet] nass werden **I**
ghost [gəʊst] Geist **II**
giant [dʒaɪənt] riesig ⟨**IV EL, 101**⟩
girl [gɜ:l] Mädchen **I**
girlfriend ['gɜ:lfrend] Freundin *(in einer Paarbeziehung)* **III**
*to **get** the **gist** [ˌget ðə ˈdʒɪst] das Wesentliche erfassen **III**

*to **give** [gɪv] geben; schenken **I**
    to give a talk [ˌgɪv ə ˈtɔ:k] einen Vortrag halten **III**
    to give sb a break [ˌgɪv əˈbreɪk] jmdm eine Chance geben ⟨**IV U5, 78**⟩
    to give somebody the bumps [ˌgɪv ðə ˈbʌmps] jemanden hochwerfen und wieder auffangen **I**
    to give up [gɪvˈʌp] aufgeben **I**
glad [glæd] froh **III**
glass [glɑ:s] Glas **II**
glasses *pl.* ['glɑ:sɪz] Brille **I**
glove [glʌv] Handschuh **III**
gm (= **gram**) [græm] Gramm **I**
*to **go** [gəʊ] gehen **I**
    to go (+ adjective) [gəʊ] werden **II**
    Let's go! [lets ˈgəʊ] Lass(t) uns gehen! **I**
    to be going on [bi: ˌgəʊɪŋ ˈɒn] los sein **II**
    to be gone [bi: ˈgɒn] verschwunden sein **II**
    to go down [gəʊ ˈdaʊn] untergehen *(Sonne)* **II**
    to go for a walk [ˌgəʊ fər ə ˈwɔ:k] spazieren gehen **I**
    to go on [gəʊˈɒn] weitermachen, weiterführen **I**
    to go on (+ *gerund*) [gəʊˈɒn] etwas weiter/immer wieder tun **I**
    to go shopping [ˌgəʊ ˈʃɒpɪŋ] einkaufen gehen **I**
    to go to sleep [gəʊ tə ˈsli:p] einschlafen **I**
    to go wrong [gəʊ ˈrɒŋ] schief gehen **II**
goal [gəʊl] Tor; Ziel **III**
goanna [gəʊˈænə] Waran ⟨**IV U1, 16**⟩
God [gɒd] Gott **II**
    thank God [ˌθæŋk ˈgɒd] Gott sei Dank **II**
gold [gəʊld] Gold **II**
gold [gəʊld] golden **III**
golden ['gəʊldn] golden **IV F1, 22**
golf [gɒlf] Golf **III**
    golf ball ['gɒlf ˌbɔ:l] Golfball **III**
    golf club ['gɒlf ˌklʌb] Golfschläger **III**
    golf course ['gɒlf ˌkɔ:s] Golfplatz **III**
for their own **good** [fə ðərˌəʊn ˈgʊd] zu ihrem Besten **IV U1, 17**
better ['betə] besser **II**
    good [gʊd] gut **I**
    G'day (= Good day) [gəˈdaɪ] Guten Tag *(australisch)* ⟨**IV U1, 8**⟩
    I'd better = I had better [aɪd ˈbetə] Ich sollte lieber … **IV U2, 29**
    no good [nəʊ ˈgʊd] nutzlos, wertlos **II**
    not any better [ˌnɒtˌeni ˈbetə] (überhaupt) nicht besser **II**
    to be better [bi: ˈbetə] sich besser fühlen; wieder gesund sein **IV U3, 51**
    to be good at [bi: ˈgʊd ət] gut sein in **I**
Goodbye! [gʊdˈbaɪ] Auf Wiedersehen! **I**
goods *(pl.)* [gʊdz] Güter; Waren **IV F1, 23**
gorgeous ['gɔ:dʒəs] hinreißend; wunderschön ⟨**IV EL, 103**⟩
gospel ['gɒspl] Gospel **III**
*to **have** (**got**) [hæv ˈgɒt] besitzen, haben **I**
*to **gotten** *(AE)* ['gɒtn] bekommen; geworden *(past participle von 'to get' in AE)* **IV U5, 82**
government ['gʌvnmənt] Regierung **III**

to **grab** [græb] greifen; schnappen I
grade (AE) [greɪd] Klasse (AE); Note (AE) II
grader (AE) ['greɪdə] -Klässler(in) II
gradual ['grædʒʊəl] allmählich III
graffiti [grə'fi:ti] Graffiti III
grammar ['græmə] Grammatik I
grand [grænd] prächtig; großartig ⟨IV U4, 60⟩
grandma ['grænmɑ:] Oma I
grandpa ['grænpɑ:] Opa I
granite ['grænɪt] Granit ⟨IV U4, 60⟩
grape [greɪp] Traube III
grass [grɑ:s] Gras III
grave [greɪv] Grab III
gravel pit slide ['grævl pɪt ˌslaɪd] abrutschender Kies in einer Kiesgrube ⟨IV EL, 101⟩
great [greɪt] großartig, toll I; groß II
green [gri:n] grün I
greenhouse ['gri:nhaʊs] Gewächshaus IV U2, 27
to **greet** [gri:t] (be)grüßen IV F3, 91
greeting ['gri:tɪŋ] Gruß III
grey [greɪ] grau I
grid [grɪd] Gitter, Tabelle II
to **grill** [grɪl] grillen III
to **grin** [grɪn] grinsen III
to **groan** [grəʊn] stöhnen III
ground [graʊnd] Boden; Grund III
  to get off the ground [get ˌɒf ðə 'graʊnd] in Gang kommen ⟨IV U5, 80⟩
group [gru:p] Klasse; Gruppe I
  tutor group ['tju:tə ˌgru:p] Klasse (in einer englischen Schule) I
*to **grow** [grəʊ] anbauen; wachsen I; züchten; ziehen IV U2, 27
  to grow tired of sb/sth [ˌgrəʊ 'taɪəd] jmds/ einer Sache überdrüssig werden ⟨IV EL, 96⟩
  to grow up [grəʊ ˌʌp] aufwachsen, erwachsen werden II
grunge [grʌndʒ] Grunge (Musikrichtung) III
to **guess** [ges] raten, vermuten I
guest [gest] Gast II
guide [gaɪd] Führer(in) III
  guide dog ['gaɪd ˌdɒg] Blindenhund IV U3, 47
guitar [gɪ'tɑ:] Gitarre I
guitarist [gɪ'tɑ:rɪst] Gitarrist(in) II
chewing gum ['tʃu:ɪŋ ˌgʌm] Kaugummi IV U3, 49
gun [gʌn] Schusswaffe I
guy [gaɪ] Typ, Kerl; pl.: Leute II
gym(nasium) [dʒɪm; dʒɪm'neɪziəm] Turnhalle III

H

hair [heə] Haar(e) II
hairstyle ['heəstaɪl] Frisur III
half, pl. **halves** [hɑ:f; hɑ:vz] (die) Hälfte IV F2, 56
  half past (two) ['hɑ:f pɑ:st] halb (drei) I
half-time [ˌhɑ:f'taɪm] Halbzeit III
hall [hɔ:l] Flur, Diele, Korridor I; Halle, Saal II
ham [hæm] Schinken II
hamster ['hæmstə] Hamster I
hand [hænd] Hand I; Blatt (beim Kartenspiel) ⟨IV EL, 100⟩
  by clapping your hands [baɪ ˌklæpɪŋ jə 'hændz] indem ihr in die Hände klatscht ⟨IV EL, 99⟩
  on the other hand [ɒn ði ˌʌðə 'hænd] andererseits IV U4, 69
to **hand** sth down to sb [ˌhænd 'daʊn] etw. an jmdn weitergeben/überliefern ⟨IV EL, 96⟩
  to hand sth over [hænd 'əʊvə] etw. übergeben IV U1, 17
handout ['hændaʊt] Informationsblatt III
to **hang** [hæŋ] hängen IV U2, 32
*to **hang** around [ˌhæŋ ə'raʊnd] herumhängen II
  to hang out (with) (infml) [hæŋ 'aʊt] sich herumtreiben (mit) II
*to **hang up** [hæŋ ˌʌp] aufhängen IV U4, 58
to **happen** ['hæpən] geschehen, passieren I
happy ['hæpi] glücklich, froh I
  happy horseshit (infml) [ˌhæpi 'hɔ:sʃɪt] uninteressantes Zeug ⟨IV EL, 101⟩
harbour ['hɑ:bə] Hafen I
hard [hɑ:d] hart; schwer II
hardly ['hɑ:dli] kaum III
hardwood ['hɑ:dwʊd] Hartholz ⟨IV U2, 27⟩
hat [hæt] Hut II
to **hate** [heɪt] hassen, nicht mögen I
to **haunt** [hɔ:nt] spuken in; heimsuchen IV U2, 32
haunted ['hɔ:ntɪd] Spuk- IV U2, 32
*to **have** [hæv] haben II; essen; trinken II
  Had I not ... (fml) [hæd] Hätte ich nicht ... ⟨IV U5, 80⟩
  I'd better = I had better [aɪd 'betə] Ich sollte lieber ... IV U2, 29
  to have (got) [hæv 'gɒt] besitzen, haben I
  to have a baby [ˌhæv ə 'beɪbi] ein Kind bekommen IV F2, 56
  to have a look (at) [ˌhæv ə 'lʊk] anschauen II
  to have a race [ˌhæv ə 'reɪs] ein Rennen veranstalten I
  to have dinner [hæv 'dɪnə] zu Abend essen I
  to have on [hæv ˌɒn] anhaben II
  to have to (do sth) [hæv] etwas tun müssen II
he [hi:] er I
head [hed] Kopf I
  head teacher (BE) [ˌhed 'ti:tʃə] Schulleiter(in) III
headache ['hedeɪk] Kopfweh III
heading ['hedɪŋ] Überschrift I
health [helθ] Gesundheit; Gesundheitslehre II
  health club ['helθ klʌb] Fitnessklub III
healthy ['helθi] gesund III
*to **hear** [hɪə] hören I
heart [hɑ:t] Herz I
heavy ['hevi] schwer II
height [haɪt] Höhe III
helicopter ['helɪˌkɒptə] Helikopter, Hubschrauber I
Hello! [hə'ləʊ] Hallo! I
  to say hello [seɪ hə'ləʊ] Hallo sagen, sich begrüßen I
helmet ['helmət] Helm III
help [help] Hilfe, Rettung I
to **help** [help] helfen I
  help yourself [ˌhelp jɔ:'self] bediene dich!/ bedienen Sie sich! I
helpless ['helpləs] hilflos I
her [hɜ:] ihr(e); sie; ihr I
here [hɪə] hier I
  Here you are! [ˌhɪə ju: 'ɑ:] Hier bitte! Bitteschön! I
hero, pl. **heroes** ['hɪərəʊ] Held II
heroine ['herəʊɪn] Heldin II
herself [hɜ:'self] (sie) selbst; sich (selbst) III
Hey! [heɪ] He! I
Hi! [haɪ] Hi! Hallo! I
*to **hide** [haɪd] (sich) verstecken II
high [haɪ] hoch; groß I
  high school ['haɪ ˌsku:l] High School (weiterführende Schule in den USA, Oberstufe) III
highlight ['haɪlaɪt] Highlight III
hike [haɪk] Wanderung III
to **hike** [haɪk] wandern III
hill [hɪl] Berg; Hügel I
him [hɪm] ihm; ihn I
himself [hɪm'self] (er) selbst; sich (selbst) III
hip-hop ['hɪp hɒp] Hip-Hop II
his [hɪz] sein(e) I; sein(-er/-e/-es) IV U3, 46
to **hiss** [hɪs] zischen ⟨IV U2, 33⟩
historical [hɪ'stɒrɪkl] geschichtlich, historisch III
history ['hɪstri] Geschichte II
hit [hɪt] Hit II
*to **hit** [hɪt] schlagen; treffen; hier: gegen etwas fahren I
hobby ['hɒbi] Hobby II
*to **hold** [həʊld] halten II
holiday ['hɒlədeɪ] Urlaub, Feiertag I
hollow ['hɒləʊ] hohl II
Holy Jeezum! (= Jesus) (infml) [ˌhəʊli 'dʒi:zəm] Heiliger Jesus! ⟨IV EL, 100⟩
home [həʊm] Heim; nach Hause I
  at home [ət 'həʊm] zu Hause I
  old people's home [ˌəʊld pi:plz 'həʊm] Altersheim II
homeless ['həʊmləs] obdachlos III
homepage ['həʊmpeɪdʒ] Homepage II
homesite ['həʊmsaɪt] Wohnstätte ⟨IV U4, 65⟩
hometown ['həʊmtaʊn] Heimatstadt IV U4, 58
homework ['həʊmwɜ:k] Hausaufgaben I
honey ['hʌni] Honig; Schätzchen (AE) III
to **hope** [həʊp] hoffen I
hopeful ['həʊpfl] hoffnungsvoll IV U5, 78
hopefully ['həʊpfli] hoffentlich IV U5, 78
hopeless ['həʊpləs] hoffnungslos IV U1, 17
horrified ['hɒrɪfaɪd] entsetzt III
horror ['hɒrə] Horror, Schrecken II
horse [hɔ:s] Pferd I

Dictionary

to be as hungry as a horse [əz ˌhʌŋgri ˌəz ə 'hɔːs] einen Bärenhunger haben **II**
white horses [waɪt 'hɔːsɪz] Schaumkronen **I**
horseback riding [ˌhɔːsbæk 'raɪdɪŋ] Reiten **II**
happy **horseshit** *(infml)* [ˌhæpi 'hɔːsʃɪt] uninteressantes Zeug ⟨**IV EL**,101⟩
hospital ['hɒspɪtl] Hospital, Krankenhaus **II**
host [həʊst] Gastgeber(in); Talkmaster **IV F1**,22
hot [hɒt] heiß **I**; scharf **III**
hotel [həʊ'tel] Hotel **II**
hour ['aʊə] Stunde **II**
  opening hours ['əʊpnɪŋ ˌaʊəz] Öffnungszeiten **I**
house [haʊs] Haus **I**
  State House ['steɪt ˌhaʊs] Regierungsgebäude ⟨**IV U4**,60⟩
housekeeper ['haʊsˌkiːpə] Haushälterin ⟨**IV U2**,32⟩
how [haʊ] wie **I**
  How about …? ['haʊ ˌəˌbaʊt] Wie ist es mit …? **I**
  How are you? [ˌhaʊ ˈɑː juː] Wie geht es dir/euch/Ihnen? **I**
  how many [haʊ 'meni] wie viele **I**
  How much is/are …? [haʊ 'mʌtʃ ɪz/ɑː] Wie viel kostet/kosten …? **I**
  How old are you? [haʊ ˈəʊld ə juː] Wie alt bist du/sind Sie? **I**
  how to do sth [haʊ tə] wie man etwas macht **II**
however [haʊ'evə] jedoch **II**
huge [hjuːdʒ] riesig, gewaltig **I**
Huh? [hʌ; hə] Was? Hä? **I**
humid ['hjuːmɪd] feucht ⟨**IV U2**,27⟩
a **hundred** [əˈhʌndrəd] hundert **I**
Hungarian [hʌŋˈgeərɪən] ungarisch; Ungar(in) **I**
hungry ['hʌŋgri] hungrig **I**
  to be as hungry as a horse [əz ˌhʌŋgri ˌəz ə 'hɔːs] einen Bärenhunger haben **II**
to **hunt** [hʌnt] jagen **I**
in a **hurry** [ˌɪn ə 'hʌri] in Eile **IV U3**,44
to **hurry (up)** [ˌhʌri ˈʌp] (sich) (be)eilen **II**
*to **hurt** [hɜːt] verletzen, weh tun **II**
*to be **hurt** [biː 'hɜːt] verletzt sein/werden **I**
husband ['hʌzbənd] Ehemann **II**
husky ['hʌski] Husky *(Schlittenhunderasse)* **II**

I

I [aɪ] ich **I**
  I'd [aɪd] Ich würde **II**
  I'd better = I had better [aɪd 'betə] Ich sollte lieber … **IV U2**,29
  I don't get it. [aɪ ˌdəʊnt 'get ˌɪt] Das kapiere ich nicht. **III**
  I'm fine. [aɪm 'faɪn] Mir geht es gut. **I**
  I see. [aɪ 'siː] aha; ach so **II**
ice [aɪs] Eis **I**
  ice cream [aɪs 'kriːm] Eis, Eiscreme **I**
idea [aɪ'dɪə] Einfall, Idee; Ahnung **I**

No idea! [ˌnəʊ aɪ'dɪə] Keine Ahnung! **I**
to **identify (with)** [aɪ'dentɪfaɪ] (sich) identifizieren (mit) **IV U3**,49
identity [aɪ'dentəti] Identität **II**
idiot ['ɪdɪət] Idiot(in) **III**
if [ɪf] wenn, falls; ob **I**
to **ignore** [ɪg'nɔː] ignorieren **III**
ill [ɪl] krank **II**
illness ['ɪlnəs] Krankheit **III**
image ['ɪmɪdʒ] Bild; Image **IV U3**,53
imaginative [ɪ'mædʒɪnətɪv] einfallsreich, fantasievoll **I**
to **imagine** [ɪ'mædʒɪn] sich (etwas) vorstellen **II**
to **imitate** ['ɪmɪteɪt] imitieren; nachahmen ⟨**IV EL**,102⟩
immediately [ɪ'miːdɪətli] sofort, gleich **I**
immigrant ['ɪmɪgrənt] Immigrant(in), Einwanderer; Einwanderin **IV U1**,10
importance [ɪm'pɔːtn̩ts] Bedeutung, Wichtigkeit **IV U2**,27
important [ɪm'pɔːtn̩t] wichtig; einflussreich **I**
impossible [ɪm'pɒsəbl] unmöglich **IV U1**,14
to **improve** [ɪm'pruːv] (sich) verbessern **II**
in [ɪn] in; rein, herein **I**
  in advance [ˌɪn əd'vɑːnts] im Voraus **III**
  in a hurry [ˌɪn ə 'hʌri] in Eile **IV U3**,44
  in between [ˌɪn bɪ'twiːn] dazwischen **II**
  in case [ɪn 'keɪs] falls; für den Fall, dass … **II**
  in class [ɪn 'klɑːs] in/vor der Klasse **I**
  in disguise [ɪn dɪs'gaɪz] verkleidet **II**
  in fact [ɪn 'fækt] tatsächlich; eigentlich **III**
  in front of [ɪn 'frʌnt əv] vor, davor **I**
  in my opinion [ɪn ˌmaɪ əˈpɪnjən] meiner Meinung nach **IV U2**,31
  in order to [ɪn 'ɔːdə tə] um … zu **III**
  in spite of [ɪn 'spaɪt əv] trotz **III**
  in the end [ˌɪn ðiː ˈend] schließlich, zum Schluss **II**
  in the late 1100s [leɪt] im späten 12. Jahrhundert **II**
  in time for [ɪn 'taɪm fə] rechtzeitig zu **III**
income ['ɪnkʌm] Einkommen **IV U3**,55
to **increase** [ɪn'kriːs] zunehmen; vergrößern ⟨**IV U1**,15⟩
indefinite [ɪn'defɪnət] unbestimmt; indefinit **IV U3**,45
independence [ˌɪndɪ'pendənts] Unabhängigkeit **IV F2**,57
independent [ˌɪndɪ'pendənt] unabhängig **III**
Indian ['ɪndɪən] indisch; Inder(in); indianisch; Indianer(in) **I**
  Indian summer [ˌɪndɪən 'sʌmə] Altweibersommer ⟨**IV U4**,61⟩
indirect speech [ˌɪndɪrekt 'spiːtʃ] indirekte Rede **III**
individual [ˌɪndɪ'vɪdʒuəl] individuell; einzeln **IV U5**,78
industry ['ɪndəstri] Industrie **III**
infinitive [ɪn'fɪnətɪv] Infinitiv **III**
influence ['ɪnfluənts] Einfluss **III**
to **influence** ['ɪnfluənts] beeinflussen **IV F1**,22

informal [ɪn'fɔːml] informell; zwanglos **III**
information [ˌɪnfə'meɪʃn] Information(en) **I**
inhabitant [ɪn'hæbɪtn̩t] Einwohner(in); Bewohner(in) **IV U1**,9
to **inherit** [ɪn'herɪt] erben **IV U2**,34
to **injure** ['ɪndʒə] verletzen **III**
inn [ɪn] Gasthaus; Herberge **IV U2**,24
inquiry [ɪn'kwaɪəri] Ermittlung; Nachforschung; Anfrage **IV U4**,70
insect ['ɪnsekt] Insekt **III**
inside [ɪn'saɪd] innen, drin; nach drinnen **I**
to **inspire** [ɪn'spaɪə] inspirieren; anregen **IV U3**,53
instantly ['ɪnstəntli] sofort ⟨**IV EL**,100⟩
instead [ɪn'sted] stattdessen **III**
instead of [ɪn'sted əv] anstatt **III**
institution [ˌɪnstɪ'tjuːʃn] Institution; Einrichtung **IV U3**,45
instruction [ɪn'strʌkʃn] Instruktion, Anweisung **III**
instrument ['ɪnstrəmənt] Instrument **I**
intention [ɪn'tentʃn] Absicht, Intention **II**
interactive [ˌɪntər'æktɪv] interaktiv **II**
interest ['ɪntrəst] Interesse **IV F3**,90
*to be **interested** in [biː 'ɪntrəstɪd ɪn] interessiert sein an, sich interessieren für **I**
interesting ['ɪntrəstɪŋ] interessant **I**
  far more interesting [ˌfɑː mɔːr 'ɪntrəstɪŋ] weitaus interessanter **I**
interior [ɪn'tɪəriə] Innenaufnahme **IV U2**,34
international [ˌɪntə'næʃnl] international **I**
Internet ['ɪntənet] Internet **I**
to **interpret** [ɪn'tɜːprɪt] interpretieren; dolmetschen **IV U1**,15
interpretation [ɪnˌtɜːprɪ'teɪʃn] Interpretation; Auslegung **IV U5**,84
to **interrupt** [ˌɪntə'rʌpt] unterbrechen **III**
interview ['ɪntəvjuː] Interview; Befragung **I**
to **interview** ['ɪntəvjuː] interviewen **II**
into ['ɪntu; 'ɪntə] in, hinein **I**
intransitive [ˌɪn'træntsətɪv] intransitiv *(kein Objekt nach sich ziehend)* ⟨**IV U2**,26⟩
to **introduce** [ˌɪntrə'djuːs] vorstellen, einführen **II**
introduction [ˌɪntrə'dʌkʃn] Einführung; Vorstellung **II**
to **invent** [ɪn'vent] erfinden **II**
invisible [ɪn'vɪzəbl] unsichtbar **II**
invitation [ˌɪnvɪ'teɪʃn] Einladung **I**
to **invite** [ɪn'vaɪt] einladen **I**
*to get (sb) **involved** (in) [ˌget ɪn'vɒlvd] sich (oder jmdn) beteiligen (an); sich engagieren (für); sich einlassen (auf) **IV U4**,67
Irish ['aɪrɪʃ] irisch; Irisch **I**
irregular [ɪ'regjələ] unregelmäßig **I**
island ['aɪlənd] Insel **I**
issue ['ɪʃuː; 'ɪsjuː] Frage; Angelegenheit; Problem **IV U3**,44
it [ɪt] es **I**
  It's nothing to do with me. [ɪts ˌnʌθɪŋ tə ˌduː wɪð 'miː] Ich habe damit nichts zu tun. **III**

It's no use (+ gerund) [ɪts 'nəʊ ˌjuːs] Es nützt nichts ... IV U4, 63
It's your turn. ['jɔː tɜːn] Du bist/Sie sind dran. I
Italian [ɪ'tæliən] italienisch; Italiener(in); Italienisch I
its [ɪts] sein(e); ihr(e) I

J

jacket ['dʒækɪt] Jacke II
jam [dʒæm] Marmelade II; Gedränge; Klemme II
  traffic jam ['træfɪk ˌdʒæm] Stau II
January ['dʒænjuri] Januar I
Japanese [ˌdʒæpn'iːz] japanisch; Japanisch IV U1, 10
jazz [dʒæz] Jazz II
jealous (of) ['dʒeləs] eifersüchtig, neidisch II
jeans pl. [dʒiːnz] Jeans I
jelly ['dʒeli] Wackelpudding, Gelee I
jerk [dʒɜːk] Trottel II
job [dʒɒb] Arbeitsstelle, Job I
jogging ['dʒɒgɪŋ] Jogging I
to join [dʒɔɪn] beitreten, sich anschließen; verbinden II
joke [dʒəʊk] Witz II
to joke [dʒəʊk] scherzen II
journalist ['dʒɜːnlɪst] Journalist(in) I
journey ['dʒɜːni] Reise, Fahrt II
judo ['dʒuːdəʊ] Judo III
to juggle ['dʒʌgl] jonglieren II
juice [dʒuːs] Saft II
July [dʒʊ'laɪ] Juli I
to jump [dʒʌmp] springen I
June [dʒuːn] Juni I
Jurassic [dʒʊə'ræsɪk] aus dem Jura stammend ⟨IV U2, 25⟩
just [dʒʌst] gerade; nur I

K

kangaroo [ˌkæŋgr'uː] Känguru IV U1, 8
kayaking ['kaɪækɪŋ] Kajakfahren II
*to be keen on [biː 'kiːn ɒn] scharf sein auf, begeistert sein von II
*to keep [kiːp] (be)halten II
  to keep (+ doing) [kiːp] etwas weiter/immer wieder tun II
  to keep sb waiting [ˌkiːp 'weɪtɪŋ] jmdn warten lassen IV U5, 80
  to keep up [kiːp ˌʌp] aufrecht erhalten II
keeper ['kiːpə] Wärter(in), Aufseher(in) I; Wächter(in), Aufpasser(in), Hüter(in) II
key [kiː] Schlüssel III
  key ring ['kiː ˌrɪŋ] Schlüsselbund; Schlüsselanhänger III
  key word ['kiː wɜːd] Stichwort; Schlüsselbegriff III
keyboard ['kiːbɔːd] Keyboard; Tastatur IV U4, 61
to kick [kɪk] kicken, treten II
  to kick sb off a team [kɪk ˌɒf] jmdn aus dem Team werfen II
kid [kɪd] Kind; Kitz I

to kidnap ['kɪdnæp] kidnappen; entführen IV U4, 68
kidnapper ['kɪdnæpə] Kidnapper(in); Entführer(in) IV U4, 68
to kill [kɪl] töten II
kilometre ['kɪləʊˌmiːtə; kɪ'lɒmɪtə] Kilometer II
kilt [kɪlt] Kilt; Schottenrock IV U3, 42
kind [kaɪnd] Art, Sorte II
  kind of ['kaɪnd ˌəv] ziemlich IV U4, 60
kind [kaɪnd] freundlich, nett II
kindergarten ['kɪndəgɑːtn] Kindergarten I
king [kɪŋ] König I
kingdom ['kɪŋdəm] Königreich III
kiss [kɪs] Kuss IV U3, 50
to kiss [kɪs] küssen IV U3, 51
kitchen ['kɪtʃɪn] Küche I
knee [niː] Knie III
knife, pl. knives [naɪf; naɪvz] Messer I
knight [naɪt] Ritter III
knock [nɒk] Klopfen, Schlag II
to knock [nɒk] stoßen; schlagen IV U3, 50
  to knock out [nɒk ˌaʊt] k.o. schlagen; umhauen III
  to knock over [ˌnɒk 'əʊvə] umstoßen II
knocker ['nɒkə] Türklopfer ⟨IV U4, 69⟩
*to know [nəʊ] wissen; kennen I
*to be known as [biː 'nəʊn ˌæz] bekannt sein als III
to knuckle ['nʌkl] mit dem Knöchel zudrücken ⟨IV EL, 100⟩
koala [kəʊ'ɑːlə] Koala IV U1, 8

L

label ['leɪbl] Etikett; Beschriftung IV U2, 27
lad [læd] Junge ⟨IV U1, 15⟩
lady ['leɪdi] Dame, Frau I
  ladies and gentlemen [ˌleɪdiz n 'dʒentlmən] meine Damen und Herren I
lake [leɪk] See II
lamb [læm] Lamm, Lämmchen I
lamp [læmp] Lampe; Leuchte IV U4, 69
lance [lɑːnts] Lanze III
land [lænd] Land II
to land [lænd] landen I
landlord ['lændlɔːd] (Haus-)Wirt IV U2, 33
landmark ['lændmɑːk] Wahrzeichen; Markstein IV U1, 9
landscape ['lændskeɪp] Landschaft I
lane [leɪn] Gasse; Fahrspur I
language ['læŋgwɪdʒ] Sprache I
lantern ['læntən] Laterne II
laptop ['læptɒp] Laptop II
large [lɑːdʒ] groß, riesig I
  largest ['lɑːdʒɪst] (der, die, das) größte I
to last [lɑːst] dauern, anhalten II
last [lɑːst] letzte(-r/-s) I
  at last [ət 'lɑːst] endlich I
  last night [lɑːst 'naɪt] gestern Abend/Nacht II
late [leɪt] spät I
  in the late 1100s [leɪt] im späten 12. Jahrhundert II
  to be late [biː 'leɪt] zu spät dran sein, zu spät kommen I

later ['leɪtə] später I
latest ['leɪtɪst] neueste(-r/-s) II
Latin ['lætɪn] Latein II
laugh [lɑːf] Lachen IV U3, 51
to laugh [lɑːf] lachen I
law [lɔː] Gesetz IV U1, 12
*to lay [leɪ] legen ⟨IV EL, 96⟩
layout ['leɪaʊt] Layout, Anordnung II
lazy ['leɪzi] faul I
*to lead [liːd] führen IV U2, 34
leader ['liːdə] Führer(in), Anführer(in) II
leaf, pl. leaves [liːf; liːvz] Blatt II
*to lean [liːn] (sich) lehnen IV U3, 52
*to learn [lɜːn; lɜːnt] lernen I
at least [ət 'liːst] mindestens, wenigstens II
leather ['leðə] Leder III
*to leave [liːv] (ver)lassen; abfahren II
  to leave out [liːv ˌaʊt] auslassen II
  to leave sb alone [ˌliːv ə'ləʊn] jemanden in Ruhe lassen III
left [left] links; linke(-r/-s) I
  on somebody's right/left [ɒn ˌsʌmbədiz 'raɪt/'left] zur Rechten/zur Linken von jemandem I
left [left] übrig II
leg [leg] Bein I
legend ['ledʒənd] Legende, Sage II
legendary ['ledʒəndri] legendär IV U2, 24
lemonade [ˌleməˈneɪd] Limonade III
*to lend [lend] (ver)leihen IV U3, 44
less [les] weniger II
lesson ['lesn] Unterrichtsstunde, Schulstunde I
*to let [let] lassen I
  Let's check! [lets 'tʃek] Lass(t) uns überprüfen! I
  Let's go! [lets 'gəʊ] Lass(t) uns gehen! I
  Let's start! [lets 'stɑːt] Lass(t) uns anfangen I
  to let off steam [ˌlet ɒf 'stiːm] Dampf ablassen; seinem Ärger Luft machen IV U3, 46
letter ['letə] Buchstabe; Brief I
  thank you letter ['θæŋk ju ˌletə] Dankschreiben I
lettuce ['letɪs] Kopfsalat III
level ['levl] Level, Höhe, Niveau II
library ['laɪbri] Bibliothek II
licence ['laɪsnts] Lizenz; Erlaubnis IV U3, 44
  driving licence ['draɪvɪŋ ˌlaɪsnts] Führerschein IV U3, 44
to lie [laɪ] lügen II
*to lie [laɪ] liegen I
life, pl. lives [laɪf] Leben I
  to take one's own life [ˌteɪk wʌnz ˌəʊn 'laɪf] sich das Leben nehmen III
lifestyle ['laɪfstaɪl] Lebensart III
to lift [lɪft] heben IV U2, 34
light [laɪt] Licht II
*to light [laɪt] anzünden; erhellen; beleuchten IV U2, 34
lighthouse ['laɪthaʊs] Leuchtturm I
like [laɪk] Vorliebe II
to like [laɪk] mögen, gern haben I

dictionary

Would you like …? [ˌwʊd jə 'laɪk] Möchtest du/möchten Sie/möchtet ihr …? II
What's it **like**? [ˌwɒts_ɪt 'laɪk] Wie ist es? II
like [laɪk] irgendwie ⟨IV U5,77⟩
like (this/that) [laɪk 'ðɪs/ðæt] so wie (hier/dort) I
like [laɪk] als ob ⟨IV U3,51⟩
*to be **likely** (to) [bi: 'laɪkli] wahrscheinlich sein IV U1,14
limerick ['lɪmrɪk] Limerick *(bestimmte Form eines fünfzeiligen Gedichts)* ⟨IV EL,99⟩
line [laɪn] Zeile; Linie I
   time **line** ['taɪm laɪn] Zeitstrahl III
   to drop sb a **line** [ˌdrɒp_ə 'laɪn] jmdm ein paar Zeilen schreiben ⟨IV F3,90⟩
link [lɪŋk] Link; Verbindung II
lip [lɪp] Lippe IV U3,50
list [lɪst] Liste I
to **listen** (to) ['lɪsn] zuhören, (an)hören I
   to listen closely [ˌlɪsn 'kləʊsli] genau zuhören ⟨IV EL,101⟩
listening ['lɪsnɪŋ] Hören, *hier:* Hörübung I
literature ['lɪtrətʃə] Literatur IV F1,23
little [lɪtl] klein I
   a **little** [ə 'lɪtl] ein bisschen IV F3,91
to **live** [lɪv] wohnen, leben I
   to live on sth ['lɪv_ɒn] von etw leben III
live [laɪv] live IV U3,45
living room ['lɪvɪŋ rʊm] Wohnzimmer I
lobster ['lɒbstə] Hummer IV U4,59
local ['ləʊkl] lokal, örtlich III
*to be **located** [bi: ləʊ'keɪtɪd] gelegen sein II
lock [lɒk] (Fahrrad-)Schloss I
to **lock** [lɒk] abschließen III
Londoner ['lʌndənə] Londoner(in) III
lonely ['ləʊnli] einsam IV U1,8
long [lɒŋ] lang; weit I
   no **longer** [nəʊ 'lɒŋgə] nicht mehr, nicht länger I
*to have a **look** (at) [ˌhæv_ə 'lʊk] anschauen III
to **look** [lʊk] (aus)sehen; schauen I
   to look after [lʊk_'ɑːftə] aufpassen auf; hüten II
   to look at ['lʊk_ət] anschauen I
   to look for ['lʊk fɔː] suchen II
   to look forward to [ˌlʊk 'fɔːwəd] sich freuen auf II
   to look like ['lʊk laɪk] aussehen wie I
   to look out for [ˌlʊk_'aʊt fə] Ausschau halten nach; sich in Acht nehmen vor II
   to look up [lʊk_'ʌp] nachschlagen, nachschauen II
lopsided [ˌlɒp'saɪdɪd] schief; nach einer Seite hängend ⟨IV U3,50⟩
lord [lɔːd] Lord, Herr II
*to **lose** [luːz] verlieren I
   to get lost [get 'lɒst] verloren gehen, sich verirren I
a **lot** of [ə 'lɒt_əv] viele, eine Menge I
   Fat lot of good it did them. [ˌfæt lɒt_əv 'gʊd_ɪt ˌdɪd ðəm] Einen Dreck hat es ihnen genützt. ⟨IV EL,100⟩
   lots of ['lɒts_əv] viel(e) I
   you lot ['juː ˌlɒt] ihr alle I
lottery ['lɒtri] Lotterie IV U2,27

loud [laʊd] laut I
lousy ['laʊzi] lausig IV U5,79
love [lʌv] Liebe; Herzliche Grüße *(am Briefende)* I
   to be in love (with) [ˌbiː_ɪn 'lʌv] verliebt sein (in) II
*to fall in **love** (with) [ˌfɔːl_ɪn 'lʌv] sich verlieben (in) II
to **love** [lʌv] lieben, gern mögen I
lovely ['lʌvli] schön, hübsch; herrlich I
low [ləʊ] niedrig III
luck [lʌk] Glück I
*to be **lucky** [bi: 'lʌki] Glück haben I
lunch [lʌntʃ] Mittagessen I
   packed lunch [ˌpækt 'lʌntʃ] Lunchpaket; Vesper III
lunchbox ['lʌntʃbɒks] Pausenbrotbehälter I
lunchroom *(AE)* ['lʌntʃrʊm] Speisesaal II

M

MA [ˌmæsə'tʃuːsɪts] Massachusetts II
mad [mæd] verrückt; wütend II
madam ['mædəm] Gnädige Frau *(Anrede)* I
magazine [mægə'ziːn] Zeitschrift, Magazin I
   football magazine ['fʊtbɔːl mægəˌziːn] Fußballzeitschrift I
magic ['mædʒɪk] Magie, Zauberei II
magnificent [məg'nɪfɪsnt] großartig, prachtvoll III
mail [meɪl] Post IV U5,77
to **mail** [meɪl] mailen, per E-Mail schicken II
main [meɪn] Haupt- II
maize [meɪz] Mais IV U2,27
*to **make** [meɪk] machen, tun I
   Made in Britain [ˌmeɪd_ɪn 'brɪtn] Hergestellt in Großbritannien I
   to be made of [bi: 'meɪd_əv] hergestellt sein aus II
   to make friends (with) [ˌmeɪk 'frendz] Freundschaft schließen (mit) III
   to make fun of [ˌmeɪk 'fʌn əv] sich lustig machen über III
   to make it ['meɪk_ɪt] es schaffen IV F2,56
   to make matters worse [tə ˌmeɪk mætəz 'wɜːs] zu allem Überfluss; um es noch schlimmer zu machen IV U2,29
   to make one's way to a place [ˌmeɪk 'weɪ] sich an einen Ort begeben IV U2,33
   to make sb do sth [meɪk] jmdn veranlassen, etw. zu tun II
   to make sense [ˌmeɪk 'sents] Sinn machen; einleuchten IV U4,69
   to make the most of [ˌmeɪk ðə 'məʊst_əv] ausnutzen II
man, *pl.* **men** [mæn; men] Mann I
to **manage** to (do sth) ['mænɪdʒ] schaffen (etw. zu tun) III
manager ['mænɪdʒə] Manager(in), Geschäftsführer(in) II
manners *(pl.)* ['mænəz] Manieren; Benehmen IV U5,83
   adverb of manner [ˌædvɜːb_əv 'mænə] Adverb der Art und Weise II

many ['meni] viele I
how **many** [haʊ 'meni] wie viele I
map [mæp] Stadtplan, Landkarte I
   mind map ['maɪnd mæp] Wörternetz *(eine Art Schaubild)* I
maple ['meɪpl] Ahorn ⟨IV U4,68⟩
marathon ['mærəθn] Marathon III
to **march** [mɑːtʃ] marschieren III
March [mɑːtʃ] März I
to **mark** [mɑːk] markieren I
marked [mɑːkt] markiert II
market ['mɑːkɪt] Markt I
marmalade ['mɑːməleɪd] Marmelade von Zitrusfrüchten II
*to be **married** to [bi: 'mærɪd tə] verheiratet sein mit I
   to get married [get 'mærɪd] heiraten II
to **marry** ['mæri] heiraten II
marsupial [mɑː'suːpiəl] Beuteltier ⟨IV U1,15⟩
mask [mɑːsk] Maske II
mass [mæs] Masse IV F1,23
master ['mɑːstə] Herr; Meister ⟨IV F2,56⟩
mouse **mat** ['maʊs mæt] Mauspad I
match [mætʃ] Wettkampf; Spiel; Match I; Streichholz IV U1,16
to **match** [mætʃ] zusammenbringen, zusammenfügen I
mate [meɪt] Kamerad(in) III
material [mə'tɪəriəl] Material II
Math *(AE)* [mæθ] Mathematik II
Maths [mæθs] Mathematik I
matter ['mætə] Angelegenheit; Frage IV U2,29
   to make matters worse [tə ˌmeɪk mætəz 'wɜːs] zu allem Überfluss; um es noch schlimmer zu machen IV U2,29
   What's the matter? [ˌwɒts ðə 'mætə] Was ist los? Was hast du? I
may [meɪ] könnte(n) vielleicht; mögen; dürfen II
May [meɪ] Mai I
maybe ['meɪbi] vielleicht I
mayday ['meɪdeɪ] Mayday, SOS-Ruf ⟨IV U2,29⟩
mayhaps ['meɪhæps] vielleicht ⟨IV U4,63⟩
me [miː] mich; mir I
   Me, too. [ˌmi: 'tuː] Ich auch. II
meal [miːl] Mahlzeit III
*to **mean** [miːn] bedeuten; meinen I
mean [miːn] gemein II
   to be on a mean streak [bi:_ɒn_ə ˌmiːn 'striːk] schlecht drauf sein ⟨IV EL,100⟩
meaning ['miːnɪŋ] Bedeutung, Sinn II
means, *pl.* **means** [miːnz] Mittel II
   means of transport *(sg. and pl.)* [ˌmiːnz_əv 'trænspɔːt] Transportmittel, Verkehrsmittel II
meat [miːt] Fleisch II
mechanic [mə'kænɪk] (Kfz-)Mechaniker(in) IV U3,43
media *pl.* ['miːdiə] Medien I
medicine ['medsn] Medizin IV U2,27
Mediterranean [ˌmedɪtə'reɪniən] mediterran, Mittelmeer- ⟨IV U2,27⟩
medium, *pl.* **media** ['miːdiəm; 'miːdiə] Medium III

*to **meet** [miːt] (sich) treffen I
Nice to meet you. [ˌnaɪs tə ˈmiːt juː] Nett, dich/Sie/euch kennen zu lernen. II
meeting [ˈmiːtɪŋ] Meeting, Treffen III
memory [ˈmemri] Erinnerung; Gedächtnis III
to **mend** [mend] flicken, reparieren II
We switched some **mental** dial over to Mute. [wi ˌswɪtʃt səm ˌmentl daɪəl ˌəʊvə tə ˈmjuːt] Wir schalteten gedanklich ab. ⟨IV EL, 101⟩
to **mention** [ˈmentʃn] erwähnen III
Don't mention it. [ˌdəʊnt ˈmentʃn ɪt] Bitte schön!; Gern geschehen. III
menu [ˈmenjuː] Speisekarte; Menü II
mere [mɪə] bloß IV U5, 76
merry [ˈmeri] fröhlich II
mess [mes] Durcheinander; Schweinerei II
to **mess** sth up [ˌmesˈʌp] etw. durcheinanderbringen; etw. vergeigen IV U4, 69
message [ˈmesɪdʒ] Nachricht I
metre [ˈmiːtə] Meter I
Mexican [ˈmeksɪkən] mexikanisch; Mexikaner(in) II
microphone [ˈmaɪkrəfəʊn] Mikrofon II
to **microwave** [ˈmaɪkrəʊweɪv] in der Mikrowelle zubereiten III
mid [mɪd] mittel ⟨IV U5, 79⟩
middle [ˈmɪdl] Mitte; Mittel- I
Middle Ages [ˌmɪdl ˈeɪdʒɪz] Mittelalter II
middle school [ˈmɪdl ˌskuːl] Mittelschule (weiterführende Schule in den USA, Mittelstufe) II
midnight [ˈmɪdnaɪt] Mitternacht IV U2, 32
might [maɪt] könnte(n) III
mild [maɪld] mild III
mile [maɪl] Meile (brit. Längenmaß) I
milk [mɪlk] Milch I
to **milk** [mɪlk] melken I
milkman, pl. **milkmen** [ˈmɪlkmən] Milchmann II
Milky Way [ˌmɪlki ˈweɪ] Milchstraße II
millennium, pl. **millennia** [mɪˈleniəm] Jahrtausend III
million [ˈmɪljən] Million III
millionaire [ˌmɪljəˈneə] Millionär(in) III
mime [maɪm] Pantomime ⟨IV EL, 102⟩
to **mince** [mɪnts] hacken III
mind [maɪnd] Geist, Verstand II
mind map [ˈmaɪnd mæp] Wörternetz (eine Art Schaubild) I
to be out of one's mind [biː ˌaʊt əv wʌnz ˈmaɪnd] verrückt sein III
to change one's mind [tʃeɪndʒ] seine Meinung ändern II
to **mind** [maɪnd] etwas dagegen haben; nichts ausmachen I
Never mind! [ˌnevə ˈmaɪnd] Mach dir nichts draus!; Macht nichts. III
mine [maɪn] Mine II
mine [maɪn] mein(-er/-e/-es) IV U3, 46
mineral water [ˈmɪnrl ˌwɔːtə] Mineralwasser IV F3, 91
minus [ˈmaɪnəs] minus; weniger I
minute [ˈmɪnɪt] Minute I
mirror [ˈmɪrə] Spiegel III

mischievous [ˈmɪstʃɪvəs] schelmisch, zu Streichen aufgelegt II
to **miss** [mɪs] vermissen; verpassen, verfehlen II
What's missing? [ˌwɒts ˈmɪsɪŋ] Was fehlt? I
mission [ˈmɪʃn] Mission, Auftrag II
mist [mɪst] Nebel; Dunst IV U2, 27
mistake [mɪˈsteɪk] Fehler III
by mistake [ˌbaɪ mɪˈsteɪk] versehentlich III
misunderstanding [ˌmɪsʌndəˈstændɪŋ] Missverständnis IV U5, 82
to **mix** [mɪks] mixen; mischen IV U5, 82
mixed [mɪkst] gemischt II
mixed bag [ˌmɪkst ˈbæg] buntes Allerlei I
ml (= **millilitre**) [ˈmɪliˌliːtə] Milliliter I
What are you pissing and **moaning** about? (infml) [ˌwɒt ə jə ˌpɪsɪŋ ənd ˈməʊnɪŋ əbaʊt] Was machst du denn für ein Theater? ⟨IV EL, 100⟩
mobile [ˈməʊbaɪl] Handy, Mobiltelefon I
model [ˈmɒdl] Model; Modell IV U4, 68
modern [ˈmɒdn] modern II
Mom (AE) [mɒm] Mama II
moment [ˈməʊmənt] Moment, Augenblick I
Monday [ˈmʌndeɪ] Montag I
money [ˈmʌni] Geld I
pocket money [ˈpɒkɪt ˌmʌni] Taschengeld I
monitor [ˈmɒnɪtə] Monitor III
monster [ˈmɒnstə] Monster I
month [mʌnθ] Monat I
moon [muːn] Mond IV U2, 33
moral [ˈmɒrl] moralisch ⟨IV F1, 23⟩
more [mɔː] mehr I
not any more [ˌnɒt eni ˈmɔː] nicht mehr II
morning [ˈmɔːnɪŋ] Morgen; Vormittag I
most [məʊst] das meiste; die meisten II
most of all [ˈməʊst əv ˌɔːl] am meisten II
most of the time [ˈməʊst əv ðə ˌtaɪm] meistens III
to make the most of [ˌmeɪk ðə ˈməʊst əv] ausnutzen II
mother [ˈmʌðə] Mutter I
to **motivate** [ˈməʊtɪveɪt] motivieren III
motorway (BE) [ˈməʊtəweɪ] Autobahn IV U3, 44
mountain [ˈmaʊntɪn] Berg I
mountain biking [ˈmaʊntɪn ˌbaɪkɪŋ] Mountainbikefahren II
Mountain Rescue [ˌmaʊntɪn ˈreskjuː] Bergwacht II
mouse, pl. **mice** [maʊs; maɪs] Maus I
mouse mat [ˈmaʊs mæt] Mauspad I
mouth [maʊθ] Mund III
to **move** [muːv] (sich) bewegen I; umziehen III
movie [ˈmuːvi] Film II
Mr [ˈmɪstə] Herr (Anrede) I
Mrs [ˈmɪsɪz] Frau (Anrede) I
Ms [mɪz] Frau (Anrede) I
MT [mɒnˈtænə] Montana II
much [mʌtʃ] viel I
How much is/are ... ? [ˌhaʊ ˈmʌtʃ ɪz/ɑː]

Wie viel kostet/kosten ... ? I
mud [mʌd] Schlamm III
muddy [ˈmʌdi] schlammig III
muesli [ˈmjuːzli] Müsli I
mug [mʌg] Becher; Krug I
mulga [ˈmʊlgə] Mulga (australische Baumart) ⟨IV EL, 96⟩
Mum [mʌm] Mama I
muscle [ˈmʌsl] Muskel III
museum [mjuːˈziːəm] Museum I
mushroom [ˈmʌʃrʊm] Pilz III
music [ˈmjuːzɪk] Musik I
musical [ˈmjuːzɪkl] Musical II
musical [ˈmjuːzɪkl] musikalisch, Musik- III
must [mʌst; məst] müssen I
mustang [ˈmʌstæŋ] Mustang IV
We switched some **mental** dial over to Mute. [wi ˌswɪtʃt səm ˌmentl daɪəl ˌəʊvə tə ˈmjuːt] Wir schalteten gedanklich ab. ⟨IV EL, 101⟩
(my) fault [ˈmaɪ ˌfɔːlt] (meine) Schuld III
my [maɪ] mein(e) I
(my) own [əʊn] (mein) eigen(-e/-r/-s) I
My name is ... [maɪ ˈneɪm ɪz] Ich heiße ... I
myself [maɪˈself] (ich) selbst; mich (selbst) III
mystery [ˈmɪstri] Mysterium, Rätsel, Geheimnis III

N

name [neɪm] Name I
first name [ˈfɜːst ˌneɪm] Vorname IV U1, 11
My name is ... [maɪ ˈneɪm ɪz] Ich heiße ... I
to call sb names [ˌkɔːl sʌmbɒdi ˈneɪmz] beschimpfen IV U3, 50
What's your name? [ˌwɒts jə ˈneɪm] Wie heißt du/heißen Sie? I
to **name** [neɪm] benennen ⟨IV EL, 98⟩
narrator [neˈreɪtə] Erzähler(in) IV U4, 70
narrow [ˈnærəʊ] eng, schmal II
nasty [ˈnɑːsti] garstig, gemein; scheußlich II
national [ˈnæʃnl] national, landesweit I
national park [ˌnæʃnl ˈpɑːk] Nationalpark, Naturpark I
nationality [ˌnæʃnˈæləti] Nationalität, Staatsangehörigkeit II
native [ˈneɪtɪv] eingeboren III
Native American [ˌneɪtɪv əˈmerɪkən] Ureinwohner(in) Amerikas, Indianer(in); indianisch II
natural [ˈnætʃrl] natürlich, Natur- III
natural resource [ˌnætʃrl rɪˈzɔːs] Bodenschatz IV U2, 27
nature [ˈneɪtʃə] Natur III
navigation [ˌnævɪˈgeɪʃn] Navigation; Orientierung IV F1, 23
near [nɪə] nahe, in der Nähe von I
nearly [ˈnɪəli] fast, annähernd II
necessary [ˈnesəsri] notwendig, nötig III
need [niːd] Bedürfnis; Erfordernis IV F3, 90
to **need** [niːd] brauchen, benötigen I

dictionary

needle [niːdl] Nadel III
negative [ˈnegətɪv] negativ, verneint I
neighborhood (AE) [ˈneɪbəhʊd] Nachbarschaft II
neighbour [ˈneɪbə] Nachbar(in) I
nervous [ˈnɜːvəs] nervös, aufgeregt I
never [ˈnevə] nie, niemals I
Never mind! [ˌnevə ˈmaɪnd] Mach dir nichts draus!; Macht nichts. III
new [njuː] neu I
news (sg.) [njuːz] Nachricht(en), Neuigkeit(en) II
newspaper [ˈnjuːˌspeɪpə] Zeitung I
next [nekst] nächste(-r/-s) I
  the next size down [ðə ˌnekst saɪz ˈdaʊn] eine Größe kleiner III
next [nekst] als nächstes II
  next to [ˈnekst tə] neben I
nice [naɪs] nett I
  Nice to meet you. [ˌnaɪs tə ˈmiːt juː] Nett, dich/Sie/euch kennen zu lernen. II
night [naɪt] Nacht I
  last night [lɑːst ˈnaɪt] gestern Abend/Nacht II
nil [nɪl] null II
nine [naɪn] neun I
nineteen [naɪnˈtiːn] neunzehn I
nineteenth [naɪnˈtiːnθ] neunzehnte(-r/-s) I
ninety [ˈnaɪnti] neunzig I; neunzig Grad Fahrenheit = ca. 32° Celsius ⟨IV EL, 100⟩
ninth [naɪnθ] neunte(-r/-s) I
no [nəʊ] kein(e) I
  no good [nəʊ ˈgʊd] nutzlos, wertlos II
  No idea! [ˌnəʊ aɪˈdɪə] Keine Ahnung! I
  no longer [nəʊ ˈlɒŋgə] nicht mehr, nicht länger I
  No way! [nəʊ ˈweɪ] Auf keinen Fall! III
  No worries! [nəʊ ˈwʌriz] Keine Sorge! ⟨IV U1, 10⟩
no [nəʊ] nein I
  Don't take no for an answer. [ˌdəʊnt teɪk ˈnəʊ fər ən ˌɑːntsə] Akzeptiere keine Widerrede. ⟨IV U1, 10⟩
nobody [ˈnəʊbədi] niemand II
to **nod** [nɒd] nicken IV U3, 52
noise [nɔɪz] Geräusch, Lärm I
noisy [ˈnɔɪzi] laut I
none [nʌn] keine(r) III
  none of this [ˈnʌn əv ðɪs] nichts davon IV U3, 50
nonet [nəʊˈnet] Nonett (bestimmte Form eines neunzeiligen Gedichts) ⟨IV EL, 98⟩
normal [ˈnɔːml] normal IV U3, 51
Norman [ˈnɔːmən] Normanne, Normannin; normannisch II
north [nɔːθ] Norden I
nose [nəʊz] Nase I
not [nɒt] nicht I
  not any better [ˌnɒt eni ˈbetə] (überhaupt) nicht besser II
  not any more [ˌnɒt eni ˈmɔː] nicht mehr II
  not even [nɒt ˈiːvn] nicht einmal II
  not exactly [ˌnɒt ɪgˈzæktli] nicht gerade IV U5, 80
  not until [nɒt ənˈtɪl] nicht (be)vor; erst (wenn/als) III

note [nəʊt] Notiz; Zettel III; Note (Musik); Ton IV U5, 78
notes pl. [nəʊts] Notizen, Anmerkungen I
nothing [ˈnʌθɪŋ] nichts II
  It's nothing to do with me. [ɪts ˌnʌθɪŋ tə ˌduː wɪð ˈmiː] Ich habe damit nichts zu tun. III
notice [ˈnəʊtɪs] Anschlag, Notiz III
to **notice** [ˈnəʊtɪs] bemerken II
noun [naʊn] Nomen II
November [nəʊˈvembə] November I
now [naʊ] jetzt, nun I
  right now [raɪt ˈnaʊ] jetzt gleich II
nowhere [ˈnəʊweə] nirgendwo; nirgendwohin II
number [ˈnʌmbə] Zahl, Nummer I
nurse [nɜːs] Krankenschwester, Krankenpfleger II

O

o'clock [əˈklɒk] Uhr (Zeitangabe bei vollen Stunden) I
oak [əʊk] Eiche II
object [ˈɒbdʒɪkt] Objekt; Gegenstand III
obligation [ˌɒblɪˈgeɪʃn] Verpflichtung ⟨IV U3, 48⟩
obvious [ˈɒbviəs] offensichtlich IV U4, 69
to **occur** [əˈkɜː] sich ereignen; vorkommen ⟨IV U1, 15⟩
ocean [ˈəʊʃn] Ozean ⟨IV U1, 15⟩
October [ɒkˈtəʊbə] Oktober I
odd [ɒd] seltsam, nicht passend I
  Find the odd word out! [ɒd wɜːd ˈaʊt] Finde das Wort, das nicht in die Gruppe passt! (Wortschatzübung) I
of [ɒv; əv] von I
  of course [əv ˈkɔːs] natürlich, selbstverständlich I
off [ɒf] von … weg/ab/herunter I
  off to [ˈɒf tə] auf nach I
  Off to the USA! [ˌɒf tə ðə juːesˈeɪ] Auf in die USA! I
offer [ˈɒfə] Angebot I
  special offer [ˌspeʃl ˈɒfə] Sonderangebot I
to **offer** [ˈɒfə] anbieten II
office [ˈɒfɪs] Büro I
  post office [ˈpəʊstˌɒfɪs] Postamt III
officer [ˈɒfɪsə] Beamter, Beamtin III
often [ˈɒfn] oft I
oh [əʊ] oh; null I
  Oh dear! [ˈəʊ ˌdɪə] Oje! I
oil [ɔɪl] Öl IV U3, 43
  oil rig [ˈɔɪl rɪg] Bohrinsel IV U3, 43
OK [əʊˈkeɪ] OK I
old [əʊld] alt I
  How old are you? [haʊ ˈəʊld ə juː] Wie alt bist du/sind Sie? I
  old people's home [ˌəʊld piːplz ˈhəʊm] Altersheim II
old-fashioned [ˌəʊld ˈfæʃnd] altmodisch IV U4, 69
olive [ˈɒlɪv] Olive; Ölbaum IV U2, 27
omelette [ˈɒmlət] Omelett I
*to be **on** [biː ˈɒn] im Gange sein, laufen I
on [ɒn] auf I
  on business [ɒn ˈbɪznɪs] geschäftlich I

  on purpose [ɒn ˈpɜːpəs] absichtlich III
  on somebody's right/left [ɒn ˌsʌmbədiz ˈraɪt/ˈleft] zur Rechten/zur Linken von jemandem I
  on the other hand [ɒn ði ˈʌðə ˌhænd] andererseits IV U4, 69
  on the run [ɒn ðə ˈrʌn] auf der Flucht IV U1, 17
  on time [ɒn ˈtaɪm] pünktlich II
  on top (of) [ɒn ˈtɒp] obendrauf II
  on top of that [ɒn ˌtɒp əv ˈðæt] obendrein; zusätzlich IV U2, 29
  to be on a team [ˌbiː ɒn ə ˈtiːm] Mitglied eines Teams sein III
  to live on sth [ˈlɪv ɒn] von etw leben III
once [wʌns] einmal; einst I
  at once [ət ˈwʌns] sofort, plötzlich I
one [wʌn] eins; ein(e) I
onion [ˈʌnjən] Zwiebel I
online [ˌɒnˈlaɪn] online II
only [ˈəʊnli] einzige(-r/-s) II
only [ˈəʊnli] nur; erst; bloß I
onto [ˈɒntə] auf … hinauf II
Oops! [uːps] Hoppla! Huch! I
to **open** [ˈəʊpn] öffnen, aufmachen I
open [ˈəʊpn] offen; geöffnet I
open-air [ˌəʊpnˈeə] Freilicht- IV U5, 81
opening hours [ˈəʊpnɪŋ ˌaʊəz] Öffnungszeiten I
opera [ˈɒprə] Oper IV U1, 9
opinion [əˈpɪnjən] Meinung II
  in my opinion [ɪn ˈmaɪ əˌpɪnjən] meiner Meinung nach IV U2, 31
opportunity [ˌɒpəˈtjuːnəti] Gelegenheit; Chance IV F3, 90
opposite [ˈɒpəzɪt] Gegenteil II
or [ɔː] oder I
oral [ˈɔːrl] mündlich IV U3, 49
orange [ˈɒrɪndʒ] Orange II
orange [ˈɒrɪndʒ] orange I
order [ˈɔːdə] Reihenfolge, Ordnung II
  running order [ˈrʌnɪŋ ˌɔːdə] Startreihenfolge ⟨IV U5, 80⟩
  in order to [ɪn ˈɔːdə tə] um … zu III
to **order** [ˈɔːdə] bestellen II; befehlen III
to **organize** [ˈɔːgənaɪz] organisieren II
origin [ˈɒrɪdʒɪn] Ursprung III
original [əˈrɪdʒnl] original; ursprünglich III
orphanage [ˈɔːfnɪdʒ] Waisenhaus ⟨IV U2, 32⟩
other [ˈʌðə] anders; andere(-r/-s) I
  each other [ˌiːtʃ ˈʌðə] sich gegenseitig II
  the other day [ðiˌʌðə ˈdeɪ] neulich IV U3, 46
otherwise [ˈʌðəwaɪz] sonst I
otherworldly [ˌʌðəˈwɜːldli] aus einer anderen Welt ⟨IV U5, 77⟩
our [ˈaʊə] unser(e) I
out [aʊt] außerhalb, (nach) draußen, raus I
  out and about [ˌaʊt ənd əˈbaʊt] unterwegs IV U3, 44
  out of [ˈaʊt əv] aus … heraus I
  out of the corner of my eye [aʊt əv ðə ˌkɔːnər əv maɪ ˈaɪ] aus dem Augenwinkel ⟨IV U3, 52⟩

out of work [ˌaʊt əv ˈwɜːk] arbeitslos III
outback [ˈaʊtbæk] Outback *(australisches Hinterland)* IV U1, 8
outlaw [ˈaʊtlɔː] Geächtete(r), Vogelfreie(r) II
outside [aʊtˈsaɪd] (nach) (dr)außen; außerhalb I
over [ˈəʊvə] (hin)über I; vorüber II
 all over [ˌɔːl ˈəʊvə] überall IV U3, 50
 over and over [ˌəʊvər ənd ˈəʊvə] immer wieder IV U3, 50
 over there [ˌəʊvə ˈðeə] da drüben I
*to overcome [ˌəʊvəˈkʌm] überwinden III
overcrowding [ˌəʊvəˈkraʊdɪŋ] Überfüllung IV U2, 27
*to overhear [ˌəʊvəˈhɪə] belauschen; zufällig mit anhören IV U3, 46
*to oversleep [ˌəʊvəˈsliːp] verschlafen II
overweight [ˌəʊvəˈweɪt] übergewichtig II
Ow! [aʊ] Autsch! I
to own [əʊn] besitzen II
(my) own [əʊn] (mein) eigen(-e/-r/-s) I

P

pack [pæk] Packung III
to pack [pæk] packen II
 packed lunch [ˌpækt ˈlʌntʃ] Lunchpaket; Vesper II
package [ˈpækɪdʒ] Paket III
page [peɪdʒ] Seite I
pain [peɪn] Schmerz II
paint [peɪnt] Farbe III
to paint [peɪnt] (an)malen, streichen II
painting [ˈpeɪntɪŋ] Gemälde ⟨IV EL, 98⟩
pair [peə] Paar I
 a pair of [ə ˈpeər əv] ein Paar I
palm tree [ˈpɑːm ˌtriː] Palme IV U2, 25
pan [pæn] Pfanne; Kochtopf mit Stiel IV U4, 63
pancake [ˈpænkeɪk] Pfannkuchen III
panic [ˈpænɪk] Panik III
pants *(AE) (pl.)* [pænts] Hose III
paper [ˈpeɪpə] Papier IV F2, 57
parade [pəˈreɪd] Parade, Umzug II
paradise [ˈpærəˌdaɪs] Paradies IV U2, 25
paragraph [ˈpærəɡrɑːf] Paragraph, Absatz II
to paraphrase [ˈpærəfreɪz] paraphrasieren; umschreiben IV U3, 49
parents *pl.* [ˈpeərənts] Eltern I
park [pɑːk] Park I
 car park [ˈkɑː ˌpɑːk] Parkplatz; Parkhaus IV U1, 11
 national park [ˌnæʃnl ˈpɑːk] Nationalpark, Naturpark I
parliament [ˈpɑːləmənt] Parlament III
part [pɑːt] Teil I; Rolle II
 to take part (in) [teɪk ˈpɑːt] teilnehmen (an) II
part [pɑːt] teils IV U1, 16
particular [pəˈtɪkjələ] bestimmt III
particularly [pəˈtɪkjələli] besonders III
partner [ˈpɑːtnə] Partner(in) I
party [ˈpɑːti] Party, Feier I
 search party [ˈsɜːtʃ ˌpɑːti] Suchtrupp ⟨IV U1, 17⟩

to party [ˈpɑːti] feiern IV U5, 77
pass [pɑːs] Ausweis, Pass II
 boarding pass [ˈbɔːdɪŋ ˌpɑːs] Bordkarte II
to pass [pɑːs] zupassen, zuspielen; reichen III; durchgehen; vorbeigehen; bestehen IV U3, 44
passenger [ˈpæsndʒə] Passagier(in); Beifahrer(in) III
passive [ˈpæsɪv] Passiv II
passport [ˈpɑːspɔːt] (Reise-)Pass IV U2, 30
past [pɑːst] Vergangenheit I
 past perfect [ˌpɑːst ˈpɜːfɪkt] Plusquamperfekt III
past [pɑːst] vorbei, vorüber I
half past (two) [ˈhɑːf pɑːst] halb (drei) I
pasta [ˈpæstə] Pasta, Nudeln II
path [pɑːθ] Pfad, Weg II
to pause [pɔːz] Pause machen; anhalten; verharren III
pavilion [pəˈvɪljən] Pavillon; Clubhaus IV U3, 51
*to pay for [peɪ] bezahlen III
PE [ˌpiːˈiː] Sportunterricht II
peaceful [ˈpiːsfl] friedlich ⟨IV EL, 96⟩
peasant [ˈpeznt] Kleinbauer II
to peep [piːp] gucken; spähen ⟨IV U4, 71⟩
pen [pen] Füller I
pencil [ˈpensl] Bleistift; Buntstift I
 pencil case [ˈpensl ˌkeɪs] Federmäppchen I
penny, *pl.* pence [ˈpeni; pents] Penny, Pence *(brit. Währungseinheit)* I
people [ˈpiːpl] Leute, Menschen I; Volk IV U3, 47
 old people's home [ˌəʊld piːplz ˈhəʊm] Altersheim II
pepper [ˈpepə] Pfeffer; Paprikaschote III
per [pɜː; pə] pro III
percent, *pl.* percent [pəˈsent] Prozent II
past perfect [ˌpɑːst ˈpɜːfɪkt] Plusquamperfekt III
perfect [ˈpɜːfɪkt] perfekt, vollkommen III
to perform [pəˈfɔːm] aufführen, auftreten III
performance [pəˈfɔːmənts] Aufführung; Vorstellung IV U5, 80
performer [pəˈfɔːmə] Darsteller(in); Schauspieler(in); Künstler(in) IV U5, 78
perhaps [pəˈhæps] vielleicht III
period [ˈpɪəriəd] Periode; Zeitspanne III
permanent [ˈpɜːmnənt] permanent; dauerhaft IV F2, 56
person [ˈpɜːsn] Person I
perspective [pəˈspektɪv] Perspektive, Blickwinkel III
to persuade [pəˈsweɪd] überreden III
pet [pet] Haustier; Liebling I
phone [fəʊn] Telefon II
 phone booth *(AE)* [ˈfəʊn ˌbuːð] Telefonzelle IV U4, 69
to phone [fəʊn] telefonieren I
photo [ˈfəʊtəʊ] Foto, Fotografie I
 to take photos [teɪk ˈfəʊtəʊz] fotografieren, Fotos machen I
photocopy [ˈfəʊtəʊˌkɒpi] Fotokopie IV U4, 67
photographer [fəˈtɒɡrəfə] Fotograf(in) III

phrase [freɪz] Redewendung, Ausdruck I
physical [ˈfɪzɪkl] physisch, körperlich II
 Physical Education [ˌfɪzɪkl ˌedʒʊˈkeɪʃn] Sport *(Schulfach)* II
piano [piˈænəʊ] Klavier, Piano II
to pick [pɪk] pflücken III
 to pick up [pɪk ˈʌp] aufheben; abholen I
pickup [ˈpɪkʌp] Pickup II
picnic [ˈpɪknɪk] Picknick I
picture [ˈpɪktʃə] Bild I
piece [piːs] Stück II
pig [pɪɡ] Schwein I
pigsty [ˈpɪɡstaɪ] Schweinestall I
pilgrim [ˈpɪlɡrɪm] Pilger(in) IV U2, 24
pill [pɪl] Pille, Tablette III
pillow [ˈpɪləʊ] Kopfkissen III
pilot [ˈpaɪlət] Pilot(in) I
pine (tree) [paɪn] Kiefer III
pineapple [ˈpaɪnæpl] Ananas IV U2, 27
pink [pɪŋk] pink, rosa I
pint [paɪnt] Pinte *(engl. Hohlmaß: 0,57 l)* II
pirate [ˈpaɪərət] Pirat(in), Seeräuber(in) IV F1, 22
What are you pissing and moaning about? *(infml)* [ˌwɒt ə jə ˌpɪsɪŋ ənd ˈməʊnɪŋ əˌbaʊt] Was machst du denn für ein Theater? ⟨IV EL, 100⟩
clay-pit [ˈkleɪpɪt] Lehmgrube ⟨IV U2, 24⟩
gravel pit slide [ˈɡrævl pɪt ˌslaɪd] abrutschender Kies in einer Kiesgrube ⟨IV EL, 101⟩
What a pity! [ˌwɒt ə ˈpɪti] Wie schade! II
place [pleɪs] Platz, Stelle, Ort I; Heim; Haus IV U4, 69
 to take place [teɪk ˈpleɪs] stattfinden III
plain [pleɪn] Ebene II
plan [plæn] Plan I
to plan [plæn] planen II
plane [pleɪn] Flugzeug I
plant [plɑːnt] Pflanze IV U1, 8
to plant [plɑːnt] pflanzen II
plantation [plænˈteɪʃn] Plantage; Kolonie ⟨IV U4, 58⟩
plaster [ˈplɑːstə] Gips III
plastic [ˈplæstɪk] Plastik, Kunststoff IV U2, 27
plate [pleɪt] Teller I
platform [ˈplætfɔːm] Plattform, Tribüne; Bahnsteig II
platypus, *pl.* platypi [ˈplætɪpəs; ˈplætɪpaɪ] Schnabeltier ⟨IV U4, 67⟩
play [pleɪ] Spiel, Theaterstück I
 role play [ˈrəʊl pleɪ] Rollenspiel I
to play [pleɪ] spielen I
player [ˈpleɪə] Spieler, Mitspieler I
 CD player [ˌsiːˈdiː ˌpleɪə] CD-Spieler I
 DVD player [ˌdiːviːˈdiː ˌpleɪə] DVD-Player III
playground [ˈpleɪɡraʊnd] Schulhof, Pausenhof I
please [pliːz] bitte I
pleased [pliːzd] erfreut; zufrieden IV F3, 91; ⟨IV EL, 96⟩
 to be pleased [biː ˈpliːzd] erfreut sein III
plenty [ˈplenti] eine Menge IV U2, 32
plot [plɒt] Handlung ⟨IV EL, 97⟩
plural [ˈplʊərəl] Plural, Mehrzahl I
plus [plʌs] plus I

one hundred and seventy-three 173

Dictionary

pm [ˌpiːˈem] nachmittags (*Uhrzeit*) I
pocket [ˈpɒkɪt] Hosen- oder Jackentasche I
  pocket money [ˈpɒkɪt ˌmʌni] Taschengeld I
poem [ˈpəʊɪm] Gedicht I
poetry [ˈpəʊətri] Lyrik ⟨IV EL, 98⟩
point [pɔɪnt] Punkt I
  breaking point [ˈbreɪkɪŋ ˌpɔɪnt] Schmerzgrenze; kritischer Punkt ⟨IV U3, 46⟩
  point of view [ˌpɔɪnt ɒv ˈvjuː] Standpunkt; Perspektive IV U5, 78
  turning point [ˈtɜːnɪŋ ˌpɔɪnt] Wendepunkt III
  2.45 (point) [ˈtuː pɔɪnt ˌfɔː ˈfaɪv] Komma (*bei Zahlenangaben*) I
to **point** out [pɔɪntˈaʊt] hinweisen auf III
poison [ˈpɔɪzn] Gift IV U1, 13
poisonous [ˈpɔɪznəs] giftig IV U1, 8
police [pəˈliːs] Polizei I
polite [pəˈlaɪt] höflich III
to drag the **ponds** [ˌdræɡ ðə ˈpɒndz] die Teiche mit Netzen absuchen ⟨IV EL, 101⟩
pony [ˈpəʊni] Pony I
  pony trekking [ˈpəʊni ˌtrekɪŋ] Ponyreiten im Gelände II
Pooh! [puː] Pfui! Bäh! I
swimming **pool** [ˈswɪmɪŋ ˌpuːl] Schwimmbecken; Schwimmbad I
poor [pɔː; pʊə] arm I
  the poor sucker [ˌpɔː ˈsʌkə] das arme Schwein ⟨IV EL, 101⟩
pop [pɒp] Pop II
  pop star [ˈpɒp stɑː] Popstar I
popcorn [ˈpɒpkɔːn] Popcorn II
the **Pope** [pəʊp] der Papst ⟨IV F1, 23⟩
popular [ˈpɒpjələ] populär, beliebt II
population [ˌpɒpjəˈleɪʃn] Bevölkerung III
pork [pɔːk] Schweinefleisch III
porridge [ˈpɒrɪdʒ] Haferbrei IV U3, 46
port [pɔːt] Hafen I
position [pəˈzɪʃn] Position III
to **position** [pəˈzɪʃn] positionieren; aufstellen ⟨IV EL, 102⟩
positive [ˈpɒzətɪv] positiv II
possibility [ˌpɒsəˈbɪləti] Möglichkeit III
possible [ˈpɒsəbl] möglich II
post [pəʊst] Pfosten, Mast II
post [pəʊst] Post I
  post office [ˈpəʊst ˌɒfɪs] Postamt III
to **post** [pəʊst] aufgeben (*einen Brief*); abschicken III
postcard [ˈpəʊstkɑːd] Postkarte I
poster [ˈpəʊstə] Poster I
pot [pɒt] Topf III; Kanne IV U2, 24
potato, *pl.* **potatoes** [pəˈteɪtəʊ] Kartoffel II
pottery [ˈpɒtri] Töpferei III
pouch [paʊtʃ] Beutel ⟨IV U1, 15⟩
pound [paʊnd] Pfund (*brit. Währungseinheit*) I
power [ˈpaʊə] Kraft, Stärke, Macht I
  Word power [ˈwɜːd ˌpaʊə] Besondere Wortschatzübung I
powerful [ˈpaʊəfl] stark; mächtig; leistungsfähig IV F1, 22
practical [ˈpræktɪkl] praktisch IV U4, 69
practice [ˈpræktɪs] Übung I
  sound practice [ˈsaʊnd ˌpræktɪs] Hör-/Ausspracheübung I
to **practice** *(AE)* [ˈpræktɪs] üben, praktizieren II
to **pray** [preɪ] beten II
prayer [preə] Gebet II
prediction [prɪˈdɪkʃn] Voraussage II
to **prefer** [prɪˈfɜː] vorziehen II
Premiership [ˈpremɪəʃɪp] erste Division, vgl. Deutsche Bundesliga II
to **prepare** [prɪˈpeə] vorbereiten; zubereiten II
  to prepare (for) [prɪˈpeə] sich vorbereiten (auf) III
preposition [ˌprepəˈzɪʃn] Präposition II
present [ˈpreznt] Gegenwart, Präsens I; Geschenk I
to **present** [prɪˈzent] präsentieren II
presentation [ˌpreznˈteɪʃn] Präsentation IV U4, 67
president [ˈprezɪdnt] Präsident(in) IV U5, 76
press [pres] Presse IV F1, 23
  printing press [ˈprɪntɪŋ ˌpres] Druckerpresse ⟨IV F1, 23⟩
pressure [ˈpreʃə] Druck IV U1, 13
pretty [ˈprɪti] ziemlich IV U4, 60
to **prevent** sth from happening/sb from doing sth [prɪˈvent] verhindern, dass etwas passiert/dass jmd etw. tut IV U5, 81
price [praɪs] Preis IV F2, 57
prince [prɪns] Prinz II
principal *(AE)* [ˈprɪnsɪpl] Schulleiter(in) II
to **print** [prɪnt] drucken IV F1, 23
  printing press [ˈprɪntɪŋ ˌpres] Druckerpresse ⟨IV F1, 23⟩
printer [ˈprɪntə] Drucker(in) II
printout [ˈprɪntaʊt] Ausdruck IV U4, 67
prison [ˈprɪzn] Gefängnis IV U1, 12
prisoner [ˈprɪznə] Gefangene(r) III
private [ˈpraɪvɪt] privat IV U4, 68
prize [praɪz] Preis II
probably [ˈprɒbəbli] wahrscheinlich II
problem [ˈprɒbləm] Problem, Schwierigkeit I
to **produce** [prəˈdjuːs] herstellen, produzieren III
product [ˈprɒdʌkt] Produkt III
professional [prəˈfeʃnl] professionell IV U5, 80
professor [prəˈfesə] Professor(in) III
profile [ˈprəʊfaɪl] Profil; Porträt; Steckbrief II
program *(AE)* [ˈprəʊɡræm] Programm II
programme *(BE)* [ˈprəʊɡræm] Programm; Sendung III
progressive form [prəˈɡresɪv] Verlaufsform II
project [ˈprɒdʒekt] Projekt II
video **projector** [ˌvɪdɪəʊ prəˈdʒektə] Beamer (*Projektionsgerät*) IV U4, 67
promise [ˈprɒmɪs] Versprechen I
to **promise** [ˈprɒmɪs] versprechen II
pronoun [ˈprəʊnaʊn] Pronomen II
  relative pronoun [ˌrelətɪv ˈprəʊnaʊn] Relativpronomen II
to **pronounce** [prəˈnaʊnts] aussprechen III
pronunciation [prəˌnʌntsiˈeɪʃn] Aussprache III
-proof [pruːf] -sicher; -resistent IV U1, 16
to **protect** sb (from) [prəˈtekt] jmdn (be)schützen (vor) II
chief **protector** [ˌtʃiːf prəˈtektə] oberste(r) Beschützer(in) ⟨IV U1, 19⟩
to **protest** [prəʊˈtest] protestieren III
Protestant [ˈprɒtɪstnt] Protestant(in); protestantisch IV F1, 23
Protestantism [ˈprɒtɪstntɪzm] Protestantismus ⟨IV F1, 23⟩
to **prove** [pruːv] beweisen III
to **provide** sb with [prəˈvaɪd] jmdn versorgen mit IV F2, 56
psychological [ˌsaɪklˈɒdʒɪkl] psychologisch; psychisch ⟨IV EL, 100⟩
pub [pʌb] Kneipe; Gasthaus III
to **pull** [pʊl] ziehen II
pump [pʌmp] Pumpe, Luftpumpe I
pumpkin [ˈpʌmpkɪn] Kürbis II
to **punish** [ˈpʌnɪʃ] bestrafen II
punk [pʌŋk] Punk III
pupil [ˈpjuːpl] Schüler(in) I
Puritan [ˈpjʊərɪtn] Puritaner(in); puritanisch IV F2, 56
purple [ˈpɜːpl] lila, violett I
purpose [ˈpɜːpəs] Zweck III
  on purpose [ɒn ˈpɜːpəs] absichtlich III
to **push** [pʊʃ] stoßen, schieben, drücken II
pushy [ˈpʊʃi] penetrant; aggressiv IV U5, 78
*to **put** [pʊt] setzen, stellen, legen I
  to put in [pʊtˈɪn] einsetzen I
  to put on [pʊtˈɒn] anziehen II
  to put up [pʊtˈʌp] aufstellen; errichten III
puzzle [ˈpʌzl] Rätsel; Puzzle I
  crossword (puzzle) [ˈkrɒswɜːd] Kreuzworträtsel II
PX [ˌpiːˈeks] PX (*Einkaufszentrum in der Kaserne*) ⟨IV EL, 100⟩

Q

Quaker [ˈkweɪkə] Quäker(in) (*Mitglied einer bestimmten christlichen Glaubensgemeinschaft*) ⟨IV F2, 57⟩
qualified [ˈkwɒlɪfaɪd] qualifiziert ⟨IV F3, 90⟩
quality [ˈkwɒləti] Qualität; Eigenschaft IV U5, 81
quarry [ˈkwɒri] Steinbruch ⟨IV U4, 60⟩
quarter past/to [ˈkwɔːtə pɑːst/tə] Viertel nach/vor I
queen [kwiːn] Königin III
question [ˈkwestʃən] Frage I
  question tag [ˈkwestʃən ˌtæɡ] Frageanhängsel, Bestätigungsfrage II
questionnaire [ˌkwestʃəˈneə] Fragebogen III
queue [kjuː] (Warte-)Schlange IV U3, 46
quick [kwɪk] schnell II
quiet [ˈkwaɪət] leise I; still III
quite [kwaɪt] ziemlich; ganz, völlig I
  quite a [ˈkwaɪt ə] ein(e) ziemliche(-r/-s); ein(e) wirkliche(-r/-s) IV U1, 8
quiz [kwɪz] Quiz, Rätsel I

R

rabbit [ˈræbɪt] Kaninchen I
race [reɪs] Wettlauf, Rennen I
 to have a race [ˌhæv ə ˈreɪs] ein Rennen veranstalten I
racket [ˈrækɪt] Schläger I
radio [ˈreɪdiəʊ] Radio I
rag [ræg] Lumpen, Fetzen II
railway [ˈreɪlweɪ] Eisenbahn IV U1, 17
rain [reɪn] Regen I
to rain [reɪn] regnen I
rainbow [ˈreɪnbəʊ] Regenbogen II
raindrop [ˈreɪndrɒp] Regentropfen IV U1, 16
rainforest [ˈreɪnˌfɒrɪst] Regenwald IV U2, 27
rainwater [ˈreɪnˌwɔːtə] Regenwasser IV U2, 27
to raise [reɪz] anheben, erhöhen, (Kinder) großziehen, (Geld) aufbringen II
raisin [ˈreɪzn] Rosine ⟨IV EL, 100⟩
ranch [rɑːntʃ; ræntʃ] Ranch II
ransom [ˈrænsm] Lösegeld ⟨IV U4, 68⟩
rap [ræp] Rap I
rare [reə] rar, selten IV U2, 27
raspberry [ˈrɑːzbri] Himbeere III
rather [ˈrɑːðə] ziemlich IV F3, 91
RE [ɑːrˌiː] Religion (Schulfach) II
to reach [riːtʃ] erreichen III
to react [riˈækt] reagieren III
reaction [riˈækʃn] Reaktion II
***to read** [riːd] lesen I
ready [ˈredi] fertig, bereit I
real [rɪəl] echt, richtig, wirklich II
realistic [ˌrɪəˈlɪstɪk] realistisch II
reality [riˈæləti] Realität; Wirklichkeit III
to realize [ˈrɪəlaɪz] erkennen, realisieren II
really [ˈrɪəli] wirklich I
reason [ˈriːzn] Grund II
rebellion [rɪˈbeliən] Rebellion III
to receive [rɪˈsiːv] empfangen IV U5, 80
in **recent** years [ɪn ˌriːsnt ˈjɪəz] in den letzten Jahren ⟨IV U1, 15⟩
recipe [ˈresɪpi] Rezept II
to recognize [ˈrekəgnaɪz] erkennen II
record [ˈrekɔːd] Rekord IV U2, 24
to record [rɪˈkɔːd] aufnehmen; aufzeichnen III
to recover [rɪˈkʌvə] sich erholen III
re-creation [ˌriːkriˈeɪʃn] Wiedererschaffung ⟨IV U4, 63⟩
red [red] rot I
reef [riːf] Riff ⟨IV U1, 9⟩
to refer (to) [rɪˈfɜː] (sich) beziehen (auf); sprechen (von) IV U2, 27
referee [ˌrefəˈriː] Schiedsrichter(in) I
reflexive [rɪˈfleksɪv] reflexiv III
refund [ˈriːfʌnd] Rückerstattung ⟨IV U5, 81⟩
region [ˈriːdʒn] Region; Gegend III
regular [ˈregjələ] regelmäßig; gleichmäßig I
reign [reɪn] Regierungszeit IV F1, 22
relationship [rɪˈleɪʃnʃɪp] Beziehung III
relative [ˈrelətɪv] Verwandte(r) I
relative [ˈrelətɪv] relativ II

relative clause [ˌrelətɪv ˈklɔːz] Relativsatz II
relative pronoun [ˌrelətɪv ˈprəʊnaʊn] Relativpronomen II
to relax [rɪˈlæks] sich entspannen, sich ausruhen I
religion [rɪˈlɪdʒn] Religion IV F2, 56
religious [rɪˈlɪdʒəs] religiös II
 Religious Education [rɪˌlɪdʒəs ˌedʒʊˈkeɪʃn] Religionsunterricht II
to remember [rɪˈmembə] sich erinnern (an); sich merken I
to remind sb of sth/sb [rɪˈmaɪnd] (jmdn an etw./jmdn) erinnern IV U1, 17
to remove [rɪˈmuːv] entfernen III
to rent [rent] mieten III
to repair [rɪˈpeə] reparieren III
to repeat [rɪˈpiːt] wiederholen II
to replace (sth by/with sth) [rɪˈpleɪs] ersetzen (etw. durch etw.) IV U2, 26
reply [rɪˈplaɪ] Antwort IV F3, 90
to reply [rɪˈplaɪ] antworten, erwidern, entgegnen III
report [rɪˈpɔːt] Bericht IV U1, 17
to report [rɪˈpɔːt] berichten; (sich) melden III
to require [rɪˈkwaɪə] benötigen; erfordern IV U5, 80
rescue [ˈreskjuː] Rettung II
 Mountain Rescue [ˌmaʊntɪn ˈreskjuː] Bergwacht II
to rescue [ˈreskjuː] retten II
reservoir [ˈrezəvwɑː] Stausee ⟨IV EL, 101⟩
resource [rɪˈzɔːs] Ressource IV U2, 27
 natural resource [ˌnætʃrl rɪˈzɔːs] Bodenschatz IV U2, 27
responsible [rɪsˈpɒntsəbl] verantwortlich ⟨IV U1, 15⟩
rest [rest] Rest I
restaurant [ˈrestrənt] Restaurant, Gaststätte I
 fast food restaurant [ˌfɑːst fuːd ˈrestrənt] Schnellrestaurant III
result [rɪˈzʌlt] Ergebnis, Resultat II
 as a result of [əz ə rɪˈzʌlt əv] infolge (von) III
to retire [rɪˈtaɪə] sich zurückziehen; sich zur Ruhe setzen III
to return [rɪˈtɜːn] zurückgeben, zurückschlagen; zurückkehren II
revenge [rɪˈvendʒ] Rache, Revanche III
Reverend [ˈrevrnd] Pfarrer (offizieller Titel des anglikanischen Pfarrers) IV U2, 32
review [rɪˈvjuː] Kritik II
rhyme [raɪm] Reim ⟨IV EL, 98⟩
to rhyme [raɪm] (sich) reimen ⟨IV EL, 98⟩
rhythm [ˈrɪðm] Rhythmus IV U5, 84; ⟨IV EL, 98⟩
rice [raɪs] Reis II
rich [rɪtʃ] reich I; reichhaltig III
 stinking rich [ˌstɪŋkɪŋ ˈrɪtʃ] stinkreich ⟨IV U4, 68⟩
***to get rid** of [get ˈrɪd əv] loswerden II
ride [raɪd] Fahrt, Ritt II
***to ride** [raɪd] fahren; reiten I
rider [ˈraɪdə] Reiter(in) II

horseback riding [ˌhɔːsbæk ˈraɪdɪŋ] Reiten II
oil rig [ˈɔɪl rɪg] Bohrinsel IV U3, 43
right [raɪt] Recht ⟨IV U1, 15⟩
right [raɪt] richtig, korrekt I; rechts; rechte(-r/-s) I
 all right [ɔːl ˈraɪt] in Ordnung; alles klar II
 on somebody's right/left [ɒn ˌsʌmbədiz ˈraɪt/left] zur Rechten/zur Linken von jemandem I
right away [raɪt əˈweɪ] sofort, gleich I
 right now [ˌraɪt ˈnaʊ] jetzt gleich II
key ring [ˈkiː ˌrɪŋ] Schlüsselbund; Schlüsselanhänger III
***to ring** [rɪŋ] klingeln; anrufen II
risk [rɪsk] Risiko II
 to take a risk [ˌteɪk ə ˈrɪsk] ein Risiko eingehen III
to risk [rɪsk] riskieren IV U4, 68
rival [ˈraɪvl] Rivale, Rivalin; Konkurrent(in) III
river [ˈrɪvə] Fluss I
road [rəʊd] Straße I
rock [rɒk] Fels, Stein I
rock [rɒk] Rock (Musik) II
rocky [ˈrɒki] felsig IV U2, 32
rodeo [rəʊˈdeɪəʊ; ˈrəʊdiəʊ] Rodeo I
role [rəʊl] Rolle I
 role play [ˈrəʊl pleɪ] Rollenspiel I
roll [rəʊl] Brötchen II
to roll [rəʊl] rollen III
roof [ruːf] Dach I
room [ruːm] Zimmer; Platz I
 changing room [ˈtʃeɪndʒɪŋ ˌrʊm] Umkleideraum III
 living room [ˈlɪvɪŋ rʊm] Wohnzimmer I
 staff room [ˈstɑːf rʊm] Lehrerzimmer III
root [ruːt] Wurzel III
rope [rəʊp] Seil II
round [raʊnd] Runde II
round [raʊnd] um … herum I
route [ruːt; raʊt] Route II
row [rəʊ] Sträßchen; Reihe I
to row [rəʊ] rudern I
royal [ˈrɔɪəl] königlich III
rubber [ˈrʌbə] Radiergummi I
rubber [ˈrʌbə] Gummi; Kautschuk IV U2, 27
rubbish [ˈrʌbɪʃ] Müll; Quatsch II
rude [ruːd] unhöflich; unverschämt II
rugby [ˈrʌgbi] Rugby I
to ruin [ˈruːɪn] ruinieren, zerstören II
rule [ruːl] Regel I
to rule [ruːl] herrschen; regieren IV F1, 22
ruler [ˈruːlə] Lineal I
on the run [ɒn ðə ˈrʌn] auf der Flucht IV U1, 17
***to run** [rʌn] rennen, laufen I; führen, leiten III
 running order [ˈrʌnɪŋ ˌɔːdə] Startreihenfolge ⟨IV U5, 80⟩
 to run down [rʌn ˈdaʊn] leer werden II
 to run out [rʌn ˈaʊt] ausgehen IV U4, 64
runaway [ˈrʌnəˌweɪ] Ausreißer(in) IV U1, 16
to rush [rʌʃ] sich beeilen I

dictionary

S

sack [sæk] Sack II
sad [sæd] traurig, schmerzlich I
saddle ['sædl] Sattel II
safe [seɪf] Safe; Tresor **IV U4, 68**
safe [seɪf] sicher I
safety ['seɪfti] Sicherheit III
to **sail** [seɪl] segeln III
sailor ['seɪlə] Seemann, Matrose; Segler **IV F1, 22**
salad ['sæləd] Salat II
salmon, pl. **salmon** ['sæmən] Lachs III
salt [sɔːlt] Salz III
the **same** [seɪm] derselbe (die-/das-) I
sand [sænd] Sand I
sandwich ['sændwɪdʒ] Sandwich, belegtes Brot I
satellite ['sætlaɪt] Satellit III
Saturday ['sætədeɪ] Samstag I
sauce [sɔːs] Sauce III
saucer ['sɔːsə] Untertasse I
sausage ['sɒsɪdʒ] Wurst II
to **save** [seɪv] retten, bergen I; sparen III
Saxon ['sæksn] Sachse, Sächsin; sächsisch II
*to **say** [seɪ] sagen, sprechen I
  to say hello [seɪ hə'ləʊ] Hallo sagen, sich begrüßen I
scar [skɑː] Narbe II
*to be **scared** [biː 'skeəd] Angst haben, erschrocken sein I
scary ['skeəri] unheimlich, gruselig; schreckhaft II
scene [siːn] Szene; Schauplatz I
scenery ['siːnri] Landschaft III
schedule ['ʃedjuːl; 'skedʒuːl] Stundenplan; Fahrplan II
school [skuːl] Schule I
  elementary school (AE) [elɪ'mentri ˌskuːl] Grundschule II
  high school ['haɪ ˌskuːl] High School (weiterführende Schule in den USA, Oberstufe) III
  middle school ['mɪdl ˌskuːl] Mittelschule (weiterführende Schule in den USA, Mittelstufe) II
  school bag ['skuːl bæg] Schultasche I
science [saɪəns] (Natur-)Wissenschaft II
science fiction [ˌsaɪəns 'fɪkʃn] Science-Fiction (Zukunftsdichtung) ⟨**IV EL, 100**⟩
scone [skɒn] Scone (eine Art süßes Brötchen) ⟨**IV U2, 24**⟩
scooter ['skuːtə] Roller I
score [skɔː] Punktestand III
to **score** [skɔː] punkten; ein Tor schießen III
scorer ['skɔːrə] Torjäger(in); Korbjäger(in) III
Scot [skɒt] Schotte; Schottin **IV U3, 46**
Scottish ['skɒtɪʃ] schottisch **IV U3, 42**
scrapbook ['skræpbʊk] Sammelalbum II
to **scrape** [skreɪp] kratzen; schürfen ⟨**IV EL, 100**⟩
scratch [skrætʃ] Kratzer **IV U1, 13**
to **scream** [skriːm] schreien, kreischen I
screen [skriːn] Bildschirm I; Leinwand III

scuba diving ['skuːbə ˌdaɪvɪŋ] Tauchen (mit Atemgerät) ⟨**IV U1, 9**⟩
sculpture ['skʌlptʃə] Skulptur III
sea [siː] Meer I
seal [siːl] Seehund I
search party ['sɜːtʃ ˌpɑːti] Suchtrupp ⟨**IV U1, 17**⟩
to **search** [sɜːtʃ] durchsuchen III
to **search for** ['sɜːtʃ fə] suchen (nach) III
seasick ['siːsɪk] seekrank **IV U2, 29**
seaside ['siːsaɪd] Küste, Meeresküste I
  at the seaside [ət ðə 'siːsaɪd] am Meer I
season ['siːzn] Saison; Jahreszeit III
seat [siːt] Sitz, Sitzplatz II
second ['seknd] Sekunde II
second ['seknd] zweite(-r/-s) I
second-hand [ˌseknd 'hænd] gebraucht II
  second-hand shop [ˌseknd hænd 'ʃɒp] Gebrauchtwarenladen II
secret ['siːkrət] Geheimnis I
*to **see** [siː] sehen I
  I see. [aɪ 'siː] aha; ach so II
  See you! ['siː juː] Bis dann!, Bis … I
seed [siːd] Saat; Samen **IV U2, 27**
to **seem** [siːm] scheinen II
  to seem familiar [ˌsiːm fə'mɪliə] bekannt vorkommen III
*to **sell** [sel] verkaufen II
*to **send** [send] schicken I
sense [sents] Sinn; Bedeutung **IV U4, 69**
  to make sense [ˌmeɪk 'sents] Sinn machen; einleuchten **IV U4, 69**
sentence ['sentəns] Satz I
to **separate** ['sepreɪt] trennen **IV U3, 44**
separate ['seprət] separat; getrennt; verschieden III
September [sep'tembə] September I
sergeant ['sɑːdʒnt] Polizeimeister(in) ⟨**IV U4, 70**⟩
series, pl. **series** ['sɪəriːz] Serie III
serious ['sɪəriəs] ernst II
servant ['sɜːvnt] Bedienstete(r); Diener(in) ⟨**IV U1, 19**⟩; **IV F2, 56**
to **serve** [sɜːv] (be)dienen; aufschlagen (Sport) II; servieren III
service ['sɜːvɪs] Service, Dienst III; Gottesdienst **IV U2, 32**
*to **set** [set] setzen; aufstellen **IV U5, 80**
  to set fire to [set 'faɪə tə] in Brand stecken III
  to set off [ˌset 'ɒf] aufbrechen II
  to set the table [ˌset ðə 'teɪbl] den Tisch decken I
setting ['setɪŋ] Schauplatz; Rahmen **IV U5, 84**; ⟨**IV EL, 97**⟩
to **settle** ['setl] siedeln; sich niederlassen **IV F1, 23**
settlement ['setlmənt] Siedlung **IV U1, 12**
settler ['setlə] Siedler(in) **IV U1, 9**
*to **set up** [ˌset 'ʌp] einrichten; aufbauen; gründen **IV F2, 56**
seven [sevn] sieben I
seventeen [ˌsevn'tiːn] siebzehn I
seventeenth [ˌsevn'tiːnθ] siebzehnte(-r/-s) I
seventh ['sevnθ] siebte(-r/-s) I
seventy ['sevnti] siebzig I

shake [ʃeɪk] Shake, Milchshake III
*to **shake** [ʃeɪk] schütteln I; zittern III
shape [ʃeɪp] Form **IV U3, 51**
to **share** [ʃeə] teilen II
shark [ʃɑːk] Hai **IV U1, 8**
to **shave** [ʃeɪv] (sich) rasieren II
she [ʃiː] sie I
shed [ʃed] Schuppen, Stall I
sheep, pl. **sheep** [ʃiːp] Schaf I
sheepdog ['ʃiːpdɒg] Hütehund; Schäferhund I
shelf, pl. **shelves** [ʃelf; ʃelvz] Regal, Regalbrett I
shelter ['ʃeltə] Obdach; Schutz(hütte) **IV U1, 17**
sheriff ['ʃerɪf] Sheriff II
*to **shine** [ʃaɪn] scheinen; glänzen I
shiny ['ʃaɪni] glänzend II
ship [ʃɪp] Schiff I
shirt [ʃɜːt] Hemd; Shirt I
shock [ʃɒk] Schock II
shoe [ʃuː] Schuh I
*to **shoot (at)** [ʃuːt] schießen (auf) II
shop [ʃɒp] Geschäft, Laden I
  corner shop ['kɔːnə ˌʃɒp] Laden an der Ecke; Tante-Emma-Laden **IV U3, 43**
  second-hand shop [ˌseknd hænd 'ʃɒp] Gebrauchtwarenladen II
  shop assistant ['ʃɒp əˌsɪstnt] Verkäufer(in) I
shopping ['ʃɒpɪŋ] Einkaufen; Einkäufe I
  shopping centre ['ʃɒpɪŋ ˌsentə] Einkaufszentrum I
  to go shopping [ˌgəʊ 'ʃɒpɪŋ] einkaufen gehen I
short [ʃɔːt] kurz I
  short cut ['ʃɔːt kʌt] Abkürzung II
shorts (pl.) [ʃɔːts] Shorts, kurze Hose **IV U1, 13**
shot [ʃɒt] Schuss, Schlag II
should [ʃʊd] sollte(n) II
shoulder ['ʃəʊldə] Schulter I
shout [ʃaʊt] Schrei, Ruf III
to **shout** [ʃaʊt] schreien, rufen I
show [ʃəʊ] Show, Schau, Aufführung II
  game show ['geɪm ˌʃəʊ] Spielshow III
  talk show ['tɔːk ˌʃəʊ] Talkshow **IV F1, 22**
*to **show** [ʃəʊ] zeigen I
  to show sb around (a place) [ʃəʊ] jmdn (an einem Ort) herumführen III
  to show up (infml) [ˌʃəʊ 'ʌp] auftauchen **IV U5, 80**
shower ['ʃaʊə] Schauer; Dusche **IV U1, 8**
show-off ['ʃəʊ ɒf] Angeber(in) II
to **shrug (one's shoulders)** [ʃrʌg] mit den Achseln/Schultern zucken **IV U3, 51**
Shsh! [ʃ] Pssst!
*to **shut** [ʃʌt] zumachen, schließen I
shy [ʃaɪ] schüchtern **IV U4, 63**
*to be **sick** [biː 'sɪk] sich übergeben **IV U3, 50**
  to be sick with worry [biː 'sɪk wɪð ˌwʌri] krank vor Sorge sein ⟨**IV U4, 69**⟩
  to feel sick [ˌfiːl 'sɪk] Übelkeit verspüren; sich schlecht fühlen III
side [saɪd] Seite II
to **sigh** [saɪ] seufzen III

dictionary D

sight [saɪt] Sehenswürdigkeit; Sicht, Anblick II
sightseeing ['saɪtsiːɪŋ] Besichtigungstour I
sign [saɪn] Zeichen; Schild III
signal ['sɪɡnl] Signal, Zeichen II
silence ['saɪləns] Stille IV U1, 16
silent ['saɪlənt] still IV U3, 46
silly ['sɪli] Dummkopf I
silly ['sɪli] dumm, doof, albern I
silver ['sɪlvə] Silber II
similar ['sɪmɪlə] ähnlich III
simple ['sɪmpl] einfach, simpel II
since [sɪnts] seit, seitdem II; da III
sincere [sɪn'sɪə] aufrichtig ⟨IV EL, 100⟩
   Yours sincerely [jɔːz sɪn'sɪəli] Mit freundlichen Grüßen IV U5, 80
*to **sing** [sɪŋ] singen I
   to sing along [ˌsɪŋ ə'lɒŋ] mitsingen I
singer ['sɪŋə] Sänger(in) II
singular ['sɪŋɡjələ] Singular IV U3, 47
*to **sink** [sɪŋk] sinken IV U2, 29
sir (AE) [sɜː] mein Herr (Anrede) I
Sir [sɜː] Sir (Anrede für einen Ritter) III
sister ['sɪstə] Schwester I
*to **sit** [sɪt] sitzen I
   to sit (down) [sɪt 'daʊn] sich (hin)setzen I
sitcom ['sɪtkɒm] Situationskomödie III
situation [ˌsɪtju'eɪʃn] Situation II
six [sɪks] sechs I
sixteen [ˌsɪk'stiːn] sechzehn I
sixteenth [ˌsɪk'stiːnθ] sechzehnte(-r/-s) I
sixth [sɪksθ] sechste(-r/-s) I
sixty ['sɪksti] sechzig I
size [saɪz] Größe, Kleidergröße I
   the next size down [ðə ˌnekst saɪz 'daʊn] eine Größe kleiner III
skateboard ['skeɪtbɔːd] Skateboard I
skates pl. [skeɪts] Inlineskates, Rollschuhe, Schlittschuhe I
skating ['skeɪtɪŋ] Inlineskate/Schlittschuh fahren I
to **ski** [skiː] Ski fahren IV U4, 62
skiing ['skiːɪŋ] Skifahren I
skill [skɪl] Fertigkeit; Geschick III
skin [skɪn] Haut, Fell I
skirt [skɜːt] Rock I
sky [skaɪ] Himmel I
skyscraper ['skaɪskreɪpə] Wolkenkratzer I
to **slap** [slæp] schlagen; einen Klaps geben ⟨IV EL, 100⟩
slate [sleɪt] Schiefer II
sled [sled] Schlitten II
*to go to **sleep** [ɡəʊ tə 'sliːp] einschlafen I
*to **sleep** [sliːp] schlafen I
   sleeping bag ['sliːpɪŋ ˌbæɡ] Schlafsack III
gravel pit **slide** ['ɡrævl pɪt ˌslaɪd] abrutschender Kies in einer Kiesgrube ⟨IV EL, 101⟩
slight [slaɪt] leicht; gering IV U5, 82
to **slip** [slɪp] (aus)rutschen III
slippery ['slɪpri] rutschig, glitschig II
slow [sləʊ] langsam I
slowly ['sləʊli] langsam I
small [smɔːl] klein I
smell [smel] Geruch, Gestank I
*to **smell** [smel] riechen (an) II

smile [smaɪl] Lächeln I
to **smile** [smaɪl] lächeln I
smoke [sməʊk] Rauch III
to **smother** ['smʌðə] ersticken ⟨IV EL, 101⟩
to **smuggle** ['smʌɡl] schmuggeln II
smuggler ['smʌɡlə] Schmuggler(in) II
snack [snæk] Snack, Imbiss II
snake [sneɪk] Schlange I
to **sneer** [snɪə] spotten, spöttisch grinsen II
to **sneeze** [sniːz] niesen II
to **sniff** [snɪf] schnüffeln; schnuppern ⟨IV EL, 103⟩
snow [snəʊ] Schnee II
snowboarding ['snəʊbɔːdɪŋ] Snowboarden IV U4, 60
so [səʊ] so I
   so far ['səʊ fɑː] bis jetzt II
so [səʊ] also, deshalb I
   so (that) ['səʊ ðət] damit; so dass I
soap [səʊp] Seife I
soccer (AE) ['sɒkə] Fußball I
social ['səʊʃl] sozial, gesellschaftlich II
society [sə'saɪəti] Gesellschaft II
sock [sɒk] Socke I
soft [sɒft] weich; sanft IV F3, 91
software ['sɒftweə] Software (Computerprogramme) IV U3, 44
soldier ['səʊldʒə] Soldat(in) III
solution [sə'luːʃn] Lösung III
some [sʌm] einige; etwas I
somebody ['sʌmbədi] jemand I
someone ['sʌmwʌn] jemand II
something ['sʌmθɪŋ] etwas I
sometime ['sʌmtaɪm] irgendwann II
sometimes ['sʌmtaɪmz] manchmal I
somewhere ['sʌmweə] irgendwo II
son [sʌn] Sohn II
song [sɒŋ] Lied, Song I
soon [suːn] bald I
sore [sɔː] wunde Stelle IV U1, 17
sorry ['sɒri] Tut mir leid, Entschuldigung I
   to feel sorry for [fiːl 'sɒri] Mitleid haben mit; bedauern IV
to **sort** sth out [ˌsɔːt 'aʊt] etw. klären; etw. erledigen IV U2, 33
soul [səʊl] Seele III
sound [saʊnd] Ton, Geräusch I
   sound practice ['saʊnd ˌpræktɪs] Hör-/Ausspracheübung I
to **sound** [saʊnd] klingen II
soup [suːp] Suppe II
sour [saʊə] sauer III
source [sɔːs] Quelle III
south [saʊθ] Süden I
southern ['sʌðən] südlich II
souvenir [ˌsuːvə'nɪə] Souvenir, Andenken I
space [speɪs] Raum; Weltraum I
Spanish ['spænɪʃ] spanisch; Spanisch I
to **sparkle** ['spɑːkl] glitzern; funkeln ⟨IV U1, 16⟩
*to **speak** [spiːk] sprechen I
   to speak up [ˌspiːk 'ʌp] lauter sprechen ⟨IV EL, 103⟩
speaker ['spiːkə] Lautsprecher II; Sprecher(in) IV U1, 14

spear [spɪə] Speer III
special ['speʃl] besonders, speziell I
   special offer [ˌspeʃl 'ɒfə] Sonderangebot I
specialty (AE) ['speʃti] Spezialität; Besonderheit IV U4, 59
spectacular [spek'tækjələ] spektakulär IV U4, 60
speech [spiːtʃ] Sprache; Rede III
   direct speech [dɪˌrekt 'spiːtʃ] direkte Rede III
   indirect speech [ˌɪndɪrekt 'spiːtʃ] indirekte Rede III
*to **spell** [spel] buchstabieren I
   spell checker ['spel ˌtʃekə] Rechtschreibprüfprogramm ⟨IV U5, 82⟩
spelling ['spelɪŋ] Orthographie, Rechtschreibung I
*to **spend** [spend] ausgeben; verbringen I
spicy ['spaɪsi] würzig; pikant III
spider ['spaɪdə] Spinne II
*to **spill** [spɪl] verschütten III
in **spite** of [ɪn 'spaɪt əv] trotz III
splash [splæʃ] Spritzer, Planscher I
splint [splɪnt] Schiene ⟨IV U1, 13⟩
spoon [spuːn] Löffel I
sport [spɔːt] Sport I
sportsman, pl. **sportsmen** ['spɔːtsmən] Sportler III
sportswoman, (pl.)**sportswomen** ['spɔːtsˌwʊmən] Sportlerin III
to **spot** [spɒt] entdecken; erkennen IV U5, 78
*to **spread** [spred] (sich) verbreiten ⟨IV EL, 101⟩
spring [sprɪŋ] Frühling II
spur [spɜː] Sporn II
squadron ['skwɒdrn] Schwadron; Staffel ⟨IV U1, 15⟩
square [skweə] Platz I; Quadrat III
   square dance ['skweə ˌdɑːnts] Square Dance II
squid [skwɪd] Tintenfisch ⟨IV EL, 101⟩
stable ['steɪbl] Stall I
staff [stɑːf] Personal; Kollegium III
   staff room ['stɑːf rʊm] Lehrerzimmer III
stage [steɪdʒ] Bühne II
to **stagger (about)** ['stæɡə] (herum)torkeln II
stairs (pl.) [steəz] Treppe III
stall [stɔːl] Stand, Bude II
*to **stand** [stænd] ertragen, ausstehen II
   to stand (up) [stænd 'ʌp] (auf)stehen I
   to stand up for oneself [ˌstænd 'ʌp] sich verteidigen IV U3, 52
standard ['stændəd] Standard III
star [stɑː] Star; Stern I
   pop star ['pɒp stɑː] Popstar I
to **stare** [steə] starren IV U3, 52
to **start** [stɑːt] anfangen, starten I
   Let's start! [lets 'stɑːt] Lass(t) uns anfangen I
   to get (sth) started [ˌɡet 'stɑːtɪd] in Gang kommen; (etw.) in Gang bringen IV U5, 80
starter ['stɑːtə] Vorspeise II
to **starve** [stɑːv] (ver)hungern IV F2, 56

Dictionary

state [steɪt] Staat, Land **I**
  State House ['steɪt ˌhaʊs] Regierungsgebäude ⟨**IV U4**,60⟩
statement ['steɪtmənt] Aussage, Behauptung **II**
station ['steɪʃn] Haltestelle, Bahnhof **I**; Farm *(in Australien)* **IV U1**,8
statue ['stætʃuː] Statue, Standbild **I**
status ['steɪtəs] Status **II**
to **stay** [steɪ] bleiben **I**; übernachten **II**
steak [steɪk] Steak **II**
*to **steal** [stiːl] stehlen **II**
steam [stiːm] Dampf **III**
  to let off steam [ˌlet ɒf 'stiːm] Dampf ablassen; seinem Ärger Luft machen **IV U3**,46
steel [stiːl] Stahl **IV U2**,27
steep [stiːp] steil **II**
step [step] Stufe; Schritt **III**
to **step** [step] treten; steigen **IV U2**,34
stepmother ['stepmʌðə] Stiefmutter **II**
stepsister ['stepsɪstə] Stiefschwester **II**
stereo ['steriəʊ] Stereoanlage **I**
*to **stick** [stɪk] kleben; stecken **III**
  to be stuck [bi: 'stʌk] stecken bleiben, festklemmen **II**
still [stɪl] still **II**
still [stɪl] noch, immer noch **I**
stinking rich [ˌstɪŋkɪŋ 'rɪtʃ] stinkreich ⟨**IV U4**,68⟩
stone [stəʊn] Stein **I**
to **stop** [stɒp] aufhören; anhalten **I**
store [stɔː] Laden, Geschäft **III**
storehouse ['stɔːhaʊs] Lager; Speicher ⟨**IV F2**,57⟩
storm [stɔːm] Sturm **I**
story ['stɔːri] Geschichte, Erzählung **I**
straight [streɪt] gerade, geradewegs, direkt **I**
strange [streɪndʒ] fremd; seltsam; merkwürdig **III**
stranger ['streɪndʒə] Fremde(r) **II**
strawberry ['strɔːbri] Erdbeere **II**
*to be on a mean **streak** [bi: ɒn ə ˌmiːn 'striːk] schlecht drauf sein ⟨**IV EL**,100⟩
stream [striːm] Bach **III**
street [striːt] Straße **I**
stress [stres] Stress **II**
to **stress** [stres] betonen **III**
strict [strɪkt] streng; strikt **IV F1**,23
*to **strike** [straɪk] schlagen; anzünden *(ein Streichholz)* **IV U3**,50
string [strɪŋ] Schnur **III**
strip [strɪp] Streifen **IV U1**,13
stripe [straɪp] Streifen **IV F2**,57
*to **strive** [straɪv] streben; sich bemühen **IV U5**,76
strong [strɒŋ] stark **I**
structure ['strʌktʃə] Struktur; Aufbau **IV U2**,36
student ['stjuːdnt] Student(in); Schüler(in) **II**
to **study** ['stʌdi] studieren; lernen **III**
stuff [stʌf] Zeug **II**
stumpy ['stʌmpi] stummelig ⟨**IV EL**,96⟩
stupid ['stjuːpɪd] dumm, blöd **I**
style [staɪl] Stil **II**

subject ['sʌbdʒɪkt] Schulfach; Thema **I**
subordinate clause [səˌbɔːdnət 'klɔːz] Nebensatz ⟨**IV U5**,81⟩
suburb ['sʌbɜːb] Vorort **IV U1**,10
to **suburbanize** [sə'bɜːbnaɪz] eingemeinden ⟨**IV EL**,101⟩
subway ['sʌbweɪ] Unterführung *(BE)*; U-Bahn *(AE)* **IV U5**,82
success [sək'ses] Erfolg **II**
successful [sək'sesfl] erfolgreich ⟨**IV EL**,100⟩
such [sʌtʃ] solch **IV U3**,44
  such as ['sʌtʃ ˌəz] (solche) wie **III**
the poor **sucker** [ˌpɔː 'sʌkə] das arme Schwein ⟨**IV EL**,101⟩
suddenly ['sʌdnli] plötzlich, auf einmal **I**
sugar ['ʃʊgə] Zucker **III**
to **suggest** [sə'dʒest] vorschlagen **II**
suggestion [sə'dʒestʃn] Vorschlag, Anregung **I**
to **suit** [suːt] passen (zu); (jmdm) stehen **III**
suitable ['suːtəbl] geeignet; passend **III**
suitcase ['suːtkeɪs] Koffer **III**
sum [sʌm] Summe; Betrag **IV U2**,34; Rechenaufgabe ⟨**IV F2**,57⟩
summer ['sʌmə] Sommer **I**
  Indian summer [ˌɪndiən 'sʌmə] Altweibersommer ⟨**IV U4**,61⟩
to **sum up** [ˌsʌm 'ʌp] zusammenfassen **IV U4**,70
sun [sʌn] Sonne **I**
Sunday ['sʌndeɪ] Sonntag **I**
sunny ['sʌni] sonnig **I**
sunscreen ['sʌnskriːn] Sonnencreme **I**
sunshine ['sʌnʃaɪn] Sonnenschein **II**
super ['suːpə] super **II**
superlative [suː'pɜːlətɪv] Superlativ **II**
supermarket ['suːpəˌmɑːkɪt] Supermarkt **I**
sure [ʃʊə; ʃɔː] sicher **I**
surfer ['sɜːfə] Surfer(in), Wellenreiter(in) **IV U1**,15
surfing ['sɜːfɪŋ] Wellenreiten, Surfen **I**
surprise [sə'praɪz] Überraschung **I**
to **surprise** [sə'praɪz] überraschen **IV F3**,90
*to be **surprised** [bi: sə'praɪzd] überrascht sein **I**
to **surround** [sə'raʊnd] umgeben **IV U4**,58
survey ['sɜːveɪ] Umfrage; Studie **III**
to **survive** [sə'vaɪv] überleben **III**
sweatshirt ['swetʃɜːt] Sweatshirt **I**
sweaty ['sweti] verschwitzt ⟨**IV EL**,100⟩
sweets *pl.* [swiːts] Süßigkeiten, Bonbons **I**
sweet [swiːt] süß **I**
sweetcorn ['swiːtkɔːn] Mais **III**
*to **swim** [swɪm] schwimmen **I**
swimmer ['swɪmə] Schwimmer(in) **III**
swimming ['swɪmɪŋ] Schwimmen **I**
  swimming pool ['swɪmɪŋ ˌpuːl] Schwimmbecken; Schwimmbad **I**
to **switch off** [swɪtʃ 'ɒf] ausschalten **III**
  to switch on [swɪtʃ 'ɒn] einschalten **III**
  We switched some mental dial over to Mute. [wi: ˌswɪtʃt səm ˌmentl daɪəl ˌəʊvə tə 'mjuːt] Wir schalteten gedanklich ab. ⟨**IV EL**,101⟩
syllable ['sɪləbl] Silbe **IV U5**,81; ⟨**IV EL**,98⟩; ⟨**IV EL**,102⟩

symbol ['sɪmbl] Symbol **IV U1**,18
system ['sɪstəm] System **II**
systematic [ˌsɪstə'mætɪk] systematisch; gezielt **IV U4**,67

T

table ['teɪbl] Tisch **I**; Tabelle **II**
  table tennis ['teɪbl ˌtenɪs] Tischtennis **II**
  to set the table [ˌset ðə 'teɪbl] den Tisch decken **I**
taco ['tɑːkəʊ] Taco *(mexikanische gefüllte Teigtasche)* **III**
tactful ['tæktfl] taktvoll **IV F3**,91
question **tag** ['kwestʃən ˌtæg] Frageanhängsel, Bestätigungsfrage **II**
*to **take** [teɪk] (mit)nehmen; bringen **I**; dauern, (Zeit) brauchen **II**
  Don't take no for an answer. [ˌdəʊnt teɪk 'nəʊ fər ən ˌɑːntsə] Akzeptiere keine Widerrede. ⟨**IV U1**,10⟩
  to take a break [ˌteɪk ə 'breɪk] Pause machen **I**
  to take a risk [ˌteɪk ə 'rɪsk] ein Risiko eingehen **III**
  to take off [teɪk 'ɒf] abheben **I**; ausziehen **II**
  to take one's own life [ˌteɪk wʌnz ˌəʊn 'laɪf] sich das Leben nehmen **III**
  to take over [ˌteɪk 'əʊvə] übernehmen; ablösen **IV U2**,29
  to take part (in) [teɪk 'pɑːt] teilnehmen (an) **I**
  to take photos [teɪk 'fəʊtəʊz] fotografieren, Fotos machen **I**
  to take place [teɪk 'pleɪs] stattfinden **III**
  to take sb (time) to do sth [teɪk] jmdn (Zeit) kosten **II**
takeaway ['teɪkəweɪ] *(Restaurant, das Speisen zum Mitnehmen verkauft)* **II**
tale [teɪl] Geschichte, Erzählung **II**
  fairy tale ['feəri ˌteɪl] Märchen **II**
talent ['tælənt] Talent **IV U5**,78
talk [tɔːk] Vortrag; Rede **III**
  talk show ['tɔːk ˌʃəʊ] Talkshow **IV F1**,22
  to give a talk [ˌgɪv ə 'tɔːk] einen Vortrag halten **III**
to **talk** [tɔːk] sprechen, reden **I**
tall [tɔːl] groß; hoch **I**
tap [tæp] Wasserhahn **IV F3**,91
  tap water ['tæp ˌwɔːtə] Leitungswasser ⟨**IV F3**,91⟩
tape [teɪp] (Ton-)Band **II**
target ['tɑːgɪt] Ziel(scheibe) **II**
tartan ['tɑːtn] Schottenkaro *(bestimmtes Muster eines Clans; karierter Schottenstoff)* ⟨**IV U3**,42⟩
taste [teɪst] Geschmack **III**
to **taste** [teɪst] schmecken **II**
tasty ['teɪsti] schmackhaft **III**
tax [tæks] Steuer **IV U3**,42
taxi ['tæksi] Taxi **I**
tea [tiː] Tee; Abendessen **I**
  cream tea [ˌkriːm 'tiː] Cream Tea *(südwestenglische Spezialität: Tee mit süßen Brötchen, die mit sehr fester Sahne und Marmelade serviert werden)* ⟨**IV U2**,24⟩

to be sb's cup of tea [ˌkʌp əv 'tiː] jmds Fall sein ⟨IV F3, 91⟩
*****to teach** [tiːtʃ] unterrichten, lehren I
teacher ['tiːtʃə] Lehrer(in) I
  head teacher (BE) [ˌhed 'tiːtʃə] Schulleiter(in) III
team [tiːm] Gruppe, Team I
  to be on a team [ˌbiː ɒn ə 'tiːm] Mitglied eines Teams sein III
tear [tɪə] Träne III
*****to tear** [teə] (zer)reißen IV U1, 13
teatime ['tiːtaɪm] Zeit für Nachmittagstee; Abendessen I
technique [tek'niːk] Methode; Technik IV U4, 67
techno ['teknəʊ] Techno II
technology [tek'nɒlədʒi] Technologie, Computerunterricht II
teddy bear ['tedi ˌbeə] Teddybär III
teenage ['tiːneɪdʒ] jugendlich IV U5, 78
teenager ['tiːnˌeɪdʒə] Teenager; Jugendliche(r) III
telephone ['telɪfəʊn] Telefon I
telescope ['telɪskəʊp] Teleskop; Fernrohr I
television ['telɪvɪʒn] Fernsehen; Fernseher I
*****to tell (somebody)** [tel] (jemandem) sagen, mitteilen I
ten [ten] zehn I
tennis ['tenɪs] Tennis I
  table tennis ['teɪbl ˌtenɪs] Tischtennis II
tense [tens] Zeit, Zeitform (grammatisch) I
tension ['tentʃn] Spannung IV U3, 52
tent [tent] Zelt II
tentacle ['tentəkl] Tentakel; Fangarm ⟨IV EL, 101⟩
tenth [tenθ] zehnte(-r/-s) I
term [tɜːm] Trimester; Semester; Halbjahr IV U3, 50
terrible ['terəbl] schrecklich, furchtbar I
terrified ['terəfaɪd] außer sich vor Schrecken II
test [test] Test; Klassenarbeit; Schulaufgabe II
text [tekst] Text; Textnachricht (SMS) I
than [ðæn; ðən] als (bei Vergleichen) I
to thank [θæŋk] danken II
  thank God [ˌθæŋk 'gɒd] Gott sei Dank II
  thank you letter ['θæŋk juː ˌletə] Dankschreiben I
  Thank you very much! [ˌθæŋk juː veri 'mʌtʃ] Vielen Dank! Herzlichen Dank! I
thanks [θæŋks] danke I
that [ðæt; ðət] dass I
that [ðæt] das; jenes I
that [ðæt] der, dem, den, die, das (Relativpronomen) I
the [ðə; ði] der, die (auch pl.), das I
  the same [seɪm] derselbe (die-/das-) I
theatre ['θɪətə] Theater I
their [ðeə] ihr, ihre (Plural) I
theirs [ðeəz] ihre(-r/-es) IV U3, 46
them [ðem; ðəm] sie; ihnen I
then [ðen] dann I
there [ðeə] dort I
  over there [ˌəʊvə 'ðeə] da drüben I
  there are [ðeər 'ɑː] da sind; es gibt I

there's [ðeəz] (= there is) da ist, es gibt I
these [ðiːz] diese (hier) I
  these days [ˌðiːz 'deɪz] heutzutage II
they [ðeɪ] sie (Plural) I
  they're (= they are) [ðeə] sie sind I
thick [θɪk] dick (nicht für Personen); dumm (für Personen) II
thief, pl. **thieves** [θiːf; θiːvz] Dieb(in) III
thin [θɪn] dünn II
thing [θɪŋ] Sache, Ding I
  The thing is … [ðə ˌθɪŋ 'ɪz] Die Sache ist die, … IV U3, 50
*****to think (of)** ['θɪŋk əv] denken (an) I
  to think of ['θɪŋk əv] halten von II
third [θɜːd] Drittel I
third [θɜːd] dritte(-r/-s) I
thirsty ['θɜːsti] durstig III
thirteen [θɜː'tiːn] dreizehn I
thirteenth [θɜː'tiːnθ] dreizehnte(-r/-s) I
thirty ['θɜːti] dreißig I
this [ðɪs] diese(-r/-s) I
those [ðəʊz] diese dort, jene I
two thousand [ˌtuː 'θaʊznd] zweitausend III
three [θriː] drei I
thriller ['θrɪlə] Thriller; spannender Krimi; Schauergeschichte ⟨IV EL, 100⟩
through [θruː] durch I
*****to throw** [θrəʊ] werfen I
Thursday ['θɜːzdeɪ] Donnerstag I
ticket ['tɪkɪt] Ticket, Fahrschein, Eintrittskarte I
to tidy (up) ['taɪdi] aufräumen, in Ordnung bringen II
tidy ['taɪdi] sauber, ordentlich I
to tie [taɪ] binden, fesseln II
till [tɪl] bis IV U4, 60
timber ['tɪmbə] (Bau-)Holz ⟨IV U4, 63⟩
time [taɪm] Zeit I; Mal I
  all the time [ˌɔːl ðə 'taɪm] die ganze Zeit I
  in time for [ɪn 'taɪm fə] rechtzeitig zu III
  most of the time ['məʊst əv ðə ˌtaɪm] meistens III
  on time [ɒn 'taɪm] pünktlich II
  time line ['taɪm laɪn] Zeitstrahl III
  What time … ? [wɒt 'taɪm] (Um) wie viel Uhr … ? I
timetable ['taɪmˌteɪbl] Stundenplan; Fahrplan II
tin [tɪn] Dose, Büchse I
tip [tɪp] Tipp I
to tiptoe ['tɪptəʊ] auf Zehenspitzen gehen ⟨IV EL, 102⟩
tired ['taɪəd] müde I
  to be tired of (+ gerund) [biː 'taɪəd] es müde/leid sein/satt haben, etwas zu tun IV U4, 60
  to grow tired of sb/sth [ˌgrəʊ 'taɪəd] jmds/einer Sache überdrüssig werden ⟨IV EL, 96⟩
title ['taɪtl] Titel, Überschrift I
to [tʊ; tə] in; nach; zu I; bis I
toast [təʊst] Toast I
tobacco [tə'bækəʊ] Tabak IV U2, 32
today [tə'deɪ] heute I
together [tə'geðə] zusammen, miteinander I

toilet ['tɔɪlɪt] Toilette IV U2, 27
tomato, pl. **tomatoes** [tə'mɑːtəʊ] Tomate II
tomorrow [tə'mɒrəʊ] morgen I
ton [tʌn] Tonne (Gewicht) I
tone [təʊn] Ton IV U3, 44
tonight [tə'naɪt] heute Abend/Nacht II
too [tuː] auch I; zu I
  Me, too. [ˌmiː 'tuː] Ich auch. II
tool [tuːl] Werkzeug, Gerät II
tooth, pl. **teeth** [tuːθ; tiːθ] Zahn I
top [tɒp] Spitze, oberer Teil II; Top III
  on top (of) [ɒn 'tɒp] obendrauf II
  on top of that [ɒn ˌtɒp əv 'ðæt] obendrein; zusätzlich IV U2, 29
topic ['tɒpɪk] Thema I
topping ['tɒpɪŋ] Belag III
tormentor [tɔː'mentə] Peiniger(in) ⟨IV EL, 100⟩
*****to get in touch (with)** [ˌget ɪn 'tʌtʃ] in Verbindung treten (mit); kontaktieren IV F3, 90
to touch [tʌtʃ] berühren; antippen I
tough [tʌf] hart; rau; zäh IV U4, 68
tour [tʊə] Tour, Fahrt, Reise I
tourist ['tʊərɪst] Tourist I
to tow [təʊ] abschleppen IV U2, 29
towards [tə'wɔːdz] in Richtung; auf … zu, darauf zu I
towel ['taʊəl] Handtuch I
tower ['taʊə] Turm II
town [taʊn] Stadt I
toy [tɔɪ] Spielzeug II; IV F2, 56
track and field [ˌtræk ənd 'fiːld] Leichtathletik III
tracker ['trækə] Fährtenleser(in) ⟨IV U1, 16⟩
to trade [treɪd] Handel treiben IV U1, 10
tradition [trə'dɪʃn] Tradition I
traditional [trə'dɪʃnl] traditionell II
traffic ['træfɪk] Verkehr II
  traffic jam ['træfɪk ˌdʒæm] Stau II
trail [treɪl] Wanderweg III
train [treɪn] Zug I
to train [treɪn] trainieren, ausbilden II
training ['treɪnɪŋ] Training, Ausbildung II
transitive ['træntsətɪv] transitiv (ein Objekt nach sich ziehend) ⟨IV U2, 26⟩
to translate [trænz'leɪt] übersetzen III
translation [trænz'leɪʃn] Übersetzung II
transparency [træn'spærntsi] Folie IV U4, 67
transport ['træntspɔːt] Transport II
  means of transport (sg. and pl.) [ˌmiːnz əv 'træntspɔːt] Transportmittel, Verkehrsmittel II
to transport [træn'spɔːt] transportieren II
trap [træp] Falle II
*****to be trapped** [biː 'træpt] in der Falle sitzen III
trash (AE) [træʃ] Abfall, Müll II
travel ['trævl] (das) Reisen II
  travel agent's ['trævl ˌeɪdʒnts] Reisebüro II
to travel ['trævl] reisen II
treat [triːt] besondere Freude; Belohnung II

Dictionary

to **treat** [tri:t] behandeln II
tree [tri:] Baum I
  palm tree ['pɑ:m ˌtri:] Palme **IV U2, 25**
trek [trek] Wanderung; anstrengender Marsch **IV U1, 16**
to **trek** [trek] wandern, marschieren II
pony **trekking** ['pəʊni ˌtrekɪŋ] Ponyreiten im Gelände II
to **tremble** ['trembl] zittern II
tribe [traɪb] Stamm I
trick [trɪk] Trick; Streich I
to **trick** [trɪk] austricksen, täuschen I
trifle ['traɪfl] englischer Nachtisch I
trip [trɪp] Trip, Reise, Ausflug I
to **trip (over)** [trɪp] stolpern (über) II
tropical ['trɒpɪkl] tropisch **IV U2, 27**
trouble [trʌbl] Ärger, Probleme II
trousers pl. ['traʊzəz] Hose I
trout, pl. **trout** [traʊt] Forelle II
truck [trʌk] Truck, Lastwagen II
true [tru:] wahr I
  to come true [ˌkʌm 'tru:] wahr werden; in Erfüllung gehen **IV U4, 58**
trumpet ['trʌmpɪt] Trompete II
to **trust** [trʌst] vertrauen II
truth [tru:θ] Wahrheit II
to **try (on)** [traɪ ˌɒn] (an)probieren; versuchen I
T-shirt ['ti:ʃɜ:t] T-Shirt II
tucker (infml) ['tʌkə] Proviant ⟨**IV U1, 16**⟩
Tuesday ['tju:zdeɪ] Dienstag I
tune [tju:n] Melodie II
to **tune** [tju:n] einstellen; stimmen (ein Instrument) ⟨**IV EL, 101**⟩
tunnel ['tʌnl] Tunnel **IV U2, 33**
turkey ['tɜ:ki] Truthahn, Pute I
It's your **turn.** ['jɔ: tɜ:n] Du bist/Sie sind dran. I
to **turn** [tɜ:n] einbiegen, abbiegen; drehen, wenden I
  to turn (into) ['tɜ:n ˌɪntə] werden; (sich) verwandeln in III
  turning point ['tɜ:nɪŋ ˌpɔɪnt] Wendepunkt III
tutor ['tju:tə] Klassenlehrer(in) I
  tutor group ['tju:tə ˌgru:p] Klasse (in einer englischen Schule) I
TV [ti:'vi:] Fernsehen; Fernseher I
  to watch TV [ˌwɒtʃ ti:'vi:] fernsehen I
twelfth [twelfθ] zwölfte(-r/-s) I
twelve [twelv] zwölf I
twentieth ['twentiɪθ] zwanzigste(-r/-s) I
twenty ['twenti] zwanzig I
twenty-one [ˌtwenti'wʌn] einundzwanzig I
twice [twaɪs] zweimal II
to **twist** [twɪst] verdrehen; verzerren **IV U4, 70**
two [tu:] zwei I
  2-1 [ˌtu: 'wʌn] zwei zu eins II
  a two-minute walk away from … [ˌtu:mɪnɪt 'wɔ:k] zwei Minuten zu Fuß von … entfernt II
  two-lane [tu:'leɪn] zweispurig ⟨**IV EL, 101**⟩
  two thousand [ˌtu: 'θaʊznd] zweitausend III
  2.45 (point) ['tu: ˌpɔɪnt ˌfɔ: 'faɪv] Komma (bei Zahlenangaben) I

type [taɪp] Typ III
to **type** [taɪp] tippen III
typical (of) ['tɪpɪkl] typisch (für) I

U

Ugh! [ɜ:] Igitt! (Ausruf des Ekels) I
ugly ['ʌgli] hässlich **IV U3, 50**
unable [ʌn'eɪbl] unfähig III
unbelievable [ˌʌnbɪ'li:vəbl] unglaublich **IV U4, 58**
uncle ['ʌŋkl] Onkel I
uncountable [ʌn'kaʊntəbl] unzählbar **IV U3, 45**
under ['ʌndə] unter I
  down under (infml) [ˌdaʊn ˈʌndə] (Spitzname für Australien) ⟨**IV U1, 8**⟩
underground ['ʌndəgraʊnd] unterirdisch ⟨**IV U5, 82**⟩
to **underline** [ˌʌndə'laɪn] unterstreichen **IV U1, 19**
*to **understand** [ˌʌndə'stænd] verstehen I
understandable [ˌʌndə'stændəbl] verständlich **IV U5, 80**
undeveloped [ˌʌndɪ'veləpt] nicht entwickelt/erschlossen ⟨**IV EL, 101**⟩
unforgettable [ˌʌnfə'getəbl] unvergesslich **IV U4, 62**
unfortunately [ʌn'fɔ:tʃnətli] leider; unglücklicherweise **IV U5, 78**
unhappy [ʌn'hæpi] unglücklich II
uniform ['ju:nɪfɔ:m] Uniform I
unique [ju:'ni:k] einzig; einzigartig **IV U1, 15**
unit ['ju:nɪt] Kapitel; Einheit I
universe ['ju:nɪvɜ:s] Universum III
university [ˌju:nɪ'vɜ:səti] Universität **IV U4, 58**
unknown [ʌn'nəʊn] unbekannt **IV F1, 23**
unless [ən'les] wenn nicht; es sei denn, (dass) … **IV U2, 33**
unlike [ʌn'laɪk] anders als; im Gegensatz zu **IV U4, 68**
*to be **unlikely (to)** [bi: ʌn'laɪkli] unwahrscheinlich sein **IV U1, 14**
unnecessary [ʌn'nesəsri] unnötig III
to **unpack** [ʌn'pæk] auspacken III
unprofessional [ˌʌnprə'feʃnl] unprofessionell **IV U5, 80**
until [ʌn'tɪl; n'tɪl] bis I
  not until [ˌnɒt ən'tɪl] nicht (be)vor; erst (wenn/als) III
up (to) [ʌp] herbei (zu); auf … zu III
  up to ['ʌp tə] bis zu III
up [ʌp] (hin)auf, hoch I
upstairs [ʌp'steəz] (nach) oben, im Obergeschoss I
us [ʌs] wir; uns I
US [ju:'es] Vereinigte Staaten; US-amerikanisch I
It's no **use** (+ gerund) [ɪts nəʊ 'ju:s] Es nützt nichts … **IV U4, 63**
to **use** [ju:z] benutzen, verwenden I
  to be used to (+ gerund) [bi: 'ju:zt tə] gewöhnt sein an; gewohnt sein **IV U4, 60**
  to get used to (+ gerund) [ˌget 'ju:zt tə] sich gewöhnen an **IV U4, 58**

useful ['ju:sfl] nützlich II
useless ['ju:sləs] nutzlos III
usual ['ju:ʒl] üblich II
usually ['ju:ʒli] normalerweise, gewöhnlich I
utter ['ʌtə] äußerst; völlig **IV U5, 78**

V

vacation (AE) [və'keɪʃn] Ferien, Urlaub II
Valentine's card ['væləntaɪnz ˌkɑ:d] Valentinskarte III
valley ['væli] Tal II
valuable ['væljuəbl] wertvoll III
value ['vælju:] Wert **IV F1, 23**
van [væn] Lieferwagen; Transporter **IV U1, 10**
vegetable ['vedʒtəbl] Gemüse I
vegetarian [ˌvedʒɪ'teəriən] Vegetarier(in) II
verse [vɜ:s] Vers; Strophe **IV U5, 84**
version ['vɜ:ʃn] Version II
very ['veri] sehr I
vet [vet] Tierarzt, Tierärztin I
to **vibrate** [vaɪ'breɪt] vibrieren III
vicar ['vɪkə] Pfarrer **IV U2, 32**
victory ['vɪktri] Sieg III
video ['vɪdiəʊ] Video I
  video clip ['vɪdiəʊ klɪp] Videoclip III
  video projector [ˌvɪdiəʊ prəʊ'dʒektə] Beamer (Projektionsgerät) **IV U4, 67**
view [vju:] Aussicht, Sicht I
  point of view [ˌpɔɪnt əv 'vju:] Standpunkt; Perspektive **IV U5, 78**
village ['vɪlɪdʒ] Dorf I
virus ['vaɪərəs] Virus **IV U3, 50**
visit ['vɪzɪt] Besuch II
to **visit** ['vɪzɪt] besuchen; besichtigen I
visitor ['vɪzɪtə] Besucher I
visual ['vɪʒuəl] visuell; optisch **IV U4, 67**
vocabulary [vəʊ'kæbjəlri] Vokabular; Wortschatz **IV U3, 49**
vocals ['vəʊklz] Gesang **IV U3, 53**
voice [vɔɪs] Stimme I
volcano, pl. **volcanoes** [vɒl'keɪnəʊ] Vulkan III
volleyball ['vɒlibɔ:l] Volleyball **IV U1, 10**

W

to **wade** [weɪd] waten ⟨**IV U5, 77**⟩
to **wait (for)** [weɪt] warten (auf) I
  to keep sb waiting [ˌki:p 'weɪtɪŋ] jmdn warten lassen **IV U5, 80**
waiter ['weɪtə] Kellner, Bedienung II
*to **wake (somebody) up** [weɪk ˌʌp] (jemanden) aufwecken; aufwachen I
walk [wɔ:k] Spaziergang I
  a two-minute walk away from … [ˌtu:mɪnɪt 'wɔ:k] zwei Minuten zu Fuß von … entfernt II
  to go for a walk [ˌgəʊ fər ə 'wɔ:k] spazieren gehen I
to **walk** [wɔ:k] gehen, laufen I
wall [wɔ:l] Wand; Mauer I
to **want (to)** ['wɒnt tə] wollen, mögen I
  to want sb to do sth [wɒnt] wollen, dass jmd etw. tut II

dictionary D

warm [wɔ:m] warm I
to warn [wɔ:n] warnen II
to wash [wɒʃ] (sich) waschen; spülen I
   to wash up [wɒʃˈʌp] abwaschen, abspülen II
waste [weɪst] Abfall; Verschwendung III
to waste [weɪst] verschwenden **IV U1, 10**
watch [wɒtʃ] Armbanduhr III
to watch [wɒtʃ] beobachten, (sich) ansehen I
   to watch TV [wɒtʃ tiːˈviː] fernsehen I
Watch out! [wɒtʃ ˈaʊt] Achtung! Pass(t) auf! I
water [ˈwɔːtə] Wasser I
   mineral water [ˈmɪnrl ˌwɔːtə] Mineralwasser **IV F3, 91**
   tap water [ˈtæp ˌwɔːtə] Leitungswasser ⟨**IV F3, 91**⟩
to water [ˈwɔːtə] bewässern, gießen **IV U2, 27**
waterproof [ˈwɔːtəpruːf] wasserdicht III
wave [weɪv] Welle I
to wave [weɪv] winken; schwenken I
way [weɪ] Weg; Art und Weise I
   by the way [ˌbaɪ ðə ˈweɪ] übrigens III
   Milky Way [ˌmɪlki ˈweɪ] Milchstraße II
   No way! [ˌnəʊ ˈweɪ] Auf keinen Fall! III
   the wrong way round [ðə ˌrɒŋ weɪ ˈraʊnd] falsch herum **IV U1, 8**
   to be in a bad way [ɪn ə ˈbæd ˌweɪ] in schlechter Verfassung sein I
   to make one's way to a place [ˌmeɪk ˈweɪ] sich an einen Ort begeben **IV U2, 33**
we [wiː] wir I
weak [wiːk] schwach I
wealth [welθ] Wohlstand; Reichtum **IV F1, 22**
wealthy [ˈwelθi] wohlhabend; reich **IV F1, 22**
weapon [ˈwepən] Waffe III
***to wear** [weə] anhaben, tragen I
weather [ˈweðə] Wetter I
   weather forecast [ˈweðə ˌfɔːkɑːst] Wettervorhersage II
web [web] (Spinnen-)Netz **IV U1, 13**
website [ˈwebsaɪt] Website, Internetauftritt II
Wednesday [ˈwenzdeɪ] Mittwoch I
week [wiːk] Woche I
   a week [ə ˈwiːk] pro Woche, in der Woche II
   What a week! [ˌwɒt ə ˈwiːk] Was für eine Woche! II
weekend [ˈwiːkend] Wochenende I
to weigh [weɪ] wiegen I
weight [weɪt] Gewicht ⟨**IV EL, 102**⟩
to welcome [ˈwelkəm] willkommen heißen II
   You're welcome. [jɔː ˈwelkəm] Bitte schön./Gern geschehen. III
Welcome! [ˈwelkəm] Willkommen! I
well [wel] gesund III
   Get well soon! [get ˌwel ˈsuːn] Gute Besserung! III
well [wel] gut I
   as well [əz ˈwel] auch III
well [wel] also; na ja; nun gut II

welly [ˈweli] Gummistiefel I
Welsh [welʃ] walisisch; Walisisch; Waliser(in) III
west [west] Westen I
western [ˈwestən] Western-; westlich II
wet [wet] nass I
   to get wet [get ˈwet] nass werden I
   wetter and wetter [ˌwetər ənd ˈwetə] immer nasser, immer verregneter II
what [wɒt] was I
   What about you? [ˌwɒt əˈbaʊt ˈjuː] Und dir/euch/Ihnen? Und du/ihr/Sie? I
   What a pity! [ˌwɒt ə ˈpɪti] Wie schade! II
   What are you pissing and moaning about? *(infml)* [ˌwɒt ə jə ˌpɪsɪŋ ənd ˈməʊnɪŋ əˌbaʊt] Was machst du denn für ein Theater? ⟨**IV EL, 100**⟩
   What a week! [ˌwɒt ə ˈwiːk] Was für eine Woche! II
   What colour is/are …? [ˌwɒt ˈkʌlər ɪz/ɑː] Welche Farbe hat/haben …? I
   what else [ˌwɒt ˈels] was sonst/noch II
   What's … in English? [ˌwɒts … ɪn ˈɪŋglɪʃ] Was heißt … auf Englisch? I
   What's it like? [ˌwɒts ɪt ˈlaɪk] Wie ist es? II
   What's missing? [ˌwɒts ˈmɪsɪŋ] Was fehlt? I
   What's the matter? [ˌwɒts ðə ˈmætə] Was ist los? Was hast du? I
   What's your name? [ˌwɒts jə ˈneɪm] Wie heißt du/heißen Sie? I
   What time …? [ˌwɒt ˈtaɪm] (Um) wie viel Uhr …? I
wheat [wiːt] Weizen I
wheel [wiːl] Rad I
wheelchair [ˈwiːltʃeə] Rollstuhl III
when [wen] wann; als; wenn I
where [weə] wo, wohin I
   Where are you from? [ˌweər ə jə ˈfrɒm] Woher kommst du/kommt ihr/kommen Sie? I
   Where … from? [ˌweə … ˈfrɒm] Woher …? I
whereas [weəˈræz] während; wohingegen **IV U5, 77**
wherever [weəˈrevə] wo(hin) auch immer III
whether [ˈweðə] ob III
which [wɪtʃ] welche(-r/-s) I
which [wɪtʃ] der, dem, den, die, das *(Relativpronomen)* II
a while [ə ˈwaɪl] eine Weile **IV U4, 58**
while [waɪl] während I
to whip [wɪp] schlagen III
whisky [ˈwɪski] Whisky **IV U3, 42**
to whisper [ˈwɪspə] flüstern III
whistle [ˈwɪsl] Trillerpfeife III
   to blow a whistle [ˌbləʊ ə ˈwɪsl] auf einer Trillerpfeife pfeifen III
white [waɪt] weiß I
   white horses [waɪt ˈhɔːsɪz] Schaumkronen I
who [huː] wer I; wem, wen I
who [huː] der, dem, den, die *(Relativpronomen)* II
whole [həʊl] ganz II
whose [huːz] wessen I

whose [huːz] dessen, deren *(Relativpronomen)* II
why [waɪ] warum I
wide [waɪd] groß; breit; weit I
wife, *pl.* **wives** [waɪf; waɪvz] Ehefrau II
the wild [waɪld] Wildnis; freie Wildbahn **IV U2, 27**
wild [waɪld] wild II
wilderness [ˈwɪldənəs] Wildnis III
wildlife [ˈwaɪldlaɪf] Tierwelt (in freier Wildbahn) II
will [wɪl] Wille; Testament ⟨**IV EL, 96**⟩
will [wɪl] werden *(futurisch)* II
wimp *(infml)* [wɪmp] Weichei; Schlappschwanz **IV U3, 52**
***to win** [wɪn] gewinnen, siegen I
wind [wɪnd] Wind I
window [ˈwɪndəʊ] Fenster I
windsurfing [ˈwɪndsɜːfɪŋ] Windsurfen II
wine [waɪn] Wein II
to flap one's wings [ˌflæp wʌnz ˈwɪŋz] mit den Flügeln schlagen ⟨**IV EL, 96**⟩
winner [ˈwɪnə] Gewinner(in), Sieger(in) II
winter [ˈwɪntə] Winter II
to wish [wɪʃ] wünschen **IV U5, 80**
with [wɪð] mit I
without [wɪˈðaʊt] ohne I
wizard [ˈwɪzəd] Zauberer II
woman, *pl.* **women** [ˈwʊmən; ˈwɪmɪn] Frau I
wombat [ˈwɒmbæt] Wombat ⟨**IV U1, 8**⟩
wonder [ˈwʌndə] Wunder; Verwunderung **IV U1, 15**
to wonder [ˈwʌndə] sich Gedanken machen, sich fragen III
wonderful [ˈwʌndəfl] wunderbar II
won't [wəʊnt] nicht werden *(futurisch)* II
wood [wʊd] Holz III
woodchuck [ˈwʊdtʃʌk] Waldmurmeltier ⟨**IV U4, 67**⟩
wooden [ˈwʊdn] hölzern **IV F2, 56**
Woof! [wʊf] Wau! I
word [wɜːd] Wort I
   words *(pl.)* [wɜːdz] Text(e) II
   Find the odd word out! [ˌɒd wɜːd ˈaʊt] Finde das Wort, das nicht in die Gruppe passt! *(Wortschatzübung)* I
   key word [ˈkiː wɜːd] Stichwort; Schlüsselbegriff III
   Word power [ˈwɜːd ˌpaʊə] Besondere Wortschatzübung I
work [wɜːk] Arbeit I
   out of work [ˌaʊt əv ˈwɜːk] arbeitslos III
to work [wɜːk] arbeiten I; funktionieren II
workman, *pl.* **workmen** [ˈwɜːkmən] Handwerker I
to work out [ˌwɜːk ˈaʊt] herausbringen, herausfinden; ausarbeiten III
workshop [ˈwɜːkʃɒp] Workshop, Werkstatt III
world [wɜːld] Erde, Welt I
***to be worried** [bɪ ˈwʌrid] besorgt, beunruhigt sein I
worry [ˈwʌri] Sorge **IV U4, 69**
   No worries! [ˌnəʊ ˈwʌriz] Keine Sorge! ⟨**IV U1, 10**⟩

dictionary

to be sick with worry [bɪ: 'sɪk wɪð ˌwʌri] krank vor Sorge sein ⟨IV U4, 69⟩
to **worry** ['wʌri] (sich) Sorgen machen I
*to be **worth** (+ gerund) [bɪ: 'wɜ:θ] (es) wert sein (zu) IV U4, 63
would [wʊd] würde(n) II
 I'd [aɪd] Ich würde II
 would not ['wʊd nɒt] weigerte(n) sich; wollte(n) nicht IV U5, 78
 Would you like …? [ˌwʊd jə 'laɪk] Möchtest du/möchten Sie/möchtet ihr …? II
wow! [waʊ] Wow! Toll! I
wreck [rek] Wrack I
wrecker ['rekə] Strandräuber *(jmd, der Schiffe mit falschen Signalen an den Strand lockt, damit sie dort auflaufen, und sie dann plündert)* ⟨IV U2, 24⟩
*to **write** [raɪt] schreiben I
writer ['raɪtə] Schriftsteller(in) IV F1, 22
wrong [rɒŋ] falsch I
 the wrong way round [ðə ˌrɒŋ weɪ 'raʊnd] falsch herum IV U1, 8
 to be wrong [bɪ: 'rɒŋ] Unrecht haben II
 to go wrong [ɡəʊ 'rɒŋ] schief gehen II

Y

yard [jɑ:d] Hof I
yeah *(infml)* [jeə] ja I
year [jɪə] Jahr; Jahrgang I
 for many years [fə ˌmeni 'jɪəz] viele Jahre lang III
yearbook ['jɪəbʊk] Jahrbuch II
yellow ['jeləʊ] gelb I
yes [jes] ja I
yesterday ['jestədeɪ] gestern I
 the day before yesterday [ðə ˌdeɪ bɪfɔ: 'jestədeɪ] vorgestern I
yet [jet] schon; noch II
yoghurt ['jɒɡət] Joghurt II
you [ju:; jə] du, ihr, Sie I; man I
 bless you ['bles ju:] Gesundheit! II
 you lot ['ju: ˌlɒt] ihr alle I
 You're welcome. [jɔ: 'welkəm] Bitte schön./Gern geschehen. III
young [jʌŋ] jung I
your [jɔ:; jə] dein(e); euer/eure; Ihr(e) I
 It's your turn. ['jɔ: tɜ:n] Du bist/Sie sind dran. I
 Yours sincerely [ˌjɔ:z sɪn'sɪəli] Mit freundlichen Grüßen IV U5, 80
 help **yourself** [ˌhelp jɔ:'self] bediene dich!/bedienen Sie sich! II
Yuk! [jʌk] Igitt! I
yummy ['jʌmi] lecker I

Z

zipper ['zɪpə] Reißverschluss III
zone [zəʊn] Zone III
zoo [zu:] Zoo, Tierpark I

Boys' names

Adam ['ædəm] IV U3, 50
Alan ['ælən] I
Alex ['æliks] III
Amir [ˌɑ:'mi:r] IV U3, 43
Anil [æ'ni:l] I
Arthur ['ɑ:θə] I
Balujee ['bɑ:lu:dʒi:] I
Barry ['bæri] II
Bart [bɑ:t] I
Ben [ben] III
Bill [bɪl] II
Bob [bɒb] IV U1, 10
Bobby ['bɒbi] III
Brad [bræd] IV U3, 44
Brooklyn ['brʊklɪn] I
Bruce [bru:s] II
Butch [bʊtʃ] IV U4, 68
Cameron ['kæmrən] IV U3, 54
Chad [tʃæd] II
Chris [krɪs] IV U3, 51
Chuck [tʃʌk] II
Colin ['kɒlɪn] I
Daniel ['dænjəl] I
Darren ['dærn] III
Dave [deɪv] II
David ['deɪvɪd] I
Dennis ['denɪs] ⟨IV EL, 100⟩
Ed [ed] II
Eddy ['edi] I
Evan ['evn] III
Frank [fræŋk] I
Fraser ['freɪzə] ⟨IV U1, 15⟩
Gareth ['ɡærəθ] III
Gordie ['ɡɔ:di] ⟨IV EL, 100⟩
Hanif [hæ'ni:f] I
Harold ['hærəld] III
Henry ['henri] II
Hobbamock ['hɒbəmɒk] ⟨IV U4, 65⟩
Homer ['həʊmə] II
Humphrey ['hʌmpfri] IV U2, 32
Jack [dʒæk] I
Jason ['dʒeɪsn] II
Jerome [dʒə'rəʊm] III
Jerry ['dʒeri] III
Jim [dʒɪm] I
John [dʒɒn] II
José [həʊ'zeɪ] I
Joshua ['dʒɒʃjuə] I
Juan [hwɑ:n] IV U5, 82
Jules [dʒu:lz] IV F3, 90
Kevin ['kevɪn] II
Lee [li:] IV U1, 12
Lenny ['leni] I
Lou [lu:] II
Luke [lu:k] IV U3, 50
Mark [mɑ:k] I
Martin ['mɑ:tɪn] III
Marty ['mɑ:ti] III
Marvin ['mɑ:vɪn] III
Matt [mæt] IV U1, 8
Nelson ['nelsn] IV U4, 68
Nick [nɪk] III
Ollie ['ɒli] II
Owen ['əʊɪn] III
Paul [pɔ:l] I
Percival ['pɜ:sɪvl] III
Pete [pi:t] III
Philip ['fɪlɪp] II
Rajiv [rə'dʒi:v] I
Ray [reɪ] ⟨IV EL, 101⟩
Rob [rɒb] III
Robert ['rɒbət] I
Romeo ['rəʊmiəʊ] I
Rory ['rɔ:ri] IV U3, 44
Ryan [raɪən] I
Sam [sæm] I
Scott [skɒt] II
Slim [slɪm] II
Spike [spaɪk] IV U3, 50
Steve [sti:v] III
Tejinder [tə'dʒɪndə] I
Tim [tɪm] III
Tom [tɒm] I
Tommy ['tɒmi] I
Tony ['təʊni] IV U2, 33
Vern [vɜ:n] ⟨IV EL, 100⟩
Wayne [weɪn] II
William ['wɪljəm] III
Willy ['wɪli] II

Girls' names

Angela ['ændʒlə] III
Anna ['ænə] I
Annie ['æni] II
Anuja [æ'nu:dʒə] I
Ashlee ['æʃli] IV U5, 76
Barbara ['bɑ:brə] III
Becky ['beki] I
Bessy ['besi] I
Britney ['brɪtni] IV U5, 76
Bronwen ['brɒnwen] III
Caitlin ['keɪtlɪn] II
Carina [kə'ri:nə] I
Caroline ['kærlaɪn] III
Cathy ['kæθi] III
Ceri ['keri] III
Cheryl ['tʃerl] II
Daisy ['deɪzi] IV U1, 16
Donna ['dɒnə] II
Emily ['emɪli] I
Emma ['emə] II
Faye [feɪ] IV U4, 70
Fiona [fi'əʊnə] I
Gemma ['dʒemə] I
Glenda ['ɡlendə] III
Gloria ['ɡlɔ:riə] IV U4, 68
Grace [ɡreɪs] I
Gracie ['ɡreɪsi] IV U1, 16
Gwen [ɡwen] III
Hazel ['heɪzl] II
Helen ['helɪn] I
Hilary ['hɪləri] IV U5, 76
Jamila [dʒə'mi:lə] I
Janet ['dʒænɪt] I
Jeanie ['dʒi:ni] II
Jenny ['dʒeni] I
Jill [dʒɪl] III
Joan [dʒəʊn] I
Joanne [dʒəʊ'æn] II
Jody ['dʒəʊdi] IV U3, 44
Judy ['dʒu:di] II

dictionary

Kate [keɪt] IV U4, 58
Kim [kɪm] I
Kristi ['krɪsti] II
Laura ['lɔ:rə] II
Lindsay ['lɪndzi] IV U5, 76
Lisa ['li:sə] III
Liz [lɪz] II
Lizzy ['lɪzi] I
Lucy ['lu:si] III
Maggie ['mægi] III
Margaret ['mɑ:grət] I
Marge [mɑ:dʒ] III
Mari ['mɑ:ri] III
Martha ['mɑ:θə] II
Mary ['meəri] I
Mary-Beth [ˌmeəri 'beθ] I
Meg [meg] I
Milly ['mɪli] II
Molly ['mɒli] IV U1, 16
Morag ['mɔ:ræg] IV U3, 44
Naomi ['neɪəmi:; neɪ'əʊmi] III
Natalie ['nætli] IV U5, 80
Natasha [nə'tæʃə] II
Nicky ['nɪki] IV U1, 10
Noreen [nɒ'ri:n] I
Pam [pæm] III
Pat [pæt] I
Peggy ['pegi] I
Polly ['pɒli] II
Rebecca [rɪ'bekə] IV U2, 32
Rikki ['rɪki] IV U5, 79
Rita ['ri:tə] I
Rosa ['rəʊzə] I
Sally ['sæli] II
Sarah ['seərə] I
Sharon ['ʃærən] II
Shelby ['ʃelbi] IV U3, 50
Shelley ['ʃeli] IV U5, 82
Sue [su:] I
Susie ['su:zi] III
Tina ['ti:nə] II
Tricia ['trɪʃə] III
Vanessa [və'nesə] I
Vicky ['vɪki] III
Victoria [vɪk'tɔ:riə] I

Surnames

Baker ['beɪkə] IV U5, 79
Batty ['bæti] III
Baxter ['bækstə] III
Bebb [beb] IV U2, 32
Bellows ['beləʊz] IV U2, 32
Blackwell ['blækwel] IV U5, 82
Brower ['braʊə] ⟨IV EL, 101⟩
Bryan [braɪən] II
Burton ['bɜ:tn] I
Campbell ['kæmbl] IV U3, 43
Chung [tʃʌŋ] II
Conway ['kɒnweɪ] IV U3, 50
Cooper ['ku:pə] I
Croft [krɒft] I
Csonka ['tʃɒŋkə] II
Dahlie ['deɪli] ⟨IV EL, 100⟩
Dane [deɪn] I
Dashworth ['dæʃwɜ:θ] IV F3, 90
Dixon ['dɪksən] I

Donovan ['dɒnəvən] IV U1, 8
Eden ['i:dn] III
Eglamore ['egləmɔ:] II
Fernandez [fɜ:'nændez] II
Flanagan ['flænəgn] IV U1, 17
Fleetwood ['fli:twʊd] II
Franklin ['fræŋklɪn] III
Gerlernter [gə'lɜ:ntə] II
Gooch [gu:tʃ] II
Gray [greɪ] II
Griffiths ['grɪfɪθs] III
Grimson ['grɪmsn] III
Hamilton ['hæmltən] II
Hammersmith ['hæməsmɪθ] IV U4, 68
Holden ['həʊldən] II
Hudson ['hʌdsn] III
Jergensen ['dʒɜ:gənsn] II
Johnson ['dʒɒntsn] II
Jones [dʒəʊnz] I
Kellerman ['keləmən] II
Kelly ['keli] IV U4, 70
Kershaw ['kɜ:ʃɔ:] II
Lepage [lə'peɪdʒ] II
Lewinsky [lu:'ɪnzki] III
Lo [ləʊ] III
Logan ['ləʊgən] II
MacAlister [mə'kælɪstə] IV U3, 42
MacDonald [mək'dɒnld] I
MacLean [mə'kleɪn; mə'kli:n] IV U3, 44
Matthews ['mæθju:z] IV U3, 51
McGill [mə'gɪl] IV U4, 68
Miller ['mɪlə] IV F2, 56
Morgan ['mɔ:gn] II
Morrison ['mɒrɪsn] IV U3, 44
Murdoch ['mɜ:dɒk] IV U3, 46
Neville ['nevl] ⟨IV U1, 19⟩
O'Brien [əʊ'braɪən] III
Parfitt ['pɑ:fɪt] IV U2, 32
Patel [pə'tel] IV U3, 50
Pengelly [ˌpen'geli] IV U2, 33
Penrose ['penrəʊz] I
Peterson ['pi:təsn] ⟨IV U1, 15⟩
Pilewski [pɪ'levski] I
Pledger ['pledʒə] II
Potter ['pɒtə] I
Preston ['prestən] II
Robinson ['rɒbɪnsn] II
Rollins ['rɒlɪnz] II
Rudd [rʌd] I
Shaw [ʃɔ:] ⟨IV EL, 98⟩
Simons ['saɪmənz] IV U5, 80
Simpson ['sɪmpsən] III
Singh [sɪŋ] I
Slater ['sleɪtə] IV U3, 43
Smith [smɪθ] I
Snyder ['snaɪdə] III
Spencer ['spentsə] II
Taylor ['teɪlə] III
Tessio ['tesiəʊ] ⟨IV EL, 101⟩
Todd [tɒd] IV U2, 32
Wainwright ['weɪnraɪt] IV U4, 68
Wallace ['wɒlɪs] I
Walters ['wɒltəz] II
Wang [wæŋ] IV U1, 10
Wray [reɪ] I

Place names

Aberdeen [ˌæbə'di:n] IV U3, 43
Aberfan [ˌæbə'væn] III
Aberystwyth [ˌæbə'rɪstwɪθ] III
Adelaide ['ædleɪd] IV U1, 15
Arndale Road [ˌɑ:ndeɪl 'rəʊd] I
Arnot Hill Park [ˌɑ:nət hɪl 'pɑ:k] I
Baker Street ['beɪkə ˌstri:t] III
Baltimore ['bɔ:ltɪmɔ:] IV U4, 58
Bamburgh ['bæmbrə] I
Barre ['bæri] IV U4, 58
Barrowland ['bærəʊlənd] IV U3, 44
Belfast [bel'fɑ:st] I
Belsize Road [ˌbelsaɪz 'rəʊd] III
Berwick-upon-Tweed [ˌberɪk əppn 'twi:d] I
Billings ['bɪlɪŋz] I
Birmingham ['bɜ:mɪŋəm] I
Blackpool ['blækpu:l] I
Boston ['bɒstn] I
Brisbane ['brɪzbən] IV F3, 90
Broadway ['brɔ:dweɪ] I
Caerleon [kɑ:'li:ən] III
Caernarfon [kə'nɑ:vn] III
Cambridge ['keɪmbrɪdʒ] IV U4, 58
Camden ['kæmdən] III
Camden Town ['kæmdən ˌtaʊn] III
Camelot ['kæmələt] III
Cardiff ['kɑ:dɪf] I
Central Park [ˌsentrl 'pɑ:k] I
Chamberlain ['tʃeɪmblɪn] ⟨IV EL, 101⟩
Chapel Bar [ˌtʃæpl 'bɑ:] I
Chicago [ʃɪ'kɑ:gəʊ] II
Chinatown ['tʃaɪnətaʊn] I
Conwy ['kɒnwi] III
Delhi ['deli] I
Denver ['denvə] I
Dundee [dʌn'di:] I
Durham ['dʌrəm] ⟨IV EL, 101⟩
Edinburgh ['edɪnbrə] I
Everglades National Park [ˌevəgleɪdz ˌnæʃnl 'pɑ:k] I
Exchange Walk [ɪksˌtʃeɪndʒ 'wɔ:k] I
Exeter ['eksɪtə] IV U2, 30
Falmouth ['fælməθ] IV U2, 24
Faywood ['feɪwʊd] IV U4, 58
Fort Augustus [ˌfɔ:t ɔ:'gʌstəs] IV U3, 43
Fort Benning [ˌfɔ:t 'benɪŋ] ⟨IV EL, 100⟩
Fort William [ˌfɔ:t 'wɪljəm] IV U3, 54
Glasgow ['glɑ:zgəʊ] IV U3, 42
Gotham City [ˌgɒθəm 'sɪti] II
Greyfriars [ˌgreɪ'fraɪəz] IV U3, 55
Harvard ['hɑ:vəd] IV U4, 58
Hastings ['heɪstɪŋz] III
Haywood ['heɪwʊd] I
Heathrow [ˌhi:'θrəʊ] I
Highbury ['haɪbri] II
Holyhead [ˌhɒli'hed] III
Honister ['hɒnɪstə] II
Honolulu [ˌhɒn'lu:lu:] IV U4, 70
Hull [hʌl] I
Jamestown ['dʒeɪmztaʊn] IV F2, 56
Jigalong ['dʒɪgəlɒŋ] ⟨IV U1, 16⟩
Johannesburg [dʒəʊ'hænɪsbɜ:g] I
Kendall Farm [ˌkendl 'fɑ:m] IV F3, 90
Kensington ['kenzɪŋtən] III
Keswick ['kezɪk] II
King Street ['kɪŋ ˌstri:t] I

Dictionary

Lakewood ['leɪkwʊd] II
Larwood Grove [ˌlɑːwʊd 'grəʊv] I
Leicester Square [ˌlestə 'skweə] III
Lewiston ['luːɪstn] ⟨IV EL, 101⟩
Lexington ['leksɪŋtən] II
Liverpool ['lɪvəpuːl] I
Llandudno [læn'dɪdnəʊ] III
London ['lʌndən] I
Los Angeles [lɒsˌ'ændʒɪliːz] I
Madison Square Garden [ˌmædɪsn ˌskweə 'gɑːdn] I
Manchester ['mæntʃɪstə] I
Manhattan [mæn'hætn] I
Mansfield Road [ˌmænsfiːld 'rəʊd] I
Market Square [ˌmɑːkɪt 'skweə] I
Market Street ['mɑːkɪt ˌstriːt] I
Massachusetts [ˌmæsə'tʃuːsɪts] II
Miami [maɪ'æmi] II
Montpelier [mɒnt'piːliə] IV U4, 60
Motton ['mɒtn] ⟨IV EL, 101⟩
Mount Street ['maʊnt ˌstriːt] I
Munich ['mjuːnɪk] München I
Naples ['neɪplz] Neapel I
Newcastle-upon-Tyne [ˌnjuːkɑːslˌəpɒn 'taɪn] I
Newport ['njuːpɔːt] III
New York [ˌnjuː 'jɔːk] I
New York City [ˌnjuː jɔːk 'sɪti] I
Nottingham ['nɒtɪŋəm] I
Nottingham Road [ˌnɒtɪŋəm 'rəʊd] I
Notting Hill [ˌnɒtɪŋ 'hɪl] III
Oxford Circus [ˌɒksfəd 'sɜːkəs] III
Penzance [pen'zænts] IV U2, 32
Perth [pɜːθ] IV U1, 16
Philadelphia [ˌfɪlə'delfiə] I
Piccadilly [ˌpɪkə'dɪli] III
Plimoth ['plɪməθ] IV U4, 58
Plymouth ['plɪməθ] IV U2, 24
Pontypridd [ˌpɒntɪ'priːð] ⟨IV EL, 101⟩
Portland ['pɔːtlənd] ⟨IV EL, 101⟩
Pownal ['paʊnl] ⟨IV EL, 101⟩
Roanoke ['rəʊənəʊk] IV F2, 56
Rockdale ['rɒkdeɪl] IV U1, 10
San Diego [ˌsæn di'eɪgəʊ] I
San Francisco [ˌsæn frən'sɪskəʊ] II
Seahouses ['siːhaʊzɪz] I
Seattle [si'ætl] II
Sherwood ['ʃɜːwʊd] I
South Parade [ˌsaʊθ pə'reɪd] I
South Street Seaport [ˌsaʊθ striːt 'siːpɔːt] I
South Warren Street [saʊθ 'wɒrn striːt] IV U5, 80
St Austell [sntˌ'ɔːstl] IV U2, 24
St Dominic [snt 'dɒmɪnɪk] ⟨IV U2, 32⟩
Swansea ['swɒnzi] III
Swiss Cottage [ˌswɪs 'kɒtɪdʒ] III
Sydney ['sɪdni] IV U1, 9
Thoresby Park [ˌθɔːzbi 'pɑːk] I
Tintagel ['tɪntædʒl] IV U2, 24
Torquay [ˌtɔː'kiː] IV U2, 29
Tower Hill [ˌtaʊə 'hɪl] III
Trenton ['trentən] IV U5, 80
Washington, D.C. [ˌwɒʃɪŋtən ˌdiː'siː] I
the West End [west 'end] III
Westminster [west'mɪntstə] III
Yellowstone National Park [jeləʊstəʊn ˌnæʃnl 'pɑːk] II

Geographical names

Alaska [ə'læskə] I
Alps [ælps] Alpen II
America [ə'merɪkə] I
Asia ['eɪʃə] Asien III
Atlantic [ət'læntɪk] II
Australia ['ɒstreɪliə] I
the Baltic ['bɔːltɪk] Ostsee IV U2, 36
Bavaria [bə'veəriə] Bayern IV U4, 60
Ben Nevis [ˌben 'nevɪs] IV U3, 54
Bermuda [bə'mjuːdə] III
Big Harcar Rock [bɪg ˌhɑːkə 'rɒk] I
Bondi Beach [ˌbɒndaɪ 'biːtʃ] ⟨IV U1, 11⟩
Botany Bay [ˌbɒtni 'beɪ] ⟨IV U1, 12⟩
California [ˌkælɪ'fɔːniə] I
Cape Cod [ˌkeɪp 'kɒd] IV U4, 58
Cascade Mountains [ˌkæskeɪd 'maʊntɪnz] III
the Channel [ðə 'tʃænl] Ärmelkanal (Teil der Nordsee zwischen Großbritannien und Frankreich) IV U2, 29
China ['tʃaɪnə] II
Colorado [ˌkɒlr'ɑːdəʊ] II
Cornwall ['kɔːnwɔːl] I
Cumberland ['kʌmblənd] II
Dartmoor ['dɑːtmɔː] IV U2, 24
Denmark ['denmɑːk] Dänemark II
Derwentwater ['dɜːwəntˌwɔːtə] II
Devon ['devn] I
Dinosaur Ridge [ˌdaɪnəsɔː 'rɪdʒ] II
England ['ɪŋglənd] I
Europe ['jʊərəp] Europa II
Exmoor ['eksmɔː] IV U2, 24
Farne Islands [ˌfɑːn 'aɪləndz] I
Florida ['flɒrɪdə] I
the River Forth [fɔːθ] IV U3, 48
France [frɑːnts] I
Georgia ['dʒɔːdʒə] ⟨IV EL, 100⟩
Germany ['dʒɜːməni] Deutschland I
Glamorgan [glə'mɔːgən] III
Gondwana [gɒnd'wɑːnə] ⟨IV U1, 15⟩
Grand Canyon [ˌgrænd 'kænjən] I
Great Barrier Reef [ˌgreɪt ˌbæriə 'riːf] IV U1, 9
Great Gable [ˌgreɪt 'geɪbl] II
the Highlands ['haɪləndz] IV U3, 42
Hudson River [ˌhʌdsn 'rɪvə] I
Hungary ['hʌŋgri] Ungarn II
India ['ɪndiə] I
Ireland ['aɪələnd] I
Jamaica [dʒə'meɪkə] IV U2, 24
Kansas ['kænzəs] III
Lake District ['leɪk ˌdɪstrɪkt] II
Loch Ness [ˌlɒx 'nes; ˌlɒk 'nes] IV U3, 42
Maine [meɪn] ⟨IV EL, 100⟩
Maryland ['meərɪlænd] IV F2, 56
Mexico ['meksɪkəʊ] I
Midwest [ˌmɪd'west] Mittlerer Westen III
Mississippi River [ˌmɪsɪsɪpi 'rɪvə] I
Montana [mɒn'tænə] II
Mount Rainier [ˌmaʊnt 'reɪniə] III
Mount St. Helens [ˌmaʊnt snt 'helənz] III
New England [ˌnjuːˌ'ɪŋglənd] Neuengland III
New Zealand [ˌnjuː 'ziːlənd] Neuseeland III
Niagara Falls [naɪˌægrə 'fɔːlz] I
Normandy ['nɔːməndi] die Normandie III
Northern Ireland [ˌnɔːðn 'aɪələnd] I
North Sea [ˌnɔːθ 'siː] I
Northumbria [nɔː'θʌmbriə] I
Omaha ['əʊməhɑː] II
Pacific Rim [ðə pəˌsɪfɪk 'rɪm] Rand des Pazifik ⟨IV U1, 10⟩
Puget Sound [ˌpjuːdʒət 'saʊnd] III
Queensland ['kwiːnzlənd] IV U1, 13
Republic of Ireland [rɪˌpʌblɪk əvˌ'aɪələnd] I
Riviera [ˌrɪvi'eərə] Riviera (Mittelmeerküste im Bereich Frankreich/Italien) IV U2, 25
Rocky Mountains [ˌrɒki 'maʊntɪnz] I
Scotland ['skɒtlənd] I
Sherwood Forest [ˌʃɜːwʊd 'fɒrɪst] I
Snowdon ['snəʊdn] III
Snowdonia [snəʊ'dəʊniə] III
South Africa [ˌsaʊθˌ'æfrɪkə] I
Spain [speɪn] Spanien IV F1, 23
Tasmania [tæz'meɪniə] Tasmanien IV U1, 12
Texas ['teksəs] I
the Thames [temz] I
UK [juː'keɪ] Vereinigtes Königreich von Großbritannien und Nordirland I
Ullswater ['ʌlzˌwɔːtə] II
United Kingdom [juːˌnaɪtɪd 'kɪŋdəm] Vereinigtes Königreich von Großbritannien und Nordirland I
United States of America [juːˌnaɪtɪd 'steɪtsˌəv ə'merɪkə] Vereinigte Staaten von Amerika I
USA [juːes'eɪ] USA I
Van Diemen's Land [ˌvæn 'diːmənz lænd] ⟨IV U1, 12⟩
Vermont [və'mɒnt] IV U4, 58
Virginia [və'dʒɪnjə] IV F2, 56
Wales [weɪlz] I
Washington ['wɒʃɪŋtən] I
Yorkshire ['jɔːkʃə] I

Other names

Arena [ə'riːnə] II
Armada [ɑː'mɑːdə] Armada (Name der spanischen Flotte) ⟨IV F1, 22⟩
Ballard ['bæləd] III
Bamburgh Castle [ˌbæmbrə 'kɑːsl] I
Barker ['bɑːkə] I
Beacon Hill [ˌbiːkn 'hɪl] IV U4, 69
Big Apple [ˌbɪgˌ'æpl] I
Big Ben [ˌbɪg 'ben] III
Boogaloo [ˌbuː'gluː] ⟨IV EL, 103⟩
Buckingham Palace [ˌbʌkɪŋəm 'pælɪs] III
the Capitol [ðə 'kæpɪtl] IV U4, 60
Causeway Street ['kɔːzweɪ ˌstriːt] IV U4, 69
Charlestown Bridge [ˌtʃɑːlztaʊn 'brɪdʒ] IV U4, 68
City Ground [ˌsɪti 'graʊnd] II
Cooper Courier [ˌkuːpə 'kʊriə] II
Crow [krəʊ] Name eines Indianerstammes II
Day Rider Ticket [ˌdeɪ 'raɪdəˌtɪkɪt] I
Disney World ['dɪzniˌwɜːld] I
Earth Keepers ['ɜːθˌkiːpəz] Umweltschutzorganisation II
Easter ['iːstə] Ostern II

dictionary D

Eden ['iːdn] (der Garten) Eden **IV U2, 24**
elfinpower ['elfɪnˌpaʊə] **IV U5, 82**
Empire State Building [ˌempaɪə 'steɪt ˌbɪldɪŋ] **I**
Evening Post [ˌiːvnɪŋ 'pəʊst] Abendpost (Name einer Zeitung) **II**
FA Cup [ˌef eɪ 'kʌp] Pokal des englischen Fußballverbands, vgl. DFB-Pokal **II**
Flash [flæʃ] **IV U5, 80**
Giants ['dʒaɪənts] **I**
the Globe Theatre ['gləʊb ˌθɪətə] das Globe-Theater **III**
Golden Gate Bridge [ˌgəʊldn ˌgeɪt 'brɪdʒ] **I**
Grace Darling Museum [ˌgreɪs ˌdɑːlɪŋ mjuːˈziːəm] **I**
Halloween [ˌhæləʊˈiːn] Halloween (Tag vor Allerheiligen) **II**
Hanover Street [ˈhænəʊvə ˌstriːt] **IV U4, 69**
Haywood School [ˈheɪwʊd ˌskuːl] **I**
Hillside Farm [ˌhɪlsaɪd 'fɑːm] **I**
Hogwarts [ˈhɒgwɒts] **II**
the Houses of Parliament [ðə ˌhaʊzɪz əv 'pɑːləmənt] the Houses of Parliament (britisches Parlamentsgebäude) **III**
Jubilee Line [ˈdʒuːbɪliː ˌlaɪn] **III**
Kennedy Space Center [ˌkenədi 'speɪs ˌsentə] **I**
Lazy G [ˌleɪzi 'dʒiː] **II**
Legolas [ˈlegəʊləs] **IV U5, 77**
Logan International Airport [ˌləʊgən ˌɪntəˌnæʃnl 'eəpɔːt] **IV U4, 70**
London Eye [ˌlʌndən 'aɪ] **I**
Longstone Lighthouse [ˌlɒŋstəʊn 'laɪthaʊs] **I**
Major Oak [ˌmeɪdʒər ˈəʊk] **II**
Mayflower [ˈmeɪflaʊə] **IV U2, 24**
Military Tattoo [ˌmɪlɪtri təˈtuː] Musikparade des Militärs ⟨**IV U3, 42**⟩
Monny [ˈmɒni] **I**
Moore River [ˌmʊə 'rɪvə] ⟨**IV U1, 16**⟩
MTV [ˌemtiːˈviː] **II**
National Museum of the American Indian [ˌnæʃnl mjuːˈziːəm əv ðɪ əˌmerɪkn 'ɪndɪən] **I**
the Olympics (Olympic Games) [əʊˈlɪmpɪks; əʊˌlɪmpɪk 'geɪmz] Olympiade, Olympische Spiele **II**
Oxford Street [ˌɒksfəd 'striːt] **III**
Oz (infml) [ɒz] Oz (Spitzname für Australien) ⟨**IV U1, 10**⟩
Philco [ˈfɪlkəʊ] ⟨**IV EL, 101**⟩
Pike Place Market [ˌpaɪk pleɪs 'mɑːkɪt] **III**
Reformation [ˌrefəˈmeɪʃn] Reformation (historische Periode der Trennung der protestantischen von der katholischen Kirche) ⟨**IV F1, 23**⟩
Renaissance [rəˈneɪsns] Renaissance (historisches Zeitalter: Wiedergeburt der klassischen Werte, Beginn der Moderne) ⟨**IV F1, 22**⟩
Rock City [ˌrɒk 'sɪti] **II**
Rockefeller Center [ˌrɒkəfelə 'sentə] **I**
Romeo and Juliet [ˌrəʊmɪəʊ ənd 'dʒuːlɪət] Romeo und Julia **III**
Rusty [ˈrʌsti] **II**
Seafair [ˈsiːfeə] **III**
Space Needle [ˌspeɪs ˌniːdl] **III**
Springfield Farm [ˌsprɪŋfiːld 'fɑːm] **II**
Stanford Street [ˈstænfəd ˌstriːt] **IV U4, 69**
Statue of Liberty [ˌstætʃuː əv 'lɪbəti] **I**
St Peter's Church [snt ˌpiːtəz 'tʃɜːtʃ] **I**
Strong Wind [ˌstrɒŋ 'wɪnd] **II**
Tabby [ˈtæbi] **I**
Tate Modern [ˌteɪt 'mɒdn] **III**
Thanksgiving [ˌθæŋksˈgɪvɪŋ] **II**
The Tales of Robin Hood [ˌteɪlz əv rɒbɪn 'hʊd] **II**
The Underdogs [ðɪ ˈʌndədɒgz] **I**
Tower Bridge [ˌtaʊə 'brɪdʒ] **III**
the Tower of London [ðə ˌtaʊər əv 'lʌndən] **III**
Underground [ˈʌndəgraʊnd] Londoner U-Bahn **III**
Wampanoag [ˌwɒmpəˈnəʊəg] **IV U4, 64**
Wongutha [ˌwɒŋˈgʌθə] ⟨**IV EL, 96**⟩

Famous names

Alan a Dale [ˌælən ə 'deɪl] **II**
Amelia Earhart [əˌmiːlɪə 'eəhɑːt] **III**
Andy Dunlop [ˌændi 'dʌnlɒp] **IV U3, 53**
Arsenal [ˈɑːsnl] **II**
Atomic Kitten [əˌtɒmɪk 'kɪtn] **II**
Avril Lavigne [ˌævrɪl ləˈviːn] **IV U5, 76**
Batman [ˈbætmæn] **II**
Blondie [ˈblɒndi] **I**
Boudicca [ˈbuːdɪkə] **III**
Bruce Springsteen [ˌbruːs 'sprɪŋstiːn] **III**
Calvin [ˈkælvɪn] ⟨**IV F1, 23**⟩
Christopher Columbus [ˌkrɪstəfə kəˈlʌmbəs] **IV F1, 23**
Christopher Wren [ˌkrɪstəfə 'ren] ⟨**IV EL, 98**⟩
Cinderella [ˌsɪndrˈelə] Aschenputtel **II**
Dante Thomas [ˌdænti 'tɒməs] **IV U5, 85**
David Beckham [ˌdeɪvɪd 'bekəm] **I**
Donald Duck [ˌdɒnld 'dʌk] **II**
Doris Pilkington [ˌdɒrɪs 'pɪlkɪŋtən] ⟨**IV U1, 18**⟩
Dougie Payne [ˌdʌgi 'peɪn] **IV U3, 53**
Edmund Clerihew Bentley [ˌedmənd ˌklerɪhjuː 'bentli] ⟨**IV EL, 98**⟩
Edward Lear [ˌedwəd 'lɪə] ⟨**IV EL, 99**⟩
Ellen MacArthur [ˌelən məˈkɑːθə] **IV U2, 24**
Elton John [ˌeltn 'dʒɒn] **IV U5, 87**
Everlyn Sampi [ˌevəlɪn 'sæmpi] ⟨**IV U1, 19**⟩
Francis Drake [ˌfrɑːntsɪs 'dreɪk] **IV F1, 22**
Fran Healy [ˌfræn 'hiːli] **IV U3, 53**
Friar Tuck [ˌfraɪə 'tʌk] **II**
Grace Darling [ˌgreɪs 'dɑːlɪŋ] **I**
Hadrian [ˈheɪdrɪən] **III**
Harry Potter [ˌhæri 'pɒtə] **II**
Hermione Granger [hɜːˌmaɪəni 'greɪndʒə] **II**
Huckleberry Finn [ˌhʌklberi 'fɪn] **II**
the Hulk [hʌlk] **II**
Jack Nicholson [ˌdʒæk 'nɪklsn] ⟨**IV EL, 100**⟩
Jennifer Lopez [ˌdʒenɪfə 'ləʊpez] **IV U5, 76**
John Rolfe [ˌdʒɒn 'rɒlf] **II**
the Joker [ˈdʒəʊkə] **II**
Jon Bon Jovi [ˌdʒɒn bɒn 'dʒəʊvi] **I**
Kenneth Branagh [ˌkenɪθ 'brænə] ⟨**IV U1, 19**⟩
Lara Croft [ˌlɑːrə 'krɒft] **II**
Laura Monaghan [ˌlɔːrə 'mɒnəhən] ⟨**IV U1, 19**⟩
Lenny Kravitz [ˌleni 'krævɪts] **I**
Little John [ˌlɪtl 'dʒɒn] **II**
Luther [ˈluːθə] ⟨**IV F1, 23**⟩
Madonna [məˈdɒnə] **I**
Maid Marian [ˌmeɪd 'mærɪən] **II**
Manchester United [ˌmæntʃɪstə juːˈnaɪtɪd] **I**
Marilyn Monroe [ˌmærɪlɪn mənˈrəʊ] **IV U5, 89**
Marla Runyan [ˌmɑːlə 'rʌnjən] **III**
Metallica [məˈtælɪkə] **IV U5, 86**
Michael Jackson [ˌmaɪkl 'dʒæksn] **II**
Mickey Mouse [ˌmɪki 'maʊs] **II**
Morgan Freeman [ˌmɔːgn 'friːmən] ⟨**IV EL, 100**⟩
Natalie Cole [ˌnætli 'kəʊl] **IV U4, 62**
Nat King Cole [ˌnæt kɪŋ 'kəʊl] **IV U4, 62**
Old Moses [ˌəʊld 'məʊzɪz] **II**
Orlando Bloom [ɔːˌlændəʊ 'bluːm] **IV U5, 77**
Paragons [ˈpærəgənz] **II**
Phillip Noyce [ˌfɪlɪp 'nɔɪs] ⟨**IV U1, 19**⟩
Pocahontas [ˌpɒkəˈhɒntəs] **II**
Pras [prɑːz] **IV U5, 85**
Renée Zellweger [ˌreneɪ 'zelwegə] **IV U5, 76**
Robbie Williams [ˌrɒbi 'wɪljəmz] **I**
Robin Hood [ˌrɒbɪn 'hʊd] **I**
Robin Hood and his Merry Men [ˌrɒbɪn ˌhʊd ənd hɪz ˌmeri 'men] **II**
Ron Weasley [ˌrɒn 'wiːzli] **II**
Rosie Rushton [ˌrəʊzi 'rʌʃtən] **IV U3, 50**
Rowan Atkinson [ˌrəʊən 'ætkɪnsn] **IV U5, 76**
Sherlock Holmes [ˌʃɜːlɒk 'həʊmz] **III**
Sir Guy of Gisborne [sɜːˌgaɪ əv 'gɪzbɔːn] **II**
Sir Kay [ˌsɜː 'keɪ] **III**
Sir Lancelot [ˌsɜː 'lɑːntsəlɒt] **III**
Stephen Hawking [ˌstiːvn 'hɔːkɪŋ] **III**
Stephen King [ˌstiːvn 'kɪŋ] ⟨**IV EL, 100**⟩
Superman [ˈsuːpəmæn] **II**
The men they couldn't hang [ðə ˌmen ðeɪ ˌkʊdnt 'hæŋ] **IV U2, 35**
Tianna Sansbury [tiˌænə 'sænzbri] ⟨**IV U1, 19**⟩
Tom Hanks [ˌtɒm 'hæŋks] ⟨**IV EL, 100**⟩
Tom Sawyer [ˌtɒm 'sɔːjə] **II**
Travis [ˈtrævɪs] **IV U3, 53**
U2 [juːˈtuː] **I**
the Virgin Queen [ˌvɜːdʒɪn 'kwiːn] die jungfräuliche Königin (Elizabeth I. wurde so genannt, weil sie nie heiratete.)⟨**IV F1, 22**⟩
Voldemort [ˈvɒldəmɔːt] **II**
Walter Ralegh (Raleigh) [ˌwɔːltə 'rɔːli] **IV F1, 22**
William Shakespeare [ˌwɪljəm 'ʃeɪkspɪə] **III**
Will Smith [ˌwɪl 'smɪθ] **IV U5, 76**

revision 1–3
Test yourself solutions

Erklärung: Test yourself!

1. Ermittle anhand der Lösungen, in welchem Bereich du die meisten Fehler gemacht hast (A, B, C oder D), am besten mit Hilfe einer Strichliste.

2. Schau dir dann im Workbook die zugehörigen *Doctor-G*-Seiten an. Dort ist bei jeder Übung angegeben, welchen Bereich (A, B, C oder D) du damit üben kannst.

3. Wähle anhand deiner Strichliste die diesem Bereich zugeordneten Übungen aus, um gezielt deine Schwachstellen zu verbessern. *Doctor G* hält zu jedem Bereich einen Grammatiktipp bereit, mit dem du dir den Stoff wieder ins Gedächtnis rufen kannst, den du für die einzelnen Übungen brauchst.

revision 1

3 People and places (Seite 39)

a) 1. Matt doesn't come from Melbourne.
2. The Wangs don't speak Japanese.
3. Matt didn't meet her parents in the street.
4. The Donovans haven't got a tennis court.

b) Where do you live? Where does your family come from? When did you come to Australia? Where did you live first? Why did you move? Does your mother work, too? What language do you speak at home? What do you like/hate?

Welcher Bereich ist verbesserungsbedürftig?

a) A Falsche Verbform.

b) A Falsche Verbform.
B Falsches Fragewort.
C Fehler bei der Wortstellung.
→ Workbook, S. 25

4 Questions with and without "do"

1. Oh? Who did you meet? 2. Really? What happened? 3. Great! Who sent it? 4. Right. Who do you want to invite? 5. Who plays in it? 6. Yes. Which do you prefer? 7. OK, so which ones fit best? 8. Really? What does she do?

Welcher Bereich ist verbesserungsbedürftig?

A Verwendung von *do*-Umschreibung statt normaler Wortstellung.
B Verwendung von normaler Wortstellung statt *do*-Umschreibung.
→ Workbook, S. 26

5 Jack and the ghost

1. In 1785, Jack had news from an uncle (who(m)/that) he had never heard of. 2. St Dominic was the name of the village (which/that) Jack was sent to. 3. His uncle, the vicar, had a housekeeper whose daughter was called Rebecca. 4. Jack enjoyed the stories (which/that) Rebecca told him about Cornwall. 5. Rebecca knew about a captain whose ship went down in a storm in 1720. 6. Wreckers stole all the wine and tobacco which/that was on the ship. 7. After that, people were scared by the story of a ghost which/that appeared on the beach at night. 8. Years later, the people of St Dominic enjoyed the wine (which/that) the vicar used at his Sunday services. 9. But in 1785, on a dark night (which/that) Jack and Rebecca would never forget, the vicar disappeared for ever! 10. The Reverend Todd is the name of the man who/that is vicar of St Dominic now.

Welcher Bereich ist verbesserungsbedürftig?

A Falsches Relativpronomen.
B *Contact clause* nicht richtig erkannt.
C Präpositionen im Relativsatz falsch benutzt.
→ Workbook, S. 26–27

rev. 2

4 Girls and boys in Scotland (Seite 73)

a) 1., 3., 7. for 2., 4., 5., 6. since
b) 1., 4., 9., 14. since 2. has been looking 3. have known 5. have been 6., 8., 12., 15. for 7. have been trying 10. have had 11. has been changing 13. has not seen 16. have been going.

Welcher Bereich ist verbesserungsbedürftig?

A Falsche Verwendung von *since* und *for*.
B Falsche Verbform?
C Falsche Verwendung der *simple* und *progressive* Form.
→ Workbook, S. 54–55

186 one hundred and eighty-six

revision 1–3
Test yourself solutions

5 Visitors to the 1627 Pilgrim Village

1. anyone 2. some 3. any 4. anyone's 5. some
6. anything 7. any 8. something 9. someone 10. anywhere 11. someone 12. somewhere

Welcher Bereich ist verbesserungsbedürftig?

A Falsche Verwendung von *some* und *any*.
B Verwechslung der Zusammensetzungen.
C Unklarheit beim Gebrauch von *some* in Fragen und *any* in bejahten Aussagesätzen.
➔ **Workbook, S. 55–56**

3 Bad news (Seite 93)

1. My bike has been stolen! 2. The South-East of England was hit by stormy weather yesterday. 3. Were many trees blown down? 4. Our TV set can't be repaired – it's too old. 5. If the thieves had been recognized, they would have been arrested sooner. 6. The terrible damage that was done by the storm will never be forgotten. 7. A lot of road accidents are caused by bad driving. 8. All the young crops in these fields have been destroyed by rabbits. 9. If the ransom isn't paid, the child may be hurt – or even killed – by the kidnappers. 10. Swimmers and surfers are sometimes attacked by sharks. That's why some people think these sharks should be killed.

Welcher Bereich ist verbesserungsbedürftig?

A Falsche Zeitform.
B Falsche Passivform.
C Probleme mit Passivformen der Modalverben (z. B. *can't be repaired*).
D Falsche Verwendung des *by-agent*.
➔ **Workbook, S. 72–73**

4 Jody and her dad

1. I told Dad (that) I'd been looking forward to this concert so much. I said (that) you and the others would be so disappointed if I couldn't go with you.
2. Dad told me (that) he understood how I was feeling. But he said (that) Rory wasn't an experienced driver yet – and added that none of us knew what the weather was going to be like at the weekend. He said (that) it might be foggy again. He remembered that there had been a bad accident in the fog on that motorway only a week or two ago.
3. I admitted that I hadn't forgotten. But I asked how Rory would ever become an experienced driver if he never got the chance to use the car at night.
4. Dad explained that he was only thinking of my safety. He wanted me to try to understand his position, too.
5. I asked him what he suggested. I wondered whether/if he expected me to stay at home while you and the others went without me.
6. Dad said (that) he had a suggestion. He advised us all to go by train. He asked (me) what I thought of the idea.
7. I said (that) I wasn't sure. I told him (that) I'd no idea what times the trains were on Saturday.
8. He told me to get the timetable. He said (that) he was sure there'd be a good connection.
9. I told him (that) I'd discuss the train times with you and (that) we'd go by train. And I thanked him for letting me go.
10. He said (that) he was glad I was happy about it now. He told me that if I let him know what the train ticket cost, he'd give me the money.

Welcher Bereich ist verbesserungsbedürftig?

A Falsche Zeit durch Nichtbeachtung der Zeitverschiebung.
B Falsche Zeitformen.
C Fehler bei der Anpassung der Personalpronomen bzw. -begleiter.
D Fehler bei Infinitivkonstruktionen (z. B. *nach tell sb. to …, advise sb. to …*)
➔ **Workbook, S. 73–74**

in the classroom

Talking to the teacher

Can you help me, please?	Können Sie mir bitte helfen?
I don't understand this.	Ich verstehe das nicht.
Can you explain that again, please?	Können Sie das bitte noch einmal erklären?
What do we have to do?	Was müssen wir denn machen?
What's that in English/German?	Was heißt das auf Englisch/Deutsch?
Can I say: …?/What does … mean?	Kann ich sagen: …?/Was bedeutet …?
Can you paraphrase …, please?	Können Sie bitte … umschreiben?
How do you do this exercise?	Wie macht man diese Übung?
Is this right? I'm not sure.	Ist das richtig? Ich bin nicht sicher.
Sorry, I don't know.	Tut mir leid, das weiß ich nicht.
Can you write it on the board, please?	Können Sie das bitte an die Tafel schreiben?
Can I ask a question, please?	Kann ich bitte eine Frage stellen?
Pardon? Can you repeat the question/sentence, please?	Wie bitte? Können Sie die Frage/den Satz bitte wiederholen?
Can you play the CD again, please?	Können Sie die CD bitte noch mal abspielen?
Can we do another example, please?	Können wir noch ein Beispiel machen?
Whose turn is it?	Wer ist dran?
What's for homework, please?	Was haben wir als Hausaufgabe auf?
I'm not feeling well.	Ich fühle mich nicht gut.
I've got a headache.	Ich habe Kopfweh.
Can I open the window, please?	Darf ich bitte das Fenster öffnen?
Can I go to the toilet, please?	Darf ich bitte auf die Toilette gehen?

Talking about stories, poems, songs, …

I like/don't like this story.	Diese Geschichte gefällt mir/gefällt mir nicht.
I think it's good, interesting, brilliant, funny, really exciting.	Ich finde sie gut, interessant, toll, witzig, wirklich spannend.
I think it's sad, terrible, boring.	Ich finde sie traurig, schrecklich, langweilig.
It was OK, but I've read better ones.	Sie ist ganz nett, aber ich habe schon bessere gelesen.
The characteristics of this story are …	Die Kennzeichen/Merkmale dieser Geschichte sind …
The key words here are …	Die Schlüsselwörter sind hier …
I can't identify with the idea …	Ich kann mich mit der Idee … nicht identifizieren.

Talking about diagrams and numbers

As you can see in this diagram …	Wie man in diesem Diagramm sehen kann, …
The diagram shows …	Das Diagramm zeigt …
The results show that …	Die Ergebnisse zeigen, dass …
More than half/a third/20 percent …	Mehr als die Hälfte/ein Drittel/20 Prozent …
Less than half/a third/20 percent …	Weniger als die Hälfte/ein Drittel/20 Prozent …
It's surprising that …	Es ist erstaunlich, dass …

Discussion phrases

What do you think?/What's your opinion?	Was meinst du?
Would you like to comment on …?	Würdest du gerne etwas zu … sagen?
In my opinion …	Meiner Meinung nach …
As far as I know …	Soweit ich weiß, …
According to … it's …	Laut … ist es …
It's a fact that …	Tatsache ist, dass …
Actually, …	Tatsächlich/Eigentlich …
Basically, …	Im Grunde …
I think you are right/wrong.	Ich denke, du hast Recht/Unrecht.
That can't be right, surely.	Das kann sicher nicht stimmen.
I agree./I disagree.	Ich stimme zu./Ich bin anderer Meinung.
Well, it's true that …, but …	… ist zwar richtig, aber …
Well, I must admit that …, but …	Ich muss zwar zugeben, dass …, aber …
Furthermore …	Darüber hinaus …
There's no /an easy solution to the problem.	Es gibt zu dem Problem keine/eine einfache Lösung.
However, …	Jedoch …
On the one hand …, on the other hand …	Einerseits …, andererseits …
I would have expected …	Ich hätte … erwartet.
Let's compare our expectations with …	Lasst uns unsere Erwartungen mit … vergleichen.

Presentation phrases

I'm going to talk about …	Ich werde über … sprechen.
My topic is …	Mein Thema ist …
I'd like to begin with …	Ich würde gerne mit … anfangen.
I wanted to find out …	Ich wollte herausfinden, …
The aim of my presentation is …	Das Ziel meines Vortrags ist …
First of all, …	Zuallererst …
Secondly, …	Zweitens …
Finally, …	Abschließend …
Now let's turn to …	Nun lasst uns zu … kommen.
Another important point is …	Ein weiterer wichtiger Punkt ist …
Apart from that, …	Außerdem …
Here you can see …	Hier könnt ihr … sehen.
This is the reason why …	Dies ist der Grund, warum …
I'd like to mention …	Ich möchte … erwähnen.
I'd like to point out that …	Ich möchte darauf hinweisen, dass …
The purpose of this is to …	Der Zweck ist, … zu zeigen.

grammar
irregular verbs

List of irregular verbs

infinitive	simple past	past participle	German
to awake [əˈweɪk]	awoke [əˈwəʊk]	awoken [əˈwəʊkn]	erwachen
to be [biː]	was/were [wɒz; wɜː]	been [biːn]	sein
to beat [biːt]	beat [biːt]	beaten [ˈbiːtn]	besiegen, schlagen
to become [bɪˈkʌm]	became [bɪˈkeɪm]	become [bɪˈkʌm]	werden
to begin [bɪˈgɪn]	began [bɪˈgæn]	begun [bɪˈgʌn]	beginnen
to bend [bend]	bent [bent]	bent [bent]	beugen
to bet [bet]	bet [bet]	bet [bet]	wetten
to bite [baɪt]	bit [bɪt]	bitten [ˈbɪtn]	beißen
to blow [bləʊ]	blew [bluː]	blown [bləʊn]	blasen
to break [breɪk]	broke [brəʊk]	broken [ˈbrəʊkn]	brechen
to bring [brɪŋ]	brought [brɔːt]	brought [brɔːt]	bringen
to build [bɪld]	built [bɪlt]	built [bɪlt]	bauen
to burn [bɜːn]	burned/burnt [bɜːnd; bɜːnt]	burned/burnt [bɜːnd; bɜːnt]	brennen
to burst [bɜːst]	burst [bɜːst]	burst [bɜːst]	bersten, platzen
to buy [baɪ]	bought [bɔːt]	bought [bɔːt]	kaufen
to catch [kætʃ]	caught [kɔːt]	caught [kɔːt]	fangen
to choose [tʃuːz]	chose [tʃəʊz]	chosen [ˈtʃəʊzn]	(aus)wählen
to cling [klɪŋ]	clung [klʌŋ]	clung [klʌŋ]	(sich) festhalten
to come [kʌm]	came [keɪm]	come [kʌm]	kommen
to cost [kɒst]	cost [kɒst]	cost [kɒst]	kosten
to creep [kriːp]	crept [krept]	crept [krept]	schleichen; kriechen
to cut [kʌt]	cut [kʌt]	cut [kʌt]	schneiden
to deal (with) [diːl]	dealt [delt]	dealt [delt]	(be)handeln
to do [duː]	did [dɪd]	done [dʌn]	tun, machen
to draw [drɔː]	drew [druː]	drawn [drɔːn]	zeichnen
to dream [driːm]	dreamed/dreamt [driːmd; dremt]	dreamed/dreamt [driːmd; dremt]	träumen
to drink [drɪŋk]	drank [dræŋk]	drunk [drʌŋk]	trinken
to drive [draɪv]	drove [drəʊv]	driven [ˈdrɪvn]	fahren
to eat [iːt]	ate [et; eɪt]	eaten [ˈiːtn]	essen
to fall [fɔːl]	fell [fel]	fallen [ˈfɔːlən]	fallen
to feed [fiːd]	fed [fed]	fed [fed]	füttern
to feel [fiːl]	felt [felt]	felt [felt]	(sich) fühlen
to fight [faɪt]	fought [fɔːt]	fought [fɔːt]	streiten, kämpfen
to find [faɪnd]	found [faʊnd]	found [faʊnd]	finden
to fly [flaɪ]	flew [fluː]	flown [fləʊn]	fliegen
to freeze [friːz]	froze [frəʊz]	frozen [ˈfrəʊzn]	erstarren, gefrieren
to forget [fəˈget]	forgot [fəˈgɒt]	forgotten [fəˈgɒtn]	vergessen
to get [get]	got [gɒt]	got [gɒt] (BE) gotten [gɒtn] (AE)	(be)kommen; werden
to give [gɪv]	gave [geɪv]	given [ˈgɪvn]	geben
to go [gəʊ]	went [went]	gone [gɒn]	gehen
to grow [grəʊ]	grew [gruː]	grown [grəʊn]	wachsen; anbauen
to hang [hæŋ]	hung [hʌŋ]	hung [hʌŋ]	hängen
to have [hæv]	had [hæd]	had [hæd]	haben
to hear [hɪə]	heard [hɜːd]	heard [hɜːd]	hören
to hide [haɪd]	hid [hɪd]	hidden [ˈhɪdn]	(sich) verstecken
to hit [hɪt]	hit [hɪt]	hit [hɪt]	schlagen; treffen
to hold [həʊld]	held [held]	held [held]	halten
to hurt [hɜːt]	hurt [hɜːt]	hurt [hɜːt]	verletzen, weh tun
to keep [kiːp]	kept [kept]	kept [kept]	behalten; weitermachen
to know [nəʊ]	knew [njuː]	known [nəʊn]	wissen
to lay [leɪ]	laid [leɪd]	laid [leɪd]	legen
to lead [liːd]	led [led]	led [led]	führen

infinitive	simple past	past participle	German
to lean [li:n]	leaned/leant [li:nd/lent]	leaned/leant [li:nd/lent]	(sich) lehnen
to learn [lɜ:n]	learned/learnt [lɜ:nd; lɜ:nt]	learned/learnt [lɜ:nd; lɜ:nt]	lernen
to leave [li:v]	left [left]	left [left]	(ver)lassen
to lend [lend]	lent [lent]	lent [lent]	leihen
to let [let]	let [let]	let [let]	lassen
to lie [laɪ]	lay [leɪ]	lain [leɪn]	liegen
to light [laɪt]	lit [lɪt]	lit [lɪt]	anzünden, beleuchten
to lose [lu:z]	lost [lɒst]	lost [lɒst]	verlieren
to make [meɪk]	made [meɪd]	made [meɪd]	machen
to mean [mi:n]	meant [ment]	meant [ment]	bedeuten; meinen
to meet [mi:t]	met [met]	met [met]	(sich) treffen
to pay [peɪ]	paid [peɪd]	paid [peɪd]	zahlen
to put [pʊt]	put [pʊt]	put [pʊt]	stellen, legen, setzen
to read [ri:d]	read [red]	read [red]	lesen
to ride [raɪd]	rode [rəʊd]	ridden ['rɪdn]	reiten; fahren
to ring [rɪŋ]	rang [ræŋ]	rung [rʌŋ]	klingeln; anrufen
to run [rʌn]	ran [ræn]	run [rʌn]	rennen, laufen
to say [seɪ]	said [sed]	said [sed]	sagen
to see [si:]	saw [sɔ:]	seen [si:n]	sehen
to sell [sel]	sold [səʊld]	sold [səʊld]	verkaufen
to send [send]	sent [sent]	sent [sent]	schicken
to set [set]	set [set]	set [set]	setzen, legen, stellen
to shake [ʃeɪk]	shook [ʃʊk]	shaken ['ʃeɪkn]	schütteln
to shine [ʃaɪn]	shone [ʃɒn]	shone [ʃɒn]	scheinen, glänzen
to shoot [ʃu:t]	shot [ʃɒt]	shot [ʃɒt]	schießen
to show [ʃəʊ]	showed [ʃəʊd]	shown [ʃəʊn]	zeigen
to shut [ʃʌt]	shut [ʃʌt]	shut [ʃʌt]	schließen
to sing [sɪŋ]	sang [sæŋ]	sung [sʌŋ]	singen
to sink [sɪŋk]	sank [sæŋk]	sunk [sʌŋk]	sinken
to sit [sɪt]	sat [sæt]	sat [sæt]	sitzen
to sleep [sli:p]	slept [slept]	slept [slept]	schlafen
to smell [smel]	smelled/smelt [smeld; smelt]	smelled/smelt [smeld; smelt]	riechen
to speak [spi:k]	spoke [spəʊk]	spoken ['spəʊkn]	sprechen
to spell [spel]	spelled/spelt [speld; spelt]	spelled/spelt [speld; spelt]	buchstabieren
to spend [spend]	spent [spent]	spent [spent]	ausgeben; verbringen
to spill [spɪl]	spilled/spilt [spɪld; spɪlt]	spilled/spilt [spɪld; spɪlt]	verschütten
to spread [spred]	spread [spred]	spread [spred]	(sich) verbreiten
to stand [stænd]	stood [stʊd]	stood [stʊd]	stehen
to steal [sti:l]	stole [stəʊl]	stolen ['stəʊlən]	stehlen
to stick [stɪk]	stuck [stʌk]	stuck [stʌk]	kleben; stecken
to strike [straɪk]	struck [strʌk]	struck [strʌk]	schlagen; anzünden
to strive [straɪv]	strove [strəʊv]	striven ['strɪvn]	streben
to swim [swɪm]	swam [swæm]	swum [swʌm]	schwimmen
to take [teɪk]	took [tʊk]	taken ['teɪkn]	nehmen
to teach [ti:tʃ]	taught [tɔ:t]	taught [tɔ:t]	lehren
to tear [teə]	tore [tɔ:]	torn [tɔ:n]	reißen
to tell [tel]	told [təʊld]	told [təʊld]	sagen, erzählen
to think [θɪŋk]	thought [θɔ:t]	thought [θɔ:t]	denken
to throw [θrəʊ]	threw [θru:]	thrown [θrəʊn]	werfen
to understand [ˌʌndəˈstænd]	understood [ˌʌndəˈstʊd]	understood [ˌʌndəˈstʊd]	verstehen
to wake [weɪk]	woke [wəʊk]	woken ['wəʊkn]	aufwachen; wecken
to wear [weə]	wore [wɔ:]	worn [wɔ:n]	tragen, anhaben
to win [wɪn]	won [wʌn]	won [wʌn]	gewinnen
to write [raɪt]	wrote [rəʊt]	written ['rɪtn]	schreiben

Bildquellen: US1: (1) Corbis/Zaunders; (2) Avenue Images GmbH/Corbis RF; (3) Avenue Images GmbH/Rubberball RF; (4) iStockphoto/RF; S. 3: Bananastock RF; S. 8: (1) Fotosearch RF/Brand X Pictures; (2) Klett-Archiv/Negenborn; (3) laif/Emmler; (4) Alamy Images RF; (5) ZEFA/Carnemoll; (6) Klett-Archiv; S. 9: (1) Corbis/Reuters; (2) Corbis/Johnson; (3) Mauritius/Bayer; (4) Klett-Archiv/Negenborn; (5) Corbis/Free Agents Limited; S. 10: (1) Alamy Images RM/Allison; (2) Getty Images/Taxi; S. 11: (1) Mauritius/Bayer; (2) Fotosearch RF/Brand X Pictures; (3) Alamy Images RM/Travel-Shots; S. 13: (1) Getty Images RF/PhotoDisc; (2) RFDS National Office; (3) Natural History Phot. Agency/A.N.T. PHOTO LIBRARY; S. 14: Corbis/Garwood & Ainslie; S. 15: (1) Avenue Images GmbH/Ingram; (2) Corel Corporation; (3) Silvestris/Kelvin; S. 16: (1) Interfoto; (2) Warner Books Inc, MiramaxBooks; S. 18: Global Pictures/defd; (2) MEV; S. 19: British Film Institute; (2) MEV; S. 20: MEV; S. 21: (1) MEV; (2) Punch Library; S. 22: (1–2) AKG; (3) Corbis/Bettmann; S. 23: (1,3) ullstein bild/The Granger Coll.; (2) AKG; (4) Corbis/Gianni Dagli Orti; (5) BPK; (6) Ingram Publishing; S. 26: Klett-Archiv; S. 27: (1) Corbis/Edifice; (2–3) Alamy Images RM/Elmtree Images; S. 30: (1) MEV; (2) PhotoDisc; S. 31: (1) PhotoAlto; (2) Avenue Images GmbH/PhotoDisc; (3) Klett-Archiv/Nierhoff; S. 34: (1) Corbis/Edmondson; (2) MEV; S. 36: (1–2) AKG; S. 37: Fotosearch RF/PhotoDisc; S. 38: Klett-Archiv/Dangelmaier; S. 39: Fotosearch RF/Brand X Pictures; S. 41: Punch Library; S. 42: (1) MEV; (2) mecom/ddp/Lenz; (3) Alamy Images RM/Eureka; (4) Cinetext; (5) Corbis/Free Agents Limited; (6) Alamy Images RM/Chmura; (7) Alamy Images RM/Lyons; S. 43: (1) Avenue Images GmbH/Corbis RF; (2) Corbis/LWA-Stephen Welstead; (3) Fotosearch RF/PhotoDisc; (4) Corbis/Paterson/Reuters; (5) Getty Images RF/Photodisc; (6) Alamy Images RM/Houghton; (7) Alamy Images RM/Photofusion Picture Library; (8) Alamy Images RM/HARRIS; (9) Mauritius/PowerStock; S. 44: (1) Avenue Images GmbH/Banana Stock; (2) Picture Press/camerapress; (3) Redferns; S. 46: Avenue Images GmbH/Ingram Publ.; S. 48: Alamy Images RM/Hale-Sutton; S. 49: (1) Picture-Alliance/Curtis; (2–3) Avenue Images GmbH/CorbisRF; (4) Corbis/Garten; S. 52: Image 100; S. 53: Corbis/Isard; S. 55: (1) Alamy Images RM/Levy; (2) Alamy Images RM/J.P. Photography; (3) Alamy Images RM/Elmtree Images; S. 57: (1) Fotofinder/Bridgeman; (2) Comstock; (3) Creativ Collection Verlag GmbH; (4) Mauritius/Pöhlmann; S. 58: (1) Getty Images/Harding; (2–3) Corbis/Kraft; (4–5) MEV; (6) Ingram Publishing; S. 59: (1) Alamy Images RM; (2) Corbis/Sedam; (3) Corbis/Snyder/Reuters; (5) Avenue Images GmbH/Ingram Publishing; S. 60: (1) Corbis/Fleming; (2;3) Mauritius/Superstock; S. 61: Corbis/Muench; S. 62: Klett-Archiv/Jung; S. 63: (1,4) Mauritius/age; (2) AP/Rowlings; (3) Fotofinder/Freelens/Tack; (5) Corbis/Fleming; S. 64: Mauritius/Superstock; S. 65: (1) AP/Rowlings; (2) AP/Loh; S. 66: (1) AP/Curtin; (2) Avenue Images GmbH/Index Stock; S. 67: (1) MEV; (2) Corbis/Brakefield; (3) Okapia/Root; (4) PhotoDisc; S. 68: Global Pictures/Defd; S. 69: Corbis/J Springer Collection; S. 70: Corbis/Bettmann; S. 71: Corbis/Stewart; S. 72: Getty Images/PhotoDisc; S. 73: Avenue Images GmbH/image 100; S. 74: Corel Corporation; S. 75: Corbis/Bettmann; S. 76: (1) Corbis/O'Reagan; (2) Corbis/Winn; (3) Corbis/Sands; S. 77: (1) GOODSHOOT; (2,4–5) Cinetext; (3) Corbis/Hird/Reuters; (6) Corbis/Hanai/Reuters; S.78: Picture-Alliance/Kalaene; S. 79: (1) Image 100/RF; (2) Corbis/Brendan; S. 80: (1) Avenue Images GmbH/Photodisc Grün; (2) Ingram Publishing; S. 82: (1) Avenue Images GmbH/Digital Vision; (2) Bananastock RF; (3) Fotosearch RF; (4) Avenue Images GmbH/Digital Vision); (5) Getty Images/PhotoDisc; S. 83: (1–2) Comstock; (3) Avenue Images GmbH/CorbisRF; (4) Ingram Publishing; (5–6) MEV; S. 84: Fotosearch RF/Brand X Pictures; S. 85: (1) Corbis/Steve; (2) GOODSHOOT; (3) Picture-Alliance/Carstensen; (4) Alamy Images RM/AA World Travel Lib; (5) Corbis/Doyle; S. 86: (1) Corbis/ML Sinibaldi; (2) Corbis/Goldsmith; (3) AP/Loh; S. 87: GOODSHOOT; (2) Picture-Alliance/Empics Yui Mok; (3) Creativ Collection Verlag GmbH; (4) Corbis/Underwood; S. 88: (1) MEV/RF; (2) Fotofinder/plainpicture/Kuttig; (3) Corbis/Cardinale/People Avenue; S. 89: Corbis/Ted Soqui; S. 90, 91: CartoonStock/Bath; S. 93: (1) MEV; (2) Avenue Images GmbH/Banana RF; S. 94: Avenue Images GmbH/Ingram; S. 96: (1–3) Klett-Archiv; S. 95: (1) images.de digital photo GmbH/Schulten; (2) Bilderberg/Popper; S. 97: (1) Corbis/Bennett/Dreamworks Picture/Bureau; (2) Sipa Press/Nana Productions; (3–4) Klett-Archiv/Bouillot; S. 98: (1) Corbis/Manning; (2) Ingram Publishing; (3–4); S. 99: (1) Ingram Publishing; (2) Creativ Collection Verlag GmbH; (3) Avenue Images GmbH/Ingram Publishing; S. 100: Corbis/Sygma/Thai Ted; S. 101: (1) Global Pictures/defd; (2) kpa; S. 102: (1) Fotofinder/Visum/Reinhardt/Zeitenspiegel; (2) Klett-Archiv; (3) Corbis GmbH/Mayer; S. 103: Stockfood Photo Stock Agency/Maximilian Stock; S. 107: MEV; S. 120: (1) EPD; (2) Klett/Georg; S. 122: Cartoon: © by Mark Parisi, printed with permission

Textquellen. S. 12: Song: © Written by Clayton, Adam/Mullen, Laurence/Evans, David/Hewson, Paul David; Rights: Polygram Int. Musik Publishing B.V./Für D/A/CH: Universal Music Publ. GmbH, Berlin; S. 15: Teenage friends watch in horror as surfer is torn apart by sharks/© Times World News; S. 16: Hyperion, New York/© Doris Pilkington-Nugi Garimara; S. 35: Song: © Written by Cush, Henry Stehan/Hasler, Shanne/Odgers, Philip Frederick/Simmonds, Paul Wayne; Rights: Bug Music Ltd./BUG Music Verlagsgesellschaft, München; S. 52: The kiss by Rosie Rushton/© Short stories, Waterstone's Middlesex; S. 53: Song: © Written by Healy, Francis; Rights: Sony Music Entertainment (UK) Ltd./Sony/ATV Music Publishing (Germany) GmbH, Berlin; S. 62: Song: © Written by Gordon, Irving; Rights: ELEKTRA Enertainment; LC 0192/Bourne Inc. Melodie der Welt J. Michel KG Musikverlag, Frankfurt/M.; S. 76: Interview with an actor/© www.bbc.co.uk; S. 85: Song: © Written by Nobles, Vada J/Pugh, Rasheem Sharrief; Rights: Kilosheem Pub/VNM Publ./EMI Music Publishing Germany GmbH & Co. KG, Hamburg; S. 86: Song: © Seger, Bob; Rights: Hideout-Records Distributors Inc./Melodie der Welt J. Michel KG Musikverlag, Frankfurt/M.; S. 87: Song: © Written by Taupin, Bernie; Rights: 1973 by Dick, James Music Ltd./Für D/A/CH: Universal Music Publ. GmbH, Berlin; S. 88: Song: © Written by Alspach, David Scott/Christy, Lauren/Edwards, Graham/Lavigne Avril Ramona; Rights: Almo-Music Copr. /Ferry Hills Songs/Mr. Spock Music/Rainbow Fish Publ./Warner-Tamerlane Publ. Co. NEUE WELT MUSIKVERLAG GMBH, Hamburg/Rondor Musikverlag GmbH, Berlin; S. 96: Fremantle Arts Centre Press/Australia © May O'Brian/Sue Wyatt; S. 98: (1) School/© Suzanne Honour (2002–2003); (2) Clerihews/© Ken Nesbitt; S. 99: Limericks/© Bruce Lansky; S. 100: Fall from innocence/The Body (S. 293)/Different Seasons © Stephen King, 1982; S. 103: Boogaloo/Alan Posener/The sketch Book (S. 4–8)

Every effort has been made to trace owners of copyright material. However, in a few cases this has not proved possible and repeated enquiries have remained unanswered. The publishers would be glad to hear from the owners of any such material reproduced in this book.

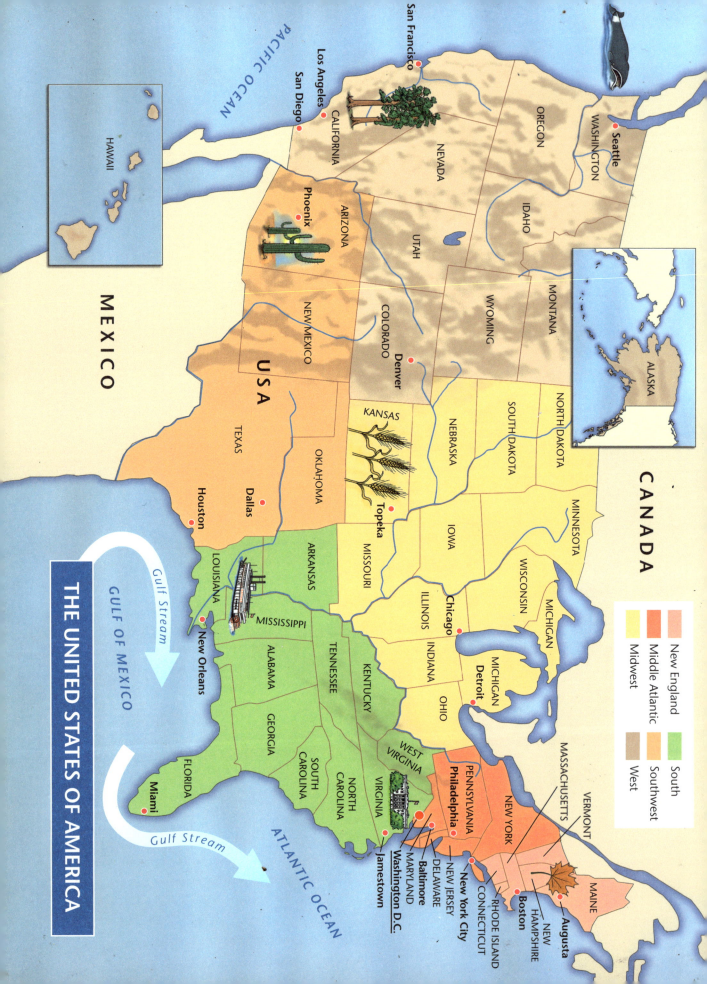